Essay Writing for Canadian Students with Readings

Roger Davis
Laura K. Davis

EIGHTH EDITION

PEARSON

Toronto

To those we have taught,
and those who have taught us.

Vice-President, CMPS: Gary Bennett

Editorial Director: Claudine O'Donnell

Acquisitions Editor: David S. Le Gallais

Marketing Manager: Jennifer Sutton

Project Manager: Kimberley Blakey

Developmental Editor: Christine Langone

Manager Content Development: Suzanne Schaan

Production Services: Cenveo® Publisher Services

Permissions Project Manager: Sue Petrykewycz

Text Permissions Research: MPS North America

Interior Design: Cenveo® Publisher Services

Cover Designer: Alex Li

Cover Image: Shutterstock

Original edition published by Pearson Education, Inc., Upper Saddle River, New Jersey, USA. Copyright © 2012 Pearson Education, Inc. This edition is authorized for sale only in Canada.

10 9 8 7 6 5 4 3 2 1 [EB]

Stewart, Kay L. (Kay Lanette), 1942-
[Essay writing for Canadian students]
    Essay writing for Canadian students with readings / Roger Davis
(Red Deer College), Laura K. Davis (Red Deer College). — Eighth edition.

Revision of: Essay writing for Canadian students / Kay L. Stewart, Marian
    E. Freeman. — Scarborough, Ont. : Prentice-Hall Canada, 1981.
Includes bibliographical references and index.
ISBN 978-0-13-349601-7 (pbk.)

    1. Exposition (Rhetoric). 2. English language—Rhetoric. I. Davis, Roger
Nathan, 1971-, author II. Title. III. Title: Essay writing for Canadian students

LB2369.S87 2015   808'.042   C2014-908172-3

ISBN 978-0-13-349601-7

Brief Contents

Contents

8 Writing Evaluation Essays 113

Part 3 Handbook for Final Editing 401

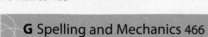
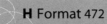

Preface to the Eighth Edition

To the Student

If you are trying to figure out how to cope with essay assignments in your college or university courses, you are the student we had in mind when we wrote this book.

We present a systematic approach to writing essays. Because we believe that writing is a skill you can learn, rather than a talent you are born with, we are convinced this method will work for most writers. Feel free to adapt it to suit your needs.

To the Instructor

If you are new to *Essay Writing for Canadian Students*, you will notice that we present the writing process as a systematic set of procedures for planning, drafting, and revising deductively organized academic essays. Like most teachers, we have found that many weaknesses in student writing stem from confused thinking about the assignment, the subject of the essay, or both. For this reason, we stress the analytic skills that help students to explore the subjects they write about more completely. We recognize that one disadvantage of this approach is that it may seem to limit creativity. The deductively organized analysis is, after all, only one kind of academic essay. Nevertheless, we believe there is value in an approach that encourages critical thinking.

Part 1 Rhetoric

The Rhetoric section takes students through the process of writing and revising a wide range of essays and writing assignments: summaries and essays in various disciplines (Chapters 2, 3, 4, and 5); essays analyzing literature, comparing, evaluating, and persuading (Chapters 6, 7, 8, and 9); and research papers (Chapters 10, 11, and 12). Part 1 emphasizes the importance of reading and thinking analytically.

In this section of the book, we have

- Expanded and updated the discussion of reading analytically and writing summaries (Chapter 2) to better reflect how those two activities are interrelated and incorporated into essay writing.
- Revised and reconfigured the discussion of evaluation essays (Chapter 8) to better reflect current topics and events.
- Expanded and reconfigured the discussion of persuasive essays (Chapter 9), emphasizing Canadian content and addressing a new sample student essay on "Canadian National Identity."
- Added a new chapter on "Writing Research Essays Across the Curriculum" to emphasize the importance and demand for writing skills in various disciplines, and to highlight the growing focus on analysing and evaluating the role and use of technology and social media in the Western world.

Part 2 Readings

We have selected essays published in a wide range of sources both to illustrate the types of writing we discuss in the Rhetoric section and to provide timely subjects for students to write about.

- About one quarter of the Readings are new to this edition.
- The Published Writings centre on four broad subject areas: language/literature, health/medicine/addiction, social justice/environmentalism/globalization, and multiculturalism/personal identity/sports, with interesting links between these categories. Students therefore have a wealth of material to analyze, compare, and evaluate.
- The new Sample Persuasive Essay, Evaluation Essay, and Research Essay show the results of the processes of gathering material, drafting, and revising covered in Chapters 8, 9, 10, 11, and 12.

Part 3 Handbook for Final Editing

The Handbook gives students the tools they need to recognize and correct problems in sentence structure, grammar, punctuation, and format.

Throughout, we've added, deleted, and changed material to make explanations and examples clearer, more useful, and more interesting.

The exercises previously interspersed throughout the Handbook section, along with the Answer Key to these exercises, have been placed in the Instructor's Manual for this edition.

How to Use This Book

Because it serves as a combined rhetoric, reader, and handbook, *Essay Writing for Canadian Students* has been used successfully in a wide variety of courses, from college and university writing courses to introductory literature to advanced writing. The scope and structure of the book allow you to tailor your course to suit your own teaching style and the needs of your students. Some instructors prefer to begin by systematically reviewing handbook material on sentence structure, grammar, and punctuation. Others plunge their students into writing essays, assigning handbook material as needed. Still others may ask students to read and respond informally to some of the published writings before assigning the first formal essay.

Your selection of rhetoric chapters will likely depend on the kind of course you are teaching. All students can benefit from Chapters 1–5, which provide an overview of the writing process and strategies for tackling essay assignments.

Writing courses

If you are teaching a writing course, you will likely use Chapter 2 on reading analytically and writing summaries, and Chapters 3, 4, and 5 on analysis essays. The latter, which examines various methods of analysis such as cause/effect analysis, process analysis, and systems analysis, lays the groundwork for students to respond to and write about texts from a wide variety of academic disciplines. Chapters 4 and 5 give detailed instructions for drafting and revising essays, with clear examples of good and weak thesis statements, topic sentences, introductions, conclusions, and middle paragraphs. You might follow up with Chapter 7, Writing Comparison Essays; the sample topic for this chapter is a comparison of two essays from the Readings. You could then introduce the more complex skills required for evaluating arguments and writing critiques found in Chapter 8. Chapter 9 calls on students to put these skills to work by constructing their own arguments about controversial issues or by writing reviews. Students could expand their persuasive essays into research papers by following the procedures set out in Chapters 10, 11, and 12.

Literature and media courses

If you are teaching a course in literature, film studies, or other media, you might emphasize the chapter devoted to writing essays on literature (Chapter 6). The sample topic for this chapter is a poem by William Carlos Williams. Chapter 1, Essay Writing: An Overview, also includes a sample essay on the film *The Matrix,* as well as a discussion of that essay. You may want students to write two or three essays analyzing a single subject before you ask them to tackle a comparison essay (Chapter 7) or an evaluative essay (Chapter 8). Classic pieces by E. M. Forster, George Orwell, W. S. Merwin, Jonathan Swift, and Virginia Woolf provide opportunities for comparison with contemporary writers in both subject and style.

However you structure your course, we hope you and your students find *Essay Writing for Canadian Students* stimulating and productive.

Supplement for Students

MyWritingLab

MyWritingLab, where practice, application, and demonstration meet to improve writing. MyWritingLab, a complete online learning program, provides additional resources and effective practice exercises for developing writers. MyWritingLab accelerates learning through layered assessment and a personalized learning path. With over eight thousand exercises and immediate feedback to answers, the integrated learning aids of MyWritingLab reinforce learning throughout the semester.

Visit **MyWritingLab** (pearsonmylabandmastering.com) to access diverse resources for composition in one easy-to-use place.

Supplements for Instructors

The **Instructor's Manual** is available for downloading from a password-protected section of Pearson Canada's online catalogue (www.pearsoncanada .ca/highered). Navigate to your book's catalogue page to access the supplement. See your local sales representative for details and access.

Learning Solutions Managers. Pearson's Learning Solutions Managers work with faculty and campus course designers to ensure that Pearson technology products, assessment tools, and online course materials are tailored to meet your specific needs. This highly qualified team is dedicated to helping schools take full advantage of a wide range of educational resources by assisting in the integration of a variety of instructional materials and media formats. Your local Pearson sales representative can provide you with more details on this service program.

Acknowledgments

First and foremost, we would like to thank Marian Allen for introducing us to this project, and for inviting us to participate in its authorship. Over the years she has created this book and contributed to it, and we express our gratitude for her guidance and mentorship. We would also like to thank Kay Stewart and Chris Bullock for the great work they have done on the previous editions of this textbook. Their insights have been invaluable, and it has been wonderful to continue work on such an excellent and successful textbook. Marian and Kay spent many summers developing the materials that led to the first edition of *Essay Writing* (1980), at that time the only university-level writing textbook by Canadian authors for Canadian students. Without Marian, Kay, and Chris's enthusiasm, hard work, and practical wisdom about students' needs, this project would never have come to fruition, nor have lasted through so many editions.

We are grateful to all our students at Red Deer College, and formerly at Grant MacEwan University and the University of Alberta. They have helped us to see what did and didn't work in teaching writing and have generously allowed us to use their writing.

We would also like to thank the reviewers who made valuable suggestions for improvements in this edition: Tim Chamberlain, Camosun College; Bernett Cody, Kwantlen Polytechnic University; Jennifer Payson, University of British Columbia; Simon Thompson, Northwest Community College; and Dat Tran, University of Ottawa.

We are grateful to our colleagues, particularly Nancy Batty and Peter Slade at Red Deer College, who have inspired and mentored us, and who provided us with feedback and suggestions for improvements on this book. Many thanks as well to the staff at Pearson Education Canada for their hard work and enthusiasm for and dedication to this project: David Le Gallais, Senior Acquisitions Editor; Joel Gladstone, Sponsoring Editor; and Christine Langone, Developmental Editor. We would also like to thank Sue

Petrykewyz, Project Manager in the Permissions Department at Pearson, for her hard work behind the scenes. For their work on previous editions of this book, we are grateful to Kathleen McGill, Sponsoring Editor; Rema Celio and Suzanne Schaan, Developmental Editors; and Avivah Wargon, Production Editor.

Finally, we would like to thank our families for their years of support, particularly our parents—who instilled in us a love for education—our siblings, and especially our three children, Rachael, Kai, and Clara, who always add fun and laughter to a hard day's work.

Rhetoric

(Part 1)

Writing Essays:
An Overview

(1)

Essay Writing: Purposes

> Writing to Learn
>
> Writing to Communicate

Essay Writing: Product

> Audience
>
> Structure
>
> Sample Essay: Analysis of a Film
>
> Discussion of the Sample Essay

Essay Writing: Process

> **Stage 1** Clarifying Essay Topics
>
> **Stage 2** Gathering Material
>
> **Stage 3** Formulating a Thesis Statement
>
> **Stage 4** Drafting
>
> **Stage 5** Revising the Thesis Statement and Essay Structure
>
> **Stage 6** Revising Individual Paragraphs
>
> **Stage 7** Final Editing

In this book we focus on essay writing for two reasons. First, the thinking skills you practise in the process of writing essays are central to the work you do in college or university. Second, the procedures you learn for writing and revising essays will help you with many other kinds of writing assignments.

Essay Writing: Purposes

Writing to Learn

How can writing essays help you develop thinking skills? One way is by encouraging you to explore your ideas. This purpose is reflected in the French word from which the term *essay* comes: *essai,* meaning "attempt." The term was first used by the French author Michel de Montaigne, who published a book of short prose pieces entitled *Essais* in 1580. This title suggests the personal, exploratory nature of Montaigne's attempts to understand the world around him by writing on everyday subjects such as the art of conversation or liars. You may study informal essays of this type in composition and literature courses, and create them as well.

Since Montaigne's day, the term *essay* has come to include formal writing on a wide range of subjects, from the nature of love in Shakespeare's *King Lear* to theories about the origins of the universe. Writing academic essays of this kind will help you develop systematic analytic thinking. It is this more formal type of essay writing that you will most often be asked to do in your university and college courses, and that we will focus on in this text.

Thinking about a **subject*** and writing about a subject are different processes. Thinking is largely internal and abstract, while writing requires you to make your thoughts external and concrete. If you were taking a painting course, you would recognize that no matter how good the instructor's lessons might be or how much you thought about painting, you would learn to paint only by painting. The same holds true for writing. Through writing essays, whether formal or informal, you develop greater awareness of the language you and others use to make meaning. What may be less obvious is that you learn the theories, concepts, and procedures of academic disciplines more thoroughly by actively employing them in writing essays.

Writing to Communicate

Some of the writing you do—such as class notes, responses to reading, drafts that go nowhere—may have no reader other than yourself. Other types of writing, like texting, have very specific, immediate purposes and may be

---

*Terms in bold are defined in the Glossary of Rhetorical Terms (497–500).

deleted without much further thought. Writing essays, however, is a means of sharing your understanding of a particular issue with others and generally involves a more sustained engagement with the issue you are writing about.

Most academic essays require an argument or opinion that will persuade the reader. Contrary to the popular belief that everyone has a right to an opinion of his or her own, not all opinions have equal merit: some opinions can be harmful (such as racism) or even incorrect (that the Earth is flat). Moving beyond mere factual information, an essay will draw conclusions about a particular topic and support a position or course of action related to that topic. The merit of an argument or opinion relies on the reasons and evidence you give to support that position as well as its ability to persuade the reader.

In an academic essay, this combination of an opinion and the reason(s) supporting it is called a **thesis**. A thesis is like a hypothesis in a scientific experiment: it is the statement or assertion that is to be proved. Proof in an academic essay consists of the logical, orderly development of your thesis through explaining your reasons and giving **evidence** (such as factual information, examples, and quotations from authorities) to support those reasons. By explaining your thesis carefully and giving evidence to support it, you are likely to persuade readers to take your opinion seriously, whether or not they agree with it.

Essay Writing: Product

If both informal essays and formal academic essays present writers' opinions on particular subjects, then the writer must consider the audience for whom a piece is being written and the presentation of the material.

Audience

Most informal essays are written for a popular audience, and the subject material is usually fairly general in nature. Magazine articles and newspaper stories often contain much factual material and are geared toward information or entertainment as a starting point for discussion. These types of essays do not represent sustained analyses of topics.

Formal essays on an academic subject, in contrast, are written for specialized audiences already familiar with the subject. Readers of these essays want to know the writer's thesis from the beginning and to have the evidence supporting the thesis laid out in a logical, orderly fashion. They also appreciate essays that are well written according to the conventions of the discipline. Most of the essays you write in college and university courses will be of this second type. You will be writing for instructors and classmates who know something about the subject and want to hear your opinion on it. For such academic audiences, then, you do not need to include broad generalizations or unnecessary summary in the essay, particularly in the introduction. Try to be as specific as possible.

Structure

Many students have learned the five-paragraph essay **structure** that includes an introduction, three body paragraphs, and a conclusion. The five-paragraph essay is an acceptable, if simple, approach to the essay. However, the five-paragraph essay can become a crutch if a writer uses it as a template for every essay. This model's main drawback is that it tends to make writers think in terms of three subpoints, which is not always the best approach to thinking about any given topic. The structure begins to dictate content, when it is generally preferable to let content dictate the structure.

Whether you write five, seven, nine, or any other number of paragraphs in your essay, it is important that you have an **introduction**, **middle paragraphs**, and a **conclusion**. Here is a brief description of these elements:

INTRODUCTION
The introduction presents the thesis of the essay. It may also establish the **context** for the discussion (for example, by defining necessary terms or giving historical background). The introduction should not include broad generalizations that will not be supported in your essay, nor should it contain references to examples or ideas that will not be analyzed.

MIDDLE PARAGRAPHS
Middle paragraphs present subpoints of your essay, which support your thesis statement. **Topic sentences** explain each subpoint and how it relates to your thesis. However, you may have two paragraphs that support a single subpoint—with a different example explained in each paragraph. One paragraph may fully explain a subpoint of your thesis, or you may need more than one paragraph to explain a subpoint. We will show you how to create an "umbrella" topic sentence—a topic sentence for two middle paragraphs—in Chapter 5.

CONCLUSION
The conclusion ties together the points developed in the middle paragraphs and mentions the wider implications of the discussion, if any.

Sample Essay: Analysis of a Film

So that you can see what this kind of essay might look like in practice, here is an example. The assignment asked students to choose their favourite film, to identify a key **theme** or topic, and to make an argument about their understanding of the material. The main structural elements of the essay have been labelled.

Writing Sample

FREE WILL AND FATALISM IN *THE MATRIX*

Introduction

Released in 1999, the movie *The Matrix* has found a central place in popular culture, certainly more so than its two sequels. Aside from its compelling action scenes, part of the film's popularity derives from its questioning of the principle of personal freedom, a principle that is usually an unchallenged assumption in North America. The film's fundamental premise is that reality is an illusion and that most humans live their lives inside a computer-generated world called "the matrix," manipulated by the machines of the future. The film asks the audience to consider the extent to which they are in control of their decisions and how much technology and other social conditions influence or determine their lives. The

Thesis statement

two characters Neo and Cypher represent opposite positions in the debate between free will and fatalism, yet the film's treatment of both characters suggests that neither free will nor fatalism is an absolute position but are related terms in the decision-making process.

Topic sentence

Through his involvement with technology, the film's main character Neo (Keanu Reeves) has the opportunity to choose between knowledge and ignorance, and ultimately to escape from his prison. An office worker by day and computer hacker by night, Neo is searching for more meaning in his life, perceiving that something is wrong with his apparent reality. It is through the hacker network that Neo meets Trinity (Carrie-Anne Moss)

Middle paragraph 1

who leads him to Morpheus (Laurence Fishburne). Morpheus offers Neo the chance to learn about the matrix, but he must make a choice between the blue pill (to remain ignorant inside the matrix) or the red pill (to learn the truth and escape the matrix). In choosing the red pill, Neo takes control of his future, which begins his quest through the film to overcome the constraints of the matrix and to become humanity's liberator. To some extent, Neo is god-like in his power at the end of the film, and he has attained this power through choosing to question his surroundings.

Transition topic sentence

In contrast to Neo, Cypher represents the opposite reaction to the realization that something is wrong with reality. Cypher has already escaped the matrix and works with Morpheus to liberate other humans from their prison. However, Cypher has grown tired of his struggle against the harsh conditions of life in the real or non–computer-generated world. Ironically, when one of the matrix's agents asks Cypher, a technical operator outside of the matrix, to betray Morpheus, Cypher willingly agrees on condition that he be reinserted back into the

Middle paragraph 2

matrix. Cypher asks to be rich and important in his new life inside the matrix and suggests the life of an actor; he wishes to remember nothing of the outside world. Essentially, Cypher consciously adopts a life inside the illusion provided by technology, a move equivalent to committing suicide in his real life so he can become an actor in a fictional world.

Topic sentence

Two extremes of the debate are therefore clear. On the one hand, Neo follows his own intuition to discover the limits of technology in order to overcome them and to live

Middle paragraph 3

in the real world. On the other hand, Cypher, who already knows the limits of technology, cooperates with technology in order to live, once again, inside the illusion of the matrix. Neo appears to embody self-determination and the triumph of free will. Cypher appears to embody resignation and fatalism.

Transition topic
sentence

However, the film complicates this simple contrast. While Cypher appears to side with an ignorant life inside the matrix, he makes a free choice to betray his friends. Although we may understand his reasons, we ultimately disagree with his decision. In the case of Neo, Morpheus and his crew believe that Neo is "the one." That is, there is a myth inside the matrix that a special person will emerge from within the matrix to liberate humanity. In other words, Neo is predestined to fulfill his role of "the one," which implies that he is not acting totally out of free will. In this way, the film reminds its viewers that our choices and situations are not as simple as they might first appear. Free will and fatalism are not discrete and separate; rather, they are intimately intertwined with one another.

Middle
paragraph 4

Conclusion

Overall, the film suggests that the very idea of free will is a concept that is, perhaps, part of our social conditioning. The contradiction the film explores is that the ability to choose—free will—may be an illusion leaving no meaningful choice. While Cypher apparently gives up in the face of real-world challenges, Neo offers hope that choice is possible, despite the influence of the matrix. Thus, the matrix represents not only technology but also larger social conditions such as politics, interpersonal relationships, and spiritual beliefs. As the internet and other technologies like social media become more pervasive in our lives, *The Matrix* reminds us to question whether these technologies allow us greater personal freedom to make our own choices and to realize our individuality or whether they limit our creativity by replacing meaningful face-to-face communication with computer-mediated friendships. The question becomes less about the possibility of free will than about the ability to understand why and how we make our choices within the circumstances in which we make them.

Discussion of the Sample Essay

"Free Will and Fatalism in *The Matrix*" illustrates the effective use of structural elements common to college and university essays. The introduction provides basic information about the film and introduces the topics of free will and fatalism. It concludes with the thesis statement, which posits that the film complicates a simple division between free will and fatalism as evidenced in the characters of Neo and Cypher. The thesis is debatable, because one could argue that free will and fatalism are distinct and separate concepts.

The thesis statement also serves as a guide to the structure of the essay as a whole. It sets out a simple proposition—that free will and fatalism are opposite terms—and establishes that this distinction does not capture the complexity of the film. The essay will demonstrate how each character represents either free will or fatalism, and it will then show how each character demonstrates the opposite position in his actions.

The middle paragraphs develop the characters in terms of the concepts under discussion by referring to specific details from the film. The first two middle paragraphs deal with separate characters to develop them individually, while the following two paragraphs deal with the characters together in comparison with each other. Also notice that this structure does not follow a simple five-paragraph essay structure that deals with three subpoints. But that does not mean that the essay has a flawed structure. Notice how the point made in each paragraph builds upon the previous one: the second paragraph contrasts Cypher to Neo, who was discussed in the first paragraph; the third paragraph develops the two contrasting characters in relation to the relevant concepts; and the fourth paragraph, developing from the third, explains the intertwining of the concepts of free will and fatalism. Each paragraph in the essay furthers the overall argument.

In the middle paragraphs of the essay, each of these points is clearly made in a topic sentence. Each topic sentence identifies the aspect of the film to be discussed and connects that aspect to the thesis by stating how it contributes to the topics of free will and fatalism. The topic sentences and some other sentences also provide transitions between one paragraph and the next.

The framework you create by establishing this kind of relationship between the thesis, topic sentences, and transitional devices will give your reader valuable assistance in following your line of thinking.

The conclusion sums up the argument of the essay and points to the wider implications of the argument. Rather than making broad generalizations, the conclusion takes a minor theme of the essay (technology) to ask further questions about how the technology in the film (*The Matrix*) might be related to our real lives (the internet, Facebook, and other social media) in terms of the major themes of the essay, namely free will and fatalism.

Essay Writing: Process

Most people don't write an essay—or anything intended to be read by others, for that matter—by sitting down with paper and pen (or computer) and rising an hour later with a finished product. The final draft is the last stage of a highly complex process of thinking and writing, rethinking and rewriting. If you want to produce an interesting, thoughtful essay like the one on *The Matrix,* you have to be prepared to give time and serious attention to your subject. Without that willingness, you will not learn how to write from this book or from any other. But if you make the effort, you can learn to write essays that have something to say and say it well.

To help you learn the skills you need, we will begin by discussing reading analytically and writing summaries, important prequels to writing an essay (see Chapter 2). Throughout the rest of the book, we will focus on the major stages of writing academic essays:

Stage 1:   Clarifying Essay Topics
Determining what your assignment requires and exploring ideas to define a topic

Stage 2:   Gathering Material
Using methods of analysis to stimulate your thinking and to organize ideas, information, and specific details about your topic

Stage 3:   Formulating a Thesis Statement
Forming a main idea and selecting points to support it from the material you have gathered

Stage 4:   Drafting
Selecting and organizing material in a first draft

Stage 5:   Revising the Thesis Statement and Essay Structure
Checking for possible problems in your thesis statement and essay structure, and making necessary changes

Stage 6:   Revising Individual Paragraphs
Checking for possible problems in your introduction, middle paragraphs, and conclusion, and making necessary changes

Stage 7:   Final Editing
Improving your sentence structure and word usage, and correcting errors in grammar, punctuation, mechanics, and format

We are not claiming that the methods and the stages we propose are the only way to write or to write effectively; we don't even claim that they reflect exactly what writers—including ourselves—do when we write. For many of us, writing is far messier and more intuitive than our model would suggest. You may find that the order in which we present writing activities suits your method of composition perfectly; on the other hand, you may find yourself writing a draft to clarify your understanding of a topic or mentally revising the structure before a word hits the page. Try out our suggestions, adjust them to your needs, and fit them into a writing process that works for you.

Exercise

Answer each of the following questions in a sentence or two.

1. We suggest that writing essays can help you think through your ideas and communicate them to other people. Which of these purposes is most relevant to you as a writer? Why?

2. What is your usual approach to writing an essay? How effective do you find this approach? Which stage(s) of the process do you find easiest? Hardest?

Reading Analytically and Writing Summaries (2)

Most of the material you need for writing essays in college and university will come from written sources. The reading you do will likely be much more difficult than your reading for high school. You may find the concepts new and the vocabulary unfamiliar. Or you may grasp the details but miss the overall point. Reading analytically is often the first step for most university- and college-level writing, so it is important that you learn how to read analytically before you begin to write about any text or texts. For this reason, we address the topic of reading analytically here, before discussing the major stages of essay writing. Along similar lines, writing a summary of a text is often a first step for developing an educated opinion (thesis) and writing an essay about it. As the main focus of essay writing is the development of a thesis statement, this chapter will also discuss the topic of writing summaries.

STAGE 1   Honing Your Reading Skills

The guidelines that follow will help you **analyze**, and therefore understand, what you read. We will explain how to analyze texts in a variety of disciplines, such as history, psychology, and political science (see Chapters 3–5). We will also aid you in explaining the relation between content and form (**literary analysis**) when you are writing about literature and film (see Chapter 6, Writing Essays on Literature). This ability to understand and analyze what you read is crucial when you are asked to explain, **compare**, or **evaluate** ideas and events you have read about (see Chapter 7, Writing Comparison Essays, and Chapter 8, Writing Evaluation Essays). It is an indispensable skill when you are writing **research papers** (see Chapter 10, Gathering Material for Research Essays). The readings in Part 2 provide many opportunities for you to practise the skills we outline in this chapter.

STAGE 2   Gathering Material: Analyzing Nonfiction Writing

STEP 1   Figuring Out the Basic Ideas

Nonfiction is a genre of writing that encompasses writing about factual or real-world events, experiences, and knowledge such as academic scholarship, newspaper and other media reports, government documents, technical manuals, and industry-related publications. It is different from the genre of fiction where writers can be purposely inventive, non-factual, or fantastical, although many writers engage in another genre called *creative nonfiction* when they take artistic licence with real-world facts.

What is the writer's *subject?*

Check the title   For most nonfiction, you will be able to identify the subject in the title or first few paragraphs. The titles of scholarly books and articles, for example, customarily state their subject: "The Effects of Television Violence on Preschoolers"; "Masculine Roles in Pat Barker's War Trilogy"; *Ukrainian Settlements in Ontario, 1870–1900.*

Not all titles, however, will identify the writer's subject so precisely. Writing intended for a general audience may have a title designed to create interest or convey the writer's attitude rather than state a subject, as in Fred Stenson's "In Search of a Modest Proposal" (Readings). Other titles may be ironic or otherwise misleading, as in W. S. Merwin's "Unchopping a Tree" (Readings).

Check the introductory paragraph(s)   Because titles can be misleading, it's always a good idea to check the first few paragraphs to confirm or correct your sense of the writer's subject. If, for example, you relied on the title of E. M. Forster's "My Wood" (Readings), you might say that Forster's subject is a piece of property he owns. From reading the introduction, however, you would find that Forster states his subject in three ways: "What is the effect of property on the character? . . . If you own things, what's their effect on you? What's the effect on me of my wood?" This introduction makes it clear that Forster is using his own experience to illustrate a broader ethical question. You might say, then, that his subject is the effects that owning things have on a person's character.

Check your sense of the whole   Sometimes identifying the subject won't be easy. The writer may seem to discuss several subjects; the details may be so fascinating that you lose the big picture; or the subject may be more complex than it initially appears. Try to think about the work as a whole. How would you describe its particular focus, in ten words or less? Consider, for instance, "My Wood" (Readings). On one level, the subject is obvious—Forster is writing about his property. But what is his attitude toward it? How would you describe his particular focus?

Reviewing your sense of the whole will help you avoid distorting what you read by assuming the first subject the writer mentions is the actual subject, or by overemphasizing a minor point. The more times you read or, more accurately, reread the piece, the better you will understand the complexities of the written work.

What is the writer's *main idea* about the subject?

Check for an explicitly stated thesis   Reread the piece, focusing on the main point the author is making about the subject. You may find a one- or two-sentence thesis statement in the introduction (as in David Suzuki's "It Always Costs" [Readings]); in the conclusion (as in Forster's "My Wood" [Readings]); or at another appropriate point (as in George Orwell's "Shooting an Elephant" [Readings]).

To make sure you understand what you have read, restate the thesis in your own words by writing down a sentence or two. By the time you reach the end of "My Wood," for example, you may recognize that the phrases "enormously stout, endlessly avaricious, pseudo-creative, intensely selfish" summarize Forster's thesis about the effects of owning property. But can you explain what Forster means by those terms in your own words? If so, you can be confident that you understand his main idea.

Restating the thesis and main points in your own words not only ensures that you understand the material but also reduces the temptation to keep quoting sentence after sentence. Use brief quotations sparingly to give a sense of the writer's tone or to define a key term that you then explain. Make sure you include the page reference for all quotations. For further information about how to handle quotations, see Part 3, Handbook for Final Editing, H2 Quotations.

If you do not understand a key term, you may miss the overall point of the piece. In the Readings, we have defined many terms for you. When you encounter unfamiliar terms in your course materials, you can look them up in your textbook or in a specialized dictionary like M. H. Abrams's *A Glossary of Literary Terms.*

Make an implied thesis explicit   In pieces that are ironic, humorous, or based on personal experience, the main idea is often strongly implied but not stated directly. In "Unchopping a Tree" (Readings), for example, the absurdity of the process Merwin describes clearly suggests an opposite meaning. But you will not find a sentence or two that spells out Merwin's point.

What do you do if there is not an explicitly stated thesis? You may have a strong enough sense of the whole to sum up its main idea from an initial reading. You will often get a more accurate sense, however, if you examine the work more closely. Jot down your initial ideas, then reconsider them after you have completed your analysis.

How does the writer develop this main idea?   Understanding how the writer organizes material to illustrate the main points will help you see the relation between main points and supporting details. When you are reading secondary sources for a research paper, keep in mind disciplinary categories (which we discuss in Chapters 3 and 6). *Disciplinary categories* are key terms specific to a discipline or field of study. In writing essays on literature, for example, literary critics may develop their interpretation through disciplinary categories such as *plot*, *characterization*, and *setting*. Or they may employ terms specific to a particular literary approach, such as *postcolonial theory* or *gender studies*. In such cases, you may need to find definitions for key terms in order to understand the main ideas. You will find more information on gathering material for research essays in Chapter 10. Pay particular attention to lists of points in the introduction, to typographical devices such as headings, to key terms in topic sentences, and to transitions. Focus on the ideas being presented, not the details. Write a sentence or two explaining the main idea of each section in your own words.

There are six main methods writers use to develop ideas in nonfiction:

1. Telling a story What are the main stages in the narrative? What point does the writer make (or what point can you make) about each stage?

In nonfiction, a narrative is a (true) story told to illustrate a point. It has a beginning and an end and several incidents in between, though the incidents may not be recounted in chronological order. The incidents are usually grouped into stages, marked by significant external or internal changes. Summarize the point made by each of the main stages: not "The first section tells about their first week kayaking up the Mackenzie," but "In their first week kayaking [stage], they had to learn to work as a team [point]."

- Key transitions
  Time words, such as *before*, *after*, *one morning*, *the next day*
  Example: Orwell, "Shooting an Elephant" (Readings)

Although we don't demonstrate how to write narrative essays in this text, we have included a few examples in the Readings to illustrate this form.

2. Analyzing causes and effects What are the main causes and/or effects? What point does the writer make (or what point can you make) about each cause and/or effect?

As we will discuss with greater detail in Chapter 3, cause/effect analysis is one of the most common ways to write about ideas and events. Watch for two types: *independent causes and effects,* and *cause and effect sequences.* Independent causes and effects are often enumerated ("one cause," "another effect," "the most important . . ."). You may find it harder to follow the development of a cause and effect sequence, where the first cause produces an effect that in turn causes a further development (as in Benjamin Franklin's caution about neglect: "For want of a nail the shoe was lost; for want of a shoe the horse was lost; for want of a horse the rider was lost.").

Independent causes/effects

- Key transitions
  Number words, such as *first, second, third;* other words signalling addition, such as *also, further, most important*
  Example: Forster, "My Wood" (Readings)

Cause/effect sequence

- Key transitions
  Words indicating cause and effect, such as *therefore, consequently, as a result*
  Example: Bruce K. Alexander, "Reframing Canada's 'Drug Problem'" (Readings)

3. Analyzing a process What are the main stages in the process? What point does the writer make (or what point can you make) about each stage?

A process has a beginning and an end, and can be divided into stages marked by significant changes. Summarize the point made by each of the main stages: not "The next stage is denial," but "The writer explains the next stage, denial, as the mind's attempt to protect the body from feeling pain."

- Key transitions
  First, next, third, final step/stage
  Example: Virginia Woolf, "[Shakespeare's Sister]" (Readings)

4. Analyzing a system What are the main parts? What point does the writer make (or what point can you make) about each part?

Anything composed of parts that work together to create a whole can be considered a system. Writers often divide their subject into parts and discuss each part in a clearly identified section of their work, such as a chapter in a book or a block of paragraphs in an essay. Identify each main part and summarize the point the writer makes about it: not "Penal institutions are one aspect of the criminal justice system," but "Penal institutions, according to the writer, are the weakest link in the criminal justice system."

- Key terms and transitions
  The parts to be discussed may be identified in the introduction.
  Watch for repetition of key terms and for terms such as these:
  aspect, element, feature, part
  Example: Virginia Satir, "Systems: Open or Closed?" (Readings)

5. Comparing and contrasting What are the main similarities and differences the writer discusses?

Comparisons are built upon analysis, and so the writer may use **methods of development** such as cause/effect, process, or systems analysis. The two basic **methods of organizing comparison essays** are the *block method* and the *point-by-point method* (see Chapter 7). Look for similar kinds of material about each subject. Make sure you note both similarities and differences.

- Key terms and transitions
  Compare, contrast, similar, different, in contrast, on the other hand, similarly, likewise
  Example: Gabor Maté, "Embraced by the Needle" (Readings)

6. Evaluating strengths and weaknesses What are the main points in the writer's argument? Are these points identified (or can you identify them) as strengths/weaknesses, costs/benefits, advantages/disadvantages? According to what **standard of evaluation**? For a detailed discussion of this term, see Stage 1, Clarifying Evaluation Topics: Checking for the Logical Standard in Chapter 8.

Writing that is intended to persuade readers is often harder to follow than other kinds of writing. There are several reasons. The subject itself may be complex, and so the writer may need to define terms; the writer's opinion about the subject may include both points in favour and points against; or the writer may introduce other opinions with which he or she agrees or disagrees. These sections may distract you from the main line of argument. Try to identify the type of analysis underlying the argument, such as cause/effect, process, or systems analysis. Use the writer's thesis as a guide to the points to watch for. Summarize each one. Then note how other points relate to the main line of argument.

- Key transitions
  Words that suggest the writer is indicating disagreement or qualification: *although, despite, nevertheless, while it is true that*
  Example: Fred Stenson, "In Search of a Modest Proposal" (Readings)

If the work you are reading does not seem to fit one of the six patterns above, don't despair. Some pieces, especially long ones, may combine different types of development. Some may simply not be well organized. Do your best to identify and summarize the main points.

What are the main types of evidence/detail the writer uses? For what purpose(s)? Each main point in a piece of nonfiction writing will be developed through evidence and details of the kinds listed below. The term *evidence* describes the specific information used to support an argument (think of the evidence offered in a murder trial). The term *details* refers specifically to particular actions in narratives and particular images in descriptions; more broadly, it refers to any material that explains or illustrates a general statement. Details may become evidence when used for a persuasive purpose (think of a Crown prosecutor reviewing the details of a murder case to decide which ones can be used as evidence of the defendant's guilt).

How much attention you pay to specific details will depend on your purpose in reading. If you are writing a research essay, you may find both the general ideas and the specific information useful to you. If you are studying for an exam, on the other hand, you may focus more on general principles, with a few selected facts or examples. If you are writing a summary of the piece as an assignment, you may be more interested in the kinds or quality of the evidence/details than in the specific information.

Note in a sentence or two which of these main types of evidence/detail the writer uses, and for what purpose.

- Examples

  Specific instances that illustrate a general point or principle. Taking a lost wallet to the police station could be used as an example of honesty.

- Facts and figures

  Specific information such as names of people, places, events; titles of publications; and names of characters

  Precise numbers, as in measurements, statistics, dates

  Research studies and other "hard" evidence

- Quotations and other references to authorities

  Quotations from people interviewed or texts consulted

  References to recognized authorities on the subject or to authoritative texts (such as the Bible, the Koran), without direct quotation

- Narrative/descriptive details

  In telling a story or describing something, a writer may use few details (as in Caesar's "I came, I saw, I conquered") or many (as in an account of kayaking from Alaska to Tierra del Fuego). The details may seem fresh and vivid or flat and clichéd. The writer may use details for purposes such as creating suspense and conveying emotion.

- Other: definitions, analogies, allusions

  To make their explanations clearer, their arguments more persuasive, or their experiences more vivid, writers may define terms, provide analogies (the behaviour of gas molecules is like the behaviour of people in an elevator), or make passing references—allusions—to well-known historical figures and events ("My hopes sank like the *Titanic*"). For more on analogies, see "Kinds of Evidence" in Stage 2, Gathering Material: Arguments and Evidence, in Chapter 8.

Analyzing a piece of nonfiction writing is often preparation for evaluating the ideas and information it presents. For suggestions about how to evaluate a writer's arguments and evidence, see Chapter 8, Writing Evaluation Essays.

STEP 2 Gaining a Broader Perspective

Once you've figured out the basic ideas in a piece of nonfiction, it's time to stand back and take another look at the work as a whole. As a result of considering the work's purpose and tone, you may modify your sense of the work's subject or thesis. Thinking about the work's context may lead you to a deeper understanding. After you've reread or thought about the whole piece, write a sentence or two answering the questions posed below.

Purpose Is the writer's main purpose to inform, to persuade, or to share personal experience? In "Girl Unprotected" (Readings), for example, Robinson's purpose is to expose and to critique the gendered underside of hockey culture. In "It Always Costs" (Readings), on the other hand, Suzuki's main purpose is to persuade readers to accept his views. Consider these possibilities carefully. You may discover that works seemingly designed to explain or to share personal experience are actually making a persuasive point.

In summarizing, choose words that show you understand the author's purpose. Use the author's name every few sentences to make clear you are stating another person's ideas, not your own.

PURPOSE	WORDS THAT CONVEY PURPOSE
To share experience	Tells the story, reflects upon, describes
To inform	Explains, discusses, examines, analyzes
To persuade	Argues, claims, makes the point, criticizes

Tone Does the writer use humour, satire, or irony? If so, how does that affect your understanding of the piece?

Context: subject What knowledge of the subject or the cultural/historical circumstances can you bring to your understanding of the work?

Take a few minutes to consider how the piece fits with other things you know about the subject. For instance, perhaps your knowledge of the "troubles" that plagued Northern Ireland for many years could enrich your understanding of Jonathan Swift's "A Modest Proposal" (Readings).

Context: writer What do you know about the writer? Does the writer mention the source of his or her knowledge about the subject? Does the writer identify herself/himself with a specific political, religious, or intellectual position? What does the work itself suggest about the writer's perspective?

Writers often give some indication of the experience or training that qualifies them to speak about their subject, as you can see in the Suzuki piece "It Always Costs" (Readings). They may also identify the political, religious, or intellectual framework that guides their thinking, as Laura Robinson specifically refuses to name one of the girls in "Girl Unprotected" (Readings) as a measure to counteract her naming in the press. The writer's perspective may be implied rather than stated. For example, Forster's biblical allusions in "My Wood" (Readings) suggest a particular religious framework. Considering the above questions will help you see the values that inform the piece of writing.

STEP 3 Writing a Summary

At first glance, writing a summary appears quite straightforward. You might assume that you simply write down what you know or what you remember from a piece of writing. However, as the preceding discussion of analysis indicates, the process of understanding the many elements and complexities of a written work can be quite challenging. Not only is it a challenge to write a summary, but also it is important to think about your purpose for writing a summary.

While some writing exercises for school may require you specifically to write a summary, there are numerous examples of where summary skills may be required or helpful in workplace environments. For example, engineers can spend much of their time writing reports and making recommendations to industry, and they may preface their reports with an executive summary to provide decision makers an overview of the project under review. Similarly, business people or entrepreneurs may rely on summary skills to pitch a product or service to potential retailers or investors. Medical practitioners may write patient histories, or teachers may write student progress reports. Even movie or book reviews are kinds of summaries. In school environments, summaries often constitute part of your writing assignments because you are responding to certain texts or sections of texts in any given discipline to demonstrate your understanding of those materials and, often, to respond to them.

Usually, the primary function of a summary is to communicate the maximum amount of information in the minimum amount (or perhaps specified amount) of space. Because a summary is usually shorter than the original work, your job as a writer is to include or to cut information. Since a summary is almost always written in your own words, you must differentiate between essential and non-essential information and organize and communicate that material in a coherent piece of writing without it sounding fragmented or excerpted from the original.

Moreover, a summary is not simply an itemization or blow-by-blow account of the original work. A good summary will tell not only *what* happened but also *how* it happened. It is a communication of both content and form, and it will communicate information as well as elements like purpose, tone, context, etc. So, for example, if you are summarizing a piece of writing that is funny, your purpose is not necessarily to be funny in your summary but to state that the original writing employs humour or comedy as a form of writing. Your task is to write a summary, not to be a comedian who makes jokes.

Finally, you should consider your own purpose when writing a summary, as it may vary in different contexts. Some summaries are to remain disinterested about the subject matter, so the summary focuses exclusively on the meaning of the original work. Other summary situations may require you to include your own opinion or evaluation of the topic or viewpoint of the original work. In the first instance, your own voice is largely absent from the text; in the latter instance, you will clearly differentiate your own view from the view of the original. Ensure you understand what is appropriate for your summary.

When you finish your analysis of the work you are summarizing, use your notes to write a brief draft summary of the piece. The summary will help you remember what you've read. You may also incorporate the summary, or parts of it, in your essay if you are using the summary for a longer work. This draft summary should include the following:

1. Complete bibliographic information about the piece: author, title, and other details as appropriate for the type of publication (see Part 3, H3 Documentation).

2. The writer's thesis, in your own words, at or near the beginning of the summary.

3. An overview of the organization of the piece and the main points in each section. State these points in your own words, but include brief quotations to capture the tone of the piece. Put quotation marks around any three or more consecutive words from the piece. If the piece is longer than a page, give page numbers in parentheses after each quotation and paraphrase. Page numbers are handy in case you need to refer to specific material again. They are crucial when you are documenting research papers.

4. The main types of evidence and an explanation of their purpose.

5. Key terms and their definitions.

Generally speaking, a summary should follow the progression and distribution of the original. In other words, your summary should spend as much time and space on a particular example or point relative to the original work. Of course, there are exceptions to this principle. For example, if the original work contains many examples, data, or statistics as its primary content, it is not very helpful or clear to select a random sampling of statistics. In a case such as this, it makes more sense to state the conclusions the original article draws from the examples, data, or statistics. You might write something like this: "The author includes an extensive analysis of the data to conclude that [X conclusion]."

For an example, see the following sample topic.

Sample Topic: Analyzing and Summarizing Laura Robinson's "Girl Unprotected"

Robinson's article "Girl Unprotected" (published on www.playthegame .org, November 19, 2008) is reprinted in the Readings. You will follow this example more easily if you read Robinson's article first.

STEP 1   Figuring Out the Basic Ideas

What is the subject? Upon a first reading or overview, this article appears to be about hockey, but the title suggests that it may be more about gender and safety than hockey. The brief author biography on the first page of the text tells us that Robinson is a reporter who frequently writes about gender in sport, so we might expect her to discuss gender in relation to hockey.

What is the main idea? Robinson's text is a good example of how it can be difficult to identify the main idea of a text on a first reading. Initially, this writing appears to be about hockey. We quickly realize it is also about how women are involved in hockey. Robinson also raises the issue of sexual abuse not only of women but also of men in hockey. At this point, we might think that Robinson as a reporter is merely commenting that sexual abuse exists in the broader hockey culture. Yet, she goes further than this. She follows the trial under question to raise questions around the reporting, the believability, and the prosecution of sexual abuse in hockey. In essence, the main idea of Robinson's work is about the process and the possibility of justice, generally, as it relates to hockey, gender, and sexual abuse, specifically.

How does the writer develop this main idea? Like many writers, Robinson does not rely solely on one method of development. Primarily, she employs both storytelling and system analysis, but she also incorporates process analysis, comparison and contrast, and evaluation, to a lesser degree. She begins her writing by situating the reader as the parent of a hypothetical girl in a hockey scenario, and she continues to tell a story of how the situation unfolds. Overall, she is critical of the justice system and how it fails to protect women in the hockey system. As part of this system analysis, she demonstrates the process of the justice system (process analysis), the unequal treatment of the different genders (compare and contrast), and the shortcomings she perceives in the system (evaluation).

What are the main types of evidence/detail the writer uses? For what purpose(s)? Robinson relies almost exclusively on examples in her piece. She draws her primary examples from the Danton case in Deseronto, but she does not limit her analysis to this single example. She begins to generalize from these examples by drawing upon Robin Warshaw's book about sexual assault on university campuses as well as another hockey example of Graham James in Swift Current. Many Canadians, if they are not familiar with these specific examples, will likely be familiar with hockey and hockey culture.

STEP 2   Gaining a Broader Perspective

Purpose and tone Robinson's main purpose is to expose some of the negative experiences within Canada's hockey culture and to question the possibility of attaining justice regarding any wrongdoing against people playing or surrounding the sport. Her focus is on the power inherent in the relationships between coaches, players, girlfriends, families and the justice system, particularly as it pertains to freedom of choice and sexuality. Her tone is primarily critical and serious, yet she draws upon imaginative and rhetorical statements to provoke the reader into thinking about his or her own response to the material.

Context Hockey is Canada's winter national sport (lacrosse is the summer sport), and it contributes greatly to our national imagination of our own country. Along with our polite and apologetic traits, we frequently invoke hockey as a defining characteristic of Canada, and we have enjoyed great success at the Olympics with Canadians winning gold for women in 2002, 2006, 2010, and 2014, and men in 2002, 2010, and 2014. When the occasional story breaks about violence or abuse in the sport, or if someone begins debating the appropriateness of fighting in hockey, Canadians may feel defensive about the sanctity of the game or uncomfortable with some of the ugly details of the sport. While it is easy to enjoy the on-ice skill of the game and the competition and rivalry between teams, there are other contexts for hockey beyond the role of player and fan. There are parents who drive children to practices at early hours, coaches who are hired and fired on the basis of their success, players who face extraordinary time and family sacrifices to excel at training, and all the other people who surround the sport. Robinson invokes the less obvious contexts for hockey by focusing on the parental perceptions of the game, the girlfriends of the players, the power of the coaches, and the capability of the justice system to investigate our national sport. Her approach may risk alienating her audience, and she must be careful not to offend her readers.

STEP 3   Writing a Summary

Now that you have gathered information for an analysis of a piece of nonfiction writing, you can clarify the connections among your points by writing a summary.

Sample Summary

"GIRL UNPROTECTED"

Laura Robinson's essay "Girl Unprotected" (www.playthegame.org, 19 Nov. 2008) uses the 2004 criminal conspiracy case of Mike Danton and the NHL to expose how the justice system's handling of the case fails to address adequately all the potential victims of and wrongdoings in hockey abuses, particularly in relation to gender and sexuality. Robinson begins her article with a second-person address to her reader to imagine having a daughter whose boyfriend is a promising hockey player. After raising hopes for the future, Robinson moves ahead in time and introduces the criminal charges against Mike Danton as an example of a player's dreams going tragically wrong. Alongside this real-life case, she maintains the reader's fictional daughter to highlight the other potential real-life victims who are pressured into sex both by their boyfriends and by the coaches. Referring to Robin Warshaw's study of perceptions and definitions of rape, Robinson demonstrates how the court system treats incidents of criminal conspiracy between men and sexual assault cases against women with a double standard of justice based on the sufficiency of evidence in each case: Danton is considered a victim of a crime perpetuated by his coach while the women are considered willing participants in a sexual assault. The male case is legitimate; the female case is not. The author draws upon her history of research to argue that courts often ignore criminal acts in hockey to "[prop] up the hockey mythology" (327) while simultaneously ignoring issues of gender, sexuality, and free choice. Robinson concludes by citing other examples of physical and sexual abuse in hockey culture to demonstrate that even the occasional stories about abuses between players and coaches do not tell all the other stories, particularly women's stories, associated with the negative elements of hockey.

Working on Your Own Assignment

Develop better reading strategies to help you understand nonfiction, such as articles in books, magazines, newspapers, and scholarly journals.

- Figure out the basic ideas by identifying the writer's subject, thesis, main points, and supporting evidence.
- Deepen your understanding of the material by considering the writer's purpose, tone, and context.
- Write a brief summary that will help you remember what you have read.

Exercises

A. Write a summary of one of the following essays from Part 2, Readings. Use the sample topic above as a guide.

- David Suzuki, "It Always Costs"
- Robert Bringhurst, "The Persistence of Poetry and the Destruction of the World"

B. Write two or three sentences identifying the major strengths and weaknesses of the following summary. Then revise the summary. You will find E. M. Forster's "My Wood" in Part 2, Readings.

> "What is the effect of property on the character?" E. M. Forster asks in "My Wood," and then proceeds to give us the answer (246). "In the first place, it makes me feel heavy" he says (246), referring to the fact that owning things weighs people down both physically and morally. "In the second place, it makes me feel it ought to be larger" he continues (247). "A little more, and then a little more" he says (247), pointing to our greed for more and more possessions. Furthermore, "property makes its owner feel that he ought to do something to it" (247). He realizes, however, that his impulse to change things "spring[s] from a foolish desire to express myself and from an inability to enjoy what I have got" (247). The final effect of property is to make a person selfish. As Forster says, "I shall wall in and fence out until I really taste the sweets of property" (248). He sums it all up by saying that his property has made him "[e]normously stout, endlessly avaricious, pseudo-creative, intensely selfish" (248).

Writing Analysis Essays: Clarifying Essay Topics and Gathering Material

Sample Topic: Nostalgia in Tim Bowling's "Na Na Na Na, Hey Hey Hey, Goodbye"

Stage 1   **Clarifying Essay Topics**

          Step 1   Defining Unfamiliar Terms and Understanding Your Assignment

          Step 2   Exploring Your Subject

Stage 2   **Gathering Material**

          Step 1   Analyzing the Text

          Step 2   Choosing Methods of Analysis

          Step 3   Choosing Disciplinary or Analytic Categories

          Step 4   Choosing Methods of Proof

          Step 5   Tying It All Together

Special Categories for Analyzing Texts

          A.   Identifying Textual Features

          B.   Connecting the Parts to the Whole

Sample Topic: Nostalgia in Tim Bowling's "Na Na Na Na, Hey Hey Hey, Goodbye"

Stage 1   **Clarifying Essay Topics**

Stage 2   **Gathering Material**

We turn now to the writing of analysis essays. As we discussed in Chapter 2, it is important to have reading and comprehension skills in order to write about a text or a subject in any discipline. It is also important to be able to summarize what you have read. Now that you understand and have worked on those skills, you are ready to learn how to analyze a text and communicate your analysis to others. In other words, you are ready to write an analysis essay.

When you write analysis essays, you focus both on the content of your source material and on how it is presented: you pay attention to what is said and how it is said. You may examine behaviour, data, events, written works, and other sources of information and ideas. Every written text is created from particular materials available to its writer. In a history course, for example, you may be asked to survey various historical documents and writings in order to answer a question about a particular aspect of World War I. In a literature course, you may be asked to analyze characters' national or gendered identities in order to determine the author's and characters' relationship to the world in which they live.

STAGE 1   Clarifying Essay Topics

STEP 1   Defining Unfamiliar Terms and Understanding Your Assignment

Make sure that you understand all the terms used in the assignment. Learning about a subject includes learning the vocabulary that specialists in the subject use. In psychology courses, you may learn the meaning of such terms as *conditioned response*, *narcissism*, and *depression*. In literature courses, you are likely to discuss the meaning of such terms as *myth*, *point of view*, and *tragedy*. As these examples suggest, the specialized vocabulary of each discipline is likely to include terms seldom used outside the field as well as terms used in a more restricted way than you would use them in everyday speech. You can often clarify the meaning of terms by consulting your course text(s) or specialized dictionaries. Many texts contain glossaries that briefly define concepts and other specialized terms.

Understanding what your assignment is asking of you is also important when you begin the process of writing an essay. Essays can take a variety of forms: they may be largely descriptive or they may be highly analytic. Knowing what an essay can do and what type of essay your topic requires will help you deliver a more effective assignment.

No matter what subject you are studying, you will write essays that present arguments—you will be using *rhetoric* (the title of Part 1), the art of persuasive speech or writing. The tradition of rhetoric dates back to ancient times: one of the first written accounts was Aristotle's *On Rhetoric*. Rhetoric is concerned with not only the argument but also the language that makes the argument. This tradition is related to current essay writing because it is the foundation of the thesis statement: an opinion (the argument) with evidence (the reasons, expressed in language, why the argument is worth believing).

When you are writing an essay that requires you to make an argument, you need to think about your subject in two related ways: analysis and critique. *Analysis* is a process in which you break down something into its various distinct parts. Related to analysis, *critique* involves an evaluation of (that is, forming an opinion or making a judgment about) some or all of those distinct parts that you identify in the analysis. For example, you could dismantle your car into all its identifiable parts: tires, hubcaps, windows, handles, fans, belts, spark plugs, and so on. However, if something were wrong with your car, you would need the critical capacity to evaluate which part is faulty. You might be able to identify all the parts, yet you might or might not be able to determine what is wrong.

The beginning chapters of the rhetoric section primarily address analysis and what we call methods of analysis. The latter chapters of the rhetoric section address evaluation and critique. However, the main focus of essay writing is the development of a thesis statement, so you will find elements of both analysis and critique in these early chapters, because a thesis involves both these processes. Engaging in an analysis is not the same as holding an opinion; similarly, having an opinion does not necessarily presuppose a thorough analysis.

STEP 2 Exploring Your Subject

Most essay topics set limits on what you should cover: the concept of the state in Plato's *Republic;* the use of the vampire myth in *Dracula* and *Interview with the Vampire;* Canadian and US policies on endangered species. Occasionally, however, you may face a fairly indefinite topic, such as "Write a 1000-word essay on how technology affects your life," or you may be invited to come up with a topic of your own.

Whether your topic is narrowly defined or open-ended, you can use various techniques—such as freewriting, brainstorming, and tree diagramming—to explore your topic and to define its limits. Limiting your topic allows you to examine your subject thoroughly enough to speak as an expert to less well-informed readers. If you try to write a five-page essay on a broad subject, such as computers or every aspect of a novel, your treatment is likely to be superficial. Narrowing your focus enables you to examine your subject in greater depth. It also helps you organize your information gathering and your writing. If you are unsure of the scope or intent of your assignment, ask for clarification from your instructor.

Here are three quick ways of generating ideas about your topic:

Freewriting   Each time you come up with an idea, does another part of your brain say, "That's no good," or "You'll look silly if you say that"? Freewriting is one way of circumventing this mental critic. If you tend to agonize over a blank page, then freewriting may set your mind in motion.

Freewriting consists of writing continuously for ten minutes or longer, without stopping to organize, correct, or evaluate what you are doing. If your first attempt at freewriting does not give you a clear sense of what you might want to focus on in your essay, try variations on the freewriting process. You might, for example, look over your first freewriting material for the idea that seems most promising and then use this idea as a springboard for a second spurt of freewriting. Or, if you are trying to find an aspect of a text that interests you, you might freewrite a fantasy dialogue with the author, asking questions and recording the replies. This dialogue may reveal possibilities that you would not have reached by more conventional means.

Brainstorming   This is another way of circumventing your mental critic. Brainstorming consists of putting down, in point form, everything you can think of about your topic, however obvious or bizarre the ideas may seem. Begin by writing your subject in the middle of a page and then jot down ideas as they come to you. When you have finished, you will have a mixture of generalizations and details radiating from your central subject. You can then draw lines to connect related points. For example, if you wanted to explore the film *The Matrix*, as discussed in Chapter 1, you might come up with a brainstorming diagram such as the one in Figure 3.1.

Much of the material you generate while brainstorming will never make it into a final version of your essay, but it's always better to have too much material than too little. From the diagram, you might pursue the aesthetics of action and violence in the film as an essay topic, or you could choose to explore the problematic opposition of free will and fatalism, as shown in the sample essay in Chapter 1.

Tree diagramming   Tree diagramming is a more systematic form of brainstorming. When you use this technique, you divide your broad subject into categories and subcategories in the form of an ever-expanding tree. Because

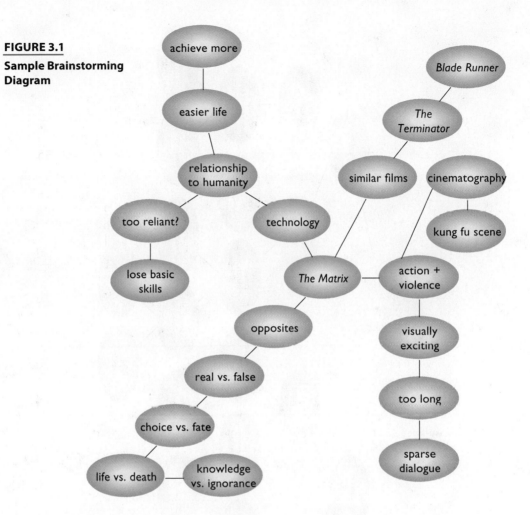

FIGURE 3.1

Sample Brainstorming Diagram

a tree diagram encourages you to develop equivalent categories, it is especially useful for narrowing comparison topics and developing arguments for and against something. For example, you might construct a tree diagram as a means of exploring arguments for and against Canada's role as a peacekeeper. Figure 3.2 represents the type of diagram you would generate by using this technique.

These discovery techniques are obviously useful for narrowing a broad subject such as technology. Even when the topic is limited, you can use these techniques to prime your thinking or to discover an angle that interests you.

FIGURE 3.2
Sample Tree Diagram

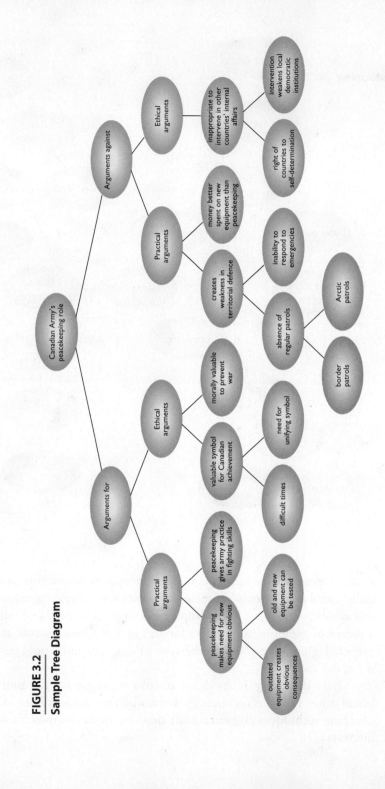

STAGE 2 **Gathering Material**

STEP 1 **Analyzing the Text**

Writers write essays on *texts*—a term that we use broadly to encompass not only disciplinary texts (history or anthropology textbooks, for example), but also interviews, advertisements, emails, signs, and visual or performance art. In an analysis essay, you gather material by thinking about the text you are considering and by breaking it down into parts in order to understand its meaning and its importance in culture and society. To gather material for an analysis essay, then, you must analyze the text and identify what is important and noteworthy about it.

STEP 2 **Choosing Methods of Analysis**

Writers have identified various methods of analysis (sometimes called rhetorical modes) that are useful in examining subjects. The following list of modes is not exhaustive, but it includes basic definitions of some major methods of analysis that you may be asked to use when you are writing essays for college or university courses.

In this section, we will touch briefly on the modes of *description*, *narration*, *division and classification*, and *comparison and contrast*, followed by a more detailed discussion of **definition**, **cause/effect analysis**, **process analysis**, and **systems analysis**. The latter four methods of analysis are common to most academic disciplines and to analytic thinking in general.

Because of its importance and prominence in many courses, we have included an entire chapter on how to write a comparison essay (see Chapter 7). In that chapter you will learn how to analyze the similarities and differences between works.

Description Description mostly involves giving details about a person or thing. The most obvious type of description is spatial and physical. For example, if you were describing a person, you might give details such as hair colour, eye colour, height, weight, and clothes worn (physical details), and organize them in a logical structure by starting from head to toe, back to front, or side to side, depending on the subject of description (spatial details). Other possibilities for description might include temporal and abstract details. You could, for example, write about a building in a city where certain historical aspects are significant. Such descriptive writing might include abstract ideas like what the building means to the citizens of the city. Good descriptive writing will avoid a shopping list approach to detail in favour of an analysis of the importance of the included details.

Narration Narration is the act of telling in language; generally speaking, all writing has an element of narration. Most frequently, narration involves telling a story, as seen in all types of writing from newspaper articles to memoirs to fiction to how-to manuals. Narration usually relates the details of what happened and in what order, although many writers toy with narrative strategies by telling events out of order or through other experimentation. Narration is similar to description, but description primarily focuses on the person or thing itself while narration is more concerned with the sequence of details over time. In some cases, both happen simultaneously.

Division and classification Division and classification are basic human ways of thinking that allow us to separate units into groups and subgroups, often in some logical structure. For example, the classification of biological organisms into kingdom-phylum-class-order is a top-down ordering. The organization of books into alphabetical order is a left-to-right ordering. The palette of colours with red-yellow-blue in the centre and orange-green-purple (and other colours) surrounding it in various combinations is a centre-out ordering. To produce good division and classification writing, it is essential that the *basis of classification* be clearly defined. There can be different reasons for dividing groups of things into subgroups. For example, we may want to classify foods in terms of their colours, their protein values, their availability, or their cost.

Comparison and contrast Comparison and contrast writing analyzes the similarities and differences of two or more things. Like division and classification, good comparison and contrast writing will identify the **basis of comparison** and explain the reason(s) for the comparison. In academic writing, comparison and contrast writing will examine related opinions or theses on any given topic. For example, a biology class might ask you to write a paper on Lamarck's and Darwin's competing theories of evolution. An economics class might ask that you analyze the benefits and drawbacks of owning a car versus taking public transit. Similarly, an environmental studies class might ask the same question about transportation, but the basis of comparison could be quite different, one being economic in nature, the other environmental. Unless the objects are identical, comparison and contrast always involves both similarity and difference.

Definition Definition is very common in college and university writing. The most obvious source for definitions is the dictionary, but dictionaries sometimes make poor sources for academic definitions because they are written for brevity. As we discussed earlier, most disciplines develop a specialized vocabulary for their own purposes, and dictionary definitions fail to capture this depth or complexity. For example, claiming you are "depressed" would mean one thing to a friend and quite another thing to a clinical psychiatrist. Given that most academic writing is aimed at a specialized audience, it is preferable to use definitions that are more thorough, developed, or specific within that particular discipline. Avoid using simple definitions from sources such as a standard student dictionary or dictionary. com. If you feel compelled to use a dictionary, the most exhaustive dictionary of the English language is the *Oxford English Dictionary* (*OED*), which traces all words back to their first appearance in written English.

Later in this chapter we explain that disciplinary categories (for example, the category of *human needs* in psychology) must be understood within the context of the discipline or course of study. Definitions of terms can also be discipline specific. This specificity is why it is important to understand terms used in your assignment in relation to your course, not just in relation to a standard dictionary. It may be necessary to refer to terms as they are outlined in your textbook or in a specialized dictionary, such as a glossary of literary terms.

If you are using a definition method of analysis, you will need to employ an *extended definition*. Whereas a *formal definition* is a short, specific definition, as outlined in a dictionary, for example, an extended definition is more complex and multifaceted. It is a sustained and thorough definition of a concept or an idea, often as it applies to a particular discipline, context, or situation. If your essay topic asks you to explore a particular concept or term in sufficient detail, then you may want to use a definition method of analysis.

The following essay topics (based on works reprinted in the Readings) would be conducive to a definition method of analysis: "Explore the meaning of *addiction* as it is outlined by Gabor Maté in 'Embraced by the Needle' and Bruce K. Alexander in 'Reframing Canada's "Drug Problem"'"; "With reference to David Suzuki's 'It Always Costs,' and W. S. Merwin's 'Unchopping a Tree,' explain *environmentalism*." Such assignments ask you to explore the complexities of a term and how that term might be understood by different authors and in various contexts.

A definition method of analysis works best when the term you are defining is open to different interpretations. For instance, if asked to respond to the essay assignment "What success means to you," no two students will write the same answer. Similarly, environmentalism might be understood and explained differently by Suzuki and Merwin. If the term or concept you are examining is vague or multidimensional, then it is particularly important to engage in an analysis of the term and to explain clearly what it means within the context of your essay. A definition can expand or limit the scope of a term, depending on the purpose of the exercise.

When employing the definition method of analysis, you can divide the concept you are defining into different parts. What is it that can provide your readers with a sense of the whole? The parts that you recognize in your concept are your categories for analysis. For example, if you are writing an essay on environmentalism and drawing upon an essay by Merwin (Readings), then you might recognize that conservation or preservation is important to the author's understanding of environmentalism. Merwin wishes to preserve forests in "Unchopping a Tree." The idea of conservation, then, can be one of the categories through which you explain environmentalism.

Conversely, you may wish to place your term within the context of a larger concept—explain your term in relation to a larger whole. If you are writing an essay on the notion of environmentalism, you can relate it to the larger concept of *ecology*. While placing your concept in a larger category, it is important to explain exactly how it fits into that larger notion. Doing so will make clear the term's meaning and your understanding of it.

You may also want to analyze your term by comparing or contrasting it with other similar concepts. If you are defining *social worker*, for instance, you may compare and contrast the role of social worker with that of a psychologist or counsellor. If you are comparing your term to something similar, then make sure to point out the difference(s) in order to make the specific meaning of your term clear. Another way of providing an extended definition of your term is to provide examples of it.

You may use one or more of these techniques in order to define your term. Above all, it is important to make clear to your readers how the works you are analyzing use the term and how you—as the author of your essay—understand the term. Analyzing definitions is therefore an important method since you can use it to exemplify your understanding and to communicate specific meanings or concepts to your readers.

Cause/effect Cause/effect analysis explores the factors that have brought about a behaviour, event, or other phenomenon (its causes, in other words) or the changes that this phenomenon has itself brought about (its effects). Analysis of causes answers *why* questions: Why do some people become addicted and others not? Why do we disapprove of hockey violence and yet keep watching the game? Analysis of effects answers *what* questions: What are the effects of addiction on parenting, or on self-esteem? What are the consequences of accepting violence in sports?

In writing cause/effect analysis essays, your eventual goal is to arrive at a thesis—an opinion about causes, effects, or the relationship between causes and effects. However, you need to be modest about your claims. As ecologist David Suzuki points out in "It Always Costs" (Readings), we can't necessarily predict the effects of our actions. Nor can we always identify causes with certainty. The relationship between causes and effects is complex and often quite conjectural, even in the sciences. Certainly most phenomena do not have either a single cause or a single effect. For example, Gabor Maté in "Embraced by the Needle" (Readings) and Bruce K. Alexander in "Reframing Canada's 'Drug Problem'" (Readings) offer somewhat different causes of addiction. Both accounts have much validity, as C. Jones points out in her comparison essay "Perspectives on Addictions" (Readings: Sample Essays).

Because the goal of most academic disciplines is to probe beneath the surface of the phenomena they study, cause/effect analysis is often required in academic essay assignments. Assignments containing the word *why* usually ask you to analyze causes, as in "Write an essay discussing the reasons why addiction to prescription drugs is so common in North America." Assignments that require you to analyze effects usually indicate this focus by using words such as *effects, consequences,* or *results.* If you are unsure whether cause/effect analysis suits your subject, try turning the essay topic into a *why* or *what* question. If rewording the assignment in this way does not make cause/effect analysis obviously appropriate, you may want to consider other types of analysis.

In the early stages of planning your essay, of course, you may not know the answer to your question about causes or effects. You still may decide that this kind of analysis is the best way to explore your subject. For example, in "Na Na Na Na, Hey Hey Hey, Goodbye" (Readings), Tim Bowling's subject is his ambivalence toward hockey, which he can explain only by exploring the reasons why his attitude exists. Thus his subject provides a strong motivation for writing a cause/effect analysis essay.

Process analysis A process generally has a beginning and an end, with various stages in the middle. Like cause and effect, it is a progression of related events through time. Unlike cause and effect, however, a process analysis deals with larger stages that may differ from the isolated events of cause and effect. The process may consist of either a sequence of actions directed toward a definite end, such as the process of making a handicraft or a machine, or a series of identifiable changes over time, such as the process of aging. We divide the process into stages according to the points at which changes occur in the actions or states that make up the process.

Using this textbook as an example, the rhetoric section could be read as a process analysis. Disregarding the stages and steps this textbook discusses, a writer could simply produce an introduction, three body paragraphs, and a conclusion. The resulting five-paragraph essay might look like an essay, but it would lack the necessary stages of development, the comprehensive working through of the process that yields a good, persuasive essay. For example, missed developmental stages could mean the essay lacks the intellectual deliberation upon other viewpoints that may conflict with or contradict the essay's thesis. The essay, by definition, is a process of working through an idea and cannot be achieved through a formulaic approach to writing offered by some simple how-to essay writing guides.

When you are writing a process analysis essay, your goal is to develop a thesis about the relationship between the stages that make up your subject. Remembering this purpose will help you avoid slipping into two kinds of writing that superficially resemble process essays but actually have very different goals: *how-to writing* and *narrative essays*.

- How-to writing consists of sets of instructions that tell you, for example, how to finger the easiest chords on your new guitar or how to minimize the use of pesticides in your garden. How-to writing may seem similar to process analysis essays about actions directed toward an end. You can avoid confusing these two kinds of writing if you remember that the aim of how-to writing is to enable the reader to *do* something, while the aim of a process analysis essay is to have the reader *believe* something, namely the author's thesis about the relationship between the action stages. A handbook on fingering guitar chords, for instance, would explain how to move from simple chords like A and E to more complex chords like F and B minor, whereas an essay analyzing the process of learning folk guitar might present the thesis that the process is unexpectedly complex because the early stages are interdependent.

- The second kind of writing that can be confused with process analysis, the narrative essay, uses nonfictional material to tell a story with a more or less explicit thesis. George Orwell's "Shooting an Elephant" (Readings) is a narrative essay in which the author describes the stages of his own awakening to the evils of imperialism. Not all narrative essays have an emphasis on stages; the ones that do, like Orwell's, may seem hard to distinguish from process essays that analyze identifiable changes over time. The key distinction is that narrative essays deal with *individual* stages; process essays analyze *general* stages of development. Thus in "Shooting," Orwell presents the stages through which one particular "young and ill educated" Englishman, a police officer, struggles to understand his true role in the East. Are these stages common to everybody who comes to a similar understanding of the significance of imperialism? It is not part of Orwell's aim to answer this question. A process analysis essay on the same subject might claim, for example, that many representatives of colonial powers go through the same process of psychological denial followed by recognition, then social accommodation followed by alienation.

Process analysis topics in academic disciplines may require you to analyze a series of directed actions, such as the procedure for casting bronze, the steps necessary to stage a Greek tragedy, or the steps required to improve the habitat for spotted owls. Analyzing a series of changes over time is a common assignment in disciplines like history (for example, analyzing the stages in the development of parliamentary democracy), psychology (analyzing the development of cognitive thinking), or anthropology (analyzing the development of Mayan religious iconography). Notice the key words in these assignments: *procedure, steps, stages, development*. Similar terms, such as *emergence, evolution, growth,* and *progress,* may also indicate process analysis.

Process analysis may also be one of several possible ways of responding to a general topic. For example, if you were given the topic "Write an essay exploring the significance of globalization," you might decide to analyze globalization in terms of its historical evolution. This is the analysis that underpins James Howard Kunstler's "Globalisation's Time Is Up" (Readings). The process approach supports his point that globalization is a transient phenomenon, rising and falling with the passage of time.

Two kinds of stages that you may develop in your process analysis essay are *chronological stages* and *action stages*.

Chronological stages Since process is an unfolding over time, periods of time form natural categories for process analysis. However, chronological stages should not be arbitrarily divided segments of time; each should correspond to a marked change in the ongoing process.

Action stages When you are analyzing a process that consists of a series of actions, action stages are useful categories for gathering material. Look for points at which the nature of the action changes. Each of these changes marks a new stage in the process. If initially you come up with only one or two action stages, think of the actions that necessarily precede and/or follow the actions you have identified.

The following assignment is an example of a process analysis essay topic.

- **Discuss** the gradual way in which the character of Neo in the film *The Matrix* comes to realize that his world is fictional.

The assignment asks you to examine Neo's process of change and discovery. You would divide the process of discovery into stages and analyze each stage. In developing the essay, you would focus each paragraph on a different stage in the process; the stage would become the topic of the paragraph and the main point would be about the significance of the stage. This method works well in theory and in expert hands, but process essays about texts often fall into the trap of just retelling the story. Be aware of this tendency if you choose the process analysis method of development.

Essentially, if your subject can be divided into stages, process analysis is one way of gathering material. Whether it is the best way depends on the kind of point you eventually want to make.

Systems analysis Whereas a *process* is the progression through general stages to some kind of end, a *system* is a combination of interrelated parts that constitutes a unified whole. To use the essay as an example, the writing of an essay is a process; the product of an essay is a system. The various parts of the essay—the thesis, the development of details, the wider implications, the audience, the context of the writing—all contribute to how the essay works. So, for example, if an essay lacked the development of details, the reader might understand the point of the argument (the thesis) but not how the writer arrived at the thesis (development of details). Or, if a writer failed to consider the essay's audience, the writer might risk alienating that audience by not considering their viewpoint. In other words, a writer who is "for" a particular position will write differently for an audience who shares similar views than for an audience who is "against" that position. In any case, when one part of a system fails to function properly or adequately, the entire system may be compromised. The system may fail, or it may find a new equilibrium. Good writing about systems will consider all parts of the system in order to make an argument.

In school you have no doubt studied planetary systems and the many systems that make up the human body. Out of school, your activities and even your mood may be influenced by the prevailing weather system. The news is filled with debates about the health care system. Yet you may not fully understand why each of these is called a system.

A system is a unified whole that is made up of many parts. This meaning can apply to a set of events, such as the French Revolution; a set of data, such as a bookkeeping system; a set of phenomena, such as an ecosystem; or a set of ideas, such as neo-liberal economic theory. It even applies to essays whose parts (thesis statement, topic sentences, and the like) contribute to a whole (the essay itself).

Whether it involves a set of phenomena or a set of ideas, a system will have *essential parts,* which are those elements needed to keep the system going, and a *goal* or *function,* which is what the system is in place to do. When writing systems analysis essays, you need to be particularly thorough in gathering material, because you cannot afford to leave out any essential part.

The purpose of systems analysis essays is to analyze the parts in order to understand the system as a whole and its goal or function. If you were analyzing the criminal justice system within a democracy, for example, you might conclude that the parts (lawmakers, courts, lawyers, juries, prisons, and so forth) are designed to achieve the goal of balancing the defendant's rights with the rights of society. In contrast, the criminal justice system in a dictatorship would have a different function, such as maintaining the authority of those in power.

Essay assignment topics may specifically ask for systems analysis. For example, an assignment could ask you to identify the key features of J. K. Galbraith's economic theories, the elements necessary for a salmon stream to be viable, the main aspects of verbal and non-verbal communication in families, the key beliefs of the '70s generation of feminists, or the defining components of systems of poetic metre. Notice the adjectives (*key, necessary, main, defining*) and nouns (*features, elements, aspects,* and *components*) in these topics. Words like these refer to essential parts of something, and thus indicate that you are being asked to view the subject as a system. Assignments may also ask you to focus on the function of one or more parts in relation to the whole, as in "Discuss the role played by planning committees in the organization of the 2015 Canada Winter Games in Prince George, British Columbia."

As a way of seeing the world, systems analysis has become increasingly common since the mid-twentieth century, when disciplines like ecology reinforced the interconnectedness of human society with the whole surrounding environment. For assignments that do not specify the method of analysis you are to use, systems analysis is a good choice if your subject can be divided up into essential parts and if you can make a valid and thoughtful point about the interconnectedness of these parts.

When you are writing a systems analysis essay, check first to see whether there is an appropriate set of disciplinary categories for the system you are analyzing. If you were analyzing the needs of wilderness forests as a system, for example, the ecological categories of carbon cycle, water cycle, nutrient cycle, and energy cycle would give you comprehensive categories for collecting material. As you move your attention away from the sciences toward culture and society, decisions about which parts are essential become a matter of informed, well-educated, or researched opinion. It is obvious that trees need water, but is an emphasis on equal pay an essential part of the ideology of 1970s feminism?

When you are writing about subjects that are governed mainly by informed opinion, it will be the details you gather that will make your claims about essential parts more or less convincing to your reader. If you are having trouble coming up with categories of essential parts, try brainstorming. Or, if the function of the whole seems more important than a detailed analysis of the parts, you may find that you can explain the significance of one system more forcefully by comparing it with a similar system. Systems analysis is a method often used in writing essays on literature. In analyzing a literary text (a poem, a film, an essay) as a work of art, you are examining it as a system of interrelated parts. The artistic choices about such matters as verse form, structure, and **style**, in particular **diction**, help shape literature's meaning—the whole work of literature as a system. Analyzing a literary text as a system gives you practice in examining a text closely. You could, however, also use cause/effect or process analysis to analyze literary texts. For instance, you could look at the historical, social, economic, or psychological causes that may have shaped a particular text, or at the text's aesthetic or social effects. This kind of cause/effect analysis is increasingly popular in literature courses, as we attempt to understand how literature "means" in our historical and contemporary world. You could also examine the process by which a text was composed, published, or performed. This kind of process analysis would be helpful, for example, if you were learning to publish or perform a creative text yourself. For more on writing essays on literature, see Chapter 6.

As is clear from the preceding discussion, many of these methods of analysis (rhetorical modes) are related to, or build upon, each other. For example, the method of division and classification shares traits with comparison and contrast. The cause/effect method is similar to process and systems analyses. An essay using a comparison and contrast analysis may need to define or describe the two things being compared. Any given essay may therefore use one method of analysis for the entire essay or, more usually, draw upon two or more methods of analysis.

If you were writing an essay on the causes and effects of addiction for Maté and Alexander (Readings), you would be using the cause/effect method of analysis. It would also be important, however, to analyze what *addiction* means to the authors and to provide an explanation of those meanings in your essay. Thus you would also be using the definition method of analysis.

If you were to compare and contrast the reasons Tim Bowling likes or dislikes hockey in "Na Na Na Na, Hey Hey Hey, Goodbye" (Readings) with the reasons Kofi Annan thinks sports are important to politics in "Football Envy at the UN" (Readings), you would be using both comparison and cause/effect for your methods of analysis. Because you are comparing two works, you are using a comparison method of analysis; because you are examining the *reasons* for the author's beliefs, you are using a cause/effect method of analysis.

STEP 3   Choosing Disciplinary or Analytic Categories

When you gather material for writing analysis essays, you often do so within the framework of a particular academic discipline, such as education, Spanish, or psychology. Academic disciplines all define their own content (the area or areas of knowledge with which they are concerned) and develop specialized vocabularies for categorizing their material. We call these *disciplinary categories.* For example, in one school of psychology, the needs for safety, belonging, love, respect, self-esteem, and self-actualization are categorized together as human needs.

Sometimes ready-made disciplinary categories are not available to you. Suppose that in an essay for a literature course, you wish to examine how several Anglo-Canadian writers represent First Nations and Métis characters in their writing. You might look at how such characters are represented in the literature socially, economically, and physically (for example, physical appearance). These categories are not literary categories *per se*. Rather, they are your own categories around which you might wish to gather material for an essay: they are not disciplinary but *analytic categories.* By contrast, in an essay for a literature course, you may be asked to determine how the form of a poem conveys its meaning. In this case, you may choose the disciplinary categories of figurative language, diction, and **tone** to structure your essay. When you gather material for an essay, you will need to place that material into categories. Those categories may be either disciplinary or analytic. The categories you choose in the planning stage of your essay will be determined by the methods of analysis you intend to employ.

STEP 4   Choosing Methods of Proof

As stated earlier, engaging in an analysis is not the same thing as proving an argument. An argument involves critique because it involves an evaluation or a judgment. In his writing *On Rhetoric*, Aristotle identified three main methods of proof: *ethos*, *logos*, and *pathos*. A persuasive essay will use at least one of these three methods of proof to persuade the audience that the thesis is worth believing. While much contemporary writing about essays will focus on *logos*, it is worth considering the other methods of proof when writing your essays. The main purpose of evaluation is to determine the strengths and weaknesses of something, and the proofs will set the standards of evaluation.

Ethos The Greek term *ethos* gives us our current word *ethics*. In terms of essay writing, *ethos* means two things. First, the person making the argument (the writer) should have an ethical character. That is, he or she should appear to have integrity and honesty, and is, therefore, believable rather than questionable. Second, the argument should be worthy of public consideration because it serves the public good. In this way, it is ethical in nature. In Aristotle's time, arguments were made in the interests of the public, a fact that is sometimes lost in today's classroom environments.

Logos The Greek term *logos* gives us our current word *logic*. In terms of essay writing, *logos* also means two things. First, the argument should be logical and reasonable; that is, we can work through its internal logic and arrive at a sound conclusion. Second, *logos* has connotations of writing, language, and words, so the words we choose when discussing a topic are important. For example, if we were trying to persuade someone to eat spinach, saying "Eat your spinach because I say so" is quite different from saying, "Spinach is high in vitamins, calcium, and fibre, so eating it would be good for you." The purpose is the same (eat your spinach), but the expression is different (command versus explanation). The second example is more persuasive because it provides specific details to support the argument and uses more appropriate language and tone.

Pathos The Greek term *pathos* refers to the emotions. While some might argue that emotion should not factor significantly into essays, emotion is nonetheless an effective tool to persuade a reader. While manipulating the reader's emotions would contradict the value of the writer's *ethos*, emotion can influence your reader when used appropriately. Like *logos*, you can invoke emotion by choosing the correct words to write an effective essay. For example, using a word like *murder* or *killing* has a different emotional effect than the more legal term *homicide*. However, keep your audience in mind because specialists in a field will expect a certain terminology and may dislike or resent blatant emotionally charged terminology.

Other methods for proving arguments can include practical and aesthetic considerations, which can be considered in terms of *ethos, logos*, and *pathos*. For example, an aesthetic evaluation considers taste (*pathos*) as well as character (*ethos*) when deciding if a particular person would enjoy a particular movie. A practical evaluation considers the most reasonable course of action (*logos*) given the people involved (*ethos*) with the least amount of disturbance (*pathos*).

STEP 5 ## Tying It All Together

Depending on which method(s) of analysis you have chosen, you have categorized your information according to a definition, sequences of causes and effects, stages in a process (chronological or action), aspects of a concept, or parts of a system. The way in which you connect these parts and see the information you have gathered working together will help you determine your overall argument: your thesis statement. We will explore this stage in the essay writing process in Chapter 4.

Special Categories for Analyzing Texts

When you are gathering materials for your essay from behaviour, data, events, and/or written or visual works—all texts—you can ask particular questions in order to develop your analysis. Here are some questions you can ask yourself when analyzing your subject, and when you are choosing disciplinary or analytic categories and connecting parts to the whole. While asking these questions, you are paying attention to *how* the work means, not just *what* it means. You may ask a few or many of these questions, depending on what kind of text you are analyzing.

A. Identifying Textual Features

Subject, genre/subgenre, context

1. What issue, idea, event, or person is this work about?
2. Does this work belong to a particular **genre and subgenre** (genre: novel, film, essay, poem; subgenre: fantasy novel, science fiction film, personal essay, lyrical poem)?
3. Can you identify the likely audience for this work (for example, academic, popular)? Is knowledge of the intended audience and/or the social, historical, or cultural situation in which the work was produced relevant to understanding the work?

Evidence and detail The material used to support evaluative or analytic points, or to give substance to explanation, narration, or description.

1. What material does the author use to support evaluative or analytic points? Examples? Facts? Statistics? References to, or quotations from, authorities on the subject? Imaginary situations? Predictions? (See Chapter 8 for kinds of evaluative arguments and detail.)

2. Does the author give substance to narration by extended accounts of a small number of events or by brief accounts of many events? Is description panoramic (using selected details to summarize a wide range of experience) or dramatic (using lots of details to convey a particular experience)?

Structure The selection and arrangement of points, narrative incidents, and/or descriptive detail.

1. Does the work use the structure appropriate to a particular genre and subgenre (for example, inductive reasoning for a personal essay)?

2. Does the work use the structure appropriate to a particular mode of discourse?

   a. Is the main purpose of the work to present an analysis, summary, or evaluation? If so, what principle determines the order in which points are presented (for example, order of ascending interest, pro–con structure)?

   b. Is the main purpose of the work to present a narrative or a description? If so, what principle governs the order (for example, past to present, near to far)?

   c. If the work mixes analysis, summary, and/or evaluation with narration and/or description, what is the organizing principle?

   d. Does the work use spatial or chronological principles of structure? (For example, are flashbacks used, or are events summarized?)

   e. Is the work divided into parts? Do these parts correspond to stages in the development of the action?

Diction

1. Is the level of usage in the work that of formal, educated speech; informal, everyday speech; the colloquial speech associated with a particular dialect or subculture; or a mixture of these levels? Are there shifts between levels of usage?

2. Is a specialized vocabulary (for example, the vocabulary of a biologist or a banker) important to this work?

3. Are there significant patterns of word choices (for example, euphemisms designed to hide unpleasant facts)?

Sentence structure

1. What are the characteristic features of the author's sentences? Long or short? Simple or complex? Is there a distinctive use of parallelism or other rhetorical devices?

2. Are there significant exceptions to, or changes in, the author's habitual sentence structure?

Tone

1. How would you describe the tone of the work?

2. Is there a narrator or speaker who is distinctly different from the author? How would you characterize the narrator's or speaker's attitude toward the subject and/or the reader? How would you characterize the author's attitude toward the reader?

3. How is the tone conveyed?

4. Are there shifts in tone? If so, where, and to what purpose?

5. How apparent, and how important to the work, is the personality of the author?

B. Connecting the Parts to the Whole

1. If the work belongs to a distinct genre and/or subgenre, in what ways does it conform to and depart from the conventions of the genre?

2. How does the title relate to the work as a whole?

3. What is the relationship between structure and evidence/detail? For example, is one part of the evaluation or analysis supplied with more evidence or detail than another?

4. What is your interpretation of the author's thesis or theme, based on your analysis of the work and your sense of how its elements are related?

5. Does the author state a thesis or theme directly?

Sample Topic: Nostalgia in Tim Bowling's "Na Na Na Na, Hey Hey Hey, Goodbye"

The aim of this section is to demonstrate ways of gathering material for a sample essay assignment. Essay assignments will ask you to analyze a text or texts. Whether those texts consist of documents, data gathered from inter-views, newspaper clippings, or a work of literature, your task will be to scrutinize the text(s) closely and present an educated opinion, a thesis on your findings. The sample essay we discuss here analyzes Tim Bowling's essay "Na Na Na Na, Hey Hey Hey, Goodbye" in relation to the notion of *nostalgia*. Bowling's essay can be found in the Readings section of this textbook; the sample student essay on Bowling's work—the one we explain here—can be found in the Sample Essays section of the Readings. We recommend that you read both Bowling's essay and the sample student essay before you continue to read this section.

STAGE 1   Clarifying Essay Topics

STEP 1   Defining Unfamiliar Terms and Understanding Your Assignment

Let's suppose that your instructor has asked for a 1000-word essay on Tim Bowling's attitude toward hockey in "Na Na Na Na, Hey Hey Hey, Goodbye" (Readings). There do not seem to be any terms that you need to look up in order to clarify your understanding of the essay topic. *Attitude* seems clear enough. Just to be sure, though, you look up *attitude* in a dictionary and find that you need to pay attention to the tone that comes through in Bowling's work. At this point, you may also want to ask yourself relevant questions for identifying textual features, as discussed earlier in Special Categories for Analyzing Texts. You want to make sure, for example, that you are clear on the genre of the work. Thus you determine that the genre is an essay and that the subgenre is a personal essay. As you read through Bowling's essay, you pay attention to details, structure, diction, tone, and so on. You will also need to understand the subject (professional hockey) and the context (1993 semifinals of the Stanley Cup) of the work.

What kind of parts does Bowling's essay break down into? What is the whole—the thesis—that Bowling is trying to convey? These are questions you will ask in order to understand Bowling's essay more thoroughly. You need to understand how Bowling's essay works in order to plan and write your own essay.

STEP 2   Exploring Your Subject

You may engage in freewriting, brainstorming, or tree diagramming to further explore the topic of your essay.

STAGE 2   ## Gathering Material

STEP 1   ## Analyzing the Text

There are different ways to gather material, depending upon what kind of essay you are writing. As you will see in Chapter 8, you will gather material for a comparison essay by thinking about and itemizing the similarities and differences between texts, events, or concepts. As you will see in Chapter 10, for example, you will gather material for a research essay by finding and reading scholarly articles and books on your topic. In an analysis essay, you gather material by analyzing the text at hand. Whether that text is a historical document, an advertisement, or a literary essay, you will break it down into parts in order to discover the whole—how it means and why it is important. What is Bowling's point? What is his thesis? As you answer these questions, you engage in an analysis of the text.

Because Bowling writes a personal essay, not a formal essay, his thesis statement is implicit rather than explicit. Unlike the formal essay you will write, he does not provide a concrete thesis statement near the beginning of his essay. Therefore, you will need to determine the answer to his questions by interrogating the text as a whole. Upon doing so, you find that Bowling does not really answer his own question. He neither solely likes nor dislikes hockey. He remains ambivalent about the game throughout the essay. You discover Bowling's attitude, in part, by how he ends his essay. He seems to have given up on it, deciding to dislike it, when he says, "I won't be watching" (239). But then he qualifies that stance by questioning whether or not he really will be able to stop watching (239). You decide that Bowling's thesis is that there are positive and negative aspects to the sport of hockey—he remains both drawn to it and aware of the problems within it. This kind of thesis, one that is not a simple either/or position, is common in academic work. Often the issues that writers discuss are complicated and cannot be simplified into a single or easy stance.

STEP 2   ## Choosing Methods of Analysis

Reread Bowling's essay. This time, you think more about the essay topic—Bowling's attitude toward hockey—and try to read between the lines, looking to see how Bowling's attitude might come across in the essay. You notice that there are various notions that keep arising in Bowling's essay. For example, Bowling keeps referring to his childhood and to Canada and what it means to be Canadian. In order to understand how these notions arise in Bowling's text, you brainstorm and freewrite. Here is the chart that you write to gather your material and organize your thoughts.

Childhood	playing hockey with marbles in the kitchen as a kid (par. 2)
	boards were blank; you could hear the whistle being blown (par. 14)
Canada	2002 Winter Olympics, loonie under the ice, Canada's win (par. 11)
	Don Cherry (par. 12), Tim Hortons, Tragically Hip (par. 7)
	millions of Canadians "grew up on the lore of the game" (par. 7)
Violence	Sheldon Kennedy and Todd Bertuzzi (par. 10)
	says the game has "outdated machismo code" (par. 6)
	Al Purdy's comment that hockey is "ballet and murder" (par. 9)
Hockey as narrative/story	"primal pull of narrative" (par. 7) hockey as the "Great Canadian Novel" (par. 7)

After you have engaged in freewriting, brainstorming, note-taking, and making charts such as the one above, you will probably have a rough idea about the kinds of parts—analytic categories—into which your essay can be divided. Upon examining these categories you can decide on a method of analysis. In terms of the work you have done on Bowling's essay, you notice that the categories you have identified above are not causes and effects, nor are they stages in a process. They are also not aspects of a definition. Rather, they seem to be parts of a whole of some sort. You don't know what that whole is, because you have not yet determined it: you have not yet created your thesis statement or argument. However, you sense that upon further examination of these categories, you might be able to understand what kind of attitude Bowling has toward hockey. Note that the list of categories you have created through brainstorming, freewriting, note-taking, and charting will probably be much longer than what you end up using in your final essay. That's okay. It's better to have too much material to work with than too little. You can eliminate some of your categories once you have decided upon a thesis statement and started to draft your essay.

Upon examining the various possible methods of analysis, you decide that a systems analysis will work best. The various categories in your chart—childhood, Canada, and so on—will lead to a thesis statement and will be able to relate to an overall argument. You have determined your method of analysis and some possible parts or categories to use in your essay. Now you can work on formulating an argument and creating a tentative thesis statement, which we will discuss in the next chapter.

As you work on your assignment, know that it's okay to go back and forth between the analysis of the text itself—looking at its parts, thinking of their importance in relation to the whole—and the method(s) of analysis and categories that you will use in order to express those ideas. Learning to analyze a text, to break it down and really understand it in an intellectual way, can be one of the most difficult but rewarding things you will learn. Your analysis of a text is intimately related to how you organize and write about it. For that reason, gathering material and writing about that material are really very closely linked in analysis essays. We remind you, as we did in Chapter 1, that although we outline how to work toward an analysis essay in stages and steps, the writing process doesn't always occur in such a linear way—it's fine to go back and forth between these stages and steps as you work on your assignment.

Working on Your Own Assignment

Clarifying the demands of your topic is a necessary first step toward writing a good essay.

- Identify terms that need to be defined and what your assignment is asking of you.
- Use freewriting, brainstorming, or tree diagramming to discover an aspect of your subject that interests you.

The purpose of writing analysis essays is to come to a better understanding of the nature and significance of your material by dividing it into relevant parts.

- Analyze the text by breaking it down into parts and thinking about what is most important.
- Decide whether you should define, or use cause/effect, process analysis, or systems analysis (or a combination of them).
- Decide on which disciplinary or analytic categories you will use.
- Decide on a method of proof: *logos*, *ethos*, or *pathos*, or a combination of them.

Exercise

Respond to each of the following questions in a sentence or two.

1. What is the main purpose of writing an analysis essay?

2. What kinds of texts might you analyze in your preparation to write an analysis essay?

3. How do you gather material for a textual analysis essay?

4. What is the difference between causal analysis (cause and effect) and a systems analysis?

5. What is the difference between a summary of a text and an analysis of a text?

6. Which method of proof is most common in contemporary writing about essays? Why do you think that most academics focus on this method of proof?

7. What kinds of questions could you ask yourself when gathering material and preparing to write a textual analysis essay?

Writing Analysis Essays: Formulating a Thesis Statement and Drafting

(4)

In Chapter 3 we discussed the early stages of writing analysis essays: clarifying essay topics and gathering material. In this chapter we will show you how to use your material to formulate a thesis statement and draft an essay. The principles discussed will apply to most of the writing you do for college and university courses.

STAGE 3　Formulating a Thesis Statement

At the heart of every essay is the writer's thesis, the main idea that gives shape and meaning to the piece of writing. Writers of informal essays (essays based on personal experience) may not state their theses directly, leaving readers to work out how details add up to a main idea. In formal academic writing, by contrast, readers expect to find a thesis statement, usually one or two sentences stating the writer's opinion about the subject and the main reasons or support for that opinion. We will demonstrate how to arrive at a tentative thesis statement that will serve as the starting point for drafting your essay.

STEP 1　Forming an Opinion

An opinion is a belief or judgment based on your interpretation of events, ideas, behaviours, or other phenomena. Consider a simple example. "The temperature is 30°C" is a statement of fact; the statement can be proved to be true or false. "It's too hot for a hike" is a statement of opinion; your hiking partner might disagree, but the opinion would nevertheless be true for you. Similarly, if you were writing an essay on World War I, you would not try to prove that particular battles were fought on particular days. That information is a matter of fact, not opinion. But not everyone agrees about the main causes of the war. So your thesis might be that the main causes of the war were economic rather than political.

When you write about familiar subjects, you may have an opinion before you begin. When the subject is new to you, as in most academic writing, your opinion usually emerges as you perceive connections among the categories you have used for your analysis. Even if you are writing about a familiar subject, you may find that new materials, evidence, and perspectives cause you to alter your opinion on that subject.

From the material that you generated by analyzing Tim Bowling's "Na Na Na Na, Hey Hey Hey, Goodbye" (Readings), for instance, you could arrive at opinions like these:

- Tim Bowling likes hockey because it has been part of his life since he was a child [causal analysis]

- Tim Bowling works through his reasons, one by one, for liking and disliking hockey [systems analysis]
- Tim Bowling dislikes violence in hockey [definition if examining the meaning of violence; systems analysis if looking at violence as a system with various kinds of violence within it]
- Tim Bowling expresses nostalgia when reminiscing about hockey [definition if examining the meanings of nostalgia; systems analysis if looking at nostalgia as a system with parts]

Opinions by themselves are incomplete. Opinions become thesis statements only when they are shaped by the reasoning used to support them.

Check your opinion against your essay topic to make sure you are still on track. In the sample topic we have been working with, the instructor asked for an essay on "Tim Bowling's attitude toward hockey in 'Na Na Na Na, Hey Hey Hey, Goodbye.'" Do all the thesis opinions above relate to the essay topic? Let's examine each of them. The first thesis opinion, analyzing Bowling's reasons for liking or disliking the sport, comes too close to repeating Bowling's own method of analysis and thesis statement. The second thesis opinion, considering Tim Bowling's reasons as a process the author goes through, doesn't really show Bowling's attitude toward the sport. The third thesis opinion, Bowling's dislike for violence in the sport, does show Bowling's attitude toward hockey. This topic could be promising, although it might not demonstrate the entirety of Bowling's opinion, since he also seems to like the sport. The fourth thesis opinion, on Bowling's feeling of nostalgia toward hockey, adheres to the essay topic. Nostalgia—one's longing for a home or past—can be seen as a kind of attitude.

Sometimes you will find that one opinion stands out as the most relevant to the essay topic. If this is the case (as we have just seen), then use that one. If you have several possibilities for a thesis opinion and each represents a good gathering of material and is an appropriate response to the assignment, then you should choose the one that you are most interested in exploring. Or, you may want to consider the possibility of combining or synthesizing two or more possibilities into a single opinion. Be careful not to take on too much material.

STEP 2   ## Supporting Your Opinion

A good thesis statement requires not only an opinion but also one or more reasons to support it. Without reasons that emphasize your particular interpretation of your subject, a thesis opinion merely sounds like a vague generalization. If you want your reader to be interested in what you have to say and to take your opinion seriously, you have to give good reasons.

Reasons—your support for your thesis—need to be grounded in evidence. The evidence you use will depend upon the discipline within which you are working. In literature courses, your evidence will be found in your primary text or **primary source** (the work of literature you are analyzing) and, if the essay requires research, in **secondary sources** (works of critics who have written about the text). In history courses, your evidence may be found in historical documents (primary sources) and in writings about those documents (secondary sources). In psychology courses, your evidence may be found in data from interviews or psychological studies. All disciplines require evidential support for thesis opinions.

Your reasons will be a short form of the points you plan to develop in detail in the body of your essay. At this stage of the writing process, you may not have worked through your material completely enough to give precise reasons. You can often use your methods of analysis to guide you as you write your draft. If you added the analytic categories of your systems analysis (see Chapter 3) to the corresponding thesis opinion that we discussed earlier, you would come up with a tentative thesis statement like this:

Tentative thesis statement	Tim Bowling expresses nostalgia when reminiscing about hockey: he dislikes violence in hockey, but he longs for his childhood, his Canadian home, and hockey as story.

This tentative thesis statement now includes both an opinion and the main points—analytic categories—you will cover in your essay. It still sounds tentative, though, because it lacks the specific insights that will later distinguish your final copy from your draft. Writing a draft often helps you clarify and deepen your thinking about your subject. In Chapter 5 you will see how to revise your thesis statement to incorporate new insights and to make it more forceful.

STAGE 4 Drafting

Write your draft well before your essay is due. It's tempting to wait until you feel inspired or until the night before the due date, but it's better to take a cue from professional writers. They cannot afford to wait for inspiration, nor do they expect to produce a perfect piece of writing the first time. Their method is almost always to write out a rough draft, let it sit for a while, and then submit it to a process of revision and fine-tuning. This is the method we recommend.

Some writers find an outline helpful at this stage, and in this chapter we explain how to develop a *draft outline* to guide the process of drafting.

Others prefer to write a draft and then use a *revision outline* to organize their material. We will illustrate that method in Chapter 5.

Since you will eventually revise what you have written, let the writing flow, even if you find yourself departing from your outline or mental plan. You may discover new and better ideas as you write. You can revise your thesis statement, structure, and individual paragraphs when you finish drafting (see Chapter 5). Resist the temptation to polish sentences that you may discard when you revise.

STEP 1   ## Selecting Material and Making Points

In formulating your tentative thesis statement, you focus on the analytic categories that provide the best support for your thesis. You may discover, however, that these categories give you too much material. It is always better to explain a few points in depth than to skim over a great many. In a short essay (500–1000 words), you can usually develop two to five main points. Thus the first step in writing a draft is to consider which paragraph topics and material to include.

- Take another look at the material generated by analyzing Tim Bowling's "Na Na Na Na, Hey Hey Hey, Goodbye" in Chapter 3. You may not be able to include all of these ideas in a short essay. Upon examining the analytic categories you've generated—childhood, Canada, violence, and hockey as narrative/story—you find that violence is not as relevant to your thesis opinion on nostalgia as are the other categories. You might decide to focus, then, on the three categories that are most relevant to your thesis opinion. But don't discard your notes on violence, including your freewriting and brainstorming. You may be able to discuss some of your ideas on violence in the text in relation to one of the three analytic categories you've chosen. Now you can turn your material into points that relate to your thesis statement. From your selected categories you arrive at the following paragraph topics and points:

TOPIC	POINT
Childhood	Bowling desires a return to his childhood, which is characteristic of nostalgia
Canada	Bowling links hockey to his Canadian home, and nostalgia is a longing to go back home
Hockey and narrative/story	Bowling says that the narrative of hockey "pull[s]" (par. 7) him into it, just as nostalgia draws one into one's past and one's home

STEP 2 Organizing Your Material

When organizing your material, there are two issues to consider:

- Whether to organize your essay with a **deductive** or **inductive structure**
- How to present your points in an effective sequence

In each case, the audience for whom you are writing will influence your choice.

Choosing deductive or inductive structure When you argue deductively, you start with a premise and test it against examples to prove its validity. Try to think of counter-examples that would disprove or contradict the premise. Your thesis will likely say something about the validity of the premise (for example, its strength or its applicability in various contexts) and the reasons for testing the validity. This structure provides a framework that makes it easier for readers to grasp the significance of specific details. Most academic writing on literature and in the humanities follows this pattern (for an example, see D. Jones's "The Complexity of Power and Gender Relations: An Evaluative Essay on Scott Russell Sanders' 'The Men We Carry in Our Minds'" [Readings: Sample Essays]). You will find deductive structure appropriate for writing essays and research papers in academic courses where your readers are familiar with the subject and want to know your interpretation of it.

In contrast, when you reason inductively, you start from a specific case or cases and move toward the principles involved. To organize an essay inductively, you present events, points, or details first and withhold the thesis to be derived from them until later. Inductive structure is often used to create interest in narrative and descriptive essays (for an example, see George Orwell's "Shooting an Elephant" [Readings] and E. M. Forster's "My Wood" [Readings]). Inductive reasoning can also be useful in writing for hostile audiences who may disagree with an explicit thesis. However, in most formal academic writing, you should state your thesis early in the writing and then walk the reader through the points of development to show how you came to that thesis statement. An essay that is structured inductively can still state the thesis in the introduction, but the rest of the essay (the body paragraphs) will follow an inductive structure.

When organizing your essay, avoid organizing your points chronologically. This method of narration, or telling a story, is usually not a good method for developing an analysis essay. Avoid the temptation to describe the unfolding of a plot or to list historical events, throwing in some commentary on the details as you go. The problem with this method is that your comments stay isolated from one another. You will be much less likely to fall into this kind of summary plus commentary if you have gathered material systematically and worked out a thesis statement to guide the writing of your draft.

Sequencing your points effectively Depending on the method of analysis you are using, the best order for presenting your material may not be obvious. For example, if you are writing a process analysis essay, you might present your points in *chronological order*. But what if you are writing a definition essay or a systems analysis essay? For these types of essays, it might be more difficult to determine the best order to present your points. The most common arrangement for these types of essays is in *order of ascending interest*. You begin with your least important point and end with your most important point. That way, you more easily keep your readers' attention and leave the strongest impression.

- In organizing your essay on Tim Bowling's "Na Na Na Na, Hey Hey Hey, Goodbye," for example, you might decide to begin with Bowling's individual relationship to his childhood and move to the wider context, that of nation and narrative. By progressing in this manner, you will highlight the importance of hockey and nostalgia beyond Bowling's individual experience.

You will face the basic decisions about organizing material—choosing deductive or inductive structure and sequencing your points effectively— no matter what kind of essay you are writing. Some types of essays bring other considerations as well. You will find suggestions for organizing comparison essays in Chapter 7; for using pro–con structure to organize a persuasive essay in Chapter 9; and for organizing research papers in Chapters 10, 11, and 12.

STEP 3   Making a Draft Outline

At this point, you may find it useful to make a draft outline to guide you as you write your draft. Put your tentative thesis statement at the top of the page. Remember to change the sequence of support, if necessary, in response to decisions you have made about organizing your draft. Then list your main points and subpoints in the sequence you have decided upon. You may also want to note the most important evidence that supports each point, such as specific examples.

STEP 4 Drafting Individual Paragraphs

Sketching the introduction You can sketch out the introduction by writing a sentence or two about the context of your topic and then stating your thesis (if you are giving your essay a deductive structure) or asking the question your essay will answer (if you are using an inductive structure). If you can't get started without a polished introduction, consult Revising Your Introduction in Chapter 5.

Drafting middle paragraphs Use each point in your draft outline as the basis for a topic sentence for one or more paragraphs. Paragraphs, like essays, can be organized either deductively or inductively, so your topic sentence may appear at the beginning or end of the paragraph. In academic essays, it is most common and often advisable to organize your paragraphs deductively. When you are writing analysis essays, try not to bury your topic sentence in the middle of a paragraph where your main point may be overlooked. Explain the point fully by such methods as defining terms, referring to authorities, and providing additional information. Support each point by giving examples, citing facts and figures, and using other specific details. We discussed how writers develop their material in Chapter 2.

Sketching the conclusion Rather than slapping a perfunctory summary on your draft, let your thinking carry you naturally into your conclusion. Often ideas come together as you write, and a better thesis emerges—if you let it. Your conclusion should never be an exact or nearly exact reproduction of your introduction.

When you have finished your draft, let it sit for a day or two. Then revise it, using the suggestions in Chapter 5 as a guide.

Working on Your Own Assignment

- Formulate a tentative thesis statement by figuring out what main idea connects your analytic categories.
- Decide what points to make and how to organize them.
- Make a draft outline to keep you on track as you write.
- Write a draft, paying most attention to developing your middle paragraphs.

Exercises

A.   Respond to each of the following in a sentence or two.

1. Explain the difference between a fact and an opinion, using an example of your own.

2. What is a thesis statement?

3. What are the advantages of writing a draft?

4. Explain the difference between inductive structure and deductive structure. How would you decide which one to use?

5. Define the term *order of ascending interest* and give an example.

B.   Work out a draft outline for an essay on a selection from the Readings section of this book. Put your thesis statement at the top of the page. List your main points in the order you plan to discuss them. Note the most important evidence you will use to support each point.

C.   Write a draft of your essay, paying particular attention to developing each of your points. Keep your draft for later use.

Writing Analysis Essays: Revising

(5)

Sample Topic: Nostalgia in Tim Bowling's "Na Na Na Na, Hey Hey Hey, Goodbye"

Stage 5   **Revising the Thesis Statement and Essay Structure**
- **Step 1**   Making a Revision Outline
- **Step 2**   Revising Your Thesis Statement
- **Step 3**   Revising Your Essay Structure

Stage 6   **Revising Individual Paragraphs**
- **Step 1**   Revising Your Introduction
- **Step 2**   Revising Your Middle Paragraphs
- **Step 3**   Revising Your Conclusion

Stage 7   **Final Editing**

Revision means literally "re-vision," seeing again. When you write a first draft, you are essentially writing it for yourself, to clarify your ideas and to try out your tentative plan for the essay. If you continue reading your work from this perspective, however, you may find it hard to see what changes are needed because you know what you mean to say. To "see again," you have to be able to adopt the perspective of your reader, to evaluate what you have written as it would appear to your intended audience.

Allow enough time before the due date to let your draft sit for a day or two after you have completed Stages 1 through 4. You will then be able to examine it more objectively when you revise.

The goal of revision is to improve your writing on three levels:

- The conceptual level: Does this essay reflect the best thinking you are capable of doing about the topic?

- The organizational level: Have you organized and presented your ideas effectively?

- The stylistic level: Is your writing clear, engaging, and free from errors?

This chapter will guide you through the process of evaluating and revising your work on the conceptual and organizational levels. You will find many suggestions for improving your style in Part 3, Handbook for Final Editing.

STAGE 5   Revising the Thesis Statement and Essay Structure

Before you begin rewriting, read through your draft to assess its overall strengths and weaknesses in content and organization. Then examine your thesis statement and essay structure, as outlined below, to see if you can improve the framework of ideas in your essay. One of the difficulties in writing analysis essays is maintaining a clear boundary between the essay you are writing and the text or texts you are writing about. We will look at different aspects of this problem and how to overcome them at each stage of revising.

STEP 1   Making a Revision Outline

You can keep track of the changes you need to make by using a revision outline—an outline of the draft you have actually written, together with suggestions for changes. Using two columns, you note in the left-hand one the points you make in your introduction, each of your middle paragraphs, and your conclusion. Record these points exactly as they stand in the draft, not as you intended them to be. As you go through the revision process, enter suggestions for changes in the right-hand column. You will find an example of a revision outline for the sample topic on nostalgia in Tim Bowling's "Na Na Na Na, Hey Hey Hey, Goodbye" on page 66.

STEP 2 ## Revising Your Thesis Statement

Whether you write a draft as soon as you have gathered material or follow the suggestions for formulating a tentative thesis statement given in Chapter 4, you will likely need to revise your thesis statement because writing the draft has helped you understand your subject better.

Check both the *content* of your thesis statement and its *presentation*. To assess the effectiveness of your thesis statement, check that it

- gives an opinion with reasons or points to support it
- suggests you have a good understanding of your subject
- interests readers in your interpretation of your subject
- is a response to the essay assignment, but does not simply repeat it
- is supported by reference to aspects of the text or texts you are analyzing in your essay

If you find any of the following problems with your thesis statement, revise as indicated.

PROBLEMS WITH THESIS STATEMENTS	EXAMPLES/SOLUTIONS	
Merely restating the subject	**AVOID**	"I will discuss nostalgia in Tim Bowling's 'Na Na Na Na, Hey Hey Hey, Goodbye.'"
	USE	"Bowling's nostalgia for hockey as it was in the past is evident in his references to his own childhood, his linking of hockey to distinctly Canadian icons, and his understanding of hockey as narrative."
Merely stating facts	**AVOID**	"Tim Bowling knows a lot about hockey."
	USE	"Tim Bowling's knowledge of the history of hockey is demonstrated in his description of events surrounding the 1993 Stanley Cup semifinals and in his reference to many hockey icons and legends."

(Continued)

(Continued)

Failing to give reasons	AVOID	"There are many reasons why Tim Bowling likes hockey."
	USE	"While Tim Bowling's knowledge of hockey shows an admiration for the sport, his criticism of the violence in hockey reveals a more conflicted attitude toward it."
Failing to separate your opinion from other writers' opinions	AVOID	"Many writers have discussed violence in hockey."
	USE	"Although many writers have discussed violence in hockey, I argue that Tim Bowling provides a more nuanced take on the problem than other writers do, since he also recognizes 'the grace and beauty of the game when played well' (237)."
Failing to signal essay structure	REVISE	. . . thesis statement or paragraph order so that points follow the order suggested by the thesis statement.
No longer fits content of essay	CHECK	. . . for better thesis statement in draft conclusion.
Too vague or mechanical	AVOID	"Tim Bowling shows his like and dislike for hockey."
	USE	"Tim Bowling demonstrates his love for the game of hockey, but he also recognizes that many real problems have become inseparable from the culture of hockey in Canada, including corporate ownership and violence."

The last problem, the tentative thesis statement that is too vague or mechanical, is the most common one. Writing your draft will often provide the insights you need to make your tentative thesis statement more precise and more interesting. Problems with thesis statements in analysis essays also arise from focusing on a critic's opinion at the expense of *your* supported opinion on these subjects.

- Take a look at the tentative thesis statement for the draft essay on nostalgia in Tim Bowling's "Na Na Na Na, Hey Hey Hey, Goodbye":

Tentative thesis statement

Tim Bowling expresses nostalgia when reminiscing about hockey: he dislikes violence in hockey, but he longs for his childhood, his Canadian home, and hockey as story.

In the process of drafting an essay to support this thesis statement, you might well decide that you could be even clearer and more specific about the points you make. You would therefore revise your thesis statement:

Writing Sample

Revised thesis statement

Bowling's nostalgia for hockey as it was in the past is evident in his references to his own childhood, his linking of hockey to distinctly Canadian icons, and his understanding of hockey as narrative.

STEP 3 Revising Your Essay Structure

Each of your middle paragraphs should constitute or contribute to one specific point that supports your thesis. The **order of your middle paragraphs** should follow the order suggested by your revised thesis statement. Use the left-hand column of your revision outline to note any of the problems discussed below and revise as suggested in the right-hand column.

PROBLEMS WITH ESSAY STRUCTURE	SOLUTIONS
Failure to paragraph	Indicate on your revision outline where each new point begins and divide your material accordingly.
Paragraphs too long	Divide paragraphs longer than half a page and use an "umbrella" topic sentence (see below).
Paragraphs too short	Combine two or more short paragraphs under one topic sentence or explain your points more fully (see below).
Paragraphs don't support revised thesis statement	Delete irrelevant material.
Point(s) made in revised thesis statement lack support	Add new paragraph(s).
Paragraphs don't follow order suggested in revised thesis statement	Indicate appropriate order on draft outline.
Paragraph order not effective	Show new order on draft outline.

"Umbrella" topic sentences Sometimes you may have more material on one aspect of your subject than you can comfortably fit into a single paragraph. If a paragraph is more than three-quarters of a page, you can often divide it and then use an "umbrella" topic sentence to tie related paragraphs together, as in the following example:

"Umbrella" topic sentence	Bowling's nostalgia is represented in his fondness for both his childhood and Canada as a nation.
Topic sentence for paragraph A	Bowling expresses a longing for his past that is characteristic of nostalgia.
Topic sentence for paragraph B	Bowling's nostalgia for the old-fashioned game of hockey is also evident in his linking of hockey to Canadian icons.

- The thinking that led you to revise the thesis statement for the sample assignment also indicates that you should examine the sequence of paragraph topics in your essay. You will now want the sequence indicated in your thesis statement. You may think of your thesis statement as moving from narrow to wide, from the individual and personal (childhood) to the national (Canada) and beyond the national (narrative in general). You can now fill in more detail in the right-hand column of your revision outline.

REVISION OUTLINE

PARAGRAPH TOPIC	**POINT**
Nostalgia and childhood	Bowling thinks about moments in his childhood that were linked with hockey and exemplifies those moments with fondness (for example, playing with marbles on the kitchen floor).
Nostalgia and Canada	Bowling connects his happy memories of hockey with Canadian icons such as the loonie—the Canadian one-dollar coin—and ex-Maple Leafs defenceman Tim Horton's doughnut chain.
Nostalgia and narrative	Bowling explains how following hockey games and newscasts about hockey is like reading a bestselling novel or work of fiction.

- For the essay that results from this revision outline, see
C. Stonehouse, "Nostalgia in Tim Bowling's 'Na Na Na Na,
Hey Hey Hey, Goodbye,'" in Part 2, Readings: Sample Essays.

STAGE 6   Revising Individual Paragraphs

Once you have revised your thesis statement and identified ways, if necessary, to improve your essay structure, you are ready to consider changes to
individual paragraphs.

STEP 1   Revising Your Introduction

Your introduction gives your readers a chance to prepare, emotionally and
intellectually, for the essay that is to follow. In the opening sentences, check
that you have identified your subject and provided a context for your essay
and the thesis statement to follow. For instance, you might give relevant
background information about historical events or define a key concept.
Also check that your introduction includes your thesis statement (for
deductively organized essays) or the question your essay will answer (for
inductively organized essays). Most academic essays in the humanities will
be organized deductively.

If you have done research, you may be tempted to display your knowledge by presenting various critical perspectives. If you are working with
a literary text, you might want to provide details of the author's life and
other publications. This practice is sometimes appropriate. In a research
essay there are good reasons to begin with a statement of the critical debate
(see Chapters 11 and 12); in a shorter analysis essay, however, you need
to introduce your thesis statement quickly rather than provide extraneous
information.

In revising your draft introduction, check that

- you provide all the necessary details to identify the work(s) you are
analyzing, such as the author and title of the work, or the historical/
psychological/sociological/cultural context and framework you are
addressing
- these details and any criticism you present are relevant to the subject identified by the assignment and to your thesis statement
- you avoid large generalizations about life or literature that are intended
to be impressive rather than to illuminate the thesis statement
- you include any other material your readers might need to understand the thesis statement or appreciate its significance

- you make an effective transition from context material to thesis statement
- you make any changes required as a result of changes to the essay structure

Check your introduction for the following problems:

PROBLEMS WITH INTRODUCTION	EXAMPLES/SOLUTIONS	
Sweeping generalizations	**NOT**	"Throughout history people have been nostalgic about their pasts." See Chapter 8 for this and other problems with argumentation.
Mechanical statements	**NOT**	"There are three ways that Bowling shows nostalgia."
	BUT	"Bowling's nostalgia for hockey as it was in the past is evident in his references to his own childhood, his linking of hockey to distinctly Canadian icons, and his understanding of hockey as narrative."
Too much detail		Keep your introduction to between four and six sentences.
		Save examples for your middle paragraphs. However, don't confuse saving examples with being vague and elusive. Even though you will provide concrete examples to demonstrate your points in your middle paragraphs, you still need to give your readers a very clear and concrete idea about your argument and your main points.
Misplaced thesis statement		Your thesis statement does not need to go in a specific place in your introductory paragraph, but you do need to include your thesis statement somewhere in the introductory paragraph. Think carefully about where to place it. You should lead up to it with context, or follow it with specific details or points about your overall argument.

- In revising your introduction, you would ask yourself what comments are necessary to set the stage for your revised thesis statement. You might decide to include a definition of nostalgia and provide a connection to the essay assignment by referring to Bowling's ambivalent relationship to hockey in connection with his feeling of nostalgia. When providing definitions of concepts, consult reliable sources. If you are using a basic dictionary, for instance, you may also want to consult a specialized dictionary on your subject—especially if you are working with a literary term or a historical or sociological concept. By adding a fuller statement of context, you might come up with a revised introduction like the one below.

Writing Sample

Revised
introduction

Tim Bowling's entertaining essay about NHL hockey, "Na Na Na Na, Hey Hey Hey, Goodbye," is an exploration of the author's own ambivalent attitude toward that sport in Canada. On the one hand, Bowling demonstrates his love and appreciation for the game. On the other hand, however, Bowling recognizes the many real problems that have become inseparable from the culture of hockey in Canada, including corporate ownership and violence. Bowling never really resolves his dilemma about hockey, remaining in a "love/hate" relationship with the game throughout the essay. Interestingly, though, while cataloguing his reasons for and against supporting the game, Bowling exemplifies a feeling of nostalgia. *The Oxford English Dictionary* explains that nostalgia derives from the Greek roots *nostos*, meaning "home," and *algia*, meaning "pain." M. H. Abrams's *A Glossary of Literary Terms* explains that "nostalgia" is a longing for a past that is pristine and idyllic—like the garden of Eden before the Fall of Adam and Eve. Thus, nostalgia is a painful separation from and longing for one's home, a home that is also construed as one's personal or ancestral past. Bowling's nostalgia for hockey as it was in the past is evident in his references to his own childhood, his linking of hockey to distinctly Canadian icons, and his understanding of hockey as narrative.

STEP 2   Revising Your Middle Paragraphs

Checking topic sentences

- Does each paragraph contain a topic sentence that announces the subject of that paragraph and makes a *point* about the subject?
- Does that point support some aspect of your thesis statement?

When you revise, make sure that each middle paragraph has a topic sentence. The topic sentence states the main idea that other sentences in the paragraph explain and support. In this way, it functions as a mini thesis statement, controlling the content of the paragraph and showing how the paragraph relates to the thesis.

Paragraphs, like essays, can be organized either deductively or inductively. If your essay is organized deductively, your reader will expect your paragraphs to be organized deductively also, with your topic sentence at or near the beginning (a transitional sentence may come first). If your essay is organized inductively, many of your paragraphs may be as well, with your topic sentence at or near the end of each paragraph.

Watch for these potential problems:

PROBLEMS WITH TOPIC SENTENCES	EXAMPLES/SOLUTIONS
No sentence stating subject and point	Add a sentence linking the main idea of the paragraph to the thesis statement.
Subject stated, no point made	"Bowling discusses his childhood." If you use a sentence like this one as a transition, make sure the next sentence states your point. Better yet, combine them: "Bowling's childhood memories of hockey are tinged with a fondness and a longing that are characteristic of nostalgia."
Point not linked to thesis	"Bowling links hockey to Canadian icons." Revise to relate to nostalgia. "Bowling's nostalgia for the old-fashioned game of hockey is not only evident in the description of his childhood but also in his linking of hockey to Canadian icons." (Note that this sentence also provides a transition from the previous paragraph, about childhood.)
Misplaced topic sentence	Don't bury topic sentences in the middle of the paragraph. Don't end a paragraph with the topic sentence for the next paragraph.

Checking paragraph development

- Is the point you make in your topic sentence sufficiently explained and supported by specific details?

Explanations serve as a bridge between main ideas and specific details. You may explain your point by defining terms, giving reasons, or moving to a subpoint. To be convincing, each point and subpoint should be supported by specific details, including facts and figures (such as names, dates, statistics); examples (such as representative instances, case studies, hypothetical examples); and quotations from or references to authorities. If you're writing an essay about literature, your evidence will include references to and quotations from the primary text, and may include references and quotations from secondary sources.

PROBLEMS WITH PARAGRAPH DEVELOPMENT	SOLUTIONS
Inadequate detail	Add examples, facts and figures, quotations, or references to texts or authorities, as appropriate.
Misleading detail	For help in identifying problems such as misleading statistics and misused authorities, see Chapter 8.
Irrelevant detail	Delete details that don't support your thesis statement.
Inadequate explanations	Add quotations, cited paraphrased material from primary or secondary texts, definitions, reasons, subpoints, and other material as necessary.

When writing an essay about literature, make sure not to slide back into telling "what happens" rather than using evidence to make a point. Sometimes we are carried away by a story, the development of a metaphor, or a compelling scene in a film or play. Use evidence such as quotations or paraphrases from the primary text to support your points.

Reread each middle paragraph carefully. Do you need to

- add examples or direct quotations? Direct quotation is often the best possible evidence. The point of your paragraph should be clearly supported. For guidelines on using quotations effectively, see Part 3, H2 Quotations.

- revise and shorten the details so that they become evidence for the point?

- explain how the evidence supports the point? Claiming that a quotation or detail supports a point is not sufficient, since other readers may understand the text differently. You need to explain the connection between your point and the quotation.

Note on your revision outline whether each paragraph follows this pattern.

REVISION OUTLINE

TOPIC SENTENCE	EVIDENCE	EXPLANATION OF EVIDENCE
Author's notion of hockey connected to his childhood memories of hockey	Memory of playing hockey with marbles on the kitchen floor	Mother as symbol of love, home, comfort

- To see how you would identify and correct problems with topic sentences and paragraph development, consider this paragraph from the draft essay on nostalgia in Tim Bowling's "Na Na Na Na, Hey Hey Hey, Goodbye":

Bowling discusses his childhood in the early 1960s. Bowling says, "I'd play with hockey cards on the linoleum floor of the kitchen, passing a marble back and forth and re-enacting great goals and saves as my mother clattered dishes in the sink nearby" (395). Bowling states, "When I was a boy, the boards, ice and score clock were free of advertising; goals and assists meant more than salaries; and players and teams had distinct characters" (395). This vision of hockey in Bowling's past is contrasted with a present day hockey game at which "you're . . . bombarded with supersonic noise and flashing lights and company logos" (239). Hockey has not yet fallen into the corruption of corporate takeover and violence.

- When you check this paragraph, you find there is no topic sentence. Your subject was intended to be how Bowling's childhood memories relate to hockey and how those memories are nostalgic, but the first sentence of the paragraph only mentions Bowling's childhood. While you provide quotations as evidence to support your point, you don't explain those quotations. You need to state your interpretation of the quotations and how they relate to the point of the paragraph and the thesis of the essay. You would note these problems on your revision outline and then use your notes as a guide to revising.

Writing Sample

Revised middle
paragraph

Bowling's childhood memories of hockey are tinged with a fondness and a longing that are characteristic of nostalgia. For instance, speaking of his childhood in the early 1960s, Bowling says, "I'd play with hockey cards on the linoleum floor of the kitchen, passing a marble back and forth and re-enacting great goals and saves as my mother clattered dishes in the sink nearby" (236). Bowling's first hockey memory is in his kitchen, the domestic space of home, and Bowling is alongside his mother, a symbol, perhaps, of love, comfort, and belonging. Furthermore, Bowling states, "When I was a boy, the boards, ice and score clock were free of advertising; goals and assists meant more than salaries; and players and teams had distinct characters" (239). Here, hockey in Bowling's childhood is understood as pristine, untouched, and not yet corrupted by corporate culture. This vision of hockey in Bowling's past is contrasted with a present-day hockey game at which "you're … bombarded with supersonic noise and flashing lights and company logos" (239). Bowling's recollection of playing hockey with marbles on his kitchen floor is nostalgic in that it exemplifies a longing for home, domesticity, and love; his recollection of the blank "boards, ice and score clock" (239) is nostalgic in its description as pure and idyllic: hockey has not yet fallen into the corruption of corporate takeover and violence.

STEP 3   Revising Your Conclusion

Many people find conclusions as hard to write as introductions. As a result, draft conclusions tend to be skimpy and mechanical. When you revise, make sure that your conclusion achieves its purpose: to leave your readers with a strong sense of the importance of what you have written.

A good conclusion for an academic essay generally summarizes and expands the thesis and main points, and sets them within a broader context. In drafting, however, you may have merely summarized your thesis and main points or, conversely, shifted into large generalizations about life or literature. Either of these choices will likely fail to satisfy your readers, who want to see what greater understanding of the text your discussion has made possible and also what the implications are for the larger issues that the assignment and text have raised.

In revising, then, ask these key questions about your draft conclusion:

1. Does your conclusion expand the original thesis statement by drawing upon the more specific ideas you have developed in the body of the essay?

2. Have you briefly discussed the broader implications of your essay? We all want to feel that what we have written is important. You can show readers that your analysis of a subject or text(s) has a broader significance by putting it within a larger context. That context might

be such things as opinions expressed by scholarly critics or reviewers, similarities to and differences from other works by the same writer, placement in a larger historical time period, movement from a specific case to a more general category, or the relevance of issues raised in the text to your readers. (In some cases, you may need to revise your introduction so that it refers to the context you will return to in your conclusion. This return to the initial context gives conclusions the sense of both extending and completing a circle.)

Finally, check to see if your draft conclusion reveals any of the following problems.

PROBLEMS WITH CONCLUSIONS	EXAMPLES	
Sweeping generalizations	**NOT**	"We all feel nostalgic about our childhood."
Mechanical repetition of thesis and points	**NOT**	"In conclusion, we have seen that Tim Bowling is nostalgic because he refers to his childhood, Canada, and narrative."

- Let's see what happens when you apply these principles to revising the conclusion of the draft essay on nostalgia in Tim Bowling's "Na Na Na Na, Hey Hey Hey, Goodbye."

Draft conclusion   In conclusion, we have seen that Tim Bowling is nostalgic because he refers to his childhood, Canada, and narrative. We can relate to the essay because, like Tim Bowling, we all feel nostalgic about our childhoods.

- This conclusion does not reflect the way the thesis statement has been developed in the essay. Furthermore, the statement of broader implications does not emerge out of the points made in the essay. It also is not true: some people have not had happy childhoods and may not long for them. You should revise to produce a conclusion that reflects what you have discovered in the process of your analysis and the implications of those discoveries. To expand a thesis and draw out its implications, you have to take the time to reflect on what your analysis has led you to discover about the subject and the text or texts you have analyzed.

Writing Sample

Revised conclusion

At the end of his essay, Bowling asks, "Can I resist the lure of *nostalgia* and the pull of narrative?" (239, my emphasis). This statement is the only one in which Bowling mentions the word "nostalgia," but the notion of nostalgia is prevalent throughout his essay. From his recollection of childhood memories of hockey, which include domestic and motherly images, to his linking of hockey to Canadian national icons, to his connection of hockey to narrative, Bowling wishes to come back to a past in which hockey was free from corruption, a past which was also supposedly idyllic, innocent, and comforting. Perhaps Bowling's desire is typical of twenty-first century Canadians who remember or have heard about their ancestor pioneers. Bowling's "Na Na Na Na, Hey Hey Hey, Goodbye" is not just an exploration of the author's reasons for liking or disliking the game of hockey: it is an engagement with the fond memories of his past, an engagement that might apply, in one way or another, to many Canadians.

After you have revised your conclusion, make adjustments to your introduction, if necessary, to ensure that the two are in accord.

STAGE 7 Final Editing

The last step in writing an analysis essay is to give your essay a final edit. Final editing is discussed in Part 3, Handbook for Final Editing. The chart at the beginning of Part 3 will help you identify problems with sentence structure, grammar, punctuation, and format.

- The sample essay that results from revisions and final editing is C. Stonehouse, "Nostalgia in Tim Bowling's 'Na Na Na Na, Hey Hey Hey, Goodbye,'" in Part 2, Readings: Sample Essays.

Working on Your Own Assignment

- Turn your draft outline into a revision outline by recording what you have actually done in your draft and what needs to be changed.
- Revise your thesis statement as necessary to reflect new ideas, changes in the structure of your essay or your introduction, and greater attention to diction and sentence structure.
- If you are providing context in your introduction, check that the context provides information that directly leads toward your thesis statement.
- Check that your thesis statement is not a description of the text or texts, but rather your supported opinion on the assignment topic.

- Check that your draft is not a running summary of the text, but rather is organized around a series of topics in ascending interest.

- Check to make sure that your middle paragraphs expand upon ideas presented in your thesis statement and that they are arranged in an effective sequence.

- Check each middle paragraph for topic sentence, transitions, supporting details, quotations and paraphrased material, and explanations.

- Check that the detail in the middle paragraphs does not simply describe a section of the text or texts, but rather is used as evidence to support a point.

- Check that the connection between point and detail in the middle paragraphs is sufficiently explained, especially in the case of direct quotations.

- Keep your reader in mind as you revise your introduction and conclusion. Check that your conclusion restates and expands the thesis and suggests broader implications appropriate to the subject and texts you are analyzing.

- When you are satisfied with the content and organization of your essay, turn to Part 3, Handbook for Final Editing, for help in improving the style.

Exercises

A.   Respond to each of the following questions in a sentence or two:

1. What should you do if you find that some of your paragraphs seem too short (one or two sentences) or too long (over a page, single spaced)? How should you revise?

2. Why is it important that each paragraph of your essay has a topic sentence? If, during your revisions, you found that some of your paragraphs had weak or no topic sentences, how should you revise? How can you make sure that you revise to write strong topic sentences?

3. What are some of the possible problems with paragraph development? How could you revise to fix those problems?

4. How can you assess your conclusion to determine what kinds of revisions it needs?

B.   E. M. Forster's "My Wood" (Readings) is an inductively organized essay, with a question at the beginning and a thesis statement at the end. Write a revision outline showing how you would change the inductive structure into a deductive structure. Consider whether changing the structure means changing the thesis statement. If yes, write the new thesis statement.

Writing Essays on Literature

(6)

Sample Topic: Tone in William Carlos Williams's "This Is Just to Say"

Stage 1   Clarifying Essay Topics

Stage 2   Gathering Material

    Step 1   Using Disciplinary or Analytic Categories

    Step 2   Connecting Textual Features to Figure Out the Work's Theme / Thesis

Sample Analysis of a Poem: William Carlos Williams's "This Is Just to Say"

Stage 3   Formulating a Thesis Statement

    Step 1   Forming an Opinion

    Step 2   Supporting Your Opinion

Stage 4   Drafting

    Step 1   Organizing Your Material

    Step 2   Making a Draft Outline

Stage 5   Revising the Thesis Statement and Essay Structure

    Step 1   Making a Revision Outline

    Step 2   Revising Your Thesis Statement

    Step 3   Revising Your Essay Structure

Stage 6   Revising Individual Paragraphs

    Step 1   Revising Your Introduction

    Step 2   Revising Your Middle Paragraphs

    Step 3   Revising Your Conclusion

In the previous three chapters we discussed how to write analysis essays, and we showed you how to clarify essay topics, gather material, formulate a thesis statement, write a draft, and revise your essay. Essays on literature are analytical, and so the stages and steps in the previous chapters are relevant to you when writing an essay on literature. Essays on literature require particular emphasis, however, because you will be paying more attention to textual features, figurative language, and how meaning is produced.

In literature courses, you may focus more on the relationship between content and form of expression than you do in other courses. In creating written texts, writers use the *material* of language. Ways of using language to achieve certain effects are *techniques*. Writers learn some techniques from studying other writers, but they may also develop new ways of using language. Thus, when you analyze written text as art, you focus on the relation between form and content. Similarly, when you analyze performances as art, as in plays, films, and television programs, you pay attention not only to the content or meaning but also to the particular ways in which the director uses the materials and techniques available. You will write essays based on information available to you from written and visual texts and documents. In literature courses, you will also write essays based on how that information is presented.

STAGE 1   Clarifying Essay Topics

Some assignments in literature classes ask you to analyze a literary text as a system, although they may not use this terminology. Such essay topics focus on the aesthetic elements of the text: how the work of literature functions as art. For example, your essay assignment might read, "Explain how the author uses figurative language in the text in order to convey a theme." You would then consider the work of literature as a system that employs metaphor, symbol, or image (categories) in order to convey a thematic message (thesis). Make sure not to confuse the literature's theme or thesis with the thesis of your own essay on the literature.

STAGE 2   Gathering Material

STEP 1   Using Disciplinary or Analytic Categories

In Chapter 3 we explained that disciplines (for example, Spanish, psychology, history, and English) develop their own vocabularies to describe concepts specific to their disciplines. When you draw upon these specialized vocabularies to analyze a text or texts and organize your essay, you use *disciplinary categories*. When you determine your own categories through your analysis of the text(s), you use *analytic categories*. Since this chapter focuses on writing essays on literature, we will explain some of the disciplinary categories available to you within the field of English. Whether you use disciplinary or analytic categories in the organization of your own essay, the disciplinary terms below will help you understand how a literary text produces meaning. You may draw upon and use these terms, whether or not you use disciplinary categories to organize your essay.

There are three basic questions for a systems analysis of a literary text: What are the parts of the text? What is their function within the work? How do the parts relate to each other? You can analyze a wide range of works by gathering material about these parts: *subject, genre, context, methods of development, structure, style, tone*, and *point of view*. Here is a brief explanation of each of these terms.

Subject Subject is the general issue(s) or concern(s) of the text, as you perceive it (them).

Sometimes your assignment will identify a subject for you, such as manhood in a Hemingway short story or the meaning of love in Emily Brontë's *Wuthering Heights.* But often you will have to decide what you think the subject is. Your statement about a text's subject(s) will be most useful to you if it is both tentative and precise: "This film seems to be about the meaning of heroism in war." If you keep your statement of subject tentative, you will find it easier to modify or change if necessary. And if you make it precise, you will have a better starting point from which to ask: how does the text treat this subject? Avoid both plot summary ("this film is about a soldier who . . .") and vague generalization ("this film is about man against man" or "this film is about war").

Genre The word *genre,* which means "kind," has traditionally been used to refer to the categories into which literary works may be grouped because of similarities in form, subject, or technique. In contemporary theory, genre has been redefined as "a form of human expression loosely adhering to certain conventions that may change over time."* This definition broadens the traditional meaning to encompass a wide range of what can be considered texts: not only literary works but also other verbal and/or visual texts such as films, television programs, speeches, and paintings.

Works can be divided into major genres and minor genres (subgenres). The major genres you are likely to study are nonfiction, fiction, poetry,

---

*Jerald Zaslove. "Bakhtin and the Image of Language: A Friendly Critique of Martin Jay's *Downcast Eyes."* Paper presented at the conference of the Canadian Association of Art History, Vancouver, 1998. Lecture.

drama, and film. Each of these has many subgenres; for example, the genre of poetry includes the subgenres of the sonnet, the ballad, and the ode, among others. Some texts cross genre boundaries. "New journalism," for instance, is nonfiction writing that uses many techniques of fiction.

Each major and minor genre has its own conventions, rules that authors either adhere to or break for their own purposes. The conventions that govern fantasy, for instance, are quite different from those that govern realist fiction. Identifying the genre and subgenre of a text makes you more conscious of the rules the author is working with or against. This knowledge will not only improve your analysis, but also help you avoid serious mistakes. Some students, for example, confuse short stories with autobiographical essays and assume that short stories are accurate accounts of the writers' own experiences. A handbook of literary or film terms will explain the conventions of many kinds of works.

Context Context means the historical and/or cultural situation in which the text was produced, including the specific audience (if any) for which it was intended.

Texts generally reflect the outlook and concerns both of the author/ director and of the era in which they are created. You may therefore find that you understand a text better if you know something about the author or director and about such factors as the historical events, social conditions, and cultural issues that enter into the work, and about the audience for which a work might have been intended. You may find this kind of information in an introduction or notes to the text itself, or you may need to look it up in the reference section of your library or online through your library catalogue or database. Be careful not to substitute information of this kind for a close analysis of the text. A poet may have had a drinking problem, for instance; that doesn't mean every poem he or she wrote is about alcoholism.

For certain kinds of essay assignments, it can be important to examine the literature you are analyzing within the historical, social, and political contexts from which it arose. For example, if you are writing an essay about the narrator's attitude toward death in a story by Edgar Allan Poe, it may be relevant to examine the story within nineteenth-century America, the movement from religious beliefs to Darwinism, or the time period's interest in psychology, spirituality, and the gothic mode. While this kind of analysis might be too much to attempt in a short essay, you may wish to incorporate it into a research essay on literature, which we discuss in Chapters 10 and 11.

Methods of development Methods of development are the specific elements, such as points, events, and descriptions, by which the author/director unfolds or elaborates the central issue or concerns of the text.

A text consists of material that develops the overall point—the theme or thesis—of the work. You can analyze this material by examining the methods of development commonly used in specific genres or subgenres. In imaginative works that tell a story (whether in poetry, fiction, drama, or film), you would pay attention to details of events, setting, and characterization. In imaginative works that do not tell a story, you might find that the theme is developed through reflections, observations, or impressions. A love poem, for example, might be developed through a list of the beloved's virtues, or a nature poem through detailed observations of the landscape. For information on characteristic methods of development in various genres, consult handbooks of literary and rhetorical terms and handbooks that focus on specific literary forms.

Structure The term *structure* refers to the way that units of material are organized to convey a theme or thesis.

In thinking about structure, you need to be aware both of the general principles of structure within various genres and of the particular ordering of material within the text you are analyzing. Novels, drama, and film often organize events into a rising and falling action; short stories more often, though not always, focus on a single moment of revelation; essays often, though not always, arrange a series of points into an order of ascending interest. In addition to these broad structural principles, each work will have its particular way of organizing material.

Consider the following points when you analyze the structure of specific texts:

Generic principles of structure Among the conventions of various subgenres are conventions about structure. If you know that a poem is a sonnet, for instance, you can anticipate that its fourteen lines will be organized into one of two structures: an octave of eight lines setting out a problem and a sestet of six lines suggesting a solution; or three quatrains of four lines, each quatrain developing one idea, and a concluding couplet that sums up the previous lines or presents them in a new light. If you find variations on these forms, think about why the author violated the conventions. You can find information about the structural conventions of various genres in dictionaries of literary and rhetorical terms and in handbooks of specific literary forms.

Spatial and chronological principles of structure Space and time often function as principles in structuring material. Notice patterns of spatial structuring: contrasts between characters identified with different settings, such as city and country; events organized as a journey; changes in a character that occur as a result of moving from a familiar to an unfamiliar place.

Time is used as a structural principle in the following ways, among others: a chronological unfolding of events; movement between the present and the past; and cycles of days, seasons, or years.

Typographical devices as indicators of structure Typographical devices often reinforce other kinds of structure. The most obvious are those that divide works into chapters or acts and scenes. Watch for the less obvious as well, such as the arrangement of lines on the page for some kinds of poetry.

Within the overall structure of the work, you may notice the way smaller blocks of material are organized. The overall structure of an essay, for example, might be chronological, but a paragraph of description within the essay might be organized according to a spatial arrangement of near to far. Making an outline of the text, or of its major divisions, will help you identify its structural principles.

Style Style is the characteristic or distinctive mode of expression within a text. In analyzing style, you examine a text at its most detailed level—the level of lines, sentences, scenes (in plays), or shots (in films). While many elements enter into the style of a work, three are most important for written texts: diction, figurative language and allusions, and the rhythm created by sentence structure and other methods.

Diction Diction refers to the kinds of words the author or characters use, in both language level (colloquial, informal, formal) and origin (for example, ethnic dialect, legal jargon). What is the effect of these choices? One essayist may use the informal language of everyday speech to seem like "one of us," for instance, while another writer may use the specialized vocabulary of economics to speak as a colleague to other experts.

Figurative language Figurative language includes *images* (figures of speech such as metaphor and simile, or visual, oral, tactile, and kinesthetic images) and *symbols* (objects or actions that stand for a more abstract idea or value, such as a pair of scales to symbolize justice).

Allusions Allusions are references to literary, historical, mythological, or religious events and figures, such as Adam and Eve. Repeated images, symbols, or allusions that form a pattern are particularly important. For instance, the images of Emily Dickinson's poem "Because I could not stop for Death" form a pattern in which life is seen as a journey with Death as a kindly companion.

Sentence structure Sentence structure determines the rhythms of prose and, with other devices, of poetry and drama. Is there a high proportion or distinctive use of basic sentences, long or short sentences, sentence fragments, parallelism, or inversion? How do line length and sound patterns contribute to the rhythms of poetry? How does the pacing of dialogue and action contribute to the effects of drama?

In analyzing the style of film and television productions, you focus on the way the camera is used, with less attention on the language. Shooting techniques, visual images and symbols, and editing techniques together create the style.

To analyze style, you may need the help of resources such as a handbook of poetics or dictionaries of slang, symbols, or film terms.

Tone   Tone refers to the attitude of the author/narrator toward the self, the subject of the text, and the reader, as conveyed by the style. In plays and films, this quality is referred to as the *mood* or *atmosphere* of the work.

When you read silently, you likely hear the words inside your head as though they were being spoken by the author or character. The voice may seem like that of a modest gentleman or a frightened child, a witty woman of the world or a dreamy adolescent. It is this sense of a voice speaking that we mean by the attitude toward the self that a written work creates.

The tone (created through stylistic choices) establishes a particular relationship among the author or narrator, the subject of the text, and the audience. The author of an essay might, for example, adopt a playful attitude toward the subject of addiction to coffee and treat the reader as either playmate or disapproving parent. Or the essayist might deliver a serious lecture about the dangers of caffeine and treat the reader either as a peer with whom to share ideas or as a pupil to be instructed. In plays and films, the tone or mood may be established through music, lighting, costuming, and other devices.

Terms commonly used to describe tone or mood include *sentimental, businesslike, authoritative, comic, nostalgic, menacing, reflective, playful,* and *serious.* The piece is ironic when we understand its meaning to be different from, or the opposite of, what is expressed.

Point of view   The perspective from which the text is presented is called point of view. On the next two pages you will read about the distinctions commonly made in analyzing point of view. Notice the difference in terminology for each genre: when referring to fiction, we say *narrator*; when referring to poetry, we say *speaker*; and when referring to nonfiction, we say *writer* or **persona**. Make sure to use the proper terminology for the genre of literature you discuss in your essay.

Fiction: Who is the narrator (storyteller)?

First-person narration

MAJOR PARTICIPANT: The story is told in the first person by an "I" who has a major role in the events (Vanessa telling the story of her encounter with Piquette in Margaret Laurence's "The Loons" [Readings]).

MINOR PARTICIPANT: The story is told in the first person by an "I" who recounts events but does not have a major role in them (the unnamed narrator of William Faulkner's short story "A Rose for Emily").

Omniscient narration The story is told in the third person by an anonymous narrator who has access to the thoughts and feelings of more than one character (as in D. H. Lawrence's short story "The Horse-Dealer's Daughter").

Limited omniscient narration The story is told in the third person by an anonymous narrator who has access to the thoughts and feelings of only one character (as in Nathaniel Hawthorne's short story "Young Goodman Brown").

Objective narration The story is told in the third person as though recorded by a camera, with no access to the thoughts or feelings of any character (as in Ernest Hemingway's short story "Hills Like White Elephants").

Poetry: Who is the speaker? Like fiction, poetry can be expressed in the first person or the third person. The most important distinction is between the first-person speaker who is a character completely separate from the poet (as in dramatic monologues such as Robert Browning's "My Last Duchess") and the first-person speaker who seems hard to distinguish from the person who wrote the poem (as in lyric poems such as Robert Frost's "Stopping by Woods on a Snowy Evening"). Although it's tempting to treat the second type as wholly autobiographical ("Frost was driving a wagon one night and . . ."), this "I" too is a literary creation, one that allows poets to transform purely individual insights and experiences into ones their readers can more easily share. That's why you ordinarily refer to the speaker of the poem rather than to the poet.

Nonfiction: Who is speaking—writer or persona? As you may have gathered by now, nonfiction writers generally speak for themselves, in either the first or third person, or they create a persona to speak for them. A persona is like a character an actor might play. The writer adopts a role, usually for purposes of humour or irony. In "A Modest Proposal" (Readings), for example, Jonathan Swift creates a persona quite different from himself to comment on conditions in Ireland.

STEP 2   Connecting Textual Features to Figure Out the Work's Theme/Thesis

In most texts, the features we have just described work together to convey an overall point about the subject. The term *thesis* is generally used to refer to the more explicit point made in essays, while *theme* refers to the more indirect points made by imaginative literature.

At first glance it may seem difficult to distinguish theme or thesis from subject. To some extent the difference is between the general and the specific. The subject is the general topic of discussion in the work; the theme or thesis is the specific point the work makes about the subject. You might describe the subject of Alice Munro's short story "Thanks for the Ride" as the dating rituals of adolescence and her theme as the necessity of recognizing the class barriers that obstruct some relationships.

A word of caution is in order here. To analyze texts effectively, you will need to formulate a clear statement of thesis or theme. But remember that it is impossible to capture everything that could be said about any complex and interesting work in a brief phrase, and the statement reflects only your current interpretation, which may change with time or reflection. There may also be discordances, gaps, or contradictions in the text that you will need to take into account. As you write your essay, keep your mind open to other possible interpretations. Remember, too, that the thesis or theme of the text is not the same as the thesis of your essay; finding your own thesis belongs to the next stage of the writing process.

Sample Analysis of a Poem: William Carlos Williams's "This Is Just to Say"

We will demonstrate how to clarify essay topics and gather material for essays on literature by working through a sample topic, an analysis of William Carlos Williams's "This Is Just to Say." You will find it easier to follow the discussion if you first read the poem carefully.

PUBLISHED WRITING

THIS IS JUST TO SAY

I have eaten
the plums
that were in
the icebox

5   and which
      you were probably
      saving
      for breakfast

      Forgive me
10   they were delicious
      so sweet
      and so cold

STAGE 1 Clarifying Essay Topics

Let's suppose that you are working on the following essay assignment:

> Write a 500-word essay in which you analyze the tone or the attitude of the speaker in William Carlos Williams's "This Is Just to Say."

Clarifying terms Tone is the one word in the assignment that may leave you feeling uncertain. The assignment seems to identify tone with the speaker's attitude. To be sure, you check a dictionary of literary terms and learn that tone is the attitude a speaker/writer takes toward the subject, reader, and self.

Recognizing genre and scope Look at Special Categories for Analyzing Texts in Chapter 3 for questions to ask when analyzing a literary text such as a poem. Also, gather material by focusing on the disciplinary categories noted earlier. Though the assignment focuses on tone, you will need to gather material in the other categories as well. You can decide which categories are most relevant to the poem and the essay assignment.

STAGE 2 Gathering Material

STEP 1 Using Disciplinary or Analytic Categories

Begin by examining relevant disciplinary categories. Make observations and take notes, as we do below.

Subject The immediate subject is the speaker telling someone (perhaps a friend or a lover) that he has eaten the "plums" in the "icebox." There may be a deeper subject, which hints at the relationship between the speaker and the person to whom he is speaking or for whom he is leaving the note. At this point, we don't know whether the speaker is a "he" or a "she." Later we decide to interpret the speaker as a "he."

Genre and context "This Is Just to Say" is a free-verse poem. William Carlos Williams is an American poet of the Modern time period. You look up *modernism* in a specialized dictionary, M. H. Abrams's *A Glossary of Literary Terms*, and find that some key elements of modernism are a break from Western culture and tradition, and a questioning of the certainty of the self and established belief systems in religion, philosophy, and politics (167).

Poetic structure You note that "This Is Just to Say" is divided into three stanzas. In the first stanza, the speaker states his action of eating the plums; in the second stanza, he speculates on his friend's or lover's intentions for the plums; in the third stanza, he apologizes for his action and describes how the plums tasted. You also note that the lines of each stanza are short, consisting of only two or three words each. The short lines and frequent line breaks create a slow reading of the poem. The reader must deliberate on each word and the cluster of words in each line.

Diction The diction in the poem is simple and easy to understand. Some of the words are sensuous and describe the taste and feel of the plums. You observe that specific and sensuous descriptions are evident in words such as "delicious," "sweet," and "cold." You look up some of the words in the poem and find that they have more than one possible meaning. The word "just," for instance, in the title of the poem, can mean either *merely* or *fair*. Upon a first reading, the poem implies that the meaning is *merely*, but keep in mind the other meaning of "just." One of the themes of the poem seems to be fairness—the speaker feels that he has done something unfair by eating the plums. He apologizes for his action. Scrutinizing the words of the poem even further, you wonder to what "this," in the title of the poem, refers. Does the word "this" refer to the note that the speaker leaves, the poem itself, or the action of eating the plums? One or more of these interpretations may be relevant. Make note of all of them.

Tone The tone of "This Is Just to Say" is perhaps the most intriguing aspect of the poem. The tone is casual rather than formal. You can imagine the speaker quickly writing a note to a friend or lover and posting it on the fridge. Upon close examination, however, the tone reveals a complexity in the relationship between the speaker and the person to whom he writes. The speaker feels a sense of guilt at his action of eating the plums, evident in the phrase "forgive me." And yet he still points out how delicious the plums were. You deduce that this poem is likely written from one lover to another.

Point of view In "This Is Just to Say," the point of view seems to be that of a speaker who is leaving a fridge note to a friend or a lover. It is written in first person narration and appears to be quite simple. We only ever receive the speaker's perspective on the situation. The speaker only speculates—but doesn't know for sure—that his friend or lover was "probably saving" the plums "for breakfast." Although the speaker could be a man or a woman, there are no indications that the speaker is a woman. You should not assume that the speaker is a man simply because the author is, but in this case, it seems to be a man who is speaking in the poem.

STEP 2   ## Connecting Textual Features to Figure Out the Work's Theme/Thesis

The material you have gathered emphasizes the complex attitude of the speaker toward his act of eating the plums and toward his lover to whom he speaks. You have examined the analytic categories that you deem relevant: subject, genre, context, poetic structure, diction, tone, and point of view. Your analysis of these categories has led you to understand the speaker's attitude as more complex than it initially appears. The speaker doesn't simply write a note and leave it on the fridge. He states his action of eating the plums, describes the sensuousness of that act, and admits his guilty feelings about the act to his lover. Your analysis has led you, then, to a deeper understanding of the poem and the speaker's attitude toward his subject.

STAGE 3   ## Formulating a Thesis Statement

You now know that when you are asked to analyze a verbal and/or visual text, you are usually expected to show the relationship between the text's content and the techniques used to create it. You also have a systematic means of gathering material in appropriate disciplinary categories, and you have worked through a sample analysis of Williams's "This Is Just to Say." Next you need to learn how to use your material effectively to draft your essay on literature, beginning with formulating a thesis statement. (See also Chapter 4 for a discussion on this stage of the writing process.)

STEP 1   Forming an Opinion

In gathering material about a text, as we have demonstrated, you start from an idea of the text's subject, analyze the text's formal elements, and then identify connections between the subject and the formal elements to arrive at an interpretation of the text's theme or thesis. The *opinion* part of the thesis statement in an essay about literature usually states this theme or thesis in a way that is shaped by the demands of the essay topic.

This does not mean, incidentally, that each text has one and only one meaning that you must discover (or borrow from someone else). It simply means that you present an interpretation of theme that you can support.

- The assignment on William Carlos Williams's "This Is Just to Say" focuses on the speaker's attitude or tone toward his subject. Combining this focus with the theme that emerged from the process of connecting textual features might give you the following thesis opinion:

  Thesis opinion: Although the speaker of William Carlos Williams's poem "This Is Just to Say" appears to take a casual tone as he writes a note of apology to his lover, he subtly reveals a more complex attitude toward his lover.

STEP 2   Supporting Your Opinion

In any thesis statement, the support for your opinion will come from the categories of material you used to arrive at the opinion. Many assignments on essays about literature require you to go through the categories of analysis, each of which focuses on a formal element of the text. To indicate support for the thesis opinion, you will refer to the most relevant disciplinary categories or formal elements. The paragraphs of your own essay may take a single formal element—a disciplinary category that you have examined—as their subject. However, they don't have to. You may weave an analysis of the categories into the paragraphs of your essay. Each paragraph will have a specific focus that is related to the thesis statement.

- To add support to your opinion on Williams's "This Is Just to Say," you would look for the categories of material that led you to that opinion. The formal elements that yielded the most material included diction, tone, and point of view. Adding a reference to these elements would give you a thesis statement like the one below.

Tentative
thesis
statement Diction, tone, and point of view in William Carlos Williams's "This Is Just to Say" indicate that the speaker's attitude toward his action of eating the plums and toward his lover is more complicated than it initially appears.

Notice that you indicate the support for your opinion by referring to the subject of the categories, not to specific details or to the points you might make. The reason is that the thesis statement sets out a proposition that you will demonstrate in the rest of the essay.

STAGE 4 Drafting

STEP 1 Organizing Your Material

Refer to Chapter 4 on choosing deductive or inductive structure for your essay. Keep in mind that most essays about literature are organized deductively, with the thesis statement in the introduction. The points derived from the thesis statement are developed in order in the middle paragraphs. This structure provides a framework that makes it easier for readers to grasp the significance of specific details. Also see Chapter 4 for a discussion on choosing a method of development and sequencing your points effectively in ascending order of interest.

STEP 2 Making a Draft Outline

Using a draft outline (described in Chapter 4) will help you avoid the problem of storytelling. Make sure your outline consists of paragraph topics and points, not of plot summary and commentary. You can easily turn your draft outline into a revision outline in the next stage of the writing process by leaving space for revision notes on the right.

- In writing a draft of your essay on Williams's "This Is Just to Say," you might decide to make a draft outline from the systems analysis approach, using the formal elements you refer to in your thesis statement as your paragraph topics and following the sequence you have there. Your draft outline, with space for revision notes, might look like this (MP stands for "middle paragraph," a paragraph in the middle of the essay):

DRAFT OUTLINE

PARAGRAPH TOPIC	POINT	REVISION NOTES
Introduction	Thesis: speaker's tone reveals complexity in relationship with lover.	
MP 1: Diction	Words such as "this" and "just" have more than one possible meaning.	
MP 2: Tone	Multiple meanings of words and sensuous descriptions complicate tone and reveal guilt and retribution.	
MP 3: Point of View	Limited point of view reveals speaker's attitude toward his own action of eating the plums and shows that he guesses his lover's reaction to it.	
Conclusion	Poem reveals that what appears simple may be more complex and intricate than one thinks.	

In writing your draft you would follow this outline, adding details and quotations from the poem to support your points.

STAGE 5   Revising the Thesis Statement and Essay Structure

If you have followed the procedures for gathering material and writing a draft, you might think your draft is unlikely to need much revision. Sometimes that is the case, but most of the time you will need to revise. It is always a good idea to review your draft a day or two after you have written it. You will then be better able to see your work with the eyes of your audience and to make any necessary revisions.

Essays on literature present problems that you may need practice in identifying and solving. In this section, we will discuss how to revise thesis statements, essay structure, and individual paragraphs for essays on literature specifically. You can find more general comments on the revising process in Chapter 5.

STEP 1   Making a Revision Outline

If you made a draft outline as described in Chapter 4 and previously in this chapter, you can easily turn it into a revision outline. See also Chapter 5 for further discussion on making a revision outline.

STEP 2   Revising Your Thesis Statement

To revise your thesis statement, check that you have an opinion and points to support it. Also check that your thesis statement relates to the essay topic. For more details on how to revise thesis statements, see Chapter 5.

Check the tentative thesis statement for the sample topic on William Carlos Williams's "This Is Just to Say":

Writing Sample

Tentative thesis statement for sample topic | Diction, tone, and point of view in William Carlos Williams's "This Is Just to Say" indicate that the speaker's attitude toward his action of eating the plums and toward his lover is more complicated than it initially appears.

Upon reviewing the tentative thesis statement, you conclude that it is weak. The focus of the thesis statement is the tone of the speaker, and yet tone appears as one of your three points. Also, while you note that the speaker's tone is complicated, you don't note what is complicated about it. The thesis statement is thus vague in that regard.

You decide to make your thesis statement less mechanical by refraining from mentioning three points that you will focus on in each of your paragraphs. While not always desirable, this method is open to you. You focus on your argument about the tone of the work. You may go back later and revise the thesis statement again, once you have revised the body paragraphs in the essay.

Revised thesis statement | If we read William Carlos Williams's poem "This Is Just to Say" with scrutiny, we can perceive the speaker's tone as vengeful and haughty—the speaker teases his lover by acknowledging not only that he can freely eat the plums but also that he can skilfully use rhetoric to justify the act and earn forgiveness.

The revised thesis statement focuses on the formal element of tone and therefore relates to the essay topic. Your interpretation of the speaker's attitude is very clear and specific. The body paragraphs of the essay will provide evidence to show how that tone is achieved.

Problems with thesis statements in essays on literature often arise from focusing on details of the work or a critic's opinion at the expense of *your* supported opinion on these subjects. Since you have not done research for this essay, you will not encounter this problem here. However, be aware of this issue when you are working on other essay assignments on literature and need to do research.

STEP 3   ## Revising Your Essay Structure

Use the revision column on your draft outline to note any problems with the analytic framework and to mark in a new order of topics and points if you need one. When you check your draft for essay structure, make sure to check that it is your analysis that provides the framework for your essay, rather than the details of the text. As we mentioned earlier in this chapter, falling into a running summary of the text is one of the most common, and most serious, weaknesses seen in essays on literature. If you find that your topic sentences and paragraph divisions correspond to the sequence of the text you are examining, you will likely need to revise your essay structure.

In reviewing the draft of the sample assignment, you discover that the first and second body paragraphs can both address diction in relation to the thesis statement on tone. The first body paragraph could focus on the multiple meanings of the words "this" and "just" and their significance in relation to the tone of the poem. The second body paragraph could focus on the phrase "forgive me"—the admission of guilt—and the sensuous description of the plums. These connotations would also be related to the thesis statement on tone. Since the essay is only to be 500 words, you can eliminate the third point. You have effectively revised your essay structure by expanding your point on diction and eliminating your point on tone (which is redundant) and your point on point of view.

STAGE 6   ## Revising Individual Paragraphs

STEP 1   ## Revising Your Introduction

In revising your draft introduction, check that you provide all the details necessary to identify the work(s), such as author/director and title(s), and that these details and any criticism you present are relevant to the subject identified by the assignment and to your thesis statement. Make sure, also, to avoid broad generalizations about literature or life that are intended to be impressive rather than to illuminate the thesis statement. See Chapter 5 for more discussion on how to revise your introduction.

Let's examine how you might revise the introduction to the essay on William Carlos Williams's poem.

- In the introduction to your draft, you focus on the idea that the tone appears simple but is actually complex. You can revise that observation to make it clearer and more specific. You will also revise your focus on the three points, a decision you already made when you revised your thesis statement and the structure of your essay. In revising your introduction, you will focus on tone through the diction of the poem. You will also need to provide a brief context for the poem by providing your interpretation of it as a note one lover leaves to another. You do not need to provide a lot of information about the author and the time period if you are writing a short essay.

Writing Sample

Revised introduction

William Carlos Williams presents his poem "This Is Just to Say" as a casual note of apology most likely written from one lover to another. Although the poem is deceptively simple, Williams leaves it open to different signifying possibilities that complicate the tone. If we read the poem on a simplistic level, we can perceive the speaker's tone as casual yet honest—in an informal manner, the speaker shows his honesty by admitting his wrong. If we read the poem with scrutiny, we can perceive the speaker's tone as vengeful and haughty—the speaker teases his lover by acknowledging not only that he can freely eat the plums but also that he can skilfully use rhetoric to justify the act and earn forgiveness.

STEP 2   Revising Your Middle Paragraphs

As we discussed in Chapter 5, check that you don't slide back into telling "what happens" in the text you are analyzing. Rather, stay with your argument and support it with concrete evidence from the text. Make sure that your middle paragraphs have a clear topic sentence and a main point. Check that the point of each paragraph is supported with examples—quotations and/or paraphrases—and explanations of those examples.

Consider this draft paragraph on tone in William Carlos Williams's "This Is Just to Say":

Draft paragraph

Diction in the poem reveals tone. The word "this" in the title of the poem is open to more than one possible meaning. It can refer to either the note of apology or to the act of eating the plums. The word "just," also in the title, is open to more than one meaning. It can mean *merely*, or it can mean *legally valid* or *fair*. These meanings show that the tone can be casual and honest or haughty and vengeful.

The topic sentence of the draft paragraph indicates the subject of the paragraph, but it is too vague. It should either be removed—if the subject of the paragraph is very clear—or revised. The indication of multiple meanings of the words in the title of the poem shows that you have paid attention to diction and the nuances in the poem. You've attempted to make a connection between diction and tone, but that connection isn't very clear. You haven't provided explanations of the evidence (quotations) you present. You could also make the transition between your discussion of the meanings of the two words more explicit. Finally, work on connecting the paragraph to the thesis statement in the introduction. Upon noting these problems, you revise to create the following middle paragraph:

Writing Sample

Revised middle paragraph

The word "this," in the title of the poem, is open to more than one possible meaning. It can refer either to the note of apology or to the act of eating the plums. If we read "this" as a reference to the note, then the speaker's tone is either honest or haughty: he either leaves the note because he wants to admit his wrong or because he wants to declare his action and thus tease his lover. If we read "this" as a reference to the act of eating the plums, then the speaker's tone is vengeful: he eats the plums as a statement of vengeance toward his lover. Similarly, the word "just," also in the title, is open to more than one possibility. It can mean *merely*, or it can mean *legally valid* or *fair*. If we read "just" as a synonym for *merely*, then the speaker takes a casual tone: he implies that his act and the note are not very important. If we read "just" as *legally valid*, then the speaker is saying "this is fair to say"—the tone is then one of retribution. Hence, the tone of the title alters between honest, haughty, casual, and vengeful according to the way in which we read the words "this" and "just."

The revised paragraph includes clear explanations of your interpretation of the diction and how it relates to the tone of the poem. You have more explicitly connected your discussion to the thesis statement, your overall argument. You have added the transitional word "similarly" to connect how the multiple meanings of the words work in the poem. The revised paragraph is well organized: two meanings of "this," followed by an ordered interpretation of each meaning; two meanings of "just," also followed by an ordered interpretation of each meaning. Finally, the paragraph has a concluding sentence that highlights the importance of multiple meanings of the words discussed.

STEP 3   Revising Your Conclusion

As we pointed out in Chapter 5, your conclusion should restate and extend your thesis, and suggest its broader context or implications. Check that your conclusion expands the original thesis statement by drawing upon the more specific ideas you have developed in the body of the essay and that it briefly discusses the broader implications of your essay.

Let's take a look at the concluding paragraph of the draft essay on Williams's "This Is Just to Say."

Draft conclusion

In conclusion, diction in the poem shows a complex rather than a simple tone. The words "this" and "just" have various meanings that hide the speaker's haughty and vengeful tone. The phrase "forgive me" and the sensuous description of the plums undermine the speaker's apology by relating how good the plums were. Overall, we can see that the speaker has a complex, even troubled, relationship with his lover.

This conclusion restates the thesis, and its general comments are very much in the spirit of Williams's poem and the points you have made in your essay. The draft conclusion is still weak, however. In a short essay assignment such as this one, it is important not to repeat points you've already made. For a more powerful conclusion, think about the broader implications of the poem. This doesn't mean that you will present large generalizations or moral statements about literature and life. Rather, consider why Williams would write such a poem in the first place and who might be his audience. Think about the poem beyond, but in relation to, the speaker and his attitude toward his lover. This kind of revising doesn't just involve editing or proofreading. It involves a second look at the poem itself, and it involves employing your critical thinking skills. Take the time to reflect on what your analysis has led you to discover about the text and the subject of the assignment.

This is the conclusion that might result from these changes:

Writing Sample

Revised conclusion

Although Williams presents his poem as a note of apology, he also presents it as a poem that appears in his collection of poems. What is Williams's purpose in presenting this poem as a piece of literature? In order to answer this question, we may view the poet in the same way that we view the speaker. Like the speaker, the poet creates a seemingly simple work that relays a casual and honest tone, as if the poem can precisely depict and justify the meaning of a particular incident. Essentially, however, he creates a complex piece of literature in which the tone is dependent upon the way we read the words. Williams thus comments on the power of language. We accept words as justifications for action, even though "just saying" is only saying. Perhaps "this" poem then, is "just to say" that there is no single truth or ideal justice that language can express.

Note that the revised conclusion includes the third possible reference to "this"—"this" as the poem itself—that you initially identified when gathering material for the essay. You can see how important it is to keep your notes, even very early ones, because you may later incorporate some of the information you gathered. Also, the broader implications in this conclusion subtly refer back to the context of the poem. When gathering material for your essay, you looked up the definition of *modernism* in M. H. Abrams's *A Glossary of Literary Terms.* The notion in your conclusion that "there is no single truth or ideal justice that language can express" is very much in the spirit of modernism's challenge to existing traditions and truths. Once again, the information you came across in the initial stages of gathering material became useful in writing the final draft of your essay.

Working on Your Own Assignment

Your main purpose in writing essays on literature is often to explain the relationship between *what* the work is about (its subject and theme) and *how* the ideas and emotions are conveyed.

- Make notes on the written text or performance in the appropriate disciplinary categories: subject, genre, context, methods of development, structure, style, tone, and point of view.

- Begin formulating your thesis statement by presenting your opinion of the text's theme or thesis, unless the assignment requires your opinion on a different element of the text.

- Complete your thesis statement by adding a reference to relevant formal elements of the text as support.

- Decide how to organize your draft, bearing in mind that presenting the elements of the text as part of a system (systems analysis) will usually work best.

- Make a draft outline to guide your writing. Leave spaces so that you can later insert revision suggestions.

- Write a draft, paying most attention to developing middle paragraphs.

- Change your draft outline into a revision outline by recording what you have actually done in your draft and what needs to be changed.

- Check that your thesis statement is not a description of the theme/thesis or form but rather your supported opinion on the assignment topic.

- Check that your draft is not a running summary of the text but rather is organized around topics of ascending interest.

- Check that the context section of your introduction provides information that directly leads toward your thesis statement.
- Check that textual detail in middle paragraphs does not simply describe a section of the text but rather is used as evidence to support a point.
- Check that the connection between point and detail in middle paragraphs is sufficiently explained, especially in the case of direct quotations.
- Check that your conclusion restates and expands the thesis and suggests broader implications appropriate to the subject of the assignment and the text.

Exercises

A. Respond to each of the following questions in a sentence or two.

1. If you are analyzing an essay, what is the difference between the writer's thesis and your own?

2. Why does "telling the story" not work as a structure for an essay about literature?

B. This two-part exercise relates to the paragraphs that appear following these instructions—the introduction and conclusion to an essay showing how three formal elements in director Terrence Malick's *The Thin Red Line* help convey the theme of the film. After completing the exercise, compare your choices with those of other class members.

1. For the introduction, mark the sentences that indicate
   - an appropriate context for the analysis
   - the principal paragraph topics the essay will cover
   - the thesis of the essay

   Cross out all material that does not relate to one of these three areas.

2. For the conclusion, mark the sentences that
   - restate the thesis
   - summarize the main points of the essay
   - suggest the wider implications of thesis and points

   Cross out all other material.

Introduction There are many levels of conflict in war. Beyond the obvious physical conflict between the armies, there is the more subtle psychological antagonism that rages inside the minds of the soldiers. This is the aspect of warfare that is explored in Terrence Malick's World War II film, *The Thin Red Line*. Malick's reputation as a film genius, along with the fact that he had not directed a movie for twenty years, caused Hollywood stars to line up for a chance to act in this project. The result was a film that has only enhanced Malick's illustrious reputation. The film claims that war is as much psychological as it is physical, and it achieves its focus on the psychology of war by using images, structure, and characterization in a very distinctive way. It is a challenging film to watch, but well worth the effort.

Conclusion Even though it was soundly beaten at the box office and the Academy Awards by *Saving Private Ryan* and many other films that were released in the same year, I believe that *The Thin Red Line* will stand the test of time. It is an extraordinarily powerful film about a topic mankind will never grow weary of analyzing. The innovative use of disjointed images, the very slow pace of the narrative, and the emphasis on collective characterization rather than individual heroism all serve to focus our attention on the psychology of the soldiers rather than their behaviour. There have been many anti-war films about war, obviously, but their messages have been undermined because they have adopted the same conventions as the heroic war film. Malick's film challenges these conventions and makes us question war in a very profound way. I think this focus will make *The Thin Red Line* widely recognized as one of the best films ever made about war. Perhaps if there were more films like this, those Academy Awards judges would start to realize that the times really are changing.

Writing Comparison Essays (7)

Sample Topic: Comparing Views of Addiction in Maté and Alexander

The comparison essay is a special type of analysis essay that you may be asked to write in many college and university courses. You could be asked to compare two poems, two models of moral development, two views of a social problem, or social organization in two tribal societies. Comparison assignments help you and your reader better understand both the things you are comparing—the *objects of comparison*—and the more general subject, concept, or focus that is the *basis of comparison.*

To illustrate how basic the process of comparison is, let's consider this question: Is someone with an income of twenty thousand dollars a year a wealthy person? In comparison to most of the planet's inhabitants, the answer would be yes; in comparison to the average North American, however, the answer would be no. Without comparison, the term *wealthy* is virtually meaningless.

Our understanding of the concept of wealth will remain fairly superficial, however, unless we take the comparison further. As we work through the similarities and differences between the situations of people with different incomes, we are forced to think not only about those specific instances, but also, and perhaps more significantly, about our own ideas of what constitutes wealth. What standard of living does each person's income provide? How many people does it support? How much of it is disposable income—that is, money that does not have to be spent on necessities such as food, clothing, and housing? Comparing the economic positions of people with different incomes would thus help us understand both the concept of wealth (the basis of comparison) and these different economic positions (the objects of comparison).

This chapter emphasizes the most problematic aspects of making comparisons: choosing a basis of comparison, arriving at a thesis, and organizing your material. You will also find general guidelines for clarifying topics, gathering material, formulating a thesis statement, and drafting and revising comparison essays. To illustrate these stages of writing, we will focus on a comparison between two essays on addiction that appear in Part 2, Readings: Gabor Maté's "Embraced by the Needle" and Bruce K. Alexander's "Reframing Canada's 'Drug Problem.'" You will follow this discussion more easily if you read the essays first.

STAGE 1 Clarifying Comparison Topics

Imagine you have been given the following choices for a comparison essay:

- Compare the explanations of addiction in Gabor Maté's essay "Embraced by the Needle" and Bruce K. Alexander's essay "Reframing Canada's 'Drug Problem.'"
- Compare any two similar short stories from your class anthology.

STEP 1   ## Checking for a Basis of Comparison

Comparison essay assignments will indicate, at least generally, the objects of comparison, the two (or more) things you are to compare. Assignments that can be stated as "Compare X and Y in terms of Z" also indicate the basis of comparison, the common element you are to focus on. The first topic above gives the basis of comparison:

> Compare Gabor Maté's essay "Embraced by the Needle" (X) and Bruce K. Alexander's essay "Reframing Canada's 'Drug Problem'" (Y) in terms of their explanations of addiction (Z).

This is the sample topic we will use for the rest of the chapter.

The second topic does not indicate a basis of comparison. To write successfully on this kind of topic, you will first need to choose objects that share a significant similarity. You might, for example, pick short stories with similar subjects, settings, or main characters. You could use one of these elements as your basis of comparison, or you might discover a more interesting basis of comparison in the process of gathering material.

STEP 2   ## Looking for Similarities and Differences

Remember that "compare" always means "compare and contrast." Look for both similarities and differences in the objects of comparison.

STAGE 2   ## Gathering Material

STEP 1   ## Using Matching Methods of Analysis and Analytic Categories

Before you can compare two things, you need to analyze each separately. To make sure you *can* compare them, you need to use the same methods of analysis for each one. The first step in gathering material, therefore, is to find appropriate methods of analysis. For example, you might use methods of analysis such as cause/effect, process analysis, or systems analysis (see Chapter 3). You will then consider the analytic or disciplinary categories to use. If you are writing a comparison essay on literature, you will consider the disciplinary categories for English discussed in Chapter 6. You will perceive similarities and differences more easily if you set out your material in matching columns.

- In the sample assignment, the phrase "explanations of addiction" indicates that you should focus on the content of the two essays, not on their literary qualities. In Chapter 2, Reading Analytically and Writing Summaries, we discussed how to figure out the basic ideas in a text. Using the categories of analysis discussed in Chapter 2, and drawing upon the methods of analysis discussed in Chapter 3, here is what you come up with:

CATEGORIES	MATÉ'S ESSAY	ALEXANDER'S ESSAY
Subject	Causes of addiction	Causes of addiction, then solutions
Main idea	Emotional pain in childhood changes brain chemistry, leading to addiction.	Social dislocations in free-market societies lead to mass addiction; integration into real communities is the most effective cure.
Development	Cause and effect analysis is framed by narratives.	Cause and effect analysis. Free-market societies create dislocation; dislocation creates addiction.
Detail	Stories of addicts; theories of effects of stress on brain chemistry	Historical examples: present day; 19th-century England; rise of capitalism
Context/ Perspective	Maté is a physician; perspective more psychological than medical.	Alexander teaches in a psychology department, but the essay is concerned more with social trends than with individuals.
Purpose	To gain sympathy for addicts' emotional suffering	To explore causes as a prompt to political action for change

Besides helping you focus on similarities and differences, a set of matching categories can reveal imbalances in your material. Occasionally you may find that a category contains a lot of material on one object of comparison, but little or none on the other. In this case you must decide whether to drop the category, find more material, or explain the imbalance.

- In the matching categories for the sample assignment, there are no major imbalances of material. But let's suppose you discovered that you had much more material in the development category for Maté's essay than for Alexander's. You would have three options:

review Alexander's essay and take more notes on its methods of development; drop this category as not relevant to your thesis; or find a reason for the imbalance. You might decide, for instance, that you have more notes on structure in the Maté essay because it is loose and unsystematic, whereas Alexander sets out the problem and its solution in a straightforward manner.

STEP 2   Clarifying the Basis of Comparison

Creating a set of matching categories will also help you clarify or decide upon a basis of comparison.

If your assignment has indicated a basis of comparison, this basis should be the focus of one set of matching categories. If the assignment has not indicated a basis, you can choose a key area of similarity and/or difference from your list of matching categories.

- The basis of comparison given in the sample assignment on addiction is "explanations of addiction." Under the category of subject, you note that both essays deal with the causes of addiction. You can thus make the basis of comparison more precise by identifying it as "explanations of the causes of addiction."

- If you had chosen the assignment asking you to compare two short stories, your matching disciplinary categories would offer you a number of possibilities to try out as a basis of comparison, such as subject, characterization, setting, style, and theme. You would choose the best basis of comparison by seeing which of these connected with the pattern of material in most other categories.

- If you chose setting, for example, could you compare not only the settings themselves, but also characters' attitudes toward the settings? The figurative language used to describe each setting? The relation between setting and theme?

STAGE 3   Formulating a Comparison Thesis Statement

STEP 1   Forming an Opinion about Each Set of Material

You arrive at a comparison thesis opinion much as you do for other analysis essays, that is, by scanning the material in your categories to see how it is linked and what point it suggests. You begin by considering what point the material in each set of categories, considered separately, makes about the basis of comparison. (We say "considered separately," but putting the columns side by side will sharpen your sense of the qualities of each object.)

- Scanning the material on "Embraced by the Needle," you may notice that Maté's point about emotional pain in childhood causing addiction is reinforced by the narrative framework and details of individual addicts' lives. The material in several categories confirms that Maté's perspective is psychological rather than medical.
- In the Alexander essay, several factors indicate a sociological perspective: the point about the social causes of addiction, the systematic cause and effect analysis, and the historical examples.

STEP 2   Forming an Opinion about Overall Similarities and Differences

The next step is to consider the relationship between the two points you came up with in the previous step. Are the objects of comparison similar or different in relation to the basis of comparison? What generalization can you make about the similarities and/or differences? Your answer to these questions becomes the *opinion* part of your thesis statement.

- "Embraced by the Needle" and "Reframing Canada's 'Drug Problem'" seem to embody quite different perspectives on the causes of addiction. You might write the opinion part of your thesis statement as follows:

Tentative thesis opinion
In "Embraced by the Needle," Gabor Maté explains the causes of addiction from a psychological perspective, whereas Bruce Alexander offers a sociological perspective in "Reframing Canada's 'Drug Problem.'"

STEP 3   Supporting Your Opinion about Similarities and Differences

As in any analysis essay, the support for your opinion comes from the categories of material you used to arrive at the opinion. The only difference in formulating a thesis statement for a comparison essay is that you draw the support from the matching categories, not from one set alone. Problems with comparison thesis statements most often come from one-sidedness, where one of the objects of comparison receives unequal treatment either in the opinion or in the support. Take care to make the thesis statement even-handed.

- In the sample assignment, the opinion part of the thesis statement focuses on perspectives, but the perspective of each essay is confirmed by the categories of main idea, development, detail, and purpose. These categories therefore provide support for the thesis opinion.

Tentative thesis statement	In "Embraced by the Needle," Gabor Maté explains the causes of addiction from a psychological perspective, whereas Bruce Alexander offers a sociological perspective in "Reframing Canada's 'Drug Problem.'" These different perspectives are evident in the writers' points and purposes, and in their handling of development and detail.

A tentative thesis statement like this gives you a starting point for exploring the similarities and differences between the things you are comparing. The process of drafting and revising often leads to deeper insights into your material.

- As you will see with the sample topic, there are important differences between a psychological and a sociological perspective. Through drafting, a better thesis emerges that explains the relationship between these two perspectives on addiction.

STAGE 4 Drafting

STEP 1 Selecting Material

As with other analysis essays, the categories of material that you found relevant in working out your thesis will become the basis for your middle paragraphs. There are two points you need to keep in mind, however:

- Because your matching categories will give you a great deal of material, you may need to limit the number of categories you use. Drop categories where your material is skimpy, imbalanced, or not relevant to your comparison. If, for instance, you were comparing two poems, one a sonnet and one not, you would likely drop the category of structure, since there would not be much point in proving the obvious differences between the two.

- Make sure you include roughly equivalent amounts of material for each of the things you are comparing.

STEP 2   Organizing Comparisons: Block and
Point-by-Point Methods

Probably the most common problem in writing comparison essays is finding an effective method of organization. There are two basic methods of organizing comparisons: the *block method* and the *point-by-point method*.

Block method   When you use the block method, you say everything you have to say about one subject before you discuss the other. This method can be effective for very short essays in which overall similarities and differences (as you might find, for instance, in a personal essay comparing good teachers and bad teachers) are more important than detailed comparisons. The block method is also useful for in-class essays and essay exams, when you are developing a few main points without extensive quotations or facts and figures as evidence.

Point-by-point method   When you use the point-by-point method, you compare things one aspect at a time. The point-by-point method usually works better for essays longer than 500 words because you can explain the significance of similarities and differences as you go along. You don't risk leaving anything unexplained or having to add another section to cover everything.

   Making a draft outline is especially valuable when you are using the point-by-point method. Note the point you intend to make about each category so you don't merely repeat the observation that the things you are comparing are similar or different. These points will become the basis for your topic sentences.

- The sample assignment seems too long and complex for the block method, so you would choose the point-by-point method. The draft outline for your middle paragraphs (MPs) might look like this:

DRAFT OUTLINE

MP 1	Thesis and perspective	Addiction is caused by emotional pain in childhood, according to Maté's psychological perspective.
		Addiction is caused by social dislocation in Alexander's sociological perspective.
MP 2	Development	Maté's causal analysis is enclosed in a narrative framework.
		Alexander's causal analysis is systematic and directly presented.
MP 3	Detail	Maté emphasizes the lives of individual addicts.
		Alexander uses non-individual historical examples.

STAGE 5   Revising the Thesis Statement and
Essay Structure

STEP 1   Revising Your Thesis Statement

In this step you ask yourself the following questions:

- Does your thesis statement present an overall opinion about similarities and differences between two (or more) objects of comparison?
- Does this opinion reflect the relationship between similarities and differences in the material you collected in matching categories?
- Is this opinion based on, and does it indicate, a common basis of comparison?
- Does the thesis statement indicate the support that you are going to present in the body of the essay?

If the answer to any of these questions is no, your thesis statement will need revision.

- Note that the following thesis statements lack some of the necessary components.

Weak thesis statements

- Maté's essay is very different from Alexander's, as I shall show by looking at their different forms and purposes. [No basis of comparison indicated]
- "Embraced by the Needle" is a psychological essay, while "Reframing Canada's 'Drug Problem'" is more systematic. [No common basis of comparison, no support]

If your thesis statement seems satisfactory, one final question remains:

- Does your draft suggest new ideas that will give you a better thesis?

As we suggested earlier, the tentative thesis statement for the sample assignment seems to have all the components mentioned above. Yet it focuses solely on differences. It does not account for the nagging sense you might have in writing the draft that while the explanations of addiction in the two essays are different, they are not incompatible. There is a link, after all, between the emotional pain suffered by individuals and the social dislocations that give rise to emotional pain. So you might revise your thesis statement to include this idea.

Writing Sample

Revised
thesis
statement
In "Embraced by the Needle," Gabor Maté explains the causes of addiction from a psychological perspective, whereas Bruce K. Alexander offers a sociological perspective in "Reframing Canada's 'Drug Problem.'" While these differences in perspective are evident in the writers' purposes and in their handling of development and detail, the main ideas expressed in the two essays are complementary rather than contradictory, for social dislocations give rise to the emotional pain experienced by individual addicts in childhood.

STEP 2   Revising Your Essay Structure

Use your draft outline, if you made one, or make a revision outline showing the points in each paragraph of your draft to check whether

- your choice of either block or point-by-point organization still seems appropriate. If your outline reveals that each block paragraph is crammed with a variety of ideas, for example, then you should probably decide to adopt the more systematic point-by-point method. On the other hand, if your paragraphs switch back and forth like a Ping-Pong ball, you may need to gather your material into larger blocks.

- your discussion includes matching points about the things you are comparing. Have you inadvertently failed to cover some aspect of one object of comparison? Have you devoted much more space to one object of comparison than another? Identify problems for correction in the next stage of revision.

- your sequence of paragraphs still seems effective. In a comparison essay, your paragraphs should lead toward the point that best illustrates the most important similarity or difference. Thus if your thesis statement suggests that differences are more important than similarities, you would discuss similarities first and then differences, ending with the most significant one. If similarities are more important, you would end with the most significant similarity.

In the sample assignment, for example, the revised thesis statement requires a rethinking of the structure. It indicates you are going to move from showing differences to showing the compatibility of psychological and sociological perspectives. You would therefore start from the most obvious difference—detail—and lead toward your comparison of these perspectives. You will see the results of this reorganization in the sample essay. See C. Jones, "Perspectives on Addictions" (Readings: Sample Essays).

STAGE 6   ## Revising Individual Paragraphs

Now that you have identified areas where your draft needs revising, it is time to tackle individual paragraphs.

STEP 1   ## Revising Your Introduction

If you have followed our advice not to worry about your introduction until the structure of the whole essay is clear, you may find that you need to fill out the statement of context that precedes your thesis statement. (See Chapters 5 and 6, Revising Your Introduction.)

Does your statement of context

- indicate your basis of comparison and establish its importance or relevance?
- provide matching information about the objects you are comparing?

In drafting your essay on the explanations of addiction, you might have begun with a statement of context like this:

Draft introduction   Understanding the causes of addiction is an important project and few people are better qualified for it than Dr. Gabor Maté. Dr. Maté works on Vancouver's Eastside, sometimes called the drug capital of North America, and his writing shows he has on-the-ground knowledge of what he is talking about. I will compare his essay entitled "Embraced by the Needle" with an essay called "Reframing Canada's 'Drug Problem'" by Bruce K. Alexander.

This statement of context successfully indicates the basis of comparison, "understanding the causes of addiction," and provides good information about Gabor Maté. It does not explain why this is an important subject, however, or give matching information on Alexander. For the revised version of this introduction, see the sample essay by C. Jones, "Perspectives on Addictions" (Readings: Sample Essays).

STEP 2   ## Revising Your Middle Paragraphs

Check to see whether

- you use topic sentences that clearly indicate your method of organization
- you use "umbrella" topic sentences when necessary to indicate the major divisions in your material
- you give roughly the same amount of space to developing points about each object, text, or concept you are comparing

Problems in developing comparison paragraphs usually come from imbalance and one-sidedness.

- In reviewing the draft for the sample assignment, for example, you might find a paragraph like the one below.

Draft middle paragraph

The most obvious contrast between "Embraced by the Needle" and "Reframing Canada's 'Drug Problem'" is in the type of detail used. In "Embraced," the detail we remember is the detail of individuals: of Anna, who "wasn't wanted"; of Carl, who "had dishwashing liquid poured down his throat"; of Wayne, a tough man, who at the end of the essay "looks away and wipes tears from his eyes." No one cries in "Reframing." In that essay, the language is abstract, the kind argumentative social scientists use.

- This paragraph was intended to compare the use of detail in the two essays. There are no examples to show the kinds of detail used in "Reframing," however, so the point of the comparison is not clear. In revising, you would both clarify the point and provide examples from "Reframing."

STEP 3   Revising Your Conclusion

It may be tempting to conclude by simply repeating what you have said about similarities and differences. Readers expect more than this, however; they want you to step back from the specific objects you have compared and explore what your essay has revealed about your subject.

You will need to check not only that your conclusion summarizes your thesis statement and main points, but also that the development of these points leads to a deeper understanding of both the basis of comparison and the objects you have compared. If either summary or development is missing, you will need to revise.

- Consider the draft conclusion to the sample assignment:

Draft conclusion

"Embraced by the Needle" and "Reframing Canada's 'Drug Problem'" are very different because their authors' handling of detail, development, and points are so different. Gabor Maté has a psychological perspective on the causes of addiction, while Bruce K. Alexander takes a sociological point of view on the issue. These are very different perspectives on this important issue, but they may be more complementary than contradictory.

- This conclusion restates the thesis but adds nothing to it. In revising, you would want to stress what you and your readers have learned from considering the causes of addiction from both a psychological and a sociological perspective.

- You will find the complete revised essay, C. Jones, "Perspectives on Addictions," in Part 2, Readings: Sample Essays.

Working on Your Own Assignment

Your purpose in comparing is to illuminate the similarities and differences between two (or more) objects of comparison in reference to a basis of comparison.

- Check your essay topics to make sure you know which ones ask you to compare. Are you given a basis of comparison or will you need to work one out?

- Gather material on both objects of comparison by using the appropriate questions for analysis essays or essays on literature. Analyze the objects separately so that you don't distort them by trying to find similarities too soon.

- Arrange your material in matching categories that contain equivalent amounts of material, focusing on the categories most relevant to your topic.

- Examine your material to determine the overall relationship between similarity and difference in reference to your basis of comparison.

- Formulate a thesis statement by making a general point about this overall relationship and giving reasons to support it.

- Organize your material by the block method or the point-by-point method, depending upon the length and complexity of your essay. Your topic sentences should make clear which method you are using.

- When you revise your draft, check to see whether your paragraphs lead toward the most important similarity or difference, and whether you have given equal attention to both objects of comparison in your thesis statement, your points and detail, and your introduction and conclusion.

Exercises

A. Work out a basis of comparison for a short essay on each of the following subjects. Compare your responses with those of other class members.

1. The celebration of Thanksgiving in your family and another family

2. Canadian and American television programs of a specific type (such as lawyer shows, family dramas, talk shows)

3. Different ways of looking at a local environmental or educational issue

B. Read the essays by Tim Bowling ("Na Na Na Na, Hey Hey Hey, Goodbye") and Kofi Annan ("Football Envy at the UN") in the Readings. What would be a workable basis of comparison for these two essays? Try several possibilities. Compare your responses with those of other class members.

C. Decide whether each of the following is a good thesis statement for a comparison essay and explain your decision.

1. For an essay comparing Sigmund Freud's view of dreams with C. G. Jung's:

> In developing a theory of dreams that emphasizes their prophetic and compensatory functions, Jung departed from the view of the unconscious upon which his mentor, Freud, had built his theory of dreams.

2. For an essay comparing the principles of solar and geothermal heating systems:

> Although solar and geothermal heating systems are similar in some respects, in others they are different.

D. Choose one of the following topics. Use the appropriate questions to gather material and formulate a thesis. Then make an outline showing how you would organize your middle paragraphs. Compare your work with the work of other class members. The essays mentioned are reprinted in Part 2, Readings.

1. Compare the authors' views of sports in relation to culture and society in the essays by Tim Bowling, Kofi Annan, and/or Jonathan Zimmerman.

2. Choose two other essays from the Readings to compare. You will need to work out your own basis of comparison.

E. Scott Russell Sanders's "The Men We Carry in Our Minds" implicitly compares and contrasts the men that his friend Anneke carries in her mind with the men that Sanders carries in his mind. Reorganize this essay so that it is a more explicit comparison essay. Make an outline showing how you would write this essay using either the block or the point-by-point method.

Writing Evaluation Essays

(8)

There is an important difference between *analysis*—identifying the causes of downtown parking problems, for example—and *evaluation*—judging whether arguments for a new downtown parking lot are logical or illogical, or whether the proposed lot will be beautiful or ugly. As this example suggests, analysis usually precedes evaluation. Whether you are arguing with a friend about whether or not a movie is worth watching, or campaigning for a political candidate, judging the value of things is an important human activity.

Making evaluations is equally important in academic disciplines, as you learn how to determine the worth of theories, experiments, technological innovations, or works of art. Analysis is the act of breaking something down into parts in order to better understand it. Evaluation is the act of judging what you have analyzed. An analysis essay in English might ask you to explain how a character attains self-fulfillment (process method of development). An evaluation essay, by contrast, might ask you to decide whether or not that character makes ethical decisions in the story. Whereas an analysis essay explains how something works—how a work of literature makes meaning, for example—an evaluation essay asks you to decide whether that work of literature or characters within it are worthy. When considering another's argument or essay, an evaluation essay judges that argument as worthy or unworthy, correct or incorrect, strong or weak.

When you write evaluative essays in an academic setting, you need to be conscious of and express the criteria you use in making judgments. Although specific criteria will vary, there are four common *standards of evaluation* that provide a broad framework for making judgments. These are the *logical*, *aesthetic*, *practical*, and *ethical* standards. In an evaluative essay or critique you use one or more of these standards to evaluate someone else's work, such as the methodology of a scientific experiment or the interpretation of a poem. When judging a work of art or a written argument, it's not convincing simply to state that you don't like the work, or that you disagree with the author's point of view. You may wish to express your opinion, but in order to make your evaluation convincing you need to state *why* the work or argument, in your opinion, is not worthy or convincing. In order to do so, you can refer to logical, aesthetic, practical, or ethical standards.

This chapter will show you how to write an evaluation essay or critique that judges the logic of stated or implied arguments. We focus on this type of critique for two reasons: to demonstrate how to separate considerations of logic from aesthetic, practical, and ethical concerns; and to give you the tools you need to evaluate your own arguments when you write persuasive essays. We will first outline the gathering, drafting, and revising process for this kind of essay, and then show the process at work in a sample assignment: evaluating the logic of an essay from Part 2, Readings.

STAGE 1 ## Clarifying Evaluation Topics: Checking for the Logical Standard

The first stage in tackling any evaluation assignment is to check what standard(s) of evaluation the assignment asks you to use. You will know to use the logical standard of evaluation if the assignment uses words like *logical, reasonable, credible, plausible,* or *valid,* and/or asks you to assess reasoning, evidence, a case, arguments, methodologies, or strategies of argumentation, as in the following:

- Does David Suzuki's "It Always Costs" present a credible case for distrusting technological innovation?
- Assess the plausibility of the evidence in Naomi Klein's "Science Says: Revolt!"

In both of these examples, you are asked not only to interpret the writers' arguments—to show how the works make meaning or to explain their content or structure—but also to evaluate the effectiveness of those arguments. You can therefore deduce that you should write an evaluation essay rather than an analysis essay.

STAGE 2 ## Gathering Material: Arguments and Evidence

Most of us have strong emotional responses, positive or negative, to a writer's position on a subject we care about. This emotional response can get in the way of a fair-minded assessment. If we disagree with a writer's views, for instance, we may be tempted to dismiss the argument without giving it serious attention. The best way to avoid this problem is to analyze the reasoning and evidence first, and only then assess the strengths and weaknesses.

STEP 1 ## Analyzing the Writer's Argument

In Chapter 2 we introduced categories for analyzing the content of nonfiction writing: subject, main idea/thesis, development, evidence/detail, purpose, and context. You use the same categories to analyze reasoning and evidence when you evaluate a piece of writing according to the standard of logic, except that you pay closer attention to types of argument (development) and kinds of evidence (detail). Make sure that you identify how the author identifies his or her main idea. Does the author tell a story? Analyze cause and effects? Analyze a process or a system? Compare or contrast? Or evaluate strengths and weaknesses?

Types of argument The important term *argument* may be used for the writer's overall case, for the structure of this case, and for individual points. In other words, a writer's argument includes his or her thesis—an educated opinion that he or she will prove—and the subpoints of that thesis, supported by evidence. The main types of argument are as follows.

Deductive argument Any argument that moves from one or more general principles to make a judgment about one or more particular cases could be called a deductive argument. The most rigorous kind of deductive argument is the *syllogism*, where a general statement (called the *major premise*) is linked to a specific case (called the *minor premise*) to produce a conclusion.

- Historians view history objectively (major premise).
- Joan is a historian (minor premise).
- Therefore Joan views history objectively (conclusion).

On a larger scale, a deductively organized essay moves from an overall point to a series of individual points that serve to confirm and develop it. In Chapter 4, Writing Analysis Essays: Formulating a Thesis Statement and Drafting, we discussed how to *structure* your own argument deductively when writing an analysis essay. When gathering material for your evaluation essay, make sure to check whether or not the author whose work you are evaluating argues deductively.

Inductive argument Any argument that moves from one or more particular cases toward a general point could be called an inductive argument. An inductive essay is structured around the movement from individual points to a more general thesis. In Chapter 4, we discussed how to structure your own argument inductively when writing an analysis essay. Instructors in the humanities and social sciences will often expect you to structure your essays deductively, with your thesis statement in your introduction rather than at the end of the essay. By contrast, instructors in the sciences will often expect you to structure your lab reports inductively, with your evidence first and your conclusion at the end of the report. When gathering material for your evaluation essay, check to see whether or not the author whose work you are evaluating argues inductively.

Cause and effect Reasoning from step to step in a process and from part to part in a system are both relatively rare, but reasoning from cause to effect is an important form of logical reasoning.

STEP 2 Evaluating the Writer's Argument

After you have analyzed a writer's argument, the next step is to evaluate the argument to determine its strengths and weaknesses. It's important to look for both strengths and weaknesses, however much you may agree or disagree with the writer's position, because your readers are more likely to be convinced when your critique seems fair-minded.

Types of argument The following guidelines will help you determine strengths and weaknesses in reasoning. Note that problems in logic are often called *logical fallacies.*

Deductive argument Deductive arguments are strong if the general principle is valid and supportable, and if the points that follow can be derived from that principle. Similarly, deductively organized essays work when the main points demonstrate the initial thesis.

Problems in deductive arguments occur when the general principle is not valid or the points do not follow from the principle. Earlier we spoke of the syllogism as the purest form of deduction. A syllogism is not valid if the major premise is untrue, the minor premise is missing, or the conclusion does not follow.

- Our earlier example of a syllogism was this: historians view history objectively; Joan is a historian; therefore, Joan views history objectively. This syllogism will not be valid if some historians do not view history objectively; if no proof is offered that Joan is a historian; or if the argument reached the conclusion that because Joan is a historian, she would make a good politician.

You are most likely to find problems in deductive arguments when the major premise is a sweeping generalization that is either unverifiable (cannot be proved to be true or false) or untrue.

- Throughout history humans have struggled for perfection. [Unverifiable]
- Hard work always leads to success. [Untrue]

This is the fallacy of *over-generalization,* a fallacy also involved when you make large conclusions from limited major or minor premises:

- Some historians are objective. [limited major premise] Joan is a historian. Therefore Joan is objective.

Another common deductive problem is the fallacy of *circular reasoning,* or begging the question, where a point that should be proved is assumed. In circular reasoning, the argument repeats itself.

- If you were to state, in an English essay, that the novel *Jane Eyre* is a story about Jane Eyre, you haven't really proved anything. If you state that one can quit smoking if he or she really wants to, you're really just saying that one can quit because he or she can quit. In both instances you're using circular reasoning, which is neither effective nor convincing.

Inductive argument An inductive argument is considered strong if the particulars are connected and if they lead plausibly to some larger conclusion. Similarly, an inductive essay works if the paragraph points are connected with each other and lead toward the concluding thesis.

Problems in inductive arguments most often occur when there is a gap between the particulars and the conclusion—thesis or argument—that the essay intends to draw from them. This gap is often called the fallacy of *hasty generalization*.

- "My neighbours never cut their lawns and the man across the street leaves his porch light on all night; these are symptoms of the moral decay of the modern world" is an ineffective inductive argument. The concluding point is too broad to emerge convincingly from these particulars.

Cause and effect Causal arguments are valid when the effect is clearly shown to follow from the cause.

- Many families with children have moved into the neighbourhood; therefore, enrolment in local schools is likely to rise. In this case, the effect (rising enrolment in schools) logically follows from the cause (families with children moving into the neighbourhood). Therefore, the causal reasoning is valid.

Problems in causal reasoning arise when the cause–effect relationship is unconvincing. Many ineffective causal arguments suffer from what is called the *post hoc fallacy*. The full phrase in Latin is *post hoc ergo propter hoc*, meaning "after this, therefore because of this." In this fallacy, because a second event follows a first, the first is taken to be the cause of the second.

- "The team ate Mighty Bites before the game; no wonder they won." Although the team won the game, there is no convincing evidence to show that they won because they ate Mighty Bites. While one follows the other, one is not the cause of the other.

A special version of *post hoc* is sometimes called the fallacy of *single cause/single outcome,* where a likely multiplicity of causes is reduced to one.

- The claim that "the increase in murders is a direct result of the suspension of the death penalty" is flawed unless further evidence is presented, since many factors are known to affect the homicide rate.

A fallacy common to several kinds of argument and evidence is the *straw man fallacy*, where an opponent's arguments are exaggerated or selectively presented to make them appear insubstantial. The name *straw man* indicates that the argument is easy to knock down. This tactic is particularly common in fallacious causal reasoning. In a straw man argument, the possible consequences of an opponent's position are misleadingly exaggerated:

- "If funding is increased for daycare centres, more children will attend them; as a result, children will cease to spend any significant time with their mothers." In this example, more funding for daycares is linked not only to more children attending them but also to the larger and unsubstantiated claim that children will not spend "*any* significant time with their mothers." This large and exaggerated claim cannot logically follow from funding increase.

- Here's another example of a straw man argument: "If we don't eat organic food, we will die from the pesticides." The effect here (death) is greatly exaggerated in relation to the cause (not eating organic food).

STEP 3   Analyzing the Writer's Evidence

Now that you have analyzed and evaluated the writer's argument, it is time to take a closer look at the writer's evidence. How does the writer prove his or her argument?

Kinds of evidence Anything used to show that a statement, argument, or thesis is true or false is considered evidence. The following list explains the most common types.

Examples An example is a detailed and specific piece of evidence intended to support a point about a larger whole. For instance, a line from a poem may support a statement about the poem's theme, or an anecdote about one mugging may support a case about the causes of street crime. Nevertheless, examples can be vivid and compelling.

Facts and figures These include statistics, research studies, and scientific observations. Facts and figures are widely used in formal scientific and applied research papers, but they are also frequently found in popular scientific essays, like David Suzuki's "It Always Costs" (Readings), and in persuasive essays, such as Elizabeth Renzetti's "Loneliness: The Trouble with Solitude" (Readings).

Reference to authorities The opinion of someone who is knowledgeable about a subject is a valid kind of evidence. Within academic disciplines you are often expected to locate your ideas within a tradition of thinking about your subject. Argument by authority is thus important in academic essays, especially research essays. When citing authorities in your evaluation essay—or assessing the validity of an author's citing of an authority—make sure that the authority you are citing is an expert in the discipline or field appropriate to the subject of your essay.

Analogies   An analogy is a comparison based on a partial similarity between the features of two unlike things. If you say that the heart is like a pump, for instance, you are using an analogy that emphasizes the similarity between the functions of the heart and the pump. When you use an analogy as part of an argument, you are arguing that one situation is like another situation and will have the same outcome, good or bad. Political arguments are often based on historical analogies: "A war in the Middle East would be another Vietnam."

Appeals to Emotion   Emotional appeals are designed to elicit strong feelings. An emotional appeal conveys a distinct attitude and invites the reader to share that attitude. Thus emotional appeals are often used in propaganda: written, visual, or spoken texts designed to persuade an audience to form a political or religious group, participate in particular social actions, or adopt a particular ideology. The feelings aroused by emotional appeals may be compatible or incompatible with a rational consideration of the subject. Thus emotional appeals are not really evidence in the logical sense at all. However, you need to be able to tell when a writer supports a position by emotional appeals rather than or in addition to reasoned arguments.

You can often identify emotional appeals by their diction and tone. The words used in emotional appeals often reflect extreme feeling: *unthinkable, dreadful, inarguable, utterly obvious, unquestionably valuable.* The tone of these appeals may be ridiculing, satiric, or humorous. In "Girl Unprotected" (Readings), Laura Robinson uses second-person narration in order to appeal to emotion. In the phrase, "*Your* daughter's boyfriend is a junior hockey player" (emphasis added) (326), she implicates the reader. She asks the reader, that is, to imagine what it would be like to have a daughter who is sexually abused by hockey players. In this way, she uses an emotional appeal.

STEP 4   Evaluating the Writer's Evidence

You have now considered the kinds of evidence that the writer uses to support his or her argument. But is the evidence valid? Does the evidence logically support the writer's overall case, argument, or thesis? In order to answer these questions, you will need to evaluate the writer's evidence.

Types of evaluation

Examples Examples are valid when they are representative of the larger point or situation they are intended to support. A single or isolated example, however, cannot prove an argument. Many examples, coupled with explanations regarding how they exemplify the argument, can make an argument convincing.

    Problems in handling examples arise when there is a questionable relationship between the particular example and the general point it intends to prove. Examples can be irrelevant to the point they are supposed to support, or generalizations can be based on too few examples, committing what we earlier called the fallacy of hasty generalization.

- "There is a flood of books being published in North America on men's problems. I saw two new titles from Australia only last week." Here, your example is irrelevant to your claim. You claim that such books are being published in *North America,* and yet your example is from *Australia.* Therefore, your example does not prove your point.

- "Clearly consideration for others is disappearing in today's society; my neighbour's parties have kept me awake three nights in a row." This example is inadequate to your claim. Having a neighbour that keeps you up does not result in a lack of consideration for others in all of society. In these two examples, your evidence is irrelevant (in the first case) and inadequate (in the second).

Facts and figures Facts and figures can be convincing evidence. As is the case with examples, facts and figures are valid if they are connected to and clearly support the argument presented.

    Problems result because statistics and other "facts" can be manipulated. Problems arise when the sources of the evidence are not current, when the evidence does not come from a reliable and appropriate source (as when statistics about the United States are assumed to apply to Canada), or when the evidence cited is extremely selective or limited. In "It Always Costs," David Suzuki points out that some studies, even if done over ten years, are still limited in their assessments, especially if they are trying to assess populations of animals or plants that must be studied over decades. The problem, he explains, is that the evidence is limited in a study in which long-term life cycles and patterns of life are important.

Reference to authorities Argument by authority is used well when the writer shows a critical awareness of the orientation and expertise of the authorities cited, the authorities have real expertise in the subject, and their ideas do not overshadow the writer's own ideas.

Problems result from citing authorities not relevant to the subject. A famous chemist is a valid authority for an essay on chemistry, but not for an essay on juvenile delinquency. Other problems include vague and unsupported references ("experts claim," "research shows"), unbalanced citation of authorities (where they are all on one side of a case, for example), and general over-reliance on authorities. Problems also occur when the authority cited is not an authority at all. All these could be called the fallacy of *inappropriate authority*, occasionally referred to as the fallacy of the *argumentum ad verecundiam* (literally, the "argument appealing to respect").

Analogies Analogies often have strong emotional appeal, and they can help explain a concept or idea to readers, but they are effective support for an argument only when they are used with other kinds of evidence.

Problems come from the fact that analogies are essentially metaphoric and emphasize similarities; when readers are aware of significant differences between the two objects being compared or see the objects through the lens of a different metaphor, they will consider that the writer has committed the fallacy of *false analogy*.

Appeals to Emotion Emotional appeals are strong in that they touch the level where beliefs are formed; they are used well when they reinforce logical arguments. Writers should not base their arguments on emotion alone, however. Emotional appeals by themselves do not prove arguments.

Problems with emotional appeals come when they are used instead of logical argument or when they are excessive. We tend to consider emotional appeals that have come unmoored from logical support as sentimental or manipulative. The common fallacy of *ad hominem* (literally "to the man") arguments—arguments directed against the arguer, not against his or her arguments—reflects a misuse of emotional appeals. So does the fallacy of *ad populum* (literally "to the populace") appeals, those designed to arouse popular unthinking sentiments. The following statements exemplify the fallacy of the *ad hominem* and *ad populum* arguments:

- "In Jean-Jacques Rousseau we see the kind of confused thinking about family and education we would expect from a man who put his own children into an orphanage." Here, the writer attacks Jean-Jacques Rousseau himself, not his argument. This statement demonstrates the fallacy of the *ad hominem* argument.

- "No one who values our pioneer past can deny that the real role for women is in the home, whether that home is a cabin in Northern Quebec or a house in suburban North York." The writer states but does not prove the idea that the place for women is the home and relies on a vague population of people who value "our pioneer past."

Neither the *ad hominem* nor the *ad populum* argument is valid or convincing.

This table summarizes the most common types of argument and evidence, along with their potential problems.

KINDS OF ARGUMENT AND EVIDENCE	FALLACIES
Deductive argument	Over-generalization, circular reasoning (begging the question)
Inductive argument	Hasty generalization
Causal argument	*Post hoc*, single cause/single outcome, straw man
Examples	Hasty generalization
Facts and figures	Outdated, inappropriate, or misleading, selective, or limited facts and figures
Reference to authorities	Appeal to inappropriate authority (*ad verecundiam*)
Analogies	False analogy
Appeals to emotion	*Ad hominem, ad populum*

Note that this is a partial list of some of the most common fallacies; for a more complete list, consult a textbook on logic or persuasive writing.

STEP 5 ## Categorizing and Charting Strengths and Weaknesses in the Writer's Argument and Evidence

Because of the complexity of evaluating reasoning and evidence, you may find it helpful to make an evaluation chart with one column for the analytic aspects of the writing, a second column for strengths, and a third column for weaknesses. If there is no key strength or weakness for a particular aspect, leave the space blank.

You will find a complete evaluation chart in the Sample Topic section of this chapter. An evaluation chart is useful for summing up the results of gathering material; it also streamlines the process of formulating a thesis statement, as you will subsequently see.

STAGE 3 ## Formulating an Evaluative Thesis Statement

An evaluative thesis statement for a critique essay should include an opinion about the relationship between strengths and weaknesses in the piece of writing, an indication of the main support for this opinion, and an indication of the standard(s) of evaluation you are using. Let us look at each of these components in turn.

STEP 1   Forming an Opinion about the Relationship between Strengths and Weaknesses

The opinion part of the thesis statement focuses on the overall relationship between strengths and weaknesses. This means you must decide whether, in general, strengths outweigh weaknesses, weaknesses outweigh strengths, or strengths and weaknesses are equally balanced. An evaluative chart makes this decision easier because you can see at a glance where you have noted strengths and weaknesses and where you have left blanks. You must still decide, of course, whether each analytic category you have used is equally important to your overall assessment.

Although you may find it difficult at first, deciding on the overall relationship between strengths and weaknesses is a skill you can acquire with practice. Simply listing some strengths and some weaknesses may be easier, but it won't give you a good thesis opinion. Similarly, claiming that there are only strengths or only weaknesses is usually an oversimplification; you would have to work hard to overcome your readers' skepticism, since few reasonable arguments are either flawless or totally flawed. Furthermore, you cannot avoid making up your mind by using the judgment that strengths and weaknesses are equally balanced. If you claim they are balanced, you will need to demonstrate the balance throughout your essay.

STEP 2   Supporting Your Opinion

An evaluation chart will also reveal the most important support for your thesis opinion, since the fullest categories will likely become the topics you use to organize the body of your essay.

STEP 3   Indicating the Standard of Evaluation

Indicating the standard of evaluation in the thesis statement is more important than you might realize. You know what standard of evaluation you are using, but unless you tell your readers, they may apply their own favoured standard and then be upset when your judgments differ from theirs. You may indicate the standard directly, by referring to logic, or indirectly, by referring to arguments or cases or by using words like *credible* or *convincing*, whichever is more suitable for your audience.

Below are examples of effective and weak thesis statements that evaluate an essay according to the logical standard.

Writing Sample

Weak thesis statements evaluating logic

- David Suzuki's "It Always Costs" is not Suzuki's typical argument about caring for the environment: it's a case against technology. [No identification of strengths or weaknesses]
- David Suzuki's "It Always Costs" provides some valid reasons for refraining from embracing technology too readily, but the argument has weaknesses. [Overall relationship of strengths and weaknesses is not clear; weaknesses are not specified; the standard of evaluation is not clear.]

Effective thesis statements evaluating logic

- Although some of his examples seem stereotyped [weakness], the use of appropriate evidence and a clear process structure [strengths supporting thesis opinion] make David Suzuki's "It Always Costs" a logically credible [standard of evaluation] essay on the costs of technology. [Putting the weakness in a dependent clause indicates that it is less important than the strengths.]
- The strength of David Suzuki's argument in "It Always Costs," its clear process structure, is more than offset [overall relationship] by its weaknesses: its stereotypical examples and excessive emotional appeals.
- Stereotypical examples and excessive emotional appeals in David Suzuki's "It Always Costs" are balanced by logical strengths in the use of appropriate evidence and a clear process structure.

STAGE 4   Drafting: Sequencing Strengths and Weaknesses

In evaluative essays or critiques, the relationship between strengths and weaknesses—as expressed in the thesis statement—determines the order of ascending interest. If weaknesses outweigh strengths, you begin with strengths and then move to weaknesses; if strengths outweigh weaknesses, then vice versa.

Once you have decided whether strengths or weaknesses come first, you will also need to decide on the order of points within each category. If you have written the support component of your thesis statement carefully, you should be able to use the sequence of topics it indicates. As for other essays, a draft outline is often helpful. For an evaluation essay or critique, make sure the draft outline indicates strengths and weaknesses as well as paragraph topics and points. You can find a sample draft outline for an evaluation essay in the Stage 4 Drafting section of the sample topic assignment later in this chapter.

STAGE 5 ## Revising the Thesis Statement and Essay Structure: Argument

The key principle to remember in revising is that your reader will judge your argument and evidence by the same standard you are using to evaluate someone else's writing. Thus you will need to review your draft to decide whether your argument as a whole is satisfactory.

STEP 1 ### Revising Your Thesis Statement: Checking for an Evaluative Point

If you are not satisfied with your argument as a whole, the problem may lie in your thesis statement.

- Does it contain an opinion about the relationship between strengths and weaknesses?
- Does it mention the specific strengths and weaknesses you discuss in your middle paragraphs, in the order you discuss them?
- Does it make clear that you are using the logical standard of evaluation?
- Has writing your draft given you new ideas about your argument?

You may have a good thesis statement and yet your argument may have changed during the writing of the draft. You may have come to a different understanding of the relationship between strengths and weaknesses or made changes in the specific strengths and weaknesses you discuss. If so, you will need to revise your thesis statement to reflect these changes.

STEP 2 ### Revising Your Essay Structure: Argument

Problems with the overall argument may lie not in the thesis statement but in the way the argument unfolds. To check essay structure, ask yourself these questions:

- Does the sequence of topics make clear the relationship between strengths and weaknesses set out in the thesis statement?
- Is the topic for each paragraph an item of support indicated in the thesis statement?
- Does the topic sentence of each paragraph make a point about one aspect of the logical standard of evaluation, such as the weaknesses of a deductive argument or the effective use of facts and figures?

If your answer to any of these questions is no, you will need to revise accordingly. You may also discover that writing the draft has revealed flaws in the argument that you planned. If so, you will need to make a revision outline to guide you as you rewrite. For a sample revision outline, see Stage 5, Step 2 in the sample topic assignment in this chapter.

STAGE 6 Revising Individual Paragraphs: *Ethos,* Argument, and Evidence

Just as you review your draft to evaluate the effectiveness of your argument as a whole, so you will need to review each paragraph to see whether you have been fair-minded and argued your points effectively with good evidence to support them.

STEP 1 Revising Your Introduction: *Ethos*

As we will discuss more extensively in Chapter 9, readers are likely to respond more strongly when values are an issue. Therefore, you need to consider your readers carefully when you write any kind of evaluative essay. When you are writing a critique of logic, you want to present yourself as reasonable and fair-minded. This is especially important in the introduction. If the introduction offends their values, readers may proceed no further.

To ensure that readers keep reading, check your introduction for what the ancient rhetorician Aristotle called *ethos*. We discussed *ethos* in Chapter 3, Writing Analysis Essays: Clarifying Essay Topics and Gathering Material. *Ethos* is the notion that the author should have an ethical character, and should put forth an argument that is worthy because it serves the public good or deserves public discussion. If you can answer yes to the following questions, your introduction is likely to seem reasonable and fair-minded.

- Do you begin by providing a clear summary of the context, subject, and thesis of the piece you are evaluating, rather than praise or critical comments?

- Have you chosen language that is as neutral as possible, rather than language that is biased in favour of or against the piece you are evaluating?

- Is the tone of the introduction as a whole that of a fair-minded, reasonable person?

If the answer to any of these questions is no, you will need to revise. The following examples will show you how.

Writing Sample

Draft introduction

Environmentalists are *always complaining* about the technology their very lives depend on. Prominent among these environmentalist *whiners* is David Suzuki, and his essay "It Always Costs" presents the *usual* illogical mixture of *prejudice* and out-of-date science for which he is becoming *notorious*.

Revised introduction

The technology we are surrounded by—from toasters to cruise missiles—has been created both by scientists' expertise and by politicians' choices. Is this technology a boon or a curse? We can perhaps help answer this question by evaluating the work of David Suzuki, a commentator on technology who is both a scientist and an environmental activist. Evaluating the logical credibility of his essay "It Always Costs" provides insights into the environmentalist view of the value of technology. [Add thesis statement.]

STEP 2　Revising Your Middle Paragraphs: Arguments and Evidence

Using the list in Stage 2, Step 2 above as a guide, check each middle paragraph to see

- which type(s) of argument and kind(s) of evidence you have used
- whether you have explained your argument fully enough
- whether you have provided enough evidence
- whether you have avoided common problems and fallacies, as discussed earlier in this chapter

Suppose, for example, you had written the following paragraph in an essay on Suzuki's "It Always Costs":

Draft middle paragraph

The way David Suzuki develops his argument is particularly impressive because he demonstrates that he can change his mind. Changing one's mind really demonstrates mental flexibility because nothing is more difficult than this. Mentioning DDT, thalidomide, and DES piles up the examples of scientific errors in a very compelling way.

This paragraph comments on Suzuki's argument, but what about your own? You may have intended to write a deductively organized paragraph to show how Suzuki develops his argument and to offer examples as evidence that this development is effective. The draft paragraph is flawed by circular reasoning, however. It asserts that Suzuki changes his mind and claims that is a good thing, but it does not explain what the change is or why it is good. The evidence is flawed by irrelevant examples, since examples concerning scientific error demonstrate nothing about change of mind. In revising the paragraph, you would present examples to show that Suzuki's essay is organized around the movement from one set of beliefs about technology to another, different set.

STEP 3   Revising Your Conclusion

In the conclusion, the emphasis shifts from the piece you have evaluated to your summation of strengths and weaknesses. You still need to leave readers with an image of yourself as fair-minded, however. One way you achieve this image is by mentioning both strengths and weaknesses. If the tone of some of your earlier comments has been sharp, now is the time to return to a more neutral, inclusive tone.

Writing Sample

Draft conclusion   If the environmental movement believes that the world is clogged up with paper products due to the pervasiveness of computer technology, perhaps some radically new decisions are called for. Stopping essays like "It Always Costs" from being printed could be the first step in this new direction. [No summary of strengths and weaknesses; biased tone]

Revised conclusion   David Suzuki's choice of obvious targets like DDT for his examples does encourage a stereotyped response, no question about that. However, this evidence is effective even if it is obvious, and the change-of-mind structure of the essay powerfully counteracts the effect of stereotyping, giving the essay finally a great deal of credibility.

Sample Topic: Critiquing the Logic of Scott Russell Sanders's "The Men We Carry in Our Minds"

In this section we will work through the essay writing process of gathering material, drafting, and revising an essay that evaluates the logic of Scott Russell Sanders's "The Men We Carry in Our Minds" (Readings). You will follow the process more easily if you read Sanders's piece first.

STAGE 1   Clarifying Evaluation Topics: Checking for the Logical Standard

Imagine you have been given the following assignment:

> Does Scott Russell Sanders present a credible case that men have not necessarily been more privileged than women? Write a 1000-word essay evaluating his argument.

By using "credible case" and "argument," the assignment indicates that you should use the logical standard of evaluation.

STAGE 2   Gathering Material: Arguments and Evidence

STEP 1   Analyzing the Writer's Argument

Before you can evaluate the essay, you will need to understand its main ideas and strategies of argumentation. To collect material on these, you use the relevant categories for analysis essays (see Chapter 3).

Subject Your reading of the essay confirms the subject suggested by the assignment: Sanders critiques a contemporary feminist movement that assumes men have been more privileged than women.

Main idea/thesis Sanders does not state his thesis explicitly, nor does he state it at the beginning of his essay. Instead, he begins his essay like a story, relating a conversation he had with his friend Anneke on gender equality. He asks himself why he has never felt that women have been disadvantaged in relation to men. He asks this question implicitly near the beginning of the essay ("I discover guilty feelings aplenty—toward the poor, the Vietnamese, Native Americans . . . But toward women I feel something more confused, a snarl of shame, envy, wary tenderness, and amazement" [329]) and explicitly in the last third of the essay ("Women . . . told me that men were guilty of having kept all the joys and privileges of the earth for themselves. I was baffled. What privileges? What joys?" [332]). Sanders answers that question throughout his essay. His thesis, which he arrives at near the end of the essay, but never states outright, is that privilege is dependent not only on gender, but also on class, race, and geographical and historical circumstances.

Types of argument Upon reviewing the strategies of argumentation outlined in Chapter 2, you deduce that the method of development used to organize this essay is narration, or telling a story. Sanders tells a story about the people he has known that differ in race, class, and gender, and how his experiences have shaped his understanding of who is privileged and who is not. It seems that Sanders shares his stories or personal experiences in order to argue that the notion of male privilege is more complex and varied than it might appear from a middle- or upper-class perspective. In addition, because Sanders begins by musing on a question—asking himself why he feels confused toward women's assertions that men are more privileged than women—he creates an inductive argument. You deduce that he provides the details of his story in an attempt to answer his own question. He reaches a conclusion or thesis at the end of his essay.

STEP 2   Evaluating the Writer's Argument

The inductive structure of the argument seems sound. Sanders moves from a specific case gradually to a more general principle about the conditions that surround privilege. He provides many descriptive and narrative details that tie to and directly lead into his conclusion (strength), although it is difficult in the first couple of pages to deduce what he will argue, since he talks about his sense of confusion rather than directly posing the question he will answer (weakness).

STEP 3   Analyzing the Writer's Evidence

Examples   Sanders uses examples to support his point that many individuals, including men, are not privileged in comparison to women. His examples consist of people he has known throughout his life, including the first men he ever saw other than his father, black convicts (330).

Appeals to Emotion   You note that in addition to his examples, Sanders draws upon emotional appeal through descriptions of disadvantaged individuals engaged in hard labour. Sanders seems to use these descriptions to appeal to the readers' emotions, evoking sympathy in the reader toward the labourers and the work they do that leads them, as Sanders notes, to an early death (331).

STEP 4   Evaluating the Writer's Evidence

Now that you have *analyzed* Sanders's evidence, you are ready to *evaluate* his material.

Examples   How relevant are Sanders's examples? Do they support his overall argument that men are not necessarily more privileged than women? You will need to look at the use of Sanders's examples to answer this question.

Upon review, you decide that Sanders's examples are directly related to and support the argument that he articulates by the end of the essay. Examples of men he knew growing up include black convicts, labourers, and soldiers. In a systematic and organized way, Sanders presents each of these examples. Through narration and description, he shows how each group was not privileged but disadvantaged. Therefore, his examples support his conclusion.

Appeals to Emotion Sanders appeals to emotion throughout the essay, through vivid descriptions. These are effective because he does not rely on an appeal to emotion alone. While invoking emotion, Sanders provides concrete evidence through examples that demonstrate his point.

While Sanders's examples and appeals to emotion work well illustrating his overall argument, you notice that Sanders does not include any other kinds of evidence. This, you decide, is the weakness in his essay. If he were to provide facts and figures or references to authorities, in addition to his examples and appeals to emotion, he might have a stronger essay. Overall, you decide that the evidence the author presents is appropriate for a literary essay such as this one.

STEP 5   Categorizing and Charting Strengths and Weaknesses in the Writer's Argument and Evidence

As an aid to seeing how strengths and weaknesses compare, you set them out briefly in an *evaluation chart*.

EVALUATION CHART

ASPECTS	STRENGTHS	WEAKNESSES
Argument	Inductive argument Method of development, narration, or telling a story	Relies on a single method of development, storytelling. Could incorporate other methods such as cause and effect to strengthen argument.
Examples	Examples provided (from narration, stories) support the argument.	Further examples, other than those related to storytelling, are not provided.
Appeals to Emotion	The appeals to emotion are combined with examples to support the logical standard.	None evident

STAGE 3   Formulating an Evaluative Thesis Statement

Looking at this chart, you decide that the strengths of the essay "The Men We Carry in Our Minds" are its inductive structure and the organized way in which it presents examples that directly support the overall argument.

Its weakness is that its use of evidence is limited to examples and appeals to emotion. In light of the fact that this is a literary essay written by a fiction writer, you decide that the evidence presented, while limited, is still quite appropriate to the subgenre—the literary essay. In addition, the examples presented and the descriptions inherent within are relevant and convincing. Therefore, in your opinion, the strengths of the essay outweigh the weaknesses. To express this relationship between the strengths and weaknesses and to express the categories that support this opinion, you come up with the following thesis statement:

Tentative thesis statement | While in "The Men We Carry in Our Minds" Scott Russell Sanders uses only examples and appeals to emotion as evidence to support his overall argument, his examples are many and varied, and they directly support his claim, while his appeals to emotion are powerful and convincing.

STAGE 4   Drafting: Sequencing Strengths and Weaknesses

Because you will argue that Sanders's essay has fewer weaknesses than strengths, you will start with weaknesses and move to strengths. Your thesis seems to suggest a workable series of paragraph topics, so you make a draft outline as a guide to writing.

DRAFT OUTLINE

PARAGRAPH TOPIC	POINT
Weakness: limited kinds of evidence presented	Sanders could use other kinds of evidence (such as facts and figures or appeals to authority) to strengthen his argument. Such evidence is missing.
Weakness: only one kind of method of development	Does not employ causal analysis or other types of methods of development in addition to storytelling
Strength: examples	Examples from Sanders's experience are strong and convincing.
Strength: appeals to emotion	Such appeals are combined with examples to adhere to the logical standard.
Strength: inductive argument	He builds his argument from varied examples.
Strength: storytelling or narration method of development	Both inductive argument and storytelling method are strong and convincing.

You then draft your essay, sketching an introduction and conclusion, and developing each of these points in a middle paragraph.

STAGE 5   Revising the Thesis Statement and Essay Structure: Reasoning

STEP 1   Revising Your Thesis Statement: Checking for an Evaluative Point

At this point, you take a critical look at your tentative thesis statement.

Relationship between Strengths and Weaknesses Writing your draft did not change your mind about the overall relationship between strengths and weaknesses, but you don't state that you believe that Sanders's essay is, overall, a strong and persuasive one. You decide to insert a sentence to make this clear. In your draft thesis statement, you don't relate anything about the content of Sanders's essay. You decide to revise to state Sanders's main argument.

Support You realize that you haven't mentioned that Sanders uses a narrative or storytelling method of development. Since this is important both to Sanders's essay and your discussion of it, you decide to state it in your thesis statement.

Indication of standard While you don't say explicitly that you are appealing to a logical standard, you feel that it is clear that you are appealing to logic. In terms of the indication of standard, no revision is necessary.

The thesis statement that results from these changes appears below.

Writing Sample

Revised thesis statement

While "The Men We Carry in Our Minds" uses only examples and appeals to emotion as evidence to support the overall argument, the examples are many and varied, and they directly support the claim, while the appeals to emotion are powerful and convincing. Sanders's essay, which he develops through storytelling and references to his own life, is an entertaining and logical piece that conveys an important argument about the complexity of gender. Power and privilege, Sanders argues, depend not only on relations of gender but also on relations of race and class.

STEP 2   ## Revising Your Essay Structure: Argument

In reviewing your draft, you note that your paragraphs move from weaknesses to strengths but that the paragraphs do not follow an order of ascending interest. The essay also seems to need a more deliberate transition from weaknesses to strengths.

Since the weaknesses of the essay are absences in the text (a lack of varied kinds of evidence, for example), your paragraphs on these topics are skimpy. You decide to discuss all the weaknesses in one paragraph, and then to order the paragraphs on the strengths in ascending order of interest. These changes will mean adjusting the order of support in your thesis statement. You make the following revision outline for the middle paragraphs (MPs):

REVISION OUTLINE

PARAGRAPH TOPIC	POINT
MP 1 Weaknesses	Lack of variety of evidence and method of development
MP 2 Strength: examples	Examples are varied and support argument point.
MP 3 Strength: appeal to emotion and inductive argument	Combined with examples, emotional appeals and inductive argument work well with storytelling method of development.

STAGE 6   ## Revising Individual Paragraphs: *Ethos,* Argument, and Evidence

STEP 1   ## Revising Your Introduction: *Ethos*

In writing your draft, you wrote the following sentence to lead up to your thesis statement:

Draft introduction   Scott Russell Sanders's "The Men We Carry in Our Minds" is a good essay about power and the relationships between men and women.

Considered logically, this sentence creates a general context for your thesis statement. It provides the name of the author and the title of the piece you'll evaluate in your essay, and it suggests Sanders's subject. The main weakness is in *ethos.* It's important to convey not only that you are fair-minded in addressing this subject, but also that there is a purpose to your essay, and, since you are arguing that Sanders's essay is convincing, to his. You decide to rewrite this sentence so that it conveys the ethical importance of Sanders's essay and your own evaluation of it.

Writing Sample

Scott Russell Sanders's essay "The Men We Carry in Our Minds" addresses a common misperception: that men have historically been more privileged than women. Sanders suggests that this assumption, held by some white middle-class feminists, needs to be questioned and critiqued. For Sanders, this misguided notion has personal and emotional impact.

Now you've implicitly stated the ethical importance of Sanders's piece by pointing out that he wants to correct the incorrect belief that men are and have been better off than women. Beliefs such as this one can have real impact in terms of society, politics, and individuals' actions.

STEP 2   ## Revising Your Middle Paragraphs: Arguments and Evidence

In checking individual paragraphs for effective argument and evidence, you find that your paragraph on Sanders's weakness in using only one kind of evidence and one kind of method of development is difficult to prove.

Draft middle paragraph

Sanders draws upon no evidence to support his point that men are not more privileged than women, other than examples. He could use facts and figures, such as statistics, to show that men are not more privileged than women. Due to the fact that many statistics show that men are more privileged than women, such as in the case of salaries, he does not draw upon such evidence. He could use analogies to show that not all men are privileged, but he does not. His argument is limited because he only uses examples from one individual's life, his own.

Upon reading and thinking about this draft middle paragraph, you decide that it is weak. It is vague and general, and doesn't discuss Sanders's essay or argument with precision or specifics. In short, you lack evidence to support your evaluation. Even though discussing gaps in an argument is somewhat difficult, you decide that you can revise to be more specific and refer more closely to the text you are evaluating.

Writing Sample

Revised
middle
paragraph

At first it might seem as though Sanders's argument is weak, since he draws only upon narrative examples for evidence and since he draws heavily on personal experience. Sanders begins his essay, for instance, with a conversation he had with his friend Anneke about the history of gender and power relations, and, after this conversation, he says that he does not feel guilt regarding a sense of so-called privilege he has supposedly had in relation to women. Rather, toward women he feels "something more confused, a snarl of shame, envy, wary tenderness, and amazement" (375). Not only does Sanders fail to express his argument here, but he also draws only upon his own feelings—"confusion, shame, and envy"— to suggest a disagreement with Anneke's point of view. Other than examples of men he has known, Sanders draws upon no evidence in his essay to support his point that men are not always in power positions in relation to women. Further kinds of evidence, such as statistics regarding the privileges some women have had in relation to men, could strengthen his argument. Sanders relies on narration, or storytelling, as a method to develop his argument. In order to strengthen his essay, Sanders might draw upon cause and effect, analyzing the causes of and effects of the history of male privilege. Or he might engage in an analysis of the system of patriarchy in American history. But he does not. Sanders's argument, one might argue, is weak because he limits his evidence to examples and relies solely on a story telling method of development.

In this revised version, you engage more closely with the text by analyzing it as you evaluate it. You refer to a specific instance in the text, Sanders's conversation with Anneke, and you quote the text. You also use the language in Sanders's essay, referring to words that express his feelings, to prove your point. Your paragraph is much more specific and therefore stronger than the draft.

STEP 3   Revising Your Conclusion

For a draft conclusion, you wrote a one-sentence summary:

Draft
conclusion

Scott Russell Sanders's "The Men We Carry in Our Minds" is a strong essay that shows how some middle-class feminist women assume that men have always held more powerful positions than women.

This concluding sentence summarizes what you've argued in your essay, but it doesn't reflect the structure of your essay, and it doesn't discuss the importance of Sanders's work or what you've said about it. It is also too short. You decide to include your discussion of Sanders's structure, inductive rather than deductive reasoning, in your conclusion, rather than in your final body paragraph. You revise both your final body paragraph and your conclusion to reflect these changes and to strengthen your essay.

Writing Sample

Clearly, "The Men We Carry in Our Minds" is a convincing essay in which the author encourages his readers to think about—and reassess—a common misperception, that men have historically been more privileged than women. While readers might deduce that the essay is weak, since it relies almost solely on a storytelling method, and since Sanders does not state his thesis explicitly at the beginning of the essay, the essay is strong: it systematically provides varied examples that support the overall argument; and, through description, it couples these examples with appeals to emotion. Sanders never explicitly states his thesis. However, his thesis—that power and privilege depend on class, race, and socio-historical conditions, as much as they do on gender—is evident and clear by the end of the essay. Therefore, Sanders strategically writes an inductively structured essay. What is more, Sanders supports his thesis with concrete, descriptive details and personal anecdotes about the men and women he has known. Overall, then, Sanders's essay is one worth reading, one in which readers find themselves rethinking long-held assumptions about the dynamics of power and privilege in our historical and contemporary world.

To read the finished version of this essay, see D. Jones, "The Complexity of Power and Gender Relations: An Evaluation of Scott Russell Sanders's 'The Men We Carry in Our Minds,'" in Part 2, Readings: Sample Essays.

Working on Your Own Assignment

Your main goal in a logical evaluation or critique essay is to assess another writer's handling of logic in writing that is itself logical and balanced.

- Check significant terms to make sure that your assignment requires the logical standard of evaluation.
- Analyze the piece of writing for subject, main idea, argument, and evidence.
- Evaluate the strengths and weaknesses of the argument and evidence.
- Formulate a thesis statement that states an opinion about the relationship between logical strengths and weaknesses in the writing, provides support for that opinion, and indicates, indirectly or directly, that you are using the logical standard of evaluation.

- Write a draft, sequencing the topics to reflect the relationship between strengths and weaknesses indicated in the thesis statement. Use a draft outline if possible.
- With the help of your draft outline or a revision outline, revise the thesis statement and overall essay structure to ensure that your argument is logical and effective.
- Check that you begin your introduction by providing a context for the writing you will discuss rather than by immediately evaluating it, so that you convey the image of yourself as fair-minded.
- Check that your middle paragraphs make strong arguments and give effective evidence.
- Check that your conclusion presents both the strengths and weaknesses of the writing you have discussed and reflects, if possible, a development of the thesis statement.
- For an example of a logical critique essay, see D. Jones, "The Complexity of Power and Gender Relations: An Evaluative Essay of Scott Russell Sanders's 'The Men We Carry in Our Minds,'" in Part 2, Readings: Sample Essays.

Exercises

A.   Write a sentence evaluating the following as thesis statements for logical critique essays.

1. In *The Hazards of Being Male*, Herb Goldberg argues that pressures to conform to a stereotyped image of masculinity force many men to live like emotional zombies. Goldberg's thesis may be correct, but there is a problem with the arguments he uses and with his narrow range of examples.

2. Charles Taylor's *The Malaise of Modernity* is one of the most rational books I have ever come across. If you want a well-reasoned book on what's wrong with the modern world, look no further.

B.   Read Naomi Klein's "Science Says: Revolt!" (Readings). Then evaluate the use of argument and evidence in the following paragraph. First, state the main idea of the paragraph. Next, identify any common fallacies. Then revise the paragraph so that it uses argument and evidence effectively:

> Naomi Klein's essay, "Science Says: Revolt!" is a good essay that has some valid points, namely that the earth is facing impending environmental disaster. The author is a well-known Canadian activist that knows a lot about this subject, and that shows in the essay. Klein makes a link between possible environmental disaster and the global system of capitalism, and she says that we cannot save the environment without changing this system. She uses some interesting evidence to support her point, although not all of her evidence is convincing. She uses good quotes from academics who know about the subject.

Writing Persuasive Essays

Sample Topic: Canadian National Identity

Stage 1   **Clarifying Evaluation Topics**
>   **Step 1**   Defining Key Terms
>   **Step 2**   Finding a Standard of Evaluation

Stage 2   **Gathering Material**
>   **Step 1**   Analyzing
>   **Step 2**   Categorizing Strengths and Weaknesses

Stage 3   **Formulating an Evaluative Thesis Statement**

Stage 4   **Drafting: Working Out a Pro–Con Outline**

Stage 5   **Revising Thesis Statement and Essay Structure**
>   **Step 1**   Revising Your Thesis Statement: Checking for an Evaluative Point
>   **Step 2**   Revising Essay Structure: Checking Sequence and Pro–Con Transitions

Stage 6   **Revising Individual Paragraphs**
>   **Step 1**   Revising Your Introduction: *Ethos*
>   **Step 2**   Revising Middle Paragraphs: Logic and Transitions
>   **Step 3**   Revising Your Conclusion: Achieving Balance

In Chapter 8, you learned how to assess the strengths and weaknesses in someone else's argument in order to write a critique essay. In this chapter, you will learn how to discover and argue your own position on a subject. Essays of this type are called *persuasive* essays because their purpose is to persuade readers to agree with your position. The following are typical assignments for persuasive essays:

1. Do Canadian citizens need a Canadian national identity?
2. Should marijuana be legalized?
3. How should institutions respond to same-sex marriage?
4. Should the summer holidays for schoolchildren be reduced to one month?

As you can see from these topics, persuasive essays generally answer a yes or no question, an argument for or against a position on a subject, but a simple "yes" or "no" answer is usually not a sufficient answer in a persuasive essay. This chapter will take you through all the steps of planning, writing, and revising a persuasive essay, using the first assignment above as the sample topic, but drawing examples from the second and third topics as well.

In the planning stages, you focus on analysis and evaluation. First you analyze your subject and your possible position on the subject—generally for or against—to determine the good and bad points, the advantages and disadvantages, the strengths and weaknesses. This analysis gives you the material you need to arrive at a considered judgment: your evaluation of overall strengths and weaknesses.

In drafting and revising, you focus on persuasion: how to present your position so that your readers are most likely to take your arguments seriously. The strategies you use depend to some extent on your audience. You may be writing for readers who are *hostile* (unlikely to agree with your position), *neutral* (likely to have an open mind), or *friendly* (likely to agree with your position). Academic writing generally assumes a neutral reader, but we will comment briefly on techniques of persuasion for hostile and friendly readers.

STAGE 1   Clarifying Evaluation Topics

STEP 1   Defining Key Terms

Understanding the key terms of the assignment and the subject is particularly important in writing persuasive essays. You will often need to define terms in your essay. Otherwise your readers may misunderstand your argument or disagree with it because they do not understand the terms in the same way.

- For an essay on legalizing marijuana, for example, you would need to be sure your readers understood the difference between legalizing the use of marijuana (making it available for sale under controlled circumstances, like liquor) and decriminalizing it (not prosecuting people who use it).

- For an essay on same-sex marriage, it would be essential for you and your readers to understand the difference between marriage as a social or religious commitment and marriage as a legal contract. You would need to define these terms for your readers.

- For the sample topic on Canadian national identity that we are focusing on in this chapter, it would be important for you to understand how national identity has been understood in the past and in the present, and also how the phrase "national identity" is similar to or differs from the phrase "national imaginary."

In many cases, one or more key terms may depend on the context of the subject you are writing about, and you will need to define that context in your essay.

- A key term in the topic on Canadian national identity is "identity." There are many ways to interpret and understand this term. For example, there are personal or individual identities, gendered identities, geographic identities, and national identities, to name just a few. In your essay, you will need to explain how national identity is different from and yet related to other kinds of identity. It will also be important for you to know that the notion of Canadian identity is not static but dynamic: it continually changes and it has held different meanings in different periods in Canadian history. You will need to acknowledge this fact as you explain and evaluate the importance of Canadian identity.

You may also need to clarify key terms, at least for yourself, by determining exactly what you are being asked to evaluate.

- For example, in the sample topic, you are being asked if Canadians need a national identity. You will therefore need to begin by establishing a working definition of Canadian national identity (a highly debatable and contested subject), and then evaluate whether or not such an identity is necessary and important for Canadian citizens. You will most definitely need to explain why you take the position you do: either why you believe that Canadians need a national identity, or why you believe that it is not important for Canadians to have a national identity. The most interesting answers to persuasive essay questions are those in which you pay heed to the complexities and nuances within the topic and the question itself.

On what basis will you make this evaluation? The answer: by finding one or more standards of evaluation, either ones indicated by the assignment or ones of your own choosing.

STEP 2 Finding a Standard of Evaluation

When you evaluate, as we pointed out in Chapter 8, you use one or more standards of evaluation as a basis for judging things. Your essay topic might explicitly ask you to consider the practical advantages and disadvantages of reducing summer holidays, the artistic merits of films, or the economic benefits of legalizing marijuana. More often, your essay topic will imply the standard(s) or expect you to figure out which ones to use. For example, if you choose to write on the artistic merits of films, you would employ an aesthetic standard of evaluation; by contrast, if you choose to write on the economic benefits of legalizing marijuana, you would need to employ a practical standard with examples and facts and figures to support your argument.

Whether you are given the standards of evaluation or have to figure them out, you will need to know how to use them. We discussed the logical standard in Chapter 8. Here is a brief discussion of the three other most useful standards of evaluation: the *aesthetic*, the *practical*, and the *ethical*.

Aesthetic standard Aesthetics is literally the study of beauty. The aesthetic standard is commonly used to judge works of art or the performance aspect of any activity, such as a political candidate's speaking skills or a figure skater's technique. When you use an aesthetic standard, you ask one or more of these questions:

- Is it well constructed, beautiful, pleasing to the senses?
- Is it well performed?
- Is it a good example of its kind?

Behind these questions are assumptions based on two key criteria for aesthetic judgments: *coherence* and *comparison*.

If something is coherent, then the parts work together to create a satisfying whole. For example, you might decide that the original *Star Wars* trilogy is good filmmaking because it has interesting characters, a suspenseful plot, and a compelling, original musical score that all combine to make definitive science fiction movies.

The judgment that something is a good example of its kind or is better than another of its kind obviously depends on comparison with typical features of the genre or kind. If you think that the original trilogy is a better, more challenging set of movies about "a galaxy far, far away" than the later trilogy, for example, you are comparing these films not just to each other but also to an ideal model of the good science fiction films as allegories of humanity, a model that values complexity over, say, entertainment and special effects.

Your evaluation of aesthetic strengths and weaknesses will be most effective when you use both comparison and coherence as your criteria.

Practical standard When you use the practical standard of evaluation, your main criteria are feasibility and usefulness. These are the key questions:

- Will this work?
- Will it be useful?
- Does it have a relevant application?

Practical judgments connect the thing being evaluated (such as a school board, a law, a product, or a proposed action) with the social situation or context in which it will be applied or the purpose it will serve. You will produce the most effective practical evaluations by considering as many aspects of the context as possible. Ask yourself questions like these: Who benefits? In what ways? What will this help us do? How much will it cost? How long will it take? What are the long-term and short-term effects?

- For example, if you were evaluating a plan to reduce summer holidays for schoolchildren to one month, you might note that the shortened vacation period could make it difficult for working parents to take holidays at the same time. On the other hand, the shorter holiday would decrease the amount of time teachers need to spend reviewing what students have forgotten and would use schools' physical plants more efficiently. Weighing these practical advantages and disadvantages against each other could lead you to a very effective judgment.

Ethical standard When you use the ethical standard, you judge an object's worth according to *moral*, *ideological*, or *religious* values. Ask questions like these:

- Is this right or wrong?
- Is this a position worth believing in?
- Is this a course of action worth following?

When you evaluate from an ethical perspective, you judge whether something is right or wrong according to a set of principles about the values that should govern behaviour. Sometimes ethical principles conflict. For one person, telling a lie may be good if the lie benefits more people than it hurts; for another, telling a lie is always bad because lying damages a person's integrity.

When you evaluate from an ideological perspective, you judge by a set of social principles. Social principles, like ethical principles, can conflict. For example, an environmentally conscious person might argue that shopping at big-box stores is socially destructive. From a practical point of view, shopping at such stores might be convenient, but her argument is based on the ideological conviction that healthy societies are based on local production and distribution.

When you evaluate from a religious perspective, you base your judgments on the doctrines of a particular religious group. Many Roman Catholics, for example, would argue against abortion on religious grounds, just as many Jehovah's Witnesses would object to blood transfusions for religious reasons. Religious principles, like ethical and social principles, may conflict over particular issues.

Values may conflict not only within each of these perspectives, but also between perspectives. For example, a person may download music from the internet, knowing that it is morally wrong to acquire copyrighted material in a way that does not benefit the artists who produced the music. The person may justify or rationalize this act by arguing that the internet represents a new kind of information sharing where copyright is less important than exposure. Therefore, the person privileges an ideological perspective (the internet benefits artists through exposure) over a moral viewpoint (it is wrong to download copyrighted materials).

Because of the wide range of values people hold, you need to take special care when you evaluate issues from an ethical perspective. Few readers are likely to accept your judgment of strengths and weaknesses simply because your system of values supports it ("Big-box stores are wrong because environmentalists say so"). Try to be aware of your own system of values and make sure those values are appropriate to your subject. Your argument will be stronger if you acknowledge ethical positions that differ from your own.

Using more than one standard of evaluation Many issues invite evaluation from more than one standard of evaluation. Some could be evaluated from all four standards that we have discussed—logical, aesthetic, practical, and ethical. You will be able to give a more balanced assessment if you gather material using all relevant standards. Your decision about which of these to include in your final essay will depend on the assignment, the subject, your own position, and the audience. It may also depend on how confident you are about handling several standards.

- If you were evaluating a film script for possible production, you might begin with its artistic merits (aesthetic standard), but you would also need to consider its audience appeal and the production costs (practical standard). If the content was potentially objectionable or offensive, you might also assess its moral strengths and weaknesses (ethical standard).

- The sample topic on Canadian national identity does not indicate a standard of evaluation. You decide to try aesthetic, ethical, logical, and practical standards. Aesthetic standards are relevant because Canada has a history of investing in culture and the arts in order to articulate a national identity, and in order to distinguish Canada from the United States. Identity, which pertains to the well-being of the individual and the country, is ethical and, more specifically, ideological. The connection between individual identity and national identity is logical, and it can be argued by inductive or deductive methods. Practical standards may be relevant if a shared national identity results in action—taking action to claim the "North" because it is part of Canadians' identity, for example.

STAGE 2   Gathering Material

STEP 1   Analyzing

If you are clear on your standard of evaluation and think you know your position on an issue, you may be tempted to skip analysis and plunge straight into evaluation. We advise you not to skip the earlier step. The process of analysis will lead you to examine more aspects of your subject, which will give you stronger arguments for your position and a greater awareness of the counter-arguments. It will also provide you with the details to make your arguments convincing.

To analyze, you need to find appropriate categories for dividing your subject into parts. The methods of analysis described in Chapter 3 (cause/effect, process, and systems analysis) will provide appropriate categories for analyzing a broad range of issues. The disciplinary categories of analysis for English described in Chapter 6, Writing Essays on Literature, will help you analyze subjects that you will evaluate by the aesthetic standard.

You can also use the standards of evaluation themselves to gather material by asking questions such as these:

- What ethical issues does this subject raise? For whom?
- What practical issues does this subject raise? For whom?

- What aesthetic issues does this subject raise? For whom?
- How valid are the arguments given about this issue? (See Chapter 8 for detailed guidelines on evaluating arguments and evidence.)

To see how you would choose categories of analysis and put them to use, let's consider the sample topic on Canadian national identity.

- The sample topic asks, "Do Canadian citizens need a Canadian national identity?" There are three possible answers: yes, no, or either yes or no, with some qualifications. In the third case, for example, you might say "yes," but qualify that answer by indicating that such an identity will also be related to and interact with a local or regional identity. As a result of defining the key terms, especially the phrase "national identity," you will be aware that the term is a debated and contentious one, and that the phrase "national imaginary" is often used instead of "national identity" to acknowledge the notion that any identity that is forged across such a vast landscape with such diverse peoples is necessarily constructed and imagined. As mentioned earlier, aesthetic questions are relevant to this topic. You decide to focus, for now, on the ethical and practical considerations. If you were to brainstorm about such considerations raised by this question, you might come up with the following list:

Ethical and Practical Issues of the Question of Whether Citizens Need a Canadian National Identity

- A Canadian identity may not speak to recent immigrants or those who practise cultural traditions different from the ones of most Canadians. Therefore, such an identity, if imposed by others, such as the government, might exclude such Canadians. [Argument: against]
- A Canadian identity might supersede or debunk local or regional identities that are stronger than national ones, thereby harming rather than enhancing Canadians' identities. [Argument: against]
- A Canadian identity might not be how individuals want to identify themselves; they might prefer choosing their identity in terms of gender, for example, rather than nation. [Argument: against]
- A national identity, set forth by the government and supported by citizens (or vice versa), might enable Canada to be stronger and to act more efficiently in international affairs. [Argument: for]
- A national identity might enable those from diverse cultural and ethnic backgrounds to come together, enhancing cross-cultural understanding within a national framework. [Argument: for]
- A sense of a Canadian citizen's national identity might enhance and build credence to one's regional or gendered identity, the various identities working together. [Argument: for)]

At this stage, it is also important to gather material from other sources, so that you can approach the topic and the question from an informed perspective. What writers and critics have discussed Canadian national identity? What are such writers' and critics' opinions on Canadian national identity, and what evidence have they provided to support their claims? Answer these questions in order to create a persuasive argument in your essay. While research can be a valuable tool in a persuasive essay, it is also important to realize that it is not absolutely necessary, as the principles of aesthetic, logical, ethical, and practical judgments have their own internal logics that can be defined and explained.

Keep in mind that by gathering material from sources, you are writing a research essay as well as a persuasive one. Determine whether you need to consult outside sources for your persuasive essay. Assessing your topic and speaking to your instructor will help you decide if and how you should do research for your persuasive essay. You may also wish to consult Chapters 10, 11, and 12 for more information and instruction on how to write research essays.

In order to make your persuasive essay current, you consult recent newspaper articles on the topic of Canadian national identity. In an article in *The Globe and Mail* on January 18, 2014, about Prime Minister Stephen Harper's belief that Canada should claim the North Pole as part of Canada, Harper states that national identity is important to him and that he is trying to foster and encourage a sense of national identity in Canadian citizens. Harper's invocation of Canadian national identity is rooted in a practical standard of evaluation, since Canada's claim on the North would also be a claim on resources, such as oil, in the Arctic.

STEP 2   Categorizing Strengths and Weaknesses

You have gathered material through analytic categories by considering arguments for and against the persuasive essay topic: Do Canadian citizens need a Canadian national identity? You have also considered what others have said about the topic, effectively gathering material on the subject through research. You are ready to begin to evaluate the material you have gathered using the appropriate standard(s) of evaluation. You first organize the material you have gathered into appropriate evaluative categories (such as strengths and weaknesses, advantages and disadvantages, arguments for and against) and then group entries within each category according to the standard of evaluation they represent.

- For the sample topic, you could categorize the points that indicate support for the importance of a Canadian national identity as *arguments for* and points that indicate opposition to the notion of a Canadian national identity as *arguments against*. You would group points within each category according to the ethical and practical standards you used in brainstorming. You would come up with the following table:

CATEGORIZING ARGUMENTS	ARGUMENTS FOR	ARGUMENTS AGAINST
NATIONAL IDENTITY FOR THE CITIZEN	Ethical: recognizes and acknowledges changing individual and collective values	Ethical: might exclude immigrant values
	Ethical: might result in peoples of different cultures and backgrounds coming together in cross-cultural understanding	Ethical: may supersede or exclude regional values
	Ethical: national identity could build credence to gender and personal identity, all working together	Ethical: gender or personal identity may be more important to many people than national identity
NATIONAL IDENTITY FOR THE STATE (FEDERAL GOVERNMENT)	Ethical: value of pluralism Practical: Canada stronger in international affairs or benefit economically (e.g., Harper invoking national identity to legitimize a claim on Northern resources)	Practical: expense of creating and promoting a national identity Practical: Such economic benefits could have a negative impact on the environment and on Inuit peoples.

STAGE 3 Formulating an Evaluative Thesis Statement

The general procedure in formulating a thesis is to identify the pattern created by the material in your categories, considered as a response to a specific essay assignment. As we pointed out in Chapter 8, the distinctive components of an evaluation thesis are an opinion about the relationship between strengths and weaknesses, an outlining of the support for this opinion, and an indication of the standard(s) of evaluation you have used.

If you are evaluating a subject about which you have an open mind, you may arrive at your opinion about the relationship between strengths and weaknesses by simply noting which category contains more points.

- Looking at the pattern of arguments for the sample topic on Canadian national identity, for instance, you might conclude that the arguments for and against a national identity are relatively balanced, but that the ethical issues outweigh the practical arguments on this topic. You would write a tentative thesis statement that reflects your own position for or against the creation and promulgation of a Canadian national identity, and you would emphasize the ethical standard of evaluation.

Tentative thesis statement (sample topic)	Though some might argue that Canadian citizens and the Canadian government need not be interested in creating, promoting, and adopting a Canadian national identity, there are many ethical and some practical reasons to suggest that a Canadian national identity is important—both for individual citizens and for the state.

As we mentioned earlier, our thinking about evaluative questions is shaped by our own values. Underlying this seemingly disinterested weighing of arguments, as you will see by reading the relevant persuasive sample essay, E. Jones, "Canadian National Identity" (Readings: Sample Essays), is an ideological belief in the value of unity and pluralism. Nevertheless, this thesis statement lays the foundation for an effective persuasive essay because it takes opposing points of view into account. This is a key consideration when you are writing for a hostile audience or, as in most academic situations, a neutral audience. These readers will be more likely to consider your position if you are fair-minded in your presentation.

On the one hand, the process of analysis may lead you to change your ideas about an issue by forcing you to consider positions different from your own. On the other hand, what happens if the opposing arguments seem stronger or more numerous than your deeply held beliefs about an issue? What do you do then? If you were writing for a friendly audience, one that shared your views, you might downplay or ignore other points of view. This tactic is not an option when you write in an academic situation, where the burden of proof is on you. You must take other positions into account while putting forward the strongest possible case for your own.

- Let's consider how you might formulate an evaluative thesis statement for the sample topic if you were opposed to the notion of a Canadian national identity on the grounds that you value individual identities over collective ones. You might, for example, concede that there are strong ethical arguments for creating and promoting a Canadian national identity, even as you argue that practical reasons, such the cost of the promotion of such an identity, suggest that Canada should not create or promote a Canadian national identity. You might also add that the promotion of a national identity could contradict or otherwise diminish individual identities. In trying to balance the opposing views, you might formulate a tentative thesis statement like this:

Tentative thesis statement (countering strong opposing arguments)	While there are ethical reasons to promote a Canadian national identity, such as the bringing together of different cultures and backgrounds in cross-cultural understanding, there are practical reasons not to promote such an identity, such as the expense that it would cost the federal government to create and promote such an identity.

STAGE 4 Drafting: Working Out a Pro–Con Outline

Formulating a thesis statement completes the work of clarifying your own position on the subject you are examining. In writing your draft you shift your focus more fully to persuasion, finding strategies that will help convince your readers to agree with your position. The most powerful tool for achieving this goal is known as *pro–con structure.*

Pro and *con* are the Latin words for *for* and *against.* The side you have decided is stronger (whether strengths or weaknesses, arguments for or arguments against) becomes the pro argument; the weaker side becomes the con argument.

- For example, if you had formulated a thesis statement asserting that the film you were reviewing had more weaknesses than strengths, your pro argument would be something like "This is a poorly written film," and your list of weaknesses would support this position. The con argument would be "This film has some strengths," an opinion supported by your list of strengths.

The principle of pro–con structure is that you systematically present the arguments against your case, conceding (admitting) their validity or refuting (arguing against) them, and then present the arguments for your case. The idea is that readers hostile to your case, or predisposed against any particular argument (likely even for neutral readers), will be more persuaded by seeing their views taken seriously before you develop your own position.

Pro–con structure may be unnecessary or inadvisable when your purpose is to reinforce the values of a friendly audience rather than to discuss them, such as when you are writing articles for your own political party. Academic writing, as we said earlier, always assumes readers need to be convinced.

There are two main ways to organize a pro–con essay:

1. State all the con arguments in a paragraph or two at the beginning of your essay, deal with these arguments, and then devote the rest of the essay to the pro arguments. This method works best for neutral (academic) readers or when strengths outweigh weaknesses, or vice versa.

   - If you were reviewing the original *Star Wars* trilogy, for example, you might concede that the special effects are not as compelling as those of the contemporary films and then go on to discuss the many strengths of the films.

2. Answer the arguments against your position point by point throughout your essay. This method is a better choice when your readers may be hostile or when there are strong arguments on both sides.

Taking con arguments into account does not mean you have to refute them all. If you concede the validity of some of the points—admit they are right or reasonable—you show more maturity and are therefore likely to be more persuasive.

You will find a draft outline invaluable for working out pro–con structure. Follow the sequence of topics and points indicated in your thesis statement. To help you keep track of your overall argument, note whether points are pro or con and what standard of evaluation they are based on. Leave spaces to record any changes you decide to make when you revise.

   - The draft outline for the sample topic would look something like this (MP stands for middle paragraph; ETH, LOG, and PRAC stand for ethical, logical, and practical, respectively):

DRAFT OUTLINE

TOPIC	POINT	REVISION NOTES
INTRODUCTION		
MP1 NATIONAL IDENTITY AND IMMIGRANTS	**Con** (ETH): a national identity might exclude immigrant values; immigrants may not feel included in national identity.	
	Pro (ETH): value of pluralism, a shared national identity might enable cross-cultural understanding.	
MP2 NATIONAL IDENTITY AND REGION	**Con** (LOG): national identity might be difficult or impossible in a vast landscape and geography, and with peoples of so many different backgrounds.	
	Pro (LOG): geographical or regional identities work alongside with and are not separate from national identity.	
MP3 NATIONAL IDENTITY AND MULTICULTURALISM	**Pro** (PRAC): national identity grounded in multiculturalism could affect immigration policies, which could enable immigrants to come to Canada and work as labourers or experts. This immigration would aid Canada economically.	
MP4 NATIONAL IDENTITY AND THE NORTH	**Con** (PRAC): following through on claims to natural resources could have negative effects on Inuit peoples and the environment.	
	Pro (PRAC): fostering a national identity rooted in the history of Anglo-explorers and settlers in the North could serve as reason to claim the North and attain natural resources for Canada—aiding Canada economically.	
CONCLUSION		

Note that the draft outline is structured in terms of a point-by-point method (presenting the con of each point, followed by the pro of each point), rather than in terms of a block method (presenting all of the cons in the first few paragraphs of your essay, and then presenting the pros for the rest of your essay).

STAGE 5   Revising Thesis Statement and Essay Structure

STEP 1   Revising Your Thesis Statement: Checking for an Evaluative Point

If you have followed all the steps in gathering material and formulating a thesis, your thesis statement should present, in a reasonable and fair-minded way,

- your opinion about the relationship between strengths and weaknesses
- your support for this opinion
- an indication of the standards of evaluation you have used

If your thesis statement is weak, you may have allowed strong opinions to carry you away, as in the first example below, or you may have ignored evidence contrary to your position, as in the second example.

Weak thesis statements
- The reasons people give for having a Canadian national identity are nonsense; if they had any sense, they should not care about a national identity and would concern themselves with more important things, such as international business. [No relationship between strengths and weaknesses, no support, no standard of evaluation]
- Though there are just as many practical reasons to support the notion of a Canadian national identity as there are to resist it, the idea of spending taxpayers' money on promoting a national identity is ridiculous. [Support contradicts opinion.]

The tentative thesis statement for the sample topic that you formulated earlier, however, meets all the requirements for an effective evaluative thesis. But when you check your indication of standards of evaluation, you notice that in your last outline you have come up with a logical reason to support a Canadian national identity—that geographical or regional identities are related to national ones. You rewrite the thesis as follows:

Writing Sample

Effective thesis
statement
(sample topic)

Though some might argue that Canadian citizens and the Canadian government need not be interested in creating and promoting a Canadian national identity, there are ethical, logical, and practical reasons to suggest that Canadian national identity is important—both for individual citizens and for the nation-state.

STEP 2 ## Revising Essay Structure: Checking Sequence and Pro–Con Transitions

You will find it useful in revising essay structure to turn your draft outline into a revision outline by identifying the points you made, as opposed to those you intended to make, and then checking for these key elements of persuasive structure:

- Have you presented your arguments in an *order of ascending interest*, ending with the most important?

- If you have used a *pro–con structure*, have you dealt with con points first and then presented the pro points, either in the essay as a whole or paragraph by paragraph?

- Do you need to *add paragraphs* in order to define terms or to make transitions from one section of your argument to another?

- Are the *transitions* between strengths and weaknesses clear in the movement *between* paragraphs?

- Do individual paragraphs reveal problems with *internal transitions* or other problems that you will need to address in the next stage of revision?

Problems in persuasive structure generally come from the difficulties writers have in distinguishing strengths from weaknesses or pro arguments from con arguments. The solution lies in learning to make the multiple transitions a good persuasive essay requires. Let us look at this issue of transitions in more detail.

In a sense, your whole essay is in transition toward your most important argument. You end with this point so that its impact is greatest on your readers. This movement will be impeded and the impact lessened if you have not dealt with the con points you have raised—or if readers are aware of points you should have raised but have not. Check to make sure you have put con points first, and responded to them, before you present your pro points.

The placement of points is not the only issue, however. The movement between paragraphs must be clearly marked by transitions so that readers know when they are moving to a paragraph beginning with a con argument, or a paragraph of definition, or a paragraph offering another aspect of the issue. (You will find additional information on this subject in Part 3, D Writing Better Paragraphs.)

STAGE 6   Revising Individual Paragraphs

STEP 1   Revising Your Introduction: *Ethos*

If *ethos*—the image a writer projects of him or herself—is important in writing introductions to critique essays, as we suggested in Chapter 8, it is even more important in persuasive essays, where readers' responses are likely to be governed by deep beliefs and emotions. The goal is to present yourself as committed but fair-minded. If you present yourself as so dogmatic that you have no sympathy for or understanding of other views, then you are unlikely to convince readers who disagree with you.

In an academic situation, where open-minded critical thinking is valued, introductory sentences like the examples below may bias the reader against your essay.

Weak introductory sentences

- The bureaucratic mind is known for its selfishness and stupidity, and recently it has come up with a proposal with just these qualities, the proposal to reduce school holidays to a month and force hard-working teachers to work twice as hard as before.
- I like the more recent *Star Wars* trilogy. It has great action sequences and killer special effects. I know you will like it, too. I have not met anyone who disliked these films.
- Who needs a Canadian national identity? Aren't there more important things in life?

The need to avoid obviously biased comments does not mean you should use deceit or conceal your position. It means that you should precede your thesis statement either with something likely to appeal to all readers or with something that establishes neutral ground, such as questions about the subject that you do not immediately answer.

- In the draft for the sample assignment, the opening of the essay consists of a question:

Draft introductory comment

Should the federal government of Canada actively promote and foster a Canadian national identity?

This is a good question to establish neutral ground, but there are still unanswered questions and background information that you will need to provide to set up your argument. So you might decide to open with this question and another, more specific one, and to follow those questions with some background about the Canadian government's attitudes toward national identity in the past. You can read the resulting introduction in E. Jones, "Canadian National Identity" (Readings: Sample Essays).

STEP 2 ## Revising Middle Paragraphs: Logic and Transitions

You may have identified problematic middle paragraphs in your review of essay structure. If not, now is the time to evaluate each middle paragraph and revise as necessary.

When you check middle paragraphs, make sure that

- each paragraph contains a topic, point, and detail that support your thesis
- you have used words, phrases, and sentences to identify pro and con arguments and to create clear transitions between these arguments, and between the arguments and the detail that supports them
- your arguments and evidence are valid

Earlier we mentioned that problems in middle paragraphs arise from the difficulty of handling transitions within a pro–con structure. This statement is true, but often problems in transitions stem from problems in logic. Many persuasive essays use the logical standard in combination with aesthetic, ethical, or practical standards. Whether you have used the logical standard or not, your readers will expect your own arguments and evidence to be free of errors in logic (see Chapter 8, Stage 2, Step 2: Evaluating the Writer's Argument).

- The following paragraph from the sample assignment exhibits typical problems with logic and transitions:

Draft middle paragraph

A national identity would be good for new immigrants. They would have a sense of how to establish themselves in the new country. Some believe that we should not have a national identity because it would exclude immigrants. How would their own values fit into a Canadian national identity? I think it would benefit everyone, though, because we could all relate to one another and have cross-cultural understanding. A multicultural identity like this would be a great national identity to have.

This paragraph meets some of the logical requirements for arguments and evidence: it includes pro and con arguments of fostering a Canadian national identity and how immigrants and non-immigrants might respond to or benefit from such an identity. The paragraph has significant omissions, however: it doesn't state how or why immigrants might feel excluded from a promoted national identity; it doesn't explain how a national identity would help immigrants fit into a new country. The organization of the paragraph is also problematic, since it goes back and forth between pros and cons, instead of systematically stating the cons first, and then proving the point by highlighting the pros. You could revise by first presenting the con argument and explaining it more specifically, then presenting a balanced statement about the benefits of a shared national identity for immigrants, being careful to explain fully why and how such a national identity would be beneficial. The resulting paragraph is the second paragraph in E. Jones, "Canadian National Identity" (Readings: Sample Essays).

STEP 3   Revising Your Conclusion: Achieving Balance

As we pointed out in Chapter 8, you should have the same concern for *ethos* in your conclusion as in your introduction. To demonstrate your fair-mindedness in the conclusion, you include the con position as well as the pro position, though you do so in a way that reinforces rather than undermines your argument. Thus in revising your conclusion you check for

- a summary and expansion of your thesis statement that refers to both strengths and weaknesses, to the relationship between them, and to the supporting topics
- a statement of broader implications that does not dismiss the weak side of the case but emphasizes the implications of the strong side

To see how you might achieve this kind of balance, consider the draft conclusion for the sample assignment:

Draft
conclusion

There are many ethical, logical, and practical reasons, however, to believe that fostering a Canadian national identity is essential. Ethical reasons include the cross-cultural understanding that national identity provides within a multicultural framework, and the personal and gender identities that a national identity can legitimate. Logical reasons include the fact that local or regional identities are tied to national ones. Practical reasons include the economic advancement that Canada could attain by fostering a national identity—one rooted in either multiculturalism or a valuing of the Canadian North. As we can see, it is important to have a Canadian national identity.

This conclusion provides a good summary of the pro argument and reiterates the topics of the body paragraphs as they relate to the thesis, the overall argument of the essay. It does not refer to the weak side of the case, however; nor does it incorporate this weak side into a clear statement of broader implications. It also doesn't highlight the importance of a national identity both for citizens and for the state: you've discussed both in your essay. In looking back over your essay, you might realize that the practical reasons you explain for the state's promotion of a national identity could conflict with ethical reasons against national identity. You will need to address this conflict and discuss its wider implications, while still highlighting the case that you've made. For the revised version, see the final paragraph of E. Jones, "Canadian National Identity" (Readings: Sample Essays).

Working on Your Own Assignment

Your main goal in writing and revising a persuasive essay is to work out your position and then persuade your readers to agree with it.

- Find a standard or standards of evaluation either in the assignment or in the process of gathering material.
- Analyze your subject by choosing appropriate categories and gathering material in them.
- Identify strengths and weaknesses by applying the appropriate standard(s) of evaluation to the material in your categories.
- Formulate a thesis that states an opinion about the relationship between strengths and weaknesses, gives reasons to support your opinion, and indicates your standard(s) of evaluation.
- Construct a draft outline according to the principle of pro–con structure and write the draft.
- Check the draft by means of a revision outline for problems in thesis statement, pro–con structure, and transitions.
- Check the introduction and conclusion for fair-mindedness; check middle paragraphs for problems in transition and logic.

Exercises

A. Identify the standard(s) of evaluation implied or stated in each of the following essay topics.

1. James Thurber's "The Catbird Seat" and Ernest Hemingway's "The Short Happy Life of Francis Macomber" are both stories about manhood. Which uses setting and characterization more effectively in conveying a theme about this subject?

2. Choose one of the educational theories we have discussed this term and evaluate whether or not it could be successfully used in either science or arts classes in your local high school.

3. Is the term *sustainable growth* an oxymoron in the twenty-first century?

4. Discuss whether feminism still remains a reasonable system of beliefs for contemporary women to adopt.

B.   Write a sentence or two evaluating the following as thesis statements for persuasive essays.

1. People describe terrorism as a complex issue. What's complex about it? You have to fight terrorism by every means available; force is the only language terrorists understand.

2. It is clear that, on moral grounds, we should have the right to interfere with customs and practices of other cultures when these customs clearly degrade one or more classes of people. Other cultures have important reasons for their customs, though; these customs are often central to their religious beliefs.

C.   Decide what point the writer of the following paragraph is trying to prove. State that point in a topic sentence. Then reorganize the paragraph, putting the con arguments first and the pro arguments second. Compare your paragraph with the paragraphs of other class members.

> Cell phones can save lives in emergencies. If your car breaks down at 3:00 a.m. on an isolated road, you can phone for help and let your family know that you will be late. Loud conversations by people using cell phones drive restaurant customers sitting at nearby tables crazy. The ringing of cell phones can destroy the climax of any movie. Cell phones are a great way to give a teenager both safety and more freedom. Drivers who talk or text on their cell phones while making a left turn are a menace on the roads.

D.   Choose one of the topics listed below and work out your own position on this issue by following the steps in this chapter for finding a standard of evaluation, gathering material, and formulating a thesis statement. Then make a draft outline indicating the sequence in which you would present the arguments for and against your position.

- Should marijuana be legalized?
- Should the summer holidays for schoolchildren be reduced to one month?
- Should the public celebration of religious or customary holidays be banned from schools and hospitals?

Gathering Material for Research Essays

Sample Topic: Margaret Laurence's "The Loons"

While different academic disciplines may have their own methods for conducting research and presenting their findings, the creation of new knowledge through research is a central activity of every discipline. Within each discipline, primary research may range from field work to laboratory work to textual work such as analyzing, interpreting, and synthesizing information. For example, sociologists can study daily workplace behaviour, or they can run controlled experiments that alter variables in the workplace environment. Furthermore, they can study all the published research on past experiments and methods, and develop new models for learning about workplace behaviour. The results of all these different kinds of research are made known to other researchers and to the general public through scholarly books and articles, the professional forms of research essays.

It is important to understand the difference between a survey of research and a research essay. In disciplines such as psychology and sociology, a research assignment may ask you to do a literature survey on a particular topic, such as depression among the elderly or youth unemployment. A literature survey requires you to examine the available scholarly publications and report on their scope and content, often without offering an interpretation or synthesis of those materials. By contrast, a research essay requires you to work out a thesis about the topic in relation to the available materials.

Although research projects may seem intimidating, research essays are quite similar to analysis, comparison, and persuasive essays. The basic principles of essay structure remain the same. The main difference is that in writing a research essay, you use secondary materials to complement the essay's overall purpose.

Research and research essays have three main purposes. They allow you

- to acquire information about a particular subject
- to become familiar with the current conventions and knowledge base of a discipline
- to add to existing knowledge by offering your own opinion or ideas

Each successive purpose builds on the preceding one. For example, if your philosophy instructor asked you to write a six-page research essay on violence, you would begin by acquiring information. In your library, you would find numerous books and articles addressing this topic from different perspectives. Since your assignment is for a philosophy course, you select materials on violence primarily from within that discipline. In reviewing these books and articles, you realize that the authors have different, if not conflicting, viewpoints and arguments about violence. You agree with some and disagree with others. You then think through the different perspectives and offer your own interpretation, opinion, or understanding of violence.

This is the basic process of research that we examine in this chapter. The next chapter will focus on writing and revising the research essay. Both chapters refer to a sample topic on Margaret Laurence's short story "The Loons" (Readings). You will better understand the procedures outlined here if you read the story first.

STAGE 1   Clarifying Research Topics

Research assignments are generally handed out at least a month before the assignment is due for good reason: research takes time. Allow at least two to three weeks to think about your topic, find material, write a draft, and revise it.

STEP 1   Understanding Directions

As soon as you receive a research assignment, make sure you understand the meaning of each possible topic, your instructor's particular requirements, and the relation between primary and secondary sources.

Specialized terms Since research assignments are usually on specialized topics, you should be alert to the specialized use of terms. For example, *narcissism* in a psychology assignment means something more specific than its popular meaning of egotism or self-absorption.

Specific requirements The way instructors phrase assignments can vary considerably. Some instructors offer broad research questions such as "Write a research essay on the debates about AIDS drugs in African countries." Other instructors give narrowly defined topics with precise guidelines about research materials, essay structure, and documentation. Some instructors may ask for a preliminary report before the final copy of the essay is due in order to ensure that you are on the right track. Take careful note of any instructions.

Primary and secondary sources Most instructors will expect you to integrate *your* views about your subject with the commentary of other writers. If your subject is something you know little or nothing about, such as, perhaps, "the debates about AIDS drugs in African countries," you would arrive at your own view by analyzing and evaluating the arguments you find in *secondary sources* (such as books and articles about the subject). On the other hand, if your subject is a *primary source* (such as a literary work you have read or a performance you have seen), you would work out your own ideas before consulting secondary sources.

Sample Topic To demonstrate how you might work through the above aspects of Step 1, we will consider the following assignments for a 1500-word research essay on Margaret Laurence's short story "The Loons" for an English class:

1. Write a research essay that examines how Margaret Laurence develops the relationship between Vanessa and Piquette in her short story "The Loons."

2. In Margaret Laurence's short story "The Loons," Vanessa says that Piquette and her family "were actually Indians, or as near as made no difference." Write a research essay that explores how Laurence treats race and race relations through the characters of Vanessa and Piquette.

3. Near the end of Margaret Laurence's short story "The Loons," Vanessa learns of Piquette's death and thinks that "As so often with Piquette, there did not seem to be anything to say." Earlier in the story, when Jules or Lazarus would get into conflict in the town, the Mounties would put them in jail "and the next morning they would be quiet again." Both the Tonnerre and MacLeod families experience silence. Write a research essay that analyzes the different types of silence in this story. You must incorporate at least three secondary sources into your essay. All quotations and citations must be in MLA format.

Notice that the primary material in each assignment is the same: Margaret Laurence's story "The Loons." The subjects are different, however; subjects vary from the depiction of a relationship to the treatment of race to the meanings of silence in the story. While only the third assignment outlines the number of secondary sources and the documentation style, you would need to use and document secondary sources in the other assignments as well. Instructors may cover this material in class or in supplementary handouts rather than in the initial assignment.

STEP 2   Choosing a Topic

It is important to think through the demands of an assignment rather than choose a topic on the basis of surface impressions. The topic that looks the easiest will not necessarily be the easiest one for you to write about. You will have a better experience writing about something you find enjoyable rather than something you find a bore. So if your assignment has different options for research, select the topic that most interests you. If your assignment does not have options but has a broad scope, ask yourself which particular area of the subject you would like to know more about. If the topic interests you, you will find yourself thinking about it even when you are not directly working on your project.

Sample Topic In the list of sample assignments above, the first assignment about the "relationship" between Vanessa and Piquette may appear to be the easiest because you are required to write about only one thing, not several things. However, even one thing can be quite complicated. How many factors enter into a relationship? Race is mentioned in the second assignment (Vanessa is white, Piquette is Métis), and so you begin to think about how race might influence the relationship. There are also differences in age, social status, and family composition. You begin to see that this topic requires you to consider different types of relationships in the same way that the third topic requires you to consider "different types of silence."

STEP 3   Defining a Preliminary Research Question

The number and variety of secondary materials available on almost any topic make researching and writing a research essay a challenge. Both tasks will be easier if you make sure your topic is manageable within the specified length of the assignment. One good strategy is to brainstorm by asking questions about your subject. From these questions, choose one that seems central to the subject (and that interests you) as your preliminary research question. We call this a *preliminary question* because it comes before you have systematically analyzed either your primary material or your secondary sources. Focusing on your preliminary research question will help you decide which secondary sources are most relevant; it will also guide you toward a clear position about one important area of your subject.

For example, if you received a political science assignment to research the conflict in the Darfur region of Sudan, you might ask questions like these: Was the conflict religiously motivated? Was the conflict racially motivated? What was the response of the international community? What were the effects on families and children? While you could conceivably try to answer all these questions in a research essay, taking one as your preliminary research question and searching for an answer would produce a more focused essay.

Sample Topic To see how you would define a preliminary research question, let us suppose you choose the first of the sample assignments on "The Loons." Brainstorming, you come up with the following questions: What is the relationship between Vanessa and Piquette? Is there much actual relationship when Piquette's presence in Vanessa's life is so minimal? Is it the relationship in Vanessa's head that is most important? If so, does this relationship change?

This last question in particular interests you because you notice that Laurence shows Vanessa's views of Piquette at three different ages, creating a passage of time that is unusually long for a short story. It seems reasonable to assume that as Vanessa grows up, she gains a greater understanding both of Piquette and of their relationship, an assumption you can test against the textual evidence of the story. Thus you decide to make this assumption into your preliminary research question: "Does Laurence portray Vanessa as attaining a more mature understanding of Piquette and of their relationship?"

STAGE 2 Finding and Gathering Materials

Once you have defined your preliminary research question, you are ready for the second stage of the research process: analyzing your primary source(s), if any; acquiring information and ideas from secondary sources; and then developing your own point of view by analyzing the relationship among your source materials.

STEP 1 Gathering Material from Primary Sources

If the starting point for your research essay is one or more primary sources (such as literary works and other written documents, or performances, experiments, or interviews), you need to know what you think about the primary source(s) before you can deal effectively with secondary sources. Working out your ideas requires choosing a method of analysis (usually systems analysis for essays on literature) and choosing disciplinary or analytic categories. We explained methods of analysis in Chapter 3, and disciplinary and analytic categories in Chapters 3 through 6. Remember that disciplinary categories are terms specific to the field of study. In English, you might consider categories such as genre, figurative language, or a specific kind of figurative language, such as metaphor. Analytic categories are your own, based on your analysis of the text. We will use the sample topic to show how a preliminary research question can lead you to the categories you need.

Sample Topic Your preliminary research question for your assignment on "The Loons" asks whether Margaret Laurence portrays her main character, Vanessa, as achieving a more mature understanding of Piquette and of their relationship. This is a question about characterization, and so a disciplinary category such as characterization will be useful. That Vanessa achieves greater maturity seems possible because of Laurence's use of time in the story, an aspect of narrative structure. When you ask yourself whether Laurence endorses Vanessa's understanding of Piquette, however, you find it hard to be sure because of the point of view: the story is written from the first-person point of view, with detail and judgment coming entirely from Vanessa. Finally, the title emphasizes the significance of the loons on the lake outside the MacLeods' summer cabin, so you add the disciplinary category of figurative language.

Analyzing the story in terms of these categories, you come up with the following chart:

ANALYSIS OF "THE LOONS"

Narrative structure

Organized around Vanessa's understanding of Piquette at different ages:

- at 11, seeing Piquette as "spr[u]ng from the people of Big Bear and Poundmaker" (273)
- at 15, feeling embarrassment, distance, and a moment of empathy
- at 19, seeing Piquette as perhaps "the only one, after all, who had heard the crying of the loons" (385)

Characterization

- Vanessa as dynamic character, with changing perceptions of Piquette (we learn little of Piquette's own desires)
- white, middle-class background, educated, daughter of doctor, Scots ancestry
- imaginative, close to father, feels guilty about not befriending Piquette as he wished

Point of view

- first-person
- enclosed within Vanessa's own perceptions; no authorial comment

Figurative language

- loons identified by Dr. MacLeod with unpeopled land
- loons identified by Piquette as "squawkin' birds"
- by end of story, loons identified by Vanessa with suffering; Piquette, victims of white development

STEP 2   Forming a Preliminary Opinion

It may be helpful, once you have analyzed any primary material, to see if this material suggests an answer to your preliminary question. This answer will be an opinion on the subject of the assignment that reflects your response to the primary material. It is a preliminary opinion, however, not a tentative thesis: a thesis statement for a research essay also needs to incorporate a response to the range of secondary material. However, having an opinion on the primary material will usually keep you from feeling overwhelmed by the range of opinions in the secondary sources. Keep in mind that you may have to change your opinion substantially once you consider this material.

Sample Topic Does Laurence portray Vanessa as achieving a more mature understanding of Piquette and of her relationship with the young Métis woman? When you look at your categories of primary material, it concerns you that the point of view makes it hard to assess Laurence's attitude toward Vanessa's perceptions. Nevertheless, your other categories seem to suggest that by the end of the story, Vanessa does develop a more realistic and empathetic understanding. So far, your analysis of the story suggests an affirmative answer to your preliminary research question.

STEP 3   Finding Secondary Sources

When you are writing on topics that do not require analysis of a primary source, such as current political events, topics of general interest, and some academic subjects, you will rely on secondary sources for information and ideas. When your starting point is the analysis of primary material, secondary sources will provide additional information and allow you to test your understanding of your material against the opinions of other writers. What exactly is a secondary source? A secondary source may be an encyclopedia entry, a specialized handbook or dictionary, CD-ROM materials, a book, or an article—in short, anything that is not a primary source but is related to your research question in a meaningful way.

Not all of these types of material are equally useful when you are writing a research essay. Perhaps the most important distinction is between *scholarly* (or **peer-reviewed**) and *non-scholarly* (or non–peer-reviewed) secondary sources. Scholarly sources, which have been reviewed by experts in the field, generally contain more accurate and more reliable information than non-scholarly sources, which have not been reviewed by experts. Using a scholarly source is one way of making an appeal to authority, as discussed in Chapter 8.

There are two main formats for scholarly sources: books and journal articles. A scholarly book may focus on a single subject, or it may address several smaller topics that fall within another category of classification. For example, a literary scholar may publish an entire book on the works of Margaret Laurence or a book on Canadian short stories that includes only one chapter on Margaret Laurence. A collection of scholarly articles, which contains multiple chapters authored by different people on a common subject, may also contain useful information about your subject even if the title does not directly indicate it.

Scholarly journals (often called *periodicals* because they appear periodically, usually between one and four times per year) consist of articles or essays that make public the research findings of experts in a field of study. They are much like magazines; however, where magazines appeal to a general audience, scholarly journals appeal to an expert audience. Because journals are published regularly and quickly, compared to books, they often contain the most up-to-date research in any given field.

Many journals also publish reviews that may help you decide whether a book is relevant to your purpose. If you want to refer to the content of the book in your essay, however, you should generally consult the original, since a review is shaped by the perspective of the reviewer and omits a great deal. Ask your instructor whether or not reviews are acceptable materials for your research essay.

Compiling a working bibliography   A working bibliography is a list of potentially useful books, articles, and other material that you put together as you search for secondary sources. You are likely to discover that some of the material is not relevant after all, and that some of it is not available, so you should aim for a working bibliography of fifteen to twenty items. From a preliminary list this size, you are almost sure to find enough good references for your essay. When you encounter a book or article that looks useful, get into the habit of printing, cutting and pasting, or copying down the bibliographic details as well as the library call number. This information will enable you to find the book or journal easily and to complete your Works Cited or References page for your essay. You may also want to make a few notes about why you think the book or article is relevant.

For most books you will require the author, the title, the city of publication, the publisher, and the year of publication. Include the editor(s) for edited books. For most journal articles you will require the author, the title of the article, the title of the journal, the volume (and issue) number of the journal, the year of publication, and the page numbers of the article. To find out exactly what bibliographic information you need for different sources, consult Part 3, H3 Documentation.

There are two main places to locate secondary sources:

- your library catalogue
- online database services

We will also discuss the advantages and disadvantages of internet sources and interlibrary loans.

The library catalogue You may find all the information you need on current events and topics of general interest in the holdings of your local public library. Your school library, which is designed to help students and instructors, will contain much more scholarly information about academic topics. If you want to find single- or multi-author books, your library catalogue is the first place to go.

You can access your school's library catalogue through a computer in the library or from your home computer via the internet. The searchable library catalogue lists all the materials your library physically contains, including books, journals, newspapers, microfilms, microfiches, CDs, CD-ROMs, and so forth.

Searching Although library catalogues vary, most allow you to search by keywords, subjects, and authors. Many also allow you to search by titles, periodical titles, call numbers, or other categories. Keyword and subject searches are probably the most useful for beginning researchers. Knowing what terms to use will help you find relevant materials. This is why it is a good idea to think about your topic *before* you begin to research, as you will have a number of key terms or key ideas to use as search strings. Often, the difficulty is not finding information but finding the right information.

Depending on the size of your school's library, any given search term will return a number of results. Some of the materials may not be relevant to your assignment, however. Rather than working your way through the whole list to find out, you can narrow your search by combining search terms. In Chapter 3, we introduced disciplinary categories as a set of terms that help define the scope of materials in a particular field of study. The library catalogue is based upon many of these disciplinary categories to allow you to search the catalogue more quickly and easily.

Some catalogues also allow you to truncate or shorten search terms so you can search numerous terms simultaneously. For example, instead of searching separately, you are able to use a term like "Canad*" to search for both "Canada" and "Canadian" or "wom?n" to search for both "women" and "woman." Consult your instructor or the reference librarian for more tips on how to better search the catalogue.

For a demonstration of how to use search terms and narrow your search, see the sample topic at the end of this section.

Online database services Academic journals are excellent research resources because they publish scholarly arguments on precise topics. If you want to find journal articles, the first place to look is the online database services. These services index scholarly and non-scholarly journals and allow you to search the contents of those journals, as well as newspapers and magazines. Some databases index journals for a specific discipline or a few related disciplines: an example is the *MLA International Bibliography,* which includes journals related to literature and literary criticism. Other databases can be very comprehensive. *Academic Search Complete,* for example, covers fields as diverse as chemistry, psychology, and the humanities. Ask your instructor or librarian to tell you what databases are available to you.

- Database searching is similar to searching a library catalogue. You rely on relevant names, concepts, keywords, and disciplinary categories to help you find articles related to your topic. You may need to search multiple databases to find the right information for your topic. Ask your instructor or reference librarian about which data bases are most suitable for your research topic.

- The results for database searches may take a number of forms: citation, abstract, full-text HTML, or full-text PDF. Essentially, some databases give you the full text of a journal article, which you can print off, download, save, or email to yourself. Full-text databases are quick and easy to use.

- Non–full-text databases return only a citation (reference) or an abstract (a brief summary) of an article. These databases usually give you details of journal, issue, and page numbers; then you must physically retrieve the journal from your library shelf and read or photocopy the article. Therefore, when searching a non–full-text database, it is important to realize that you need to check the title of the journal in your school's library catalogue to know if your school subscribes to the print journal. If your school does subscribe, you can retrieve the journal from the shelves; if the library does not subscribe, you will need to order the article through inter-library loan.

- Some databases provide you with both full-text articles and non–full-text articles. As we will explain, it is worth considering both kinds of articles.

Library catalogue and online database searches: advantages and disadvantages At this point you may be tempted to conclude that collecting books and journals is too time-consuming, so you should forget about searching the library catalogue and non–full-text databases. Why can't you just search full-text databases? Consider the strengths and weaknesses of these different methods of research:

- Many online databases include journals only from the 1990s and later; therefore, they do not include any information prior to the first year of indexing. Clearly, every discipline has important research materials prior to the digitization of knowledge.

- For financial reasons, some journals withhold online access to the most recent months or years of the print version of the journal. Consequently, the most recent information is only available in print form.

- Non–full-text databases can refer you to important information that is not available online. Many important print journals are not included in full-text online databases. Therefore, you should consider print articles as well.

- Most of your library's book holdings are not available in full-text online versions. Books contain some of the best information, so it is important to search through the books in your library. To ignore your library stacks is to ignore one of the most significant sources of information at your disposal. It is becoming increasingly common for books, as well as articles, to be online and available electronically through your school library. Even so, it is important to consider those books that are not available electronically and to look them up in your school's library stacks.

- Some databases include non-scholarly sources. Newspapers and magazines can be valuable resources if you are writing on a subject of general interest. If you are writing on an academic subject, however, you should draw your secondary sources primarily from scholarly books and articles. Some databases allow you to limit your searches to scholarly sources; some do not. In either case, you are ultimately responsible for determining the value and reliability of your secondary sources.

The internet The internet is becoming an increasingly valuable tool for researchers and the general public. For many people, it is the starting point to find information. When using the internet (as with any source of information), it is important to consider the source or origin of the information you find. Many academic, professional, and governmental organizations are publishing their materials online for public use, and these are very useful resources. Other sources, probably like your school's library and its database subscriptions, offer online access limited to members within the institution who have exclusive access to helpful resources. Generally speaking, pages like *Wikipedia* or personal blogs are not the most reliable sources of information, as just about anyone can contribute to them. They may or may not be accurate. If you are not sure about a source, consult with your instructor.

Interlibrary loan If you don't find the secondary sources you need by searching your library catalogue and online databases, you may be able to access materials through interlibrary loan. Most college and university libraries are accessible online, and you can search other library catalogues quite easily. Be aware, however, that it may take a week or a few weeks to receive materials through interlibrary loan services. For more information on interlibrary searching, consult your librarian.

Sample Topic The first step in looking for scholarly secondary materials on Margaret Laurence is searching the library catalogue. If we conducted an author search using Laurence's name, the search would return the titles of books *by* Laurence, not *about* Laurence. Luckily, most catalogues allow you to search a person's name as a *subject* of study rather than as an *author* of the text. For example, searching a college catalogue using "Laurence, Margaret" as the subject (not author) search term returned twelve results. One of these, you discover when you visit the library stacks, is a collection of articles that includes a chapter on "The Loons" by Laurence herself, entitled "Time and the Narrative Voice" (included in Readings). This material will likely prove useful because the author is discussing her own method of composition, and so you photocopy the article and take down the relevant bibliographic information. Provide the information from the source that you are viewing, as information may be available in several places—such as original publications, reprints, or online reproductions. If the source is in print, for example, your citation should specify that medium.

Laurence, Margaret. "Time and the Narrative Voice." *Margaret Laurence*. Ed. W. H. New. Toronto: McGraw-Hill Ryerson, 1977. 156-60. Print.

Using Laurence's name as a subject on a major university catalogue returned 124 items, far too many to wade through. You can narrow the results by combining search terms. If we think about Margaret Laurence as a writer, she is Canadian, a woman, from Manitoba, writing in the 1960s and 1970s. By combining the terms relevant to Laurence, terms from your class notes, and categories suggested by the story, you might come up with the following chart of possible search terms.

LITERATURE	RACE	AGE	CHARACTER
"The Loons"	Métis	adolescent	development
Laurence, Margaret	Native	youth	narrative
short story	Indian	child	narrator
short fiction	First Nations	maturity	authorial intent
Canada/Canadian	Aboriginal	family	voice
genre	Indigenous	school	point of view
women	white		
A Bird in the House	cultural assimilation		

Let's see what results you might get by combining some of these search terms.

- The four-word search string "Native and women and literature and Canada" yields eight results. Writing down the call numbers of several books, you find one in the stacks that has a whole chapter on "The Loons." This book did not turn up on your subject search of Laurence's name in the library catalogue. You take down the following bibliographic information:

  Acoose, Janice. *Iskwewak—Kah' Ki Yaw Ni Wahkomakanak: Neither Indian Princesses nor Easy Squaws.* Toronto: Women's Press, 1995. Print.

- The three-term string "Native and cultural assimilation and Canada" also yields eight items, one of which offers some interesting historical material about residential schools and the abduction or forced adoption of Aboriginal children in the 1960s and 1970s, the time when Laurence was writing this story. You add this book to your working bibliography:

  Fournier, Suzanne, and Ernie Crey. *Stolen from Our Embrace: The Abduction of First Nations Children and the Restoration of Aboriginal Communities.* Vancouver: Douglas & McIntyre, 1997. Print.

You would follow the same process for searching online databases.

You won't need to search every possible combination of terms to find materials for your project. Choose the most likely. As this last example shows, even material that does not deal directly with your subject may prove useful. It is up to you to make the connections between your secondary sources and your ideas about your primary source.

STEP 4   Evaluating Secondary Sources and Taking Notes

Once you have a significant working bibliography (fifteen to twenty entries), you are ready to read, evaluate, and take notes on your secondary sources. However, you do not have to read the whole of every book and article. Rather, begin by skimming over some of the materials. For example, read the introductory chapter of a book or the abstract or first paragraph of a scholarly essay. If the material looks promising, keep reading. If it looks irrelevant, briefly skim another section or two and then discard the material if it does not suit your essay. Make a note on why you discarded the material in case your research direction changes at a later date and the material becomes relevant.

How do you decide which secondary materials are relevant? Material is relevant if it helps answer your preliminary question. It is relevant if it agrees with your preliminary opinion; it is equally if not more relevant if it expresses different opinions. You are looking for a range of perspectives, not simply opinions that echo your own. From your initial list, choose six to eight of the most relevant sources for closer attention. You may not end up including all of them in your essay, but you should work with as many sources as possible when developing your thesis. Remember as well that you can use secondary sources to address general questions related to your specific area of research and to provide contextual material.

Once you have selected your best sources, read through the materials and isolate the key points that will help you support your ideas or answer your questions. Does this book or article support your opinion? Does it contradict your opinion? Does it necessitate a shift in your thinking? As you read further in any field, you should think about connections between secondary sources. Do you notice any trends? Are there common approaches or common assumptions? Do certain names keep appearing as major figures in the field? Furthermore, as you continue to read, you may find a book or article that makes more or less exactly the case you had in mind. Do not despair. View this as a strength because it demonstrates that you identified an important idea or argument in the field. It is likely that there are different answers to your preliminary question and that you now must recast it in terms of the research.

Occasionally you may find that none of your secondary sources answers exactly the question you are asking. This does not mean that you ask it anyway and dismiss all the secondary commentary as irrelevant. Nor does it mean that you throw away your question and settle for one that has been fully discussed already. Instead, consider whether you could broaden or alter the focus of your question in a way that will allow you to use your secondary material.

One strategy for coming to grips with your secondary sources is to read each book (or, more practically, each relevant chapter) or article once through, reasonably closely but not too slowly. If working from your own print copy, underline or highlight sections you find particularly illuminating. Upon completion, write down what you think is the author's thesis or main point. Also write down your response to this point as well as how you think it might relate to your own opinion.

Then, do a second reading that is much more meticulous. You may come across numerous discipline-specific terms that are unfamiliar to you; as a result, your research materials may seem overly wordy and unnecessarily difficult. It is your responsibility as a good researcher to look up unfamiliar terms either in a standard dictionary or in a specialized dictionary specific to the particular research field. Although this work can be time-consuming, you will find that your research materials will be more useful to you when you understand their complexities and nuances.

As you progress through the reading, keep in mind your idea about the thesis of the work. This focus will help you follow the author's argument in close detail, to understand how he or she arrives at the conclusion. As you work through the second reading, take detailed notes of relevant sections.

- Make sure that your notes are both accurate and precise. In order to avoid plagiarism, you need to distinguish between your ideas and the ideas you use from secondary sources. As you take notes, either summarize the author's ideas in your own words (see Chapter 2) or quote directly from the secondary source (see Part 3, H2 Quotations).
- When quoting, you must quote materials *exactly* as they appear in the original text. For both summary and quotation, you must include the relevant page number(s) of the materials. You should also include, in square brackets, your evaluation of this material: Why is it relevant to your essay? When you begin to write your essay, this approach will help you separate your ideas from the ideas of others.

Sample Topic Out of the fifteen or so items in your working bibliography, half a dozen present various opinions about Vanessa's relationship with

Piquette, so you don't need to modify your preliminary research question. You take more extensive notes on these sources, being particularly careful to be accurate about publication details, quotations, and summaries. You are also careful about adding your own notes on how each critic's thesis relates to your preliminary opinion, putting them in square brackets to distinguish them from the material directly from the critic. Notes on one of these items might look like this:

Acoose, Janice. "Fenced In and Forced to Give Up: Images of Indigenous Women in Selected Non-Indigenous Writers' Fiction." *Iskwewak   Kah' Ki Yaw Ni Wahkomakanak: Neither Indian Princesses nor Easy Squaws.* Toronto: Women's Press, 1995. 69-88. Print.

Thesis: that indigenous women are "misrepresented in non-Indigenous writers' texts" (70) and that W. P. Kinsella and Margaret Laurence participate in this misrepresentation.

[contradicts my claim that Laurence portrays a more mature understanding]

Development of argument: Acoose starts with the case of a young Aboriginal woman being assaulted and murdered, then shows that works by Kinsella and Laurence portray Aboriginal women as either empty and wanton (Kinsella) or worthwhile but helpless victims (Laurence). She then returns to the case of murdered Aboriginal women, suggesting that they are victims of this kind of stereotyping, and urges writers and others to see Aboriginal women as having "strength, determination, and beauty" (88).

Important quotations:

(1) "I urge readers to consider the white constructs of Indigenous women who have been variously portrayed as creatures of nature, temptresses, or femme fatales, Indian princesses, easy squaws, or suffering, helpless victims." (74)

[Does the comparison of Piquette to the loons perpetuate this idea of her as a creature of nature and as a helpless victim?]

(2) "In Margaret Laurence's 'The Loons,' protagonist Vanessa MacLeod . . . is a young white christian lower-middle-class girl whose understanding of reality is filtered through a racist, classist, and male-privileged ideological value system. Vanessa is represented as a somewhat autonomous subject, whereas Piquette Tonnerre is represented as a victim who is consistently victimized." (79)

[Contradicts my opinion, suggests Vanessa's viewpoint is static and deluded]

When you have taken detailed notes on all of the secondary sources you have selected for extensive treatment, you are ready to see how these items relate to each other and to your primary material.

STEP 5   Comparing Source Material

Since opinions vary wildly on almost every subject under the sun, your research has likely yielded relevant but differing opinions about your research question. In order to formulate a full research thesis statement, you will need to bring these opinions into relationship with each other and, if you have also analyzed a primary source (or sources), with your preliminary opinion.

If you are working solely with secondary sources, your essential task is that of comparing the opinions expressed in your sources and then figuring out how and why you agree or disagree with each one. You will find this task easier if you make a chart to show matching categories of analysis, like the chart comparing two essays on addiction (see page 102 in Chapter 7).

If you began by analyzing a primary source or sources, you can simply add the secondary source material to the categories you found for the primary material. If you have altered the preliminary question or changed your opinion in the course of your research, you may have to adjust the categories accordingly.

Putting your source material into common categories is the last step in gathering material. We will show how this technique works by referring to the sample topic.

Sample Topic   Among the items you chose for detailed notes was a book on Laurence in which Jon Kertzer argues that "In [Vanessa's] memoir she succeeds in making contact, at least in the sense of understanding and feeling compassion for Piquette's plight, but only after her friend is dead and the loons have vanished"(Kertzer 68) and an article by Peter Easingwood that speaks of Vanessa's "psychological compulsion to question [given] reality" and the "older narrator's . . . recogni[tion of this] compulsion"(Easingwood 126). You also found an article by Laurence herself that claims that Vanessa, hearing of Piquette's death, realizes that "she, too, like the entire town, is in part responsible" ("Time and the Narrative Voice," 283, Readings). These claims for Vanessa's increasing maturation are contradicted by Janice Acoose, whose work we summarized in Step 4. You found support for Acoose's position in a non-literary source, *Stolen from Our Embrace*, a book on the "abduction" of Aboriginal children in which Suzanne Fournier and Ernie Crey argue that the taking away of children was based on the belief that Aboriginal people did not have the strength to be responsible for their own communities. Remembering that articles in academic periodicals often contain the most specific criticism, you have included an article in which Tracy Ware reviews criticism of "The Loons" and argues that Acoose is correct;

while "The Loons" does contain social criticism, he maintains, it also follows a "debased master narrative that regards Natives as victims" (Ware 71). When you map these different opinions onto the categories you devised for the primary material, you come up with the following chart:

"THE LOONS"

Narrative structure
PRIMARY

Story organized around Vanessa's understanding of Piquette at different ages: at 11, seeing Piquette as "spr[u]ng from the people of Big Bear and Poundmaker," "a daughter of the forest" (273); at 15, feeling embarrassment, distance, and a moment of empathy; at 19, seeing Piquette as perhaps "the only one, after all, who had heard the crying of the loons" (374)

SECONDARY

Acoose—does not see change in Vanessa's viewpoint

Laurence, Kertzer, Easingwood—Vanessa arrives at responsibility (L), compassion (K), recognition (E)

Ware—Vanessa does change; her "distance from her youthful excesses is the source of most of the [story's] irony" (76)

Characterization
PRIMARY

Vanessa as middle class, doctor's daughter; also as dynamic character, with changing perceptions of Piquette

SECONDARY

Acoose—Vanessa as static, transmitter of ideology

Laurence, Kertzer, Easingwood—Vanessa as developing more mature understanding, within limits

Point of view
PRIMARY

Story told from first-person point of view. Effect: enclosure within Vanessa's own perceptions; no authorial comment.

SECONDARY

Acoose, Ware: Laurence sees beyond Vanessa's viewpoint, but not far enough to repudiate stereotype of indigenous woman as victim. Fournier and Crey: stereotype of Indian as victim is destructive.

Figurative language

PRIMARY

Loons identified with unpeopled land (Dr. MacLeod); "squawkin' birds" (Piquette 275); suffering, Piquette, victims of white development (Vanessa at end of story)

SECONDARY

Acoose's critique of "princess of nature" vision could apply to this identification (81)

Ware: critics identify Indian and Métis with loons, but so does Laurence

Gadpaille: identification of Métis with nature makes story a "helpless lament" (qtd. in Ware 80)

This chart allows you to see major similarities and differences among your sources at a glance, and therefore lays the groundwork for formulating your research thesis statement.

Working on Your Own Assignment

Preliminary thinking and writing about your research topic will help you plan and carry out an efficient strategy for gathering material.

- Consider each possible topic carefully to clarify its demands.
- Choose a topic that interests you and narrow your focus to one or two specific research questions.
- Use appropriate methods of analysis and disciplinary or analytic categories (see Chapter 3 and Chapter 6) to gather primary material or explore your topic.
- Compile a working bibliography of secondary sources by using your library's online catalogue and online database services.
- For each secondary source, take down complete bibliographic information.
- For the sources you select to use in your research essay, make detailed notes in point form with short, carefully selected quotations for key ideas. Include page numbers for both quoted and paraphrased material.
- Make a chart that allows you to compare notes from all your research material (primary source[s], if used, as well as secondary sources) within appropriate categories.

Exercises

A.   Suppose that you were writing a research paper using David Suzuki's essay "It Always Costs" (Readings) as your primary source material. Write brief responses to each of the following questions. Save your material for possible use in the exercises for Chapter 11.

1. Formulate three different preliminary research questions you might ask in response to this essay. Then choose the one that most interests you and brainstorm for five minutes about that question.

2. How would you go about searching your library catalogue for material by David Suzuki? For material about David Suzuki?

3. Which online databases in your school library would be most appropriate for finding secondary material on your research question?

4. List five to ten methods of analysis relevant to your research question. Use disciplinary and/or analytic categories as appropriate.

5. List five strings of search terms likely to yield relevant material on your research question. These strings may consist of terms from the methods of analysis you listed above as well as biographic material on David Suzuki (see the opening pages of his essay in Readings).

B.   Suppose that you were writing a research paper using E. M. Forster's "My Wood" (Readings) as your primary source. Write brief responses to each of the following questions. Save your material for possible use in the exercises for Chapter 11.

1. Formulate three different preliminary research questions about the literary essay. Then choose the one that most interests you and brainstorm for five minutes about that question.

2. How would you go about searching your library catalogue for material by E. M. Forster? For material about E. M. Forster?

3. Which online databases in your school library would be most appropriate for finding secondary material on your research question?

4. List five to ten methods of analysis relevant to your research question. Use disciplinary or analytic categories as appropriate.

5. List five strings of search terms likely to yield relevant material on your research question. These strings may consist of terms from the methods of analysis you listed above as well as biographic material on E. M. Forster.

C.   Make research notes on Margaret Laurence's essay "Time and the Narrative Voice" (Readings) that would be appropriate for the sample research topic.

Works Cited

Acoose, Janice. "Fenced In and Forced to Give Up: Images of Indigenous Women in Selected Non-Indigenous Writers' Fiction." *Iskwewak—Kah' Ki Yaw Ni Wahkomakanak: Neither Indian Princesses nor Easy Squaws.* Toronto: Women's P, 1995. 69-88. Print.

Easingwood, Peter. "The Realism of Laurence's Semi-Autobiographical Fiction." *Critical Approaches to the Fiction of Margaret Laurence.* Ed. Colin Nicholson. Vancouver: U of British Columbia P, 1990. 119-32. Print.

Fournier, Suzanne, and Ernie Crey. *Stolen from Our Embrace: The Abduction of First Nations Children and the Restoration of Aboriginal Communities*. Vancouver: Douglas & McIntyre, 1997. Print.

Kertzer, Jon. *"That House in Manawaka": Margaret Laurence's* A Bird in the House. Toronto: ECW P, 1992. Print.

Laurence, Margaret. "Time and the Narrative Voice." *Margaret Laurence*. Ed. W. H. New. Toronto: McGraw-Hill Ryerson, 1977. 156-60. Print.

Ware, Tracy. "Race and Conflict in Garner's 'One-Two-Three Little Indians' and Laurence's 'The Loons.'" *Studies in Canadian Literature*. 23.2 (1998): 71-84. Print.

Writing Research Essays (11)

Sample Topic: Margaret Laurence's "The Loons"

When you have completed the preliminary stages outlined in Chapter 10, you are ready to compose your research essay. If you have made initial efforts to clarify your own thinking and have taken good notes on the secondary materials, the writing process will be easier than if you have attempted to keep everything in your own mind without writing things down.

This chapter highlights the importance of synthesizing your materials as you formulate a thesis, and as you draft and revise your essay. Synthesis is the combination of different elements into a complex whole. Weak research essays often result from a lack of meaningful connections between ideas or sources, leading to a fragmented or disconnected line of argument. Good research essays, in contrast, establish and develop meaningful links between the research materials, the subject of study, and the writer's viewpoint. As you draft and revise, however, your thinking may change, requiring changes in your thesis statement and essay structure, as the sample topic on Margaret Laurence's "The Loons" will demonstrate. So you also need to have the mental flexibility to make substantial revisions when they are called for.

STAGE 3 Formulating a Research Thesis Statement

Like other essays, a research essay is built upon a thesis statement: your opinion on your subject, supported by reasons. As you work out your draft research thesis statement, you must do so in relation to the research materials you have gathered. Your thesis may be similar to positions outlined in the secondary materials or different from them all. It should not simply echo any of them, however. Even if you agree with one of these positions, you will support your opinion by your own set of reasons. Then your essay will become one voice in a discussion among informed people.

STEP 1 Forming a Research Opinion

Before you formulate the opinion part of your thesis statement, check to see whether your preliminary research question still seems valid or whether it needs adjusting in light of your secondary sources. Then examine the categories you have used to compare your sources. What patterns of response to your research question do you find?

After analyzing case studies of addiction (primary material), for example, you may have decided on the following research question: is a cognitive model sufficient to explain the causes of addiction? When you review the secondary sources, however, you find few references to cognitive causes and many references to physiological causes, so you change your question to the following: is a disease model sufficient to explain the causes of addiction? Comparing your primary and secondary material leads you to this research opinion:

Draft research opinion	Academics in medical disciplines find the disease model sufficient, while substance abuse counsellors find this model insufficient, an opinion I share.

STEP 2 Supporting Your Opinion

The support for a thesis opinion usually comes from your own ideas about your subject or your analysis of primary material, along with the secondary sources that confirm your opinion. Since it is hard to combine so much in a single sentence, writers commonly refer to secondary material in a sentence or two preceding the thesis statement. Then they give their own reasons, which represent their distinctive contribution to the discussion, after the thesis opinion.

Remember that this version is not necessarily a final thesis statement. Although you arrived at this thesis statement in a systematic way, you may change your mind or discover new ideas as you draft your research essay and revise it.

Sample Topic For an example of how you would form a research opinion and support it, let us look at the sample topic on Margaret Laurence's "The Loons" (Readings).

You found secondary sources on "The Loons" that addressed the issue of whether Laurence portrays her main character, Vanessa MacLeod, as gaining a more mature understanding of the young Métis woman, Piquette Tonnerre, so this still seems a valid research question. Your answer has changed, however. On reviewing the patterns in the materials in your chart, you find yourself convinced by the critical positions developed by Janice Acoose, Tracy Ware, and Suzanne Fournier and Ernie Crey. You are persuaded that "The Loons" presents an Aboriginal person as a victim and in doing so reinforces a destructive stereotype. So you revise your preliminary opinion to reflect this change. In a sentence or two leading into this opinion, you summarize the differences among critics as you would for a pro–con argument (see Formulating an Evaluative Thesis Statement in Chapter 9), beginning with the critics you disagree with and ending with the critics you agree with. You then add to your thesis opinion a reference to the disciplinary categories you used in analyzing the story that best supports your position. Your tentative thesis statement would look something like this:

<table>
<tr>
<td>Tentative
thesis
statement</td>
<td>While critics like Kertzer and Easingwood agree that Vanessa MacLeod grows in understanding, critics like Acoose and Ware lay more emphasis on the persistence of destructive racial stereotypes in Vanessa's views and in the story as a whole. In this essay I will examine issues in narrative structure, characterization, point of view, and figurative language in "The Loons" to show that, while it initially appears that Margaret Laurence portrays Vanessa as achieving a more mature understanding of Piquette, in some ways this understanding is not mature at all, a fact Laurence does not appear to recognize.</td>
</tr>
</table>

This thesis statement contains all the elements it needs. Nevertheless, as you will see later, it does not reflect the writer's final thoughts on the subject, nor is it in a final polished form.

STAGE 4 Drafting

STEP 1 Sequencing Topics and Points

The basic principle for sequencing research essays, as for any other essay, is to try to maintain an order of ascending interest, beginning with topics that contradict or offer only weak support for your thesis and ending with topics that give the strongest evidence in its favour. Achieving this order may be complicated by the need to integrate your own analysis with your responses to secondary material. There is not one way to meet this need. You may discuss your responses to secondary material early in the essay and then move to your analysis; or, more often, you may have a mixture of your analysis and references to secondary material in most of your paragraphs. In every case, you will have to clarify the topics you plan to cover and the point you intend to make about each topic before you can figure out an effective sequence.

STEP 2 Making a Formal Outline

Making an outline is particularly valuable for the research essay, as the complexity of research material makes it easy to lose sight of paragraph topics. Although a regular draft outline will work for this purpose, you may be asked to hand in a *formal outline* as a guide for your reader. Some writers finish the essay first and then write an outline. Others make an outline before they draft the essay in order to work out the relationship among major points, minor points, and supporting evidence. An outline will help you maintain a balance between your own analysis and the material you have found in your sources.

To make a formal outline, write your thesis statement at the top of a page. Then list your major points with Roman numerals, your subpoints under each heading with capital letters, and evidence to support each sub-point with Arabic numerals. If you need a fourth level, use lowercase letters. For an example, see the sample topic below.

Sample Topic To work out an order of ascending interest for your topics and points, you consider the categories you've used for your chart comparing primary and secondary material. The categories of characterization and narrative structure offer most support for the idea of Vanessa's maturation, an idea you no longer support. You therefore decide to start with these paragraph topics and to follow them with paragraphs on point of view and figurative language, topics that directly support your case. You then make the following formal outline as a guide for writing your draft:

Writing Sample

Thesis
statement

In this essay I will examine issues in narrative structure, characterization, point of view, and figurative language in "The Loons" to show that, while it initially appears that Margaret Laurence portrays Vanessa as achieving a more mature understanding of Piquette, in some ways this understanding is not mature at all, a fact Laurence does not appear to recognize.

Major point
Subpoint
Evidence

I. Characterization

    A. Some critics suggest that Vanessa gains a more mature understanding, within limits.

        1. Quotation from Kertzer and analysis

        2. Quotation from Easingwood and analysis

    B. Another critic implies that Vanessa is a static character.

        1. Quotation from Acoose and analysis

    C. My own reading suggests that Vanessa is a dynamic, changing character, with increasing awareness.

        1. Quotation from story and analysis

Additional
points to be
expanded

II. Narrative Structure

    A. The story's stages are based around Vanessa's developing viewpoint.

    B. Evidence shows that her changes in understanding do structure the story.

    C. Some critics confirm this point.

III. Point of View

    A. The first-person point of view raises problems.

    B. Some critics argue that these problems reflect the limits of Laurence's vision.

    C. The destructive effects of the victim stereotype are well documented.

IV. Figurative Language

    A. The loons are associated with suffering and helplessness, both in the story and in the criticism.

    B. Some critics comment on the identification of Aboriginal peoples with "creatures of nature."

    C. The limits of Vanessa's vision and maturity are evident in this metaphor.

Remember that each section of the outline corresponds not to a single paragraph but to a topic; you may need more than one paragraph to discuss a topic fully.

STEP 3   Sketching the Introduction and Conclusion

Although it's generally best not to spend much time on introductions and conclusions when you are drafting, some writers cannot proceed effectively until they have written a good introduction. We will therefore give you some guidelines that you can use while you are drafting your introduction and conclusion or when you revise.

An *introduction* for a research essay will usually need the following:

- an explanation of the primary material (if any) and/or the subject that provides the context for your research question

- an indication of your research question

- a reference to the secondary material, providing an indication of its range and highlighting any point(s) of difference relevant to answering your research question

- a thesis statement that responds to primary material and/or subject in the context of the secondary material

A research essay conclusion will usually contain the following:

- a summary of the way in which the body of the essay has confirmed and extended the thesis statement

- a statement of the further implications of your project, which might include the call for more research or suggest ways your research applies to a broader area

So that you can see these checklists in use, in the following pages we have included a draft introduction and conclusion for the sample topic at the revision stage of the writing process.

STEP 4   Writing the Draft

Your main goal in writing a first draft is to get your ideas on paper, however rough the form. At this point you are still exploring your subject and working out the connections among your sources. Your draft may be much shorter than your final essay, for in revising you may expand your discussion of your sources, add details, or even develop a whole new line of argument. Remember that *revision* means "seeing again," rethinking every part of your essay, not merely correcting errors in grammar and spelling. If you are a writer who likes to craft each paragraph before moving on, you may want to consult the checklists on revising middle paragraphs (Stage 6, Step 2) before you write your draft.

STAGE 5   ## Revising Thesis Statement and Essay Structure: Relating to Your Sources

As you drafted your essay, you may have had the sense that you were wandering off-topic or developing new ideas. Now is the time to take a broad overview of your essay. Are you satisfied with your thesis statement? If not, how does it need to change? If your thesis statement still seems satisfactory, does the overall structure of the essay develop your reasons in a logical way? If not, how does it need to change?

You may find that, like many students struggling with research material, you have relied too heavily on particular sources or, alternatively, failed to use them enough.

You can tell that you have depended too much on your sources when your entire essay completely agrees with one of them or perhaps agrees consecutively with sources that turn out to disagree with each other. It is true that your opinion about your subject may not differ from the views of other writers you have consulted. If you were researching Britain's entry into World War I, for example, you might conclude, along with the historians you had consulted, that the British were initially disorganized and inefficient. The historians might identify different causes for this inefficiency. One source might argue that the main cause was Prime Minister Herbert Asquith's indecisiveness; another might blame the arrogance of Field Marshal Earl Kitchener; a third might blame the British class system and capitalist economics. You would be relying too heavily on your sources if you merely adopted the views of one historian and followed the same line of argument, or if you presented each historian's view without evaluating them all. You would need to backtrack, analyze the strengths and weaknesses of each historian's position, and then work out a revised thesis statement and essay structure.

The second problem arises from a failure to use research material in an integrated way. The thesis statement might take no account of the secondary material, or the secondary material might be used at random rather than to answer the research question. If your draft makes little use of your sources, you may need to make sure you understand each writer's main ideas or gather material that is more relevant.

When you have reviewed your draft, revise your thesis statement, if necessary. Then make note of any changes required to your essay structure on a revision outline (see Making a Revision Outline in Chapter 5).

Sample Topic

Revising the thesis statement   In drafting your research essay on "The Loons," you had the increasing sense that you were presenting too simple a case. When you review your thesis and the development of your points, you realize that you have essentially endorsed the positions developed by Janice Acoose and Tracy Ware. You wonder, though, whether the evidence in the story confirms their position: that Laurence is misguidedly endorsing Vanessa's identification of Piquette with the loons, and thus Aboriginal people with helpless victimhood. If, as Ware points out, Laurence treats the younger Vanessa's positions ironically, why should we assume that this irony disappears in the treatment of the older Vanessa's views? When consulting the story as you drafted, you became aware of the voice of an older narrator, introduced at the beginning and present at the end. When you reread the details of the ending in light of this older, ironic voice and Laurence's comments on time in "Time and the Narrative Voice," you decide that Laurence is not endorsing Vanessa's identification of Piquette with the loons but critiquing it.

When you revise your thesis statement, then, you indicate this more independent perspective and your deeper understanding of the story by moving the category of point of view to a more emphatic position, by making your opinion and reasons more precise, and by removing the claim that Laurence is not aware of the limitations of Vanessa's understanding.

Writing Sample

Revised thesis
statement

Critics Jon Kertzer and Peter Easingwood agree that Vanessa MacLeod grows in understanding, whereas critics Janice Acoose and Tracy Ware lay more emphasis on the persistence of destructive racial stereotypes in Vanessa's views and in the story as a whole. An analysis of characterization, narrative structure, figurative language, and point of view in "The Loons" suggests that, while Laurence shows Vanessa struggling with her conceptions of Piquette and maturing in certain ways, she also demonstrates Vanessa's inability to escape the historical and social limits of her understanding.

Revising essay structure   The changes in the thesis statement will mean changes in essay structure. You also realized as you wrote your draft that characterization and narrative structure are inseparable because each stage of the narrative focuses on a stage in Vanessa's development. In the revision column of your outline you make notes to expand your discussion of narrative structure, to examine the metaphor of the loons before discussing point of view, which has become a more significant topic, and to add a point about the link between the figurative language at the end of the story and Laurence's conception of time. For the results of these changes, see F. Smith's research essay "Laurence's 'The Loons': Insight or Stereotype?" (Readings: Sample Essays).

STAGE 6 Revising Individual Paragraphs: Integrating and Documenting

STEP 1 Revising the Introduction

Even if you used the checklist for research introductions (see Stage 4, Step 3) for drafting your essay, you will find it a helpful guide to revision. Assuming that you have already revised your presentation of secondary sources and your thesis statement itself, you may find that you have not succeeded in giving the context for your subject and/or primary material in a compact way, or that you have forgotten to mention your research question. We will demonstrate the revision of these elements through the sample topic.

Sample Topic The first half of the introductory paragraph of the draft research essay on "The Loons" reads as follows:

In her short story "The Loons," Margaret Laurence uses the memories of Vanessa at different stages of her life to create a unique and dynamic relationship between Vanessa and Piquette. Their relationship moves through certain stages as Vanessa grows up and comes to realize certain truths. As an eleven-year-old, Vanessa sees Piquette "in terms of romanticized notions of Indians" ("Time" 283); at fifteen, she remembers feeling "embarrassment and pity" ("Time" 283); at eighteen, Vanessa realizes that she is somewhat responsible for Piquette's demise.

These introductory sentences present one important aspect of the story's context, Vanessa's process of development; however, they do not explain who Vanessa and Piquette are, mention the research question, or identify the source of the quotations.

You might revise like this:

Writing Sample

Revised introductory sentences

Following the main character Vanessa MacLeod's development from the age of eleven to eighteen, Margaret Laurence's short story "The Loons" focuses on the white girl's relationship with a Métis girl named Piquette Tonnerre. Vanessa's attitudes change during the story—from naive romanticism to "embarrassment and pity" (Laurence, "Time" 283) to accepting her share of collective responsibility for Piquette's death. This final change allows the reader to think that Vanessa gains insight into her would-be friend's life, what Laurence herself called "the pain and bewilderment of one's knowledge of other people" (282). But does Laurence actually portray Vanessa as achieving a mature understanding of Piquette and of their relationship by the end of the story? Laurence critics provide a range of answers to this question.

You can read the whole of the revised introduction in the finished research essay, F. Smith's "Laurence's 'The Loons': Insight or Stereotype?" (Readings: Sample Essays).

STEP 2   Revising Middle Paragraphs: Integrating Sources

In drafting your essay, you probably used your research material in each of your middle paragraphs to varying degrees. One paragraph may present a key writer's position on your subject and your response; another paragraph may draw equally upon several secondary sources; a third may be devoted to your analysis of a primary source, with little reference to secondary sources. When you are ready to revise, you may discover that you have given too much or too little attention to your sources. Or, in trying to juggle your sources, you may have lost sight of the overall point or structure of your paragraph. Use the following checklist to help you identify where you need to revise.

CHECKLIST FOR REVISING MIDDLE PARAGRAPHS: INTEGRATING SOURCES

- Are the topic of the paragraph and your own point about it clearly set out in your topic sentence? Do the topic sentences, when read sequentially, guide the reader through each step of your analysis or argument?

- Does the order of points within the paragraph develop the analysis or argument in a logical way?

(Continued)

(Continued)

- Have you provided your own evidence to explain why you agree or disagree with points made by other writers? Don't rely on quotations from secondary sources to make important points for you.

- Have you made clear distinctions between your ideas and those of your sources? Introduce quotations and paraphrases by briefly mentioning the idea you wish to highlight, using appropriate transitional words and phrases, such as "Wong's study provides further support . . .; on the other hand, Friedman argues. . . ." (For more on this topic, see Part 3, H2 Quotations.)

- Have you provided enough details from primary and/or secondary sources to support your point? Have you included explanations that make the significance of those details apparent to your reader?

When you are trying to pull together material from a wide variety of sources, it's easy to get caught up in details and lose sight of the points those details are meant to support. In the following paragraph, for instance, the writer draws on three sources: J. M. Bynner, *The Young Smoker* (London: Her Majesty's Stationery Office, 1969); Bernard Mausner and Ellen S. Platt, *Smoking: A Behavioral Analysis* (New York: Pergamon, 1971); and Richard Olshavsky, *No More Butts: A Psychologist's Approach to Quitting Smoking* (Bloomington: Indiana UP, 1977). Although the paragraph provides adequate *details* in a mixture of summary and quotation, it does not provide enough *explanation* of the relationship between the topic sentence and the various studies; indeed, one of the studies seems to contradict the others.

Draft middle paragraph

The social causes of smoking have been established in a number of studies. According to B. Mausner and E. Platt, many smokers reported that they thought of smokers as daring and sophisticated and of non-smokers as sensible and careful (7). According to Richard Olshavsky, advertising does not seem either to inhibit or to promote cigarette smoking (98). In his study of the smoking habits of British schoolboys, J. M. Bynner discovered that "Boys who smoke thought of themselves as being fairly tough but not as tough as they would like to be. They, more than any other group, saw non-smokers as completely lacking in toughness and thus the act of giving up smoking involved identification with a group which had a very unattractive characteristic" (93).

Notice how the revised version links the topic sentence with the research details, explains the apparent contradiction in the studies, and maintains the mixture of summary and quotation:

Revised middle paragraph

The social causes of smoking have been established in a number of studies. Although the image of smokers conveyed by advertising may not be important, since, as Richard Olshavsky points out, advertising does not seem either to inhibit or to promote cigarette smoking (98), there is good evidence that the image smokers have of themselves is very important. In his study of the smoking habits of British schoolboys, J. M. Bynner discovered that "Boys who smoke thought of themselves as being fairly tough but not as tough as they would like to be. They, more than any other group, saw non-smokers as completely lacking in toughness and thus the act of giving up smoking involved identification with a group which had a very unattractive characteristic" (93). Adults seem to share this kind of thinking. According to B. Mausner and E. Platt, many smokers reported that they thought of smokers as daring and sophisticated and of non-smokers as sensible and careful (7).

In this instance, the paragraph could be revised effectively by merely rearranging its parts and rewriting a few sentences. More often, middle paragraphs need to be revised substantially, a process that can be quite time-consuming. Be prepared to reread your sources, rework the points you've made, and add new material.

STEP 3   Revising Middle Paragraphs: Documenting Sources

Learning how to integrate source material is a key step in learning to write a research essay. The next step is learning how to identify or *document* the sources you have used in a clear and unambiguous way. When you document sources, you tell readers exactly where you found quotations and paraphrased material so that, if they wish, they can locate each item for themselves. Using quotations and paraphrased material without identifying the source is called *plagiarism*. More exactly, plagiarism is the act, intentional or otherwise, of copying or borrowing words or ideas without properly acknowledging the original source. Plagiarism carries serious consequences, ranging from a failing grade to expulsion, so it's important to understand the different forms that plagiarism can take. Plagiarism occurs when

- a student hands in work done wholly or in part by another person
- portions of a submitted work are taken from another source without proper reference to that source

- a student paraphrases sections of another work without acknowledging the source
- ideas in a work are borrowed, derived, or developed from another
source without reference to that source (for example, "checking a
few internet sites for ideas")

Last-minute panic or a lack of ideas leads some students into *intentional
plagiarism*—deliberately copying large sections of a published work, string-
ing together unacknowledged quotations from several works, or handing
in an essay written by someone else. If you give yourself plenty of time and
follow the guidelines we have suggested for gathering material, you won't
find yourself tempted to plagiarize.

Unintentional plagiarism, on the other hand, generally results from losing track of your sources as you take notes and draft your essay. The surest
way to avoid unintentional plagiarism is to learn how to document research
materials properly. That means giving in-text references in addition to
including full bibliographic information for each source in a Works Cited
or References page at the end. The examples of plagiarism that follow will
demonstrate how to use your source material without plagiarizing.

First, imagine writing an essay on Michael Ondaatje's novel *Coming
through Slaughter.* You might come across a published article—a hypothetical example by S. Smith—that is relevant to your essay topic.

EXCERPT OF PUBLISHED WRITING

Michael Ondaatje's fragmented writing in *Coming through Slaughter* stylistically echoes the
improvised, unpredictable music and actions of the main character, Buddy Bolden.

Plagiarized words

In *Coming through Slaughter,* Ondaatje's fragmented writing stylistically
echoes Buddy Bolden's music.

Revision

S. Smith has argued that Ondaatje's "fragmented writing . . . stylistically
echoes" (32) Buddy Bolden's music.

Here the point is attributed to the author, quotation marks and ellipses
indicate the words quoted, and the page reference ensures that readers
could find the quotation.

Plagiarized idea

Michael Ondaatje writes in a style similar to Buddy Bolden's jazz music.

Revision

Michael Ondaatje writes in a style similar to Buddy Bolden's jazz (Smith 32).

As you can see, the only difference between the plagiarized idea and the revision is the inclusion of the parenthetical reference giving the source of the idea. While it is generally better to introduce quotations and paraphrases by at least mentioning the author's name, the writer is no longer guilty of plagiarism. If you have kept track of your sources while you are gathering material, you can easily supply any missing information when you revise. You will find it difficult to document your sources accurately, however, if your notes do not distinguish quotations from paraphrases as well as paraphrases from your own ideas.

When you revise, use the following checklist to help you identify problems with documentation.

CHECKLIST FOR REVISING MIDDLE PARAGRAPHS: DOCUMENTING SOURCES

- Have you put quotation marks around all quoted material and identified the source, including page number, in the style required for your assignment?

- Are quotations accurate? Are they used effectively?

- Have you identified the source of all paraphrased material in the style required for your assignment?

- Have you documented the origin of any ideas that you borrowed, developed, or derived from another source?

- Have you given full bibliographic details for each source you used, primary or secondary, in a Works Cited or References list, in the style required?

- Does your Works Cited or References list contain *all* the works mentioned in your research essay? Does it contain *only* the works mentioned in your essay?

You will find further information on quotations and on MLA and APA documentation styles in Part 3, H3 Documentation.

Sample Topic Let us suppose that your draft research essay on Laurence's story includes the following paragraph on the metaphor of the loons. How well are the research materials used to present the various interpretations of this metaphor and to advance the thesis? Are sources appropriately introduced and documented? Keep the checklists for integrating and documenting sources in mind as you read.

The expectations imposed on Piquette along with Vanessa's "white" version of history make it nearly impossible for the two girls to see eye to eye and become friends. Vanessa's "understanding of reality is filtered through a racist, classist, and male-privileged ideological value system" (Acoose, p. 79 Fenced). She does not seem to realize that Aboriginal peoples have been among the most disadvantaged people in Canada (Fournier and Crey, p. 82), so little regarded that white people have found it justified to take away large numbers of their children for adoption. Laurence uses the loons, whose "voices belonged to a world separated by eons from [Vanessa's] neat world" (p. 385), as a metaphor for the First Nations people of Canada. Dr. MacLeod remarks that the loons must have sounded plaintive and pitiful before any person, meaning any white person, ever set foot here. In saying this, it is understood that the MacLeods believe the Aboriginal peoples of Canada to have always been as they are: destitute and powerless victims. This is a misrecognition of such people. Tracy Ware says this misrecognition is also Laurence's. Critics like Michelle Gadpaille say the story is a lament for the passing of a way of life.

These are some of the problems you might identify:

Integrating sources

- Topic sentence about loons buried in the middle of the paragraph
- No clear line of argument through the paragraph; need to reorganize
- Little use of own evidence; most points made by critics
- Not clear whose point it is in sentence beginning "In saying this, it is understood . . . "; not clear whose term "misrecognition" is
- A brief explanation of loon metaphor and details of its first occurrence, but no discussion of the metaphor at the end of the story

Documenting sources

- Quotations from the character Dr. MacLeod and the critics Gadpaille and Ware not in quotation marks; parenthetical citations not in MLA style
- Need to replace Acoose quotation with quotation more relevant to loons

- First paraphrase from Fournier and Crey documented; second paraphrase not documented
- "The Loons," Acoose, Fournier and Crey, and Ware should appear in Works Cited
- Gadpaille is quoted in Ware, which should be acknowledged, but Gadpaille should not appear as an entry in Works Cited

Revised along these lines, this paragraph expands into three, as you will see in paragraphs 10, 11, and 12 of the sample research essay by F. Smith, "Laurence's 'The Loons': Insight or Stereotype?" (Readings: Sample Essays).

STEP 4   Revising the Conclusion

You may have used the checklist for research essay conclusions (Stage 4, Step 3) in drafting your essay; you should certainly use it in revising. Does your conclusion summarize and draw together the major points of your essay? Does it show whether your research question has been answered in the way that you claimed it would? Does it sound mechanical?

You can avoid a simple repetition of your thesis by making reference to the way some of your initial ideas have been developed. You can also suggest the larger implications for your thesis; that is, you can explain how, if you had more time and space to write, you would develop your ideas in a wider context. In this way you will show that you have thought about not only the details of your subject but also the larger scope of the project.

Sample Topic Let us suppose that you have written the following conclusion to your draft:

Draft conclusion   Vanessa was raised with certain ideals and her reality has been filtered in such a way that her world has been processed to give her an inherently stereotypical view of indigenous people. As they are, they do not fit into Vanessa's little world; therefore she has an idea of what they should be like so that they will fit. This in turn affects the way she treats Piquette. Laurence works through the steps, first by making Vanessa assume that Piquette is like a historical Native, familiar with the forests and the lands of Canada. Vanessa then realizes Piquette's need to fit in, but cannot allow her to because of who she is. Finally, Piquette dies and Vanessa can only think of how uncomfortable Piquette made her, and she wants to forget the look she saw in Piquette's eyes the moment she really saw her. In her short story, Laurence has used stereotypical images of Aboriginal Canadians and their history to create an adverse relationship between Vanessa and Piquette.

This conclusion neither makes an effective summary nor develops the implications of the research. It does refer to the research question and reaffirm the thesis about Vanessa's maturation, but it presents this view in a way that does not sum up the actual analysis. This is a common mistake, springing from the desire not to repeat what has already been said.

Your aim in revising is to summarize the analysis in a way that presents the argument in an overall—and thus new—light, especially when you add a statement of implications. So you reinstate the categories you used as paragraph topics and show how your points about them have answered your research question. Then you review your judgments about the secondary sources and their contribution to the question of stereotyping. You decide that a point about the way Laurence critiques stereotyping can be your statement of the broader implications of your essay. The conclusion that results from these revisions is the final paragraph in F. Smith, "Laurence's 'The Loons': Insight or Stereotype?" (Readings: Sample Essays).

Working on Your Own Assignment

In writing and revising a research essay, your goal is to integrate your own ideas about your subject with information and ideas drawn from secondary sources.

- Formulate a thesis statement by reviewing your notes to find (a) the connections between the material you have gathered and your research question, and (b) the most important similarities and differences between your ideas and the ideas expressed in your secondary sources.

- Organize your material by making a formal outline that sets out the main ideas in your essay. Indicate in the outline where you want to bring in secondary material and the point you want to make about it.

- As you write your draft, keep track of your sources by putting the author and page number in parentheses after each quotation and after any paraphrased material (for APA style, include the year of publication).

- Check the thesis statement and overall structure of your draft against your formal outline. Watch for paragraphs that are too long. You may need to subdivide them, to shorten quotations, or to delete unimportant or irrelevant material. Make a note of any necessary changes.

- As you read through each middle paragraph, ask yourself two questions: What is the main point? How does this material support my thesis? If your topic sentence does not answer these questions, revise it. Put all the important points in your own words and include quotations, references, and other evidence to support them. Make clear why you agree or disagree with the opinions of other writers.

- In both your introduction and your conclusion, connect your own thinking with your research material.

- Make sure that you have documented all your sources, both by using parenthetical references in the essay and by giving complete bibliographical details in a list of Works Cited or References.

Exercises

A. Make a formal outline of the sample research essay, "Laurence's 'The Loons': Insight or Stereotype?" (Readings: Sample Essays). Compare this outline with the outline used in writing the draft (Stage 4, Step 2). What changes do you observe? Consider such things as the topics covered, the points made, and the secondary sources used.

B. Janice Acoose argues that Canadian literature needs more positive representations of indigenous characters by indigenous writers. Find a short story by an indigenous Canadian writer that includes positive images of indigenous characters. To find a suitable story, consult anthologies of Aboriginal writers or search the library catalogue for books by writers such as Thomas King, Lee Maracle, and Jeannette Armstrong. Find secondary sources to inform your reading of the story. Then write a research essay comparing the story you found with "The Loons." Use the material on "The Loons" in this text, including the research essay by F. Smith, in any way that suits your comparison.

C. Draft and revise a research essay on the topic you chose from Exercise A or B, Chapter 10.

Writing Research Essays across the Curriculum (12)

Sample Topic: Influences of Social Media

Stage 1   **Clarifying Research Topics**
> **Step 1**   Defining a Preliminary Research Question

Stage 2   **Finding and Gathering Materials**
> **Step 1**   Gathering Material from Primary Sources
> **Step 2**   Forming a Preliminary Opinion
> **Step 3**   Finding Secondary Sources
> **Steps 4, 5**   Evaluating Secondary Sources, Taking Notes, and Comparing
>   Source Material

Stage 3   **Formulating a Research Thesis Statement**

Stage 4   **Drafting**
> **Step 1**   Sequencing Topics and Points
> **Step 2**   Making a Formal Outline
> **Step 3**   Sketching the Introduction and Conclusion
> **Step 4**   Writing the Draft

Stage 5   **Revising the Thesis Statement and Essay Structure: Relating to Your Sources**
> **Step 1**   Revising the Thesis

Stage 6   **Revising Individual Paragraphs: Integrating and Documenting**
> **Step 1**   Revising the Introduction
> **Step 2**   Revising Middle Paragraphs: Integrating Sources
> **Step 3**   Revising the Conclusion

As a user of this text book, you will be approaching this material in the context of a writing or composition course, a literature course, a communications course, or an English course. For many, if not most, post-secondary programs, there is usually some writing requirement built in to the curriculum, as most educators would agree that the abilities to write and to express ideas clearly are valuable skills in almost all situations. As we mentioned in Chapter 1, the skills of thinking, organizing, and writing that are involved in essay writing are fundamental to almost all intellectual and professional pursuits. Engineers require math and science skills, yet they also write reports. Business people need math and economic skills, yet they also write business plans, proposals, and letters. Social workers require interpersonal and listening skills, yet they also write client reports and reviews. In fact, with the increasing versatility in technology and its various applications, writing is becoming more, rather than less, common in almost all situations, not only in work but also in life generally. As recently as twenty years ago, most people did not email or text at all; now it is a daily habit for most people in the developed world. We are constantly engaged with texts, images, videos, and all types of information. Even texting shorthand is changing the nature of language, and we need to think about the applicability and the appropriateness of our textual communications. The challenge is to produce, to receive, and to process information—in short, to make sense of it and to engage with it in meaningful ways.

The purpose of this final chapter is to demonstrate the research and the writing processes in a fairly conventional mode of academic writing. While the previous chapters on research focused on an example of literary analysis and literary research, this chapter demonstrates how those same reading, writing, and researching skills are central to all disciplines of study, not simply writing, literature, or English. As the writers of this textbook, we explicitly acknowledge our own backgrounds in writing and literature and our own possible biases, yet we also maintain that the written word (or textual production of all varieties) is probably the most central and important means to acquire and to distribute information and knowledge in our lives. Knowing how to shape and to control our language is vital to good work. The topic discussed in this chapter is one that could be addressed in an essay in any number of disciplines. It would be relevant to courses, for example, in sociology, popular culture, or general education, to name a few. This chapter is meant to be studied in conjunction with Chapters 10 and 11, and builds upon the material presented in those chapters.

The topic we present in this chapter is social media, particularly Facebook, and how it influences our daily lives and our perceptions of ourselves and our world. We will begin by demonstrating how we may approach this topic from a variety of perspectives and then proceed to narrow down the topic to the subject of identity formation. The research question we pose is this: How do people construct their identity or sense of "self" on a platform like Facebook? What features or topics influence their self-presentation? What kinds of things do people post? What role does the "like" function play in identity formation?

The broad context of social media has taken shape over the last approximately twenty years. With the development of personal computer technology in the latter half of the twentieth century and the explosion of the internet in the twenty-first century, online communication is an undeniably central force in our lives. It seems that almost every business or service has an online presence, from banking to news media to school registration to paying parking tickets to shopping and beyond. For example, traditional media outlets like television now feature so-called interactive broadcasts where they utilize online technologies to show maps of the world, weather reports, user-uploaded video, Twitter posts, and other types of content. Online communication has radically changed the speed and the ways by which we acquire and share information, and it is changing our experiences of the world, from posting pictures of our food to participating in an overthrow of a national government. Social media is one significant dimension of this evolving medium.

STAGE 1 Clarifying Research Topics

As we said at the outset of this book, writing can be a complicated and messy affair. The step-by-step approach we outline in this book is only a guide. Some steps may require more or less effort for any given project, depending on the nature of the project. You will need to think about your purpose and processes in writing when deciding what to do at any given step. For example, in the literary example of Margaret Laurence, there is considerable significance for the primary text of the short story. In this chapter, the primary text of Facebook is quite a different kind of textual example. It is not really literary. It includes alternate types of media like sound, images, and video. And, for most of us, our experiences are largely anecdotal as users. Therefore, Step 1 of Gathering Material from Primary Sources in Stage 2 of Finding and Gathering Materials from Chapter 10 may not require as much time for an analysis of Facebook as it would for a literary short story. We could certainly spend a lot of time gathering material from Facebook, but it is a rather different kind of activity from literary analysis. Laurence's deliberation about historical memory in "Time and the Narrative Voice" is perhaps not as immediately relevant to a Facebook picture of someone's lunch. Yet, we can still consider the nature and subject of representations, as Aimée Morrison does in her article about the rhetoric of Facebook (Readings).

In what follows here, we offer a similar but modified progression through the previous chapters' stages and steps for writing a research essay.

STEP 1 Defining a Preliminary Research Question

It is important to set out a preliminary research question that explains what question you will be answering, or what problem you will be addressing, in your research paper. If you are writing a history paper, you might be addressing what happened to a particular culture or group during a war. If you are writing a sociology paper about the internet, you might ask how trends of internet usage have changed in particular societies over time. The discipline in which you are working will help shape the kinds of research questions you will ask and answer for your essay.

Know your discipline so that you can answer the research question effectively. For instance, in an English class, instructors generally are not looking for essays that analyze the characters of novels psychologically, using references to psychology books and referring to characters as if they were real people: they are interested in a literary analysis, not a psychological one. Conversely, psychology instructors are generally not looking for linguistic analysis of psychological theories. It's also important that you define key terms in your research question and make sure you understand those terms from the perspective of the discipline within which you are working.

Sample Topic Let's consider how you might define a preliminary research question in relation to our sample topic, an analysis of the social media network Facebook. Upon researching and contemplating the social media network, you discover that Facebook is currently the largest and arguably the most significant social media platform. Estimates place the number of Facebook users between 800 million and one billion as of 2014. If Facebook were a country, it would be one of the largest by population on the planet. Given the size of this population, it is extremely difficult, if not impossible, to generalize about Facebook users. Perhaps the only thing all users have in common is that they have a Facebook profile. Yet it is partly this term *profile* that will concern us in this chapter. Why would someone create a profile? What is necessary to create a profile? And, what does someone do with a profile? For our purposes here, we are sticking with individual profiles, not business, group, or other types of profiles.

These broad questions may, at first, seem obvious or irrelevant. Yet these broad questions are starting points for disciplinary analysis. There is a common saying that if all you have is a hammer, then everything looks like a nail. In academic circles, this is called "groupthink," where everyone begins to see things in the same way. Establishing disciplinary categories of analysis is very useful in academic writing, yet it is also important to keep in mind that different disciplines approach the same subject from different perspectives and with different assumptions. It is often helpful to question your own, or your discipline's, assumptions about a topic.

For example, Facebook's primary colours are white and blue, and someone had to decide on these colours. This is a design or aesthetic issue, and you should consider whether or not an aesthetic standard is appropriate to your analysis. If you were working in a marketing field, the colour scheme may be relevant to your users' tastes, yet, if you were a computer programmer looking at speed and functionality, the colours may be totally irrelevant. Similarly, Facebook asks you certain questions when you register: gender, date of birth, religious and political views, relationship status, etc. This information concerns demographics, administration, and marketing, among other things. A marketer uses this data to sell or promote products; a programmer thinks about storing and correlating the data. Each Facebook profile must have a consistent style design with content display and links to friends, interests and likes, advertising, and other objects of interest. This is a design issue as well as a programming issue. As a company, Facebook must make revenue. It must market itself and its product to interested parties. Facebook has likely made very strategic decisions about these kinds of questions of interactions and objectives. What often appears to be a relatively banal process of logging in to Facebook to see a picture of your friend's cat is actually a very complex interface of programming, design, conceptualization, marketing, and other factors to deliver an easy and agreeable experience for the user. You may often simply gloss over an activity as meaningless or merely fun when, in fact, it is an incredibly frequent and resource-intensive habit that engages hundreds of millions of people on a daily basis.

While any of these topics would warrant further examination and research, you will need to narrow down the focus of your research, defining the research question you will address. You decide to examine the role and function(s) of the user on Facebook. You will analyze the ways in which users construct profiles and, by extension, versions of themselves in the online environment. You will also consider the conditions under which Facebook collects and uses user profiles. Your preliminary research opinion will be that Facebook offers a very limited and incomplete vehicle for identity formation, one that may negatively impact a user's self-esteem because of its reliance on the validation of others through the mechanism of "likes."

STAGE 2 Finding and Gathering Materials

STEP 1 Gathering Material from Primary Sources

You will need to be familiar with primary sources in the discipline within which you are working. In history, for example, primary sources are actual documents from the time period under study: a letter from Canada's first Prime Minister, a newspaper article from the Victorian period. Secondary sources in history, on the other hand, are scholarly articles, books, or textbooks written about those primary documents or written about historical events. In the social sciences, such as psychology or sociology, primary sources are often in the form of first-hand interviews or surveys. In English courses, primary sources consist of the work or works of literature that you'll be analyzing, such as novels, poems, plays, or films. Once you've determined your primary source or sources, you'll need to determine what kind of material to gather from them. Then, you'll use analytic or disciplinary categories to organize your material.

Sample Topic Facebook is a large subject of study, and it is impossible to comment on all aspects of it. It is crucial to narrow down the subject of study, and the disciplinary categories you bring to the topic will determine the kinds of materials you will gather from analyzing Facebook. For your essay on Facebook, you decide to examine how users represent themselves, how users perceive others, and how Facebook is structured.

STEP 2 Forming a Preliminary Opinion

Once you have gathered material from your primary source, think about and write down your preliminary opinion of it. As we noted in Chapter 10 (Gathering Material for Research Essays), this preliminary opinion is not yet a thesis statement, since you haven't done enough analysis and research to form a thesis statement. However, having a preliminary opinion of your material will help you start to focus your research essay. It will be helpful to take notes on your primary sources and then write your opinion about various aspects of those sources. In your notes, ask and answer pertinent questions about the primary sources in order to come to a preliminary opinion on them.

Sample Topic The primary source of Facebook is mostly your own impressions of it, based on your experiences as a user of the site. While your individual responses will be largely subjective, it is worth interrogating why you hold your beliefs. For example, have you ever considered how the "likes" on your status affect how you feel? Do you appreciate it when someone "likes" one of your posts? How often do you "like" other people's posts? Do you usually post positive or negative (or both?) status updates on Facebook? Is it important how many "friends" you have? Your responses to these types of questions will help you understand your attitudes toward Facebook. For the purposes of the sample topic, you assume the position of a writer who uses Facebook but is wary of and critical toward Facebook's ulterior interests, specifically data collection and marketing.

STEP 3   Finding Secondary Sources

Secondary sources are resources you read about your topic. As we outline in Chapter 10, there are many sources for finding information about a particular topic. Most instructors will require you to use scholarly resources, rather than general interest ones. Make sure to check with your instructor about acceptable secondary sources for your paper, but generally you will want to consult library databases and catalogues for relevant scholarly articles and books in your discipline and on your topic.

It is important to remember that any given database may house thousands or hundreds of thousands of scholarly articles, and many databases can be subject specific (say, law) or interdisciplinary (say, science or humanities). So, choosing which databases (and subsequently which journals and articles) to consult and to use will inform and shape your knowledge and writing about the subject. For example, simply using the keyword *Facebook* in the database *ProQuest Science Journals* quickly yields results from diverse sources such as *Journal of Alcohol and Drug Education*, *Anthropological Quarterly*, and *The New England Journal of Medicine*. Each of these journals will generally convey its own scholarly approach to research, as an anthropologist will likely approach the subject of Facebook with a different set of tools from a medical doctor publishing in a medical journal.

Sample Topic If you have first-hand experience with Facebook, you will have personal and anecdotal evidence that informs your opinion about Facebook. Some of us generally like it; others generally dislike it. We joined for different reasons: the urging of friends, a desire to connect with long-lost people, business relations, fan pages, work-related activities. You might have a variety of types of friends, from close friends whom we see on a regular basis in real life to people who live halfway across the world, to work colleagues, to family members, and possibly to random people or fictional personalities. There are those friends who post everything about their daily lives and those friends who never post but consistently lurk. Some post only personal information; others post social or political concerns. Some people only ever comment on others and never post about themselves. You decide that you have a relatively uncontroversial or common stance toward Facebook. You share a moderate amount of personal information with the intent of keeping interested friends informed about the progression of your significant life events.

For this example, we will use the library databases to find journal articles on the subject. In gathering secondary materials from the database *Academic Search Complete*, you conduct a search using terms like *Facebook*, *identity*, *construction*, *personality*, *subject*, and their variations. After consulting a number of secondary sources, you narrow your focus to these three articles:

> Chou, Hui-Tzu Grace, and Nicholas Edge. "'They Are Happier and Having Better Lives than I Am': The Impact of Using Facebook on Perceptions of Others' Lives." *Cyberpsychology, Behavior and Social Networking* 15.2 (2012): 117-121. Print.
>
> McNeill, Laurie. "There Is No 'I' in Network: Social Networking Sites and Posthuman Auto/Biography." *Biography* 35.1 (2012): 65-82. Print.
>
> Morrison, Aimée. "Facebook and Coaxed Affordances." *Identity Technologies; Constructing the Self Online*. Eds. Anna Poletti and Julie Rak. Madison, WI: U of Wisconsin P, 2013. 112-131. Print. (A slightly shortened version of Morrison's article appears in the Readings)

STEPS 4 and 5 Evaluating Secondary Sources, Taking Notes, and Comparing Source Material

Make sure that the secondary sources that you have consulted are relevant to your discipline and to the topic at hand. Some topics may be approached from a variety of disciplinary angles. If you are writing a research paper for a psychology class, you will want to take a psychological approach to the problem and consult articles within the field of psychology. If you are writing a research paper for a history class, by contrast, you will need to take a historical approach and consult articles and books within the field of history. Assess your secondary sources and compare the kinds of information they provide relative to your discipline and focus. You may wish to make notes, charts, or columns to help you compare and contrast the articles at hand, and to assess their relevance and importance. Consult Chapter 10 for more details and information on how to take notes for your research paper.

Sample Topic If you employ your summary skills from Chapter 2 and take the time to understand and to summarize the arguments of the secondary sources, you will find that Morrison and McNeill are longer and more qualitative in their analyses of Facebook. Chou and Edge, by contrast, are more quantitative. Qualitative analysis is more concerned with the intrinsic qualities of a subject (its qualities) and seeks to understand underlying motivations and provide insights into a problem, whereas quantitative analysis is more numerical and seeks to gather quantifiable, measurable information, like frequency and distribution, about a subject (its quantity). You can tell the difference in these critics' approaches fairly quickly by Chou and Edge use of data and statistical analysis in contrast to the rhetorical, historical, and philosophical analyses of Morrison and McNeill's. It is beyond the scope of this chapter to discuss the advantages, disadvantages, and reasons behind qualitative and quantitative approaches, but it is important to realize that you should not fall into a simple privileging of one type of research over another based on the distinction between qualitative and quantitative analyses, as most disciplines engage in both to differing degrees.

STAGE 3   Formulating a Research Thesis Statement

In forming a research opinion and supporting that opinion, you should accurately summarize and represent the research materials in your essay as they pertain to your ideas and argument. A common tendency among beginning researchers is to feel overwhelmed or exhausted by the research or to find themselves simply agreeing with the conclusions drawn from the research. While this is a common occurrence, it is important to keep in mind that there are almost always questions about any given subject. If there weren't questions to be considered, the matter would be solved (or, perhaps, unknowable) and no work would be necessary. Recognizing this need for discussion is central to understanding the reasons behind the research materials you encounter in the library and elsewhere. Be sure that your thesis statement is your educated opinion, not the opinion of critics, although you should be able to explain how the critics' opinions relate to your own, and to what extent you agree and disagree with them. The stronger thesis statements for research essays either build upon and add to the critics' opinions, or are related to but distinctly different from them.

Sample Topic

In summarizing the three articles you have chosen for your research paper on Facebook, you make the following brief assessments for your own understanding:

> Chou and Edge survey college students and conclude that Facebook users tend to represent themselves positively in status updates, and frequent users of Facebook tend to see other users as generally happier and more satisfied than themselves.

McNeill argues that the historical idea of a stable and evolving self is not necessarily the most useful model for human subjectivity in the digital age. Rather, she suggests that we reconceptualize identity as a networked self that cooperates with technology to access multiple sites and means for exchanging and constructing meaning.

Morrison focuses on the rhetorical structures of status updates and suggests that Facebook wants users to backfill their "timeline" not so much to explain what is happening now as much as to know about the histories and backgrounds of the users.

STAGE 4   Drafting

STEP 1   Sequencing Topics and Points

The major drawback of a standard five-paragraph essay model is that it presupposes that there are three points in any given essay. Students sometimes think about essays as having "three points" as a starting place to begin writing. The same kind of problem can emerge when writing research essays. As long as a writer has collected some "really good quotations" from secondary sources, then the writer may feel ready to begin writing. One problem with this approach is that it privileges the form or structure of the essay (three points or three quotations) over the content of the essay (what you really want to argue). Often, arranging and sequencing points is more complicated than simply itemizing three things in a series. Assess the material you've gathered from your primary and secondary sources, and the preliminary opinion at which you've arrived. Think about how many points you have, based on the material you've gathered, and arrange your material accordingly. As in other kinds of essays, sequence your points in ascending order of interest so that each point builds upon the previous one.

STEP 2   Making a Formal Outline

Making an outline is an important step when writing a research paper because it helps you balance your own opinion with the opinions of critics. A research paper in any discipline is not a research report. That is, it isn't a report on what others have said about the topic. Rather, it is your own argument or educated opinion on the topic, based on an analysis of critics' works. Each section of your essay should incorporate your own opinion or analysis of the topic supported by evidence from your primary and secondary sources.

Sample Topic Below is an example of an outline that you have created for your research essay on Facebook.

Writing Sample

Tentative thesis statement I argue that, while Facebook can have positive benefits of keeping people in contact with one another, the detrimental effects of inaccurate perceptions of the world and low self-esteem warrant a more critical reception of the information on the site and the amount of time spent on the site.

I. Introduction
   A. Statement of topic and context
   B. Introduction of research materials
   C. Thesis statement

II. Topic and Context
   A. Facebook and identity formation
   B. Ways of representing self
      1. positive
      2. negative
   C. Introduction of key terms
      1. friend
      2. profile
      3. affordance
      4. constraint

III. Research
   A. Morrison on data collection
      1. friend or user
      2. update or data
   B. Argument by analogy: Facebook as a mall
   C. McNeill on self
      1. discreet individual
      2. networked entity
   D. Chou and Edge: Facebook negatively impacts self-esteem

IV. Conclusion
   A. Reasons for using Facebook
      1. friends
      2. commerce
      3. other?
   B. Limit use

STEP 3   Sketching the Introduction and Conclusion

Most academic books on any given subject will begin with a chapter of introduction. Ask yourself: when do you think the author writes the introduction? Most authors will tell you that the introduction is usually written at the end of the project. That is, the introductory chapter is a fiction that makes the rest of the work look like it knew where it was going. You, like an author of an academic book, might best write your introduction after you've written the research essay. A research project, like an essay, is a working-through of an idea or argument. Many authors are not sure where they will end up, so it is quite impossible to write an introduction at the beginning of a project. An author may have some vague idea of how it might turn out, but it is only after you have arrived at a conclusion that you know where you are. Therefore, if you decide to write your introduction before you write the essay, it's important to revise your introduction substantially after you have written a draft and therefore thought through all of the implications of your topic.

So, think of it this way: the introduction is really the conclusion. The conclusion is really the next step in the process. The Canadian author bpNichol commented that the problem with conclusions is that they conclude. In other words, a conclusion is not supposed to stop or to shut down work; rather, conclusions should be seen as foundations for further work in an area. For the introduction, tell your reader about your conclusions. For the conclusion, tell your reader why it is important that you have arrived at this point and explain the possibilities for further work from this point onward.

Sample Topic   In your essay on Facebook, the introduction states both a positive and negative outcome of Facebook use. It is positive because it enables people to keep in touch. It is negative because people tend to represent themselves selectively, which can lead to detrimental effects on others' self-perceptions. The conclusion similarly states that the author will continue to use Facebook, but with a greater awareness of the drawbacks or pitfalls of the site.

STEP 4   Writing the Draft

Most people have probably heard about "writer's block," the idea that writers have trouble putting words on a page. While this is certainly a true phenomenon, an equally difficult challenge is revision. Often, there is not a clear distinction between drafting and revising, as the two can happen more or less simultaneously. You may type a sentence and then immediately go back and rewrite it. Or you may think carefully about a phrasing of a sentence before you actually write it down: the formulation or revision simply takes place in your head.

It's best to set aside a full draft for a day or two and then return to it to do some substantial revisions. This is the case even if you have been writing and rewriting as you create your essay. In order to have time to revise, it's important to begin writing your essay early, well before the deadline. Beginning early will also help you avoid unnecessary anxiety and writer's block. Drafting is a constant process of writing and revision, which cannot be easily explained or compartmentalized in a series of stages and steps. While the stages and steps outlined in this book are helpful, it's important to keep in mind that writing is often messier than these stages and steps indicate, and that writing often involves going back and forth between such stages and steps.

Sample Topic When reviewing your research materials for your essay, it may initially appear that all the authors of the articles you have chosen for your secondary sources are making a similar point, namely that Facebook has negative effects. It would be reductive simply to say that all the authors are against Facebook. Rather, good critical thinking and careful written explanation will allow a writer to express the more subtle critiques of each research source. Morrison, for example, is concerned with how the structure and writing of status updates help contribute to an autobiographical textual production while Facebook simultaneously "harvests" (298) user data alongside identity construction. McNeill has similar concerns about autobiography and identity construction, yet she foregrounds the changing possibilities for identity formation away from a discreet or singular interaction to a more complex and technological process. She does not categorically condemn these changes as inauthentic or negative; rather, she keeps open the possibility for understanding and employing these new mechanisms as, perhaps, unavoidable and, possibly, beneficial means to create more robust and dynamic identities in the future. Facebook may have negative effects, but we can work to redress them and build a better platform for self-expression; one, perhaps, free of highly commercialized interests.

STAGE 5 ## Revising the Thesis Statement and Essay Structure: Relating to Your Sources

When you re-evaluate your thesis statement and essay structure, check to see how you have integrated your secondary sources. As we explain in detail in Chapter 11, it's important to create a balance between showing that you understand the critics' views and expertise on the subject, and relating your own educated opinion on the subject in relation to theirs. Make sure, as well, that you have incorporated an analysis of both the primary sources and the secondary ones. Different disciplines will require different emphases on primary and secondary sources. In all disciplines, your own opinion in relation to the sources should be central to your argument.

It is worth noting the nature of thesis statements in relation to the work you are doing and the audience you are addressing. If we accept that one of the primary purposes of an essay is to persuade your audience into believing something and acting on that belief, then we are thinking of an essay as changing people and their behaviours. Like the difference between an explicit and implicit thesis, a thesis can be highly prescriptive in telling readers what to think and what to do, or it can be more descriptive by giving readers the necessary information to make an informed decision on their own. It is a question of style and purpose. If we use a simple and silly example like smoking, you can have a highly prescriptive thesis that commands the reader to do something ("don't smoke!"), a relatively clear cause-and-effect thesis where the direction is obvious ("if you smoke, you will get cancer"), a more descriptive thesis where the reader is left to make a decision ("smoking causes cancer"), or an (admittedly bizarre) even-handed thesis that weighs options ("smoking looks cool, but it causes cancer"). Use your judgment when crafting a thesis. People do not usually like to be told what to think and what to do, but gentle coaxing or suggestion can often be highly effective.

Sample Topic If you return to the tentative thesis statement for the sample essay on Facebook, part of it states that the findings "warrant a more critical reception of the information on the site and the amount of time spent on the site." However, this might still be a little vague: what does it mean to have "a more critical reception"? This acknowledgment of critical thinking is important to the essay because it indicates the primary point(s) that you wish to make in the paper. Further elaboration at this step would help the essay, and a return to the sources can help clarify the point. We will work through some textual examples and then offer a revised thesis.

A useful strategy in critical reading practices is to gain the ability to identify where and how authors employ critical thinking strategies in their own work. This helps you, as a reader, identify key arguments or points in published writing. We will demonstrate two common examples: the question and the argument identification.

If we return to McNeill's text, she asks a basic question about the process of identity construction on Facebook: "So who is this 'authentic' self?" (68). As we mentioned earlier, the frame of the research question is an important consideration. Probably very few Facebook users log on with the explicit goal of defining himself or herself or constructing an authentic identity. Most people simply do not operate this way. Yet, it is undeniable that our actions on Facebook contribute to our self-identity to varying degrees. Simultaneously, though, we often refer to ourselves as a "self," as if we were discreet, contained, stable identities. Therefore, in asking a question about the "authentic" self, McNeill prompts us to negotiate the difference between a traditional humanist description of the stable self and a contemporary situation where we manage different versions of ourselves in a digital environment.

McNeill makes this point about the Facebook timeline feature. She writes, "it departs from a strictly humanist understanding of the self as autonomous, and invites us to consider how the network can be a posthuman practice even with humanist foundations" (72). McNeill essentially explains that the new digital environment is not necessarily inconsistent with traditional environments, only different. And the ways in which we behave in these different environments contribute to our identities. There are clear connections to Morrison's rhetorical analysis here, where she tracks the changes in the mechanics of the status update and its representational possibilities. The environment plays a factor, if not multiple factors, in our own "authentic" self-presentation.

Furthermore, McNeill does not limit her analysis only to shifting platforms of self-identity. She continues her argument to assert that the users and their behaviours further modify the environment and its content. She writes, "our actions and proclivities shape our own experience of Facebook on all fronts: they determine which posts we see in our News Feeds, what ads appear beside our Walls, and what actions we 'need' to take to improve Facebook for ourselves and others" (78). Therefore, while we post updates and events on Facebook, the site itself responds by utilizing these data to tailor the environment to better suit our and its interests. Keep this in mind as we demonstrate the second critical reading practice.

Chou and Edge make clear some of their argumentative strategies in their analysis of their Facebook data. Regarding the data's indication that people tend to view others' Facebook lives in a positive light, they hypothesize that "one could argue that frequent Facebook users shall know the tricks others use to manage the impression; therefore, experienced Facebook users could avoid the potential distorted perception. However, the results of the research suggest that frequent Facebook users tend to perceive that others are happier" (119). This is a very clear expression of analytical thinking and writing. Chou and Edge point out one possible explanation for an argument, namely that an awareness of Facebook's distortions of perceptions would help a user negate or mitigate a faulty perception. It would seem to stand to reason that if you are aware of a bias then you should be able to ignore or minimize that bias. However, as the researchers assert, the results of the data indicate otherwise. Despite knowing about the influence of bias, people still believe in the outcome of the bias. Another name for this logical contradiction is *cognitive dissonance*.

These examples demonstrate how the logical principles from Chapter 8 on Writing Evaluation Essays manifest in published research almost all the time.

Also, the conclusions we can discern from the published writing allow us to synthesize ideas from the research materials in order to further our own arguments.

STEP 1 Revising the Thesis

From the analyses of McNeill and Chou and Edge, we can connect their two points. McNeill argues that our stable senses of self and environment are changing, and Chou and Edge point out the cognitive dissonance between knowing of a bias and retaining a belief in a bias. The purpose of working through the textual examples was to clarify what the draft thesis meant by "a more critical reception" of the materials presented on Facebook.

On the one hand, McNeill's argument claims that we willingly contribute information to our online Facebook profiles without necessarily having a full understanding of how the environment operates. That is, the more we interact with the Facebook environment, the more the Facebook environment molds itself to cater better to our own individual preferences, thereby providing a more enjoyable and desirable platform.

On the other hand, Chou and Edge's argument claims that frequent users of Facebook tend to believe that other users enjoy better lives, despite a possible awareness that this bias may be a result of Facebook's own design. Chou and Edge also state that this happens "whether consciously or unconsciously" (119), indicating that users cannot totally control or manage the environment. It is challenging to be exempt from the influence of Facebook.

With these points in mind, you might revise the thesis in the following manner:

Writing Sample

Tentative thesis statement

I argue that, while Facebook can have positive benefits of keeping people in contact with one another, the detrimental effects of inaccurate perceptions of the world and low self-esteem warrant a more critical reception of the information on the site and the amount of time spent on the site.

Revised thesis statement

While Facebook initially appears to be about expressing yourself and keeping in touch with friends, research indicates that it can overemphasize the happiness of others and, thereby, lower a user's self-esteem. With Facebook's dynamic ability to respond to user actions and tailor its content accordingly, the site contributes less to self-expression and autobiography than it does to the data-mining and commercial interests of Facebook and its customers. Therefore, while Facebook may be a commonplace tool in our daily lives, it is important to realize that the apparently benign or banal participation on the site simultaneously constructs and defines users more as customers than as people.

The revised thesis has done three primary things. It has clarified the "inaccurate perceptions" to be an overemphasis of "the happiness of others." It has also specified that one possibility for "a more critical reception" of the site is to realize that Facebook's primary commercial purpose is served by its secondary social purpose. Moreover, it takes the idea of "time spent on the site" and suggests that any participation on the site is contributing to a commercial end as well as a social end.

STAGE 6   Revising Individual Paragraphs: Integrating and Documenting

STEP 1   Revising the Introduction

Revise the introduction to your research essay after you've written a draft of the essay. You'll find that your thinking has changed throughout the writing of the essay. In a research essay, you'll discover that writing the draft has helped you understand your own opinion in relation to the critics' opinions on the subject. You'll be better able to integrate your own opinion with theirs, and you'll be better able to articulate the structure of your essay. Check that your introduction isn't incomplete, only one or two sentences, or too long, so that the reader loses focus on your research essay's topic.

Sample Topic The draft introduction of your research essay on Facebook reads as follows:

Facebook has become a global phenomenon that engages hundreds of millions of people on a daily basis. The Social Network Site (SNS) purports to give people a way to express their unique, individual identities. Yet the site simultaneously limits the user's capabilities for self-expression through its own structure in collecting information and its own reasons or ends for offering the service in the first place. As most users may agree, the general function of Facebook is to connect people to friends, which would seem to be a relatively good-natured or beneficial service where people can chat with current friends, keep in touch with old friends, and potentially meet new friends. I argue that, while Facebook can have the positive benefits of keeping people in contact with one another, the detrimental effects of inaccurate perceptions of the world and low self-esteem warrant a more critical reception of the information on the site and the amount of time spent on the site.

This draft introduction is quite good. You've clearly presented and contextualized the topic for your readers so that they know what the essay will be about. You've also provided some specific details about self-expression and Facebook, and your argument or thesis statement, at the end of the paragraph, is clear.

After writing your draft, though, you've come to a better understanding of how your own argument relates to and fits into what scholars say about the subject. You decide to mention the critics in your introduction and explicitly state how your argument relates to and differs from theirs.

You revise your introductory paragraph so that it reads as follows:

Facebook has become a global phenomenon that engages hundreds of millions of people on a daily basis. The Social Network Site (SNS) purports to give people a way to express their unique, individual identities. Yet, the site simultaneously limits the user's capabilities for self-expression through its own structure in collecting information and its own reasons or ends for offering the service in the first place. As most users may agree, the general function of Facebook is to connect people to friends, which would seem to be a relatively good-natured or beneficial service where people can chat with current friends, keep in touch with old friends, and potentially meet new friends. However, as some research indicates, Facebook can have many negative consequences. As autobiography researchers Aimée Morrison and Laurie McNeill indicate, the profiles or identities that Facebook constructs are not authentic or accurate representations of real individuals but are inaccurate and highly constructed. Moreover, other researchers like Hui-Tzu Grace Chou and Nicholas Edge have shown that Facebook users frequently misread or misunderstand Facebook posts, leading them to have faulty perceptions of their friends and their world. While Facebook initially appears to be about expressing yourself and keeping in touch with friends, the site can overemphasize the happiness of others and, thereby, lower a user's self-esteem. With Facebook's dynamic ability to respond to user actions and tailor its content accordingly, the site contributes less to self-expression and autobiography than it does to the data-mining and commercial interests of Facebook and its customers. Therefore, while Facebook may be a commonplace tool in our daily lives, it is important to realize that the apparently benign or banal participation on the site simultaneously constructs and defines users more as customers than as people.

STEP 2 Revising Middle Paragraphs: Integrating Sources

When you revise your middle paragraphs, you want to check that each paragraph has a main point that relates to the overall thesis of the research essay. Check, also, that you have used evidence from your primary and secondary sources effectively, and that you have explained and analyzed them well. Refer to Chapter 11 for a checklist on revising middle paragraphs and integrating sources.

Sample Topic

Draft middle paragraph

Facebook allows its users to formulate their identities through a profile page. As Sidonie Smith and Julia Watson have noted, the very word *profile* implies a particular approach to identity formation: "the medical history, the work history, the credit history" (quoted in McNeill, 75) of the individual. That is, a profile is based on a set of selection criteria, such as a racial profile (race) or a medical profile (health). As users set up accounts on Facebook, the site asks them for their name, gender, birthday, and email address. It additionally asks for optional information on religious views, political views, occupation, musical tastes, and relationship status, among others. Facebook allows its users to establish certain facts about their identities while it ignores or actively prohibits other types of information, such as whether or not a potential user has ever defied the laws of gravity or has a criminal record.

This paragraph focuses on a particular topic, the Facebook profile, while relating it to the overall argument of the research essay, that the site inscribes identities in certain ways. After having written the draft, though, you feel that you could do more to analyze the Facebook profile. You have thought more deeply about the subject and feel that you can add a few sentences to show that depth of thought.

You revise as follows:

Revised middle paragraph

Facebook allows its users to formulate their identities through a profile page. As Sidonie Smith and Julia Watson have noted, the very word *profile* implies a particular approach to identity formation: "the medical history, the work history, the credit history" (quoted in McNeill, 75) of the individual. That is, a profile is based on a set of selection criteria, such as a racial profile (race) or a medical profile (health). As users set up accounts on Facebook, the site asks them for their name, gender, birthday, and email address. It additionally asks for optional information on religious views, political views, occupation, musical tastes, and relationship status, among others. Facebook allows its users to establish certain facts about their identities while it ignores or actively prohibits other types of information, such as whether or not a potential user has ever defied the laws of gravity or has a criminal record. While on the surface it may appear that Facebook is asking fairly standard questions about a person's identity to formulate a profile, it nonetheless has a set of criteria for selection. Therefore, while people may manage a host of different and possibly competing variables in their real lives, a Facebook profile reveals a generally standardized set of traits of any individual on the network. People's ongoing complaints about Facebook's privacy settings demonstrate an uneasiness with the visibility of certain information, such as relationship status or political views, and they desire a means to control the publication of their information.

STEP 3   Revising the Conclusion

When revising your conclusion, ask yourself how your research question or problem has been answered, and make that answer clear to your readers. Also state the importance of the research problem and the answer to it as well as the significance of your research essay. You may want to reiterate your own position in relation to what scholars have said about the subject. See the sample essay by L. Smith, "Like Me on Facebook: Identity Construction in Social Media" (Readings: Sample Essays).

Working on Your Own Assignment

Refer to Chapter 11 for steps to follow in your own research paper assignment.

Exercises

A. Write a paragraph evaluating the strengths and weaknesses of the following introduction to a research essay on computers and learning. Focus on content rather than correctness.

> In the last fifteen years, our education system has changed. It now advocates the use of computers as tools for enhancing the education of students. Computers are viewed as machines that link us universally and consequently offer endless information to children. This technology is gaining major publicity, as people assume that computers will give future generations of children an advantage; they will have more knowledge and problem-solving skills. Whether or not this change is positive and necessary is still a topic for debate. In "It Always Costs," Suzuki boldly states that "we must understand that there is no such thing as a problem-free technology. However beneficent, technology always has a cost" (344).

B. Read the following middle paragraph of an essay on computers and learning. Underline the writer's topic sentence, main point(s), and explanations of details. Circle transitions and citation details. Then make a list similar to that in Chapter 11, Stage 6, Step 2 to show what changes you would make to create a more effective middle paragraph.

> Without motivation or stimulation, any task becomes boring or difficult to achieve. It is postulated that computers motivate children, as they can be simple and exciting. In Shlechter's *Problems and Promises of Computer-Based Training,* he asserts that "as advertisements for CBI [computer-based instruction] products have claimed, learner motivation is high for a particular CBI program because the system is easy and fun to use" (11). Science teachers, apparently, see students are able to learn just as much through computer simulations as through hands-on laboratory procedures. Motivation may indeed be lost through lengthy hands-on procedures. There is speculation that motivation may be lost through the physical stagnation involved in using a computer. Armstrong and Casement researched this field in *The Child and the Machine*

and discovered that "even if computer use instills a positive attitude towards the technology, there is no proof that this enthusiasm spills into other areas of learning." A child may be fascinated by the technology but still not have the motivation to learn on her own.

C. Discuss how you would approach essays in different disciplines, such as English, history, or psychology. Where would you go to find sources for each of these different disciplines? What kinds of research problems or questions would you address for each? Why is it important to think about the disciplinary approach you will take to your essay?

Readings

Published Writings

Sample Essays

Published Writings

Reframing Canada's "Drug Problem"

Bruce K. Alexander

A gain this year, drug users are dying in record numbers in downtown   1
eastside Vancouver, and ragged junkies are shocking tourists on city
streets. There is no general agreement on what to do about this.

But this is nothing new. Vancouver has served as display case for   2
Canada's self-destructive drug use since the early 20th century, and there
has never been a durable consensus about how to react. Instead, past decades
have seen a hotly contested waxing and waning in importance of three long-
familiar types of interventions:

1) Criminal prosecution and intensive anti-drug propaganda   3
   campaigns, which dominated the 1920s, 1950s and 1980s;
2) Medical and psychological treatment, which dominated the late   4
   1960s and early 1970s; and
3) Interventions that are now called "harm reduction" techniques,   5
   which dominate the 1990s. These include methadone maintenance,
   needle exchanges, detox centres and a unique hassle-free residence
   which provides secure housing for the sickest street people, even if they
   refuse to quit drugs.

Bruce K. Alexander is a professor emeritus of
psychology at Simon Fraser University and a
research associate with the Canadian Centre for
Policy Alternatives. His research interests include
the causes of addiction, the effects of globalization on psychological functioning, and the history of psychology.

Although proponents of each type of   6
intervention are dedicated and knowledgeable, no levels of expenditure and
no way of combining interventions has
stopped the deaths or quelled the misery
by much. Unfortunately, "new" ideas
coming to the fore are not much more
promising. These include "heroin maintenance," *i.e.*, distributing clean, injectable heroin in safe doses to addicts, and
"legalization," *i.e.*, making certain drugs

freely available and letting users face the consequences of their free choice. Although there is value in both ideas, neither is actually new, and neither can substantially reduce the problem.

Although heroin maintenance is currently being promoted as a "trial," it has been tried many times before. Clean, injectable heroin and/or morphine have been provided to addicts for years in England, the Netherlands, Switzerland, Australia and Canada. In Canada this was done illegally, by a few courageous doctors, some of whom were severely punished. The largest trials were undertaken in the US before World War II in over 40 cities and rural areas, particularly in the state of Kentucky. 7

The results of these trials are consistent. Some addicts adjust to heroin or morphine maintenance reasonably well, although they seldom quit their habit; others continue to destroy themselves in spite of maintenance; but the majority never receive maintenance because of animosity between clinicians, who want to impose stringent conditions for receiving the drug, and street addicts, who find these conditions abhorrent. Because heroin maintenance can help some addicts, it is a worthwhile addition to existing interventions, but it can have no major impact. 8

Legalization is an even older idea, since all the illicit drugs were formerly legal. Although legalization can be truly beneficial for recreational users of illegal drugs who are now senselessly prosecuted, it will not help the destructive drug users much. They can harm themselves with legal drugs as much as with illegal ones. In fact, the most lethal Canadian drug addictions are to legal drugs, particularly alcohol and tobacco. 9

The reason why the old interventions are not accomplishing much and the "new" ideas are unpromising is obvious to many people. Self-destructive drug users are responding in a tragic, but understandable way to lives that were hopelessly and cruelly dislocated before their "drug problem" began. Here I use the single word "dislocated" very broadly, to describe the absence of that essential integration and identification with family, community, society and spiritual values that makes "straight" life bearable most of the time and joyful at its peaks. 10

It is a fact of history and psychology that prolonged dislocation of individuals (for example, children abused by their families) or of groups (for example, aboriginal people whose cultures are destroyed by invasion) predictably begets desperate, obsessive attempts to find some kind of integration and identity, to somehow "get a life." In the absence of achievable, healthy possibilities, this usually takes the form of lifestyles built around vice, violence and excess, frequently including an ultimately self-defeating use of drugs. Thus, the problem on Vancouver's streets is not really a "drug problem"—drug use is only a part of a much larger pattern of response to prolonged dislocation. 11

Dislocation is increasing everywhere, because globalized, market-driven 12 societies can *only* be established and maintained by dislocation of traditional local culture, economy and human relationships. Dislocation serves to create and maintain a market in labour, land and currency that is predictably responsive to the economic laws of supply and demand, rather than to non-economic needs or traditions. This necessary connection between market-driven society and dislocation was recognized in early 19th century England, as much by Whig theoreticians like William Townsend and Herbert Spencer as by socialists like Robert Owen. Later, it was analyzed by historians like Karl Polanyi and Eric Hobsbawm. Polanyi's classic study *The Great Transformation* (1944) makes the point concisely: Establishing a "self-regulating market" "must disjoint man's relationships and threaten his natural habitat with annihilation."

The historical facts behind this analysis are well known. A full-blown 13 globalized, market-driven society was established early in 19th century England with a massive dispossession of the rural poor and their absorption into urban slums, workhouses and a brutal, export-oriented manufacturing system. There was a concomitant explosion in the destructive use of alcohol, which had not been a significant problem previously. In the later 19th and 20th centuries, both this dislocation of people and the destructive use of alcohol and drugs were transplanted from England to the settlers and natives in English colonies and to the rest of western Europe. Eventually, market-driven society and its concomitant "drug problem" were globalized.

There have been some periods of respite from painful dislocation, 14 notably during Canada's post-war Keynesian era, but as new challenges have required increased productivity and greater "flexibility," dislocation has generally increased everywhere. Increasing dislocation is the obvious result of the "progress" being achieved today, both in developing countries under the persuasive guidance of the International Monetary Fund and in developed countries, including Canada, under elected governments. Governments everywhere are manipulating economic parameters in ways that often increase unemployment and reduce vital public support for families, communities and national culture.

Obviously, deviant lifestyles and self-destructive drug use are not 15 confined to the poor, and their prevalence among the affluent is also best understood as a result of chronic dislocation. Again, Polanyi makes a complex point concisely: " . . . the most obvious effect of the new institutional system was the destruction of the traditional character of settled populations and their transmutation into a new type of people, migratory, nomadic, lacking in self-respect and discipline—crude, callous beings *of whom both labourer and capitalist were an example* (Polanyi, 1944, p. 128, italics added). At the end of the 20th century, dislocation is the norm for rich and poor. Jobs disappear on short notice; communities are weak and unstable; people routinely change spouses, occupations, technical skills, languages, nationalities and ideologies as their lives progress; as well, the continued viability of crucial ecological systems are in question. For rich and poor alike, dislocation plays havoc with the delicate interpenetrations of people, society, the physical world and spiritual values that are needed to sustain a healthy identity and a rational existence.

Futurists predict—and celebrate—more increases in dislocation as 16 impersonal networks and business dealings on the Internet further replace local ties. New, electronic communication systems are expected to even alienate people from their familiar sense of themselves as human beings— the ultimate dislocation. Harvey argued in the June 1998 issue of *Policy Options* that electronic networks ("*réseaux*") would be the source of social and personal identity in the future: "*L'introspection est un luxe, l'intériorité un mythe difficilement atteignable. Les réseaux, images, métaphores ou systèmes physiques, sont désormais le miroir de notre propre images.*"[1]

Vancouver is no more than a display case for the ubiquitous problems 17 of dislocation and its consequences. There are people in every city, town, suburb and rural area whose lifestyles are as self-destructive as those of Vancouver junkies, although their drugs of choice are more likely to be alcohol, marijuana, glue, codeine and a variety of legal stimulants and depressants (*e.g.*, Ritalin and Valium). Many self-destructive people do not use drugs, but the same pattern of self-destructive excess is seen in their addictions to gambling, food, deviant sexuality and so on.

No solution to this problem will emerge from the rivalry between 18 criminal, medical/psychological or harm reduction interventions, because all three embody the same faulty premises. All three focus on drug use as the key problem and suppose that an adequate remedy lies in some manipulation of the drug-using person. The international "harm reduction" movement, with strong Canadian participation, is demonstrating how naturally these apparently opposing interventions can work together, particularly if the more violent police interventions are reined in to some extent.

Although realistic, pragmatic integration of these interventions is for 19 the best, a century of well-intended effort and huge expenditures indicates that no combination of them is likely to succeed. Based on faulty premises, all downplay the overarching problems that keep flooding society with new addicts.

Here are the problems that Canada must address in order to formulate 20 better drug policy: 1) Many Canadians are so severely dislocated that lives of self-destructive drug use along with other forms of vice, violence and excess are the best recourse they can muster. 2) The root cause is a vast, multi-layered incommensurability between the institutions of globalized, · market-driven society and the basic psychological, social and spiritual needs of human beings. 3) This root cause is only fleetingly acknowledged in public debate. 4) Our usual forms of intervention are hugely expensive and have a barely measurable effect. 5) Illegal drug business and legal pharmaceutical industries are making huge profits from the drugs with which people harm themselves and therefore have much to gain from the status quo. 6) In an era of almost complete domination of Canadian thought by the logic of globalization, it is difficult even to conceptualize credible means of ameliorating dislocation. This is because dislocation is built into globalized, market-driven society. 7) Avoiding these formidable realities has created a stalemate and led us to endlessly persevere with weak interventions and an absurd "war on drugs."

It is time to re-frame the problem. For decades there has been a futile 21 debate about whether self-destructive drug use is a "criminal problem" or a "medical problem." I hope that it can now be clear that it is neither—it is a political problem.

Canadian society must expend the necessary effort and money to 22 reduce dislocation, despite its ever-strengthening neoliberal ideology. Of course it would be naive to suppose that we can return to any real or imagined golden age. However, it is at least as naive to suppose that we can continue to hurtle forward, ideologically blinded to the problems built into the kind of society we are building. The solution to the so-called "drug problem" is nothing less than rejecting single-minded neoliberalism and exercising sensible, humane controls over environments, corporations and public institutions for the common good. This cannot be accomplished piecemeal, but requires a broadly framed policy that at times supersedes the pursuit of wealth and ever-freer markets.

As a single example of the possibilities for reallocating resources, consider 23 that the government now spends huge amounts of money in BC scanning the countryside with low-flying helicopters and fixed wing aircraft, searching for outdoor marijuana plantations, which often contain only a few dozen plants. The quest is futile, because the province is immense and because marijuana can be grown indoors with slightly more capitalization. High grade marijuana is available throughout the province at a price per intoxication well below that of alcohol. Moreover, the great majority of users suffer no discernible ill-effects.

The side-effect of this futile criminal intervention is the transformation 24 of resourceful and prosperous growers who might be mainstays of their rural communities into a shadowy class of farmer-criminals. Community-busting is advanced further when the RCMP arrives in a local community, announces a meeting, and enlists the aid of local people to inform on their neighbours who might be growers, thus sowing further suspicion and division.

At the same time, the provincial government cannot find enough 25 money to support the local schools and hospitals in many of these same communities, dislocating children and medical patients into adjacent districts, far from families and friends. The police frequently cannot find money to investigate petty crime, embittering the life of the poor and vulnerable. There are not enough social workers to intervene in known cases of child abuse. The money now being spent to disrupt the social fabric by vainly attacking marijuana cultivation could be far better spent to prevent the dislocation of the children, the sick and the vulnerable. Reducing dislocation would help reduce the present and future "drug problem."

Although it is easy to generate examples of this kind of policy change, 26 it may be difficult to generate enthusiasm for them within the major Canadian political parties in their current mindsets. However, the apparent singleminded addiction of our politicians to neoliberal ideology may, in the end, prove as catastrophic as the addictions that are seen on the streets of downtown Vancouver. The catastrophic potential of neoliberal ideological addiction is not only environmental and social, but also psychological, since it contributes substantially to the casualties of dislocation that disquiet Vancouver's coroners and shock the tourists on the streets.

The reframing of Canadian drug policy should start with rejection of 27 the universal application of neoliberal ideology and proceed to reallocation of resources from the three familiar interventions to reducing dislocation. It is my belief that Canadians are ready for such an adventure, especially if our politicians, who obviously know better, can find the courage to kick their habit.

NOTES

[1] Pierre-Léonard Harvey's text translates as follows: "Introspection is a luxury, interiority a myth difficult to achieve. Networks, images, metaphors or physical systems are henceforth mirror images of ourselves."

VOCABULARY

Keynesian—economic policies based on the writings of John Maynard Keynes (1883–1946), a British economist who argued that state intervention was necessary in capitalist societies in order to mitigate negative effects like unemployment from market instability

neoliberal—a form of liberalism that moves away from traditional liberal principles and toward "new" forms of liberalism such as free-market principles

QUESTIONS

1. Alexander takes addiction to include behaviours like "gambling, food, deviant sexuality and so on." What definition of addiction do you think he is using in this essay?

2. Alexander refers to English history and to the history of Native Canadians as well as the predictions of "futurists." How does he link these examples with the effects of free-market society in the present? Is this argument convincing to you?

3. "Reframing Canada's 'Drug Problem'" contains both neutral and evaluative diction. Identify three to five examples of each kind. How is the use of diction linked to the essay's purpose, as you understand it?

4. In this essay, an explanation of the causes of addiction leads to a proposal for solutions. How effective is this problem–solution structure? To what extent would this structure be useful in your own writing?

SUGGESTION FOR WRITING

Alexander describes the beginning of the twenty-first century as a time of weak communities, rapid change, and instability in work, relationships, beliefs, and places of residence. Write a short essay exploring to what extent your own experience of the beginning of the twenty-first century echoes this view.

Football Envy at the UN

Kofi Annan

The World Cup[1] makes us at the UN green with envy. As the pinnacle of the only truly global game, played in every country by every race and religion, it is one of the few phenomena as universal as the UN. You could say it's more universal. FIFA[2] has 207 members; we have only 191. But there are better reasons for our envy.

This is an event in which everybody knows where their team stands, and what it did to get there. They know who scored and how and in what minute of the game; they know who saved the penalty. I wish we had more of that sort of competition in the family of nations. Countries vying for the best standing in the table of respect for human rights, and trying to outdo one another in child survival rates or enrolment in secondary education. States parading their performance for all the world to see. Governments being held accountable.

Millions of people around the planet love talking about the World Cup. In Paraguay fans will be picking over that own goal; in Japan they will be debating strategies for today's contest with Australia.[3] Everywhere people are dissecting the games, revealing an intimate knowledge of their own teams and many others. Tongue-tied teenagers suddenly become eloquent and dazzlingly analytical. I wish we had more of that sort of conversation in the world at large: citizens consumed by the topic of how their country could do better on the Human Development Index,[4] or exercised about how to reduce carbon emissions or HIV infections.

The competition takes place on a level playing field, where every country has a chance to participate on equal terms. Only two commodities matter: talent and teamwork. I wish we had more levellers like that in the global arena. Free and fair exchanges without the interference of subsidies, barriers or tariffs. Every country getting a real chance to field its strengths on the world stage.

The World Cup illustrates the benefits of cross-pollination between peoples and countries. More and more national teams now welcome coaches from other countries, who bring new ways of thinking and playing. The same goes for the players who represent clubs away from home.

Kofi Annan (b. 1938) is a Ghanaian diplomat who served two terms as the first black African Secretary General of the United Nations (1997–2006). Winner of the Nobel Peace Prize jointly with the UN in 2001, he opposed the US and British invasion of Iraq in the absence of UN support.

"Football Envy at the UN" appeared in the My Two Cents column of *The Guardian* on June 12, 2006, and is reprinted with permission of the Kofi Annan Foundation.

They inject fresh qualities into their new team and are able to contribute more to their home side when they return. In the process, they often become heroes in their adopted countries—helping to open hearts and minds.

I wish it were equally plain for all to see that human migration in general can create triple wins—for migrants, for their countries of origin, and for the societies that receive them. Migrants not only build better lives for themselves and their families, but are also agents of development— economic, social, and cultural—in the countries they go and work in, while they inspire with new-won ideas and know-how when they return.   6

Playing in the World Cup brings profound national pride. For countries qualifying for the first time—such as my native Ghana—it is a badge of honour. For those doing so after years of adversity—such as Angola[5]—it provides a sense of national renewal. And for those who are currently riven by conflict, but whose World Cup team is a unique and powerful symbol of national unity—such as Ivory Coast[6]—it inspires nothing less than the hope of national rebirth.   7

Which brings me to what is perhaps most enviable of all for us in the UN: the World Cup is an event in which we see goals being reached. I'm not talking only about the goals a country scores; I also mean the most important goal of all—being there, part of the family of nations and peoples, celebrating our common humanity. I'll try to remember that today as Ghana plays Italy in Hanover. Of course, I can't promise I'll succeed.   8

NOTES

[1] Games among the thirty-two national soccer teams qualifying for the 2006 World Cup were played at various sites in Germany during June and July 2006.

[2] "FIFA" stands for the *Federation Internationale de Football Association,* the regulatory body for international soccer.

[3] In the first round of the World Cup tournament, Paraguay lost to England 1–0 on a goal inadvertently put into his own net by a Paraguay player; Japan lost to Australia 3–1.

[4] The Human Development Index is an instrument developed in 1992 to measure countries' achievements in three basic areas: life expectancy, literacy, and standard of living.

[5] The armed wing of the Angola rebel movement was disbanded in 2002, ending twenty-seven years of civil war.

[6] Voting reforms that would have disenfranchised most of the predominantly Muslim northern region, exacerbated by an economic downturn and ethnic tensions, led to the outbreak of civil war in Ivory Coast in 2002. Under a UN mandate, French troops were dispatched as peacekeepers in the former French colony.

VOCABULARY

riven—torn apart

QUESTIONS

1. An analogy is a comparison between unlike things that emphasizes similarities and downplays differences. Kofi Annan develops his essay by means of an extended analogy between the World Cup and the UN.

   a. List the specific points of comparison paragraph by paragraph. Which aspects of this analogy do you find most effective? Least effective? (See Chapter 8, Analogies [120, 122].) Why do you think Annan chose analogy to make his case?

   b. Can you think of aspects of the game of soccer not mentioned by Annan that would complicate his argument? For example, Annan does not mention the role or influence of soccer referees in games. Who enforces rules on the world stage? In 2011, bribery was alleged around Qatar's successful bid for the 2022 World Cup, and there were allegations of rampant game fixing in professional soccer by organized crime. Are there similar scandals on the world stage?

2. Sum up in a sentence or two Annan's vision of how countries should operate. Do you agree or disagree with this vision? Why?

3. How does Annan's view of equality among nations, as presented in paragraph 4, compare with the view Polly Toynbee presents in "Inequality Is the Real Enemy" (Readings)?

SUGGESTIONS FOR WRITING

1. Kofi Annan, like Tim Bowling in "Na Na Na Na, Hey Hey Hey, Goodbye" (Readings), captures the allure of sports. Is there a sport that attracts you in a similar way? If so, write a one-page essay that conveys its special qualities. Or, in the light of the estimates that well over one billion people watched the final game of the 2006 World Cup, write an essay that argues the merits and/or drawbacks of our enthusiasm for sports.

2. Use Annan's piece as a model for writing an extended analogy comparing some aspect of everyday life with an institution such as a school, a hospital, a business, or a political party.

Na Na Na Na, Hey Hey Hey, Goodbye

Tim Bowling

It's late spring, 1993. Millions of Canadians are tuned in to Game 7 of the Stanley Cup semifinals between the Toronto Maple Leafs and the Los Angeles Kings. It's an event of operatic drama. The Leafs have not won the Stanley Cup since 1967, while the Kings, in uncharted territory, are led by none other than the Great One, Wayne Gretzky, whose 1988 trade from Edmonton to Hollywood shocked those same millions of Canadians now frozen before their TV sets. 1

I'm not one of those millions. It is true I have been a hockey fan as long as I can remember. In fact, one of my earliest memories is from the late sixties, not long after the Leafs' last Cup raising, when I'd play with hockey cards on the linoleum floor of the kitchen, passing a marble back and forth and re-enacting great goals and saves as my mother clattered dishes in the sink nearby. The NHL has always been my primary source of spectator entertainment. 2

But I'm not watching Game 7 between the Leafs and the Kings. I can't. The tension is too much for me. I *care* too much. I so loathe the Kings—representatives of everything glitzy, shallow, crass and American—and so want an all-Canadian dream final between the Leafs and Montreal Canadiens, that I'm hiding out from the game. This is not an easy thing to do when nearly the whole country is tuned in. I'm so well versed in watching televised hockey that even the faintest sound emanating from a TV set or someone watching a TV set will tip me off to developments in the game. So I have to get away. But to where? Fortunately, I'm old enough and smart enough to be resourceful. 3

While Gretzky dipsy-doodles behind the Leafs' net, I sit in a dark, nearly empty Vancouver theatre, watching *Howards End*. It's a long movie, long enough to cover three periods and at least one period of overtime. With luck, the drama, NHL style, will be over before the credits roll. 4

As humiliating as it is to recall this memory, I mention it for two reasons. 5

Tim Bowling, who now lives in Edmonton, was born in Vancouver and has worked as a deckhand on a salmon-fishing boat. He is the author of many novels and books of poetry. Of these, *Dying Scarlet* won the 1998 Stephan G. Stephansson Award for Poetry, and both *The Witness Ghost* (2003) and *The Memory Orchard* (2004) were shortlisted for the Governor General's Literary Award for Poetry. Bowling was the recipient of a Guggenheim Fellowship in 2008. He has recently published a new collection of poetry, *Tenderman* (2011).

Reprinted by permission from "Na Na Na Na, Hey Hey Hey, Goodbye," *Alberta Views*. December 2005-January 2006, pp. 46–49 by Tim Bowling.

One, it highlights the bizarre Canadian fact that many so-called sensitive, cultured men (the sort who happily watch Ivory/Merchant films) are nonetheless fervent fans of a brutal, bone-breaking, blood-spattering sport. And two, it marks my nadir as a professional hockey fan. In the spring of 1993, something had to give. Either I was going to remain a "fanatic," or I was going to put away childish things. For God's sake, I had even read several E. M. Forster novels! What the hell was I doing caring so much about professional hockey, a game so violent that its rules include penalties for drawing blood and instigating fights? I abhorred violence and even cited it as a reason why I so disliked the United States. Yet I was drawn to the NHL like a bear to a campsite, like a politician to graft, like Simone de Beauvoir to Jean-Paul Sartre. I just couldn't turn away. Only when I walked out of that theatre into the street and hailed a group of teenaged boys (obviously they'd know the result of the game), and saw them shrug and heard one say "I have no idea," did I begin the process of cultural de-programming that would find me, a decade later, completely indifferent to the labour dispute between the NHL team owners and players.

However, indifference to the business side of professional hockey, and to the NHL, whose games have so declined in quality over the past decade that a breakaway merits a mention on the national news, doesn't quite translate into disinterest. The truth is, like so many non-violent Canadian men, alternately bored and disgusted by the game's outdated machismo code, I always have one ear cocked for news of the NHL. This remains true despite the fact that I no longer watch the games or care who wins, and that I actively scorn the corporate and boorishly patriotic culture that has grown up around professional hockey in Canada. Why? What is it about the NHL that retains even a slight grip on my imagination? 6

The most compelling answer concerns the primal pull of narrative. The NHL, for better or worse, is the Great Canadian Novel, a tale replete with villains and heroes, prima donnas and blue collar types, triumph and failure, hope and revenge, all played out at high speed over generations. Like millions of Canadians, I grew up on the lore of the game, everything from Conn Smythe's infamous remark that "if you can't beat 'em in the alley, you can't beat 'em on the ice" to Paul Henderson's famous series-winning goal against the Soviets in 1972. When the Tragically Hip uncovered a great rock song in the tragic death of the Leafs' Bill Barilko—"Bill Barilko disappeared / that summer (in 1951) / he was on a fishing trip (in a plane)/ The last goal he ever scored (in overtime) / won the Leafs the Cup / They didn't win another until 1962 / the year he was discovered"—I understood. When the internationally acclaimed Canadian filmmaker Atom Egoyan directed a TV movie about Brian "Spinner" Spencer's descent from NHL 7 tough guy to drug gang shooting victim, I understood. When ex-Maple Leafs defenceman Tim Horton's doughnut chain became a Canadian cultural icon, I understood. The NHL, in short, is the book most Canadians have been reading all their lives. What other is there?

Just as King Shahryar put off killing Scheherazade[1] because he wanted to hear how the story she was telling would turn out, I can't quite kill off my interest in the NHL. Northrop Frye[2] maintained that narrative was the common denominator between high and low culture, which explains our interest in everything from opera to soap opera. That makes eminent sense to this disillusioned NHL follower—why else should I carry around ridiculous facts such as six out of seven Sutter brothers from Viking, Alberta, made the big time and Bobby Clarke overcame diabetes to realize his professional dreams, or smile with goofy fondness at the common graffiti of my childhood—"Jesus Saves, Esposito Scores on the Rebound"?   8

Canadian poet Al Purdy described hockey as a combination of ballet and murder. Certainly the grace and beauty of the game when played well remains a major reason why I'm still mildly attracted to the NHL. After all, the players are the most skilled in the world, even if expansion and relentless marketing (just how many jerseys can one team have?) have conspired to water down the talent and glaciate the pace of play. Besides, hockey requires a special skill that takes years to master. Most people can imagine doing the running and jumping and catching required by baseball, football and basketball, but if you can't skate (and many Canadians can't), you can't even take to the playing surface. Hockey is uniquely demanding at its most basic level, and therefore its beauty is all the more impressive. Even so, would a ballet lover, in expectation of a rare graceful step, put up with the prima ballerina being slammed into the scenery every few minutes?   9

This question leads directly to the most worrying explanation for my ongoing interest in the NHL: I'm not nearly as sensitive and enlightened as I think I am. When Thomas Hobbes[3] wrote that life is "nasty, brutish and short," he wasn't referring to hockey, but, like most Canadian men, I've absorbed a Hobbesian philosophy as a way to justify my imaginative commitment to a machismo culture in which 14-year-old boys are sent away from home to play junior hockey and, as in the case of Sheldon Kennedy and others, sexually abused by their coaches in the process; and in which a star player like Todd Bertuzzi can jump an opponent from behind, breaking his neck, and not be universally vilified for his actions, but rather become the particular hero of Vancouver Canucks hockey fans. In fact, Don Cherry, the wildly popular spokesman for everything bigoted and "traditional" in hockey culture, is a sort of combination Thomas Hobbes/ Don Rickles/ Buffalo Bill Cody, exploiting a dog-eat-dog philosophy to garner laughs at   10 others' expense while travelling around the country in his garish huckster's clothes. Perhaps following the NHL, and watching *Coach's Corner*, is simply akin to slowing down on the highway to gawk at an accident. We don't like what we see, but we're drawn to it in some primal way.

But that's too harsh an indictment of our fascination with the NHL. 11 A more likely reason for it is political. It's perhaps a cliché by now to point out the importance of hockey to Canada's national identity, but it's a cliché with undeniable truth. When the Canadian icemakers at the 2002 Winter Olympic games in Salt Lake City placed a loonie under the ice as good luck for Team Canada in its gold medal game with Team USA, most Canadians were delighted. And a major part of that delight lies in our undefeatable conviction that, no matter what else the world beats us at, it can't beat us at hockey. This particular form of patriotism has deep roots for my generation of hockey fans, of course. Explaining the tension of the 1972 Summit Series between Canada and the USSR, in which Team Canada won the final three games behind the Iron Curtain to retain global hockey supremacy, Phil Esposito, with no sense of embarrassment or irony, remarked, "It wasn't hockey, it was war."

Well, Phil, I was happy Canada won, and at one time I even understood 12 Bobby Clarke's vicious slash of Valeri Kharlamov, which knocked the Soviets' star player out of the series, as a patriotic act. But the summit series was not Vimy Ridge or Dieppe. Yet the link between hockey and nationhood, as currently promoted even more vociferously by media coverage of the game in Canada, is not easily broken. That Don Cherry can use his few minutes of nationally televised screen-time every week to lobby for increased support of Canada's armed forces proves just how powerfully the hockey/nationhood link is forged (and don't forget Jean Chrétien dubbed his globe-trotting trade missions Team Canada, in a desperate attempt to benefit from reflected hockey glory). One day, perhaps, our soldiers will wear their names on their backs and UN peacekeeping missions will end with the announcement of first, second and third stars.

A more honourable connection between the NHL and Canadian political 13 life does exist, however. Because professional hockey is a shared national story, it affords us a kind of grassroots democracy. Everyone is entitled to participate in the tangled discourse of finance, politics and entertainment spawned by the modern NHL. Your background doesn't matter (unless you're an American), your education and income don't matter, not even your annual beer consumption matters. If you have an opinion on salary caps or on refereeing or on the superiority of Edmonton over Calgary as a hockey city, you're welcome to share it. Whether you're in Glace Bay or Nanaimo, Guelph or Banff (or any other place that sounds like two players colliding), you can walk into a bar where *Hockey Night in Canada* is showing and feel that your opinions are a national birthright, like 5 per cent beer and bilingualism (OK, maybe not bilingualism, but you get the idea).

At this point, no doubt, many Canadians will throw up their hands 14 in frustration and say, "He's taking all this too seriously. It's just a game." Well, let's look at the NHL from the simple perspective of escapist entertainment. Into what are we escaping exactly? When I was a boy, the boards, ice and score clock were free of advertising; goals and assists meant more than salaries; and players and teams had distinct characters. If you attended a game, there was silence after the whistle so you could hear someone in the crowd heckle a ref (one I remember from the seventies, directed at referee Bruce Hood: "Hey, Bruce, take off your hood!" Not exactly Evelyn Waugh level of wit, but appreciated nonetheless). Or perhaps, instead of silence, an organist played "Three Blind Mice." Today at a game, you're so relentlessly bombarded with supersonic noise and flashing lights and company logos that you come away with two conclusions: the NHL is for 20-year-old men who love violent video games, and the games themselves are beside the point, just another way to promote a crass, materialistic, corporatist agenda.

We're deep into the NHL season now, the first in two years. Dozens 15 of players have changed teams, a dozen others have retired. There's a new phenom named Sidney Crosby who's expected to challenge the scoring statistics of Gretzky one day, and the Leafs still haven't won the Cup since 1967 (the Kings beat them back in '93, in case you were dying to know). I haven't watched a game all year, and I don't intend to, just as I didn't miss the NHL at all during its year-long absence—which was, in fact, wonderfully refreshing, like fasting after binging on double-doubles and maple creams down at the local Tim Hortons. Why should I follow a sport whose foundation in this country is made of blood and beer and an empty rhetoric around outdated and destructive notions of patriotism and manhood?

I shouldn't, and neither should you, especially if you're over 40. 16 To everything there is a season, as the Bible says, and the season for the NHL is past. As the league continues to struggle with its dinosaur code of machismo, as it expands into Arkansas and Tijuana, as the players wear jerseys with Wal-Mart and McDonald's logos, I won't be watching.

And yet, if somehow the fates conspire, and two Canadian teams meet 17 in the Stanley Cup Finals, can I resist the lure of nostalgia and the pull of narrative? Can I stop thinking and be entertained?

NOTES

[1] In the *Arabian Nights Entertainment,* Scheherazade is the wife of a Persian king who puts off executing her because he is enthralled by the stories she tells every night.

[2] Northrop Frye was a well-known Canadian literary critic, author of works on Blake, literary criticism, and the mythic imagination, among other topics. See Frye's "Preface to the *Bush Garden*" (229).

[3] Thomas Hobbes (1588–1679) was an English philosopher whose masterwork, *Leviathan,* argued for a materialist view of human motives.

QUESTIONS

1. Bowling begins his essay at a point more than a decade earlier than his time of writing. Why?

2. How can you tell that Bowling is knowledgeable about Canadian hockey? Why is knowledge of hockey important to the essay?

3. Most of Bowling's essay is organized around cause/effect analysis, as he considers the reasons for the NHL's "grip on [his] imagination." Where does he shift to cause/effect analysis (evaluating whether these reasons are worthwhile)?

4. Bowling's references range widely from poets and critics to Canadian bands like the Tragically Hip, from watching *Howards End* to insulting hockey referees. Does this range of reference help Bowling's case or weaken it? Why?

SUGGESTION FOR WRITING

Does something grip your imagination without your really knowing why? If so, use cause/effect analysis to explore this attraction. Consider whether some of Bowling's strategies could be helpful for your essay.

The Persistence of Poetry and the Destruction of the World*

Robert Bringhurst

W hat it pleases us to call the New World is in fact a very old world— just as old, at any rate, as Asia, Europe, and Africa. It is part of the ancient continent of Pangaea, born from the same geological matrix as Europe. Its rivers and forests, and its ecology and geology, were thoroughly developed long before Columbus. And it has been inhabited by thinking, speaking, knowing human beings for several thousand years. 1

But an inhabited world, with its own philosophical, artistic, scientific, and literary traditions, is not what the European conquerors and colonists wanted to find. It is therefore not what they saw. They saw instead an empty world, free and ripe for the taking. They saw a gift of God meant for no one but themselves. 2

This deliberate hallucination is still with us, like the star of a Christmas without end. 3

The European colonists' arrival in the New World marks the escalation of a war that had been fought in Europe and Asia for more than two millennia and continues even now. It is the war between those who think they belong to the world and those who think that the world belongs to them. 4

It is the war between the pagans, who know they are surrounded and outnumbered by the gods, and all the devotees of the number one—one empire, one history, one market, or one God—and who nowadays insist on the preeminence of everyone for himself: the smallest number one of all.

It is no accident that prophets of monotheism, including Plato[1] and Mohammed, have often banished the poets. These prophets understand that the poet is a pagan and polytheist by nature. In a certain sense, even Dante, Milton, San Juan de la Cruz, Teresa of Ávila, Gerard Manley Hopkins, and T. S. Eliot are pagans. Without admitting it, they 5

Robert Bringhurst (b. 1946) is a writer of considerable breadth. He has also written poetry consistently since the early 1970s. In 1992, he published *The Elements of Typographic Style*, which greatly influenced the field of typography. He also collaborated with the late Aboriginal artist Bill Reid and has translated works of oral Haida storytellers into written English. Bringhurst lives on Quadra Island, off the coast of British Columbia. This essay was originally a lecture and is collected in his 2006 book, *The Tree of Meaning: Thirteen Talks*.

Reprinted by permission from Robert Bringhurst, "The Persistence of Poetry and the Destruction of the World." From *The Tree of Meaning: Thirteen Talks* (Kentville, NS: Gaspereau Press, 2006), 40–45.

seem to understand, like the peoples of the Altiplano[2] of Bolivia and Peru, and like many Native Canadians, that it is best to interpret Christianity as one more form of paganism.

But Mohammed and Plato are poets too in their way, monotheistic 6 and tedious at times, but very much livelier and more pluralistic at others.

The great danger is single-mindedness: reducing things to one perspective, 7 one idea, one overriding rule.

A polytheistic understanding of the world survived in Europe even in 8 the time of the conquistadors, though it was then forced to take a word-less form. Music gave it refuge. It is found in polyphonic music, which is the music of multiple, simultaneous and independent voices. The churches of Europe overflowed with music of this kind in the fifteenth, sixteenth and seventeenth centuries. It did not change the course of history, but it preserved an essential perception of the plurality of being. It preserved the essential, faithful heresy that reality is not of just one mind.

European music of more recent centuries is, for the most part, 9 homophonic. It is the music of one voice that speaks in the name of all and of many voices that answer as one voice.

In the meantime, the conquest continues—in South America, North 10 America, Asia, Australia, and in Europe too. It continues in Bosnia and Hercegovina, where a tradition of oral epic poetry survived from Homer's time until even a few months ago. Now, at this moment, the villages in which those poets lived are rubble and mass graves.[3]

From Alaska to Tierra del Fuego, and from Ireland to Japan, the forests 11 fall and subdivisions replace them. The homes of the gods are supplanted by the houses and garages of human beings. It is hard work, this eviction of the gods and of all the cultures that acknowledge their existence. We keep at it even so.

The Haida poet Skaay[4] refers to human beings as *xhaaydla xitiit* 12 *ghidaay*: "plain, ordinary surface birds." Creatures with more power—killer whales, loons, grebes, sea lions, seals—know how to dive. They pierce the surface, the *xhaaydla* it is called in Haida. If we go with them—if, that is, we are *invited* to go with them—we enter the world of the myths. We come back speaking poetry.

Two thousand kilometres south of the country of the poet Skaay, in 13 the Ruby Mountains, the country of the Paiute, now part of the state of Nevada, there are pines of the species *Pinus aristata,* bristlecone pines. These trees live longer than any other creatures on the earth. The oldest individuals—not much taller than I am—are 5,000 years of age or more. A few years ago, a person who called himself a scientist found in these mountains a pine that might, he thought, be the oldest of all. He cut it down to count its rings. He killed what may indeed have been the oldest living being in the world, to convert it into a statistic. Then he published his report, without the least apology, in a scientific journal.[5]

This is not science. It is one more thoughtless manifestation of the 14 conquest, one more step in reducing the world to human terms.

The American novelist William Faulkner, when he received the Nobel 15 Prize, concluded his address by saying, "Mankind will not only survive, he will prevail." I am an admirer of Faulkner, but I think that his prediction is logically impossible. I think that if humanity survives, it can only be because it does *not* prevail, and that if we insist, like Ozymandias,[6] on prevailing, we will surely not survive.

I have been listening to the world for barely half [a] century. I do not 16 have the wisdom even of a young tree of an ordinary kind. Nevertheless, I have been listening—with eyes, ears, mind, feet, fingertips—and what I hear is poetry.

What does this poetry say? It says that what-is is: that the real is real, 17 and that it is alive. It speaks the grammar of being. It sings the polyphonic structure of meaning itself.

In the great ceiling of the Sistine Chapel there are readers rather than 18 writers. The prophets and sibyls scrutinize their folios and scrolls. Nothing is written there that we can read. The great pages in their laps and in their hands reflect what happens as if they were mirrors. In front of these blank mirrors the blind prophets are listening. There is only one writer, Jehosaphat[7] the scribe, tucked away in the corner with his scrap of paper, listening to those who really listen.

The theme of the ceiling is the poetry of the world, not the glory of the 19 poet.

It is true that the face of Michelangelo is there in the midst of the 20 chapel's big back wall. It is rendered, this self-portrait, as a face still attached to a human hide freshly peeled from someone else's living body. The sculptor is subsumed in his own tale. The listener listens to himself. In the midst of his own vision, the visionary can be seen. But he is peeled. In the midst of that most sculptural of paintings, the image of the sculptor is reduced to two dimensions.

When I was a youngster in school, someone asked me, "If a tree falls in 21 the forest with no one there to hear it, does it make a sound or not?" The question is demented. If a tree falls in the forest, all the other trees are there to hear it. But if a man cuts down the forest and then cries that he has no food, no firewood, no shade, and that his mind can get no traction, who is going to hear *him?*

Poetry is the language of being: the breath, the voice, the song, the 22
speech of being. It does not need us. We are the ones in need of it. If we
haven't learned to hear it, we will also never speak it.

Beings eat one another. This is the fundamental business of the world. 23
It is the whole, not any of its parts, that must prevail, and this whole is
always changing. There is no indispensable species, and no indispensable
culture. Especially not a culture that dreams of eating without being eaten,
and that offers the gods not even the guts or the crumbs.

When he sees his own people destroying the world, what is the poet to 24
say? *Stop?* Or more politely, *Please stop, please?*

All the poets of all times can only say one thing. They can say that 25
what-is is. When he sees his people destroying the world, the poet can say,
"we're destroying the world." He can say it in narrative or lyric or dramatic
or meditative form, tragic or ironic form, short form or long form, in verse
or prose. But he cannot lie, as a poet, and offer himself as the savior. He can
believe or not believe that salvation is possible. He can believe in one God
or in many gods or in none. He can believe or not believe in belief. But he
cannot finally say anything more than the world has told him.

When he sees that, in absolute terms, we human beings are now too 26
numerous—in addition to the fact that we seem too powerful as a
species—what is the poet going to do? Pull the trigger? Sing a song of praise
to Herod[8] or to Hitler? It is hard to say it to other humans, and humans, of
course, are loath to believe it, but this is the fact: human beings have built a
world in which humans need to die more and faster than they do. Yet even
in this condition, murder is not the answer.

Long ago, in a book of poems protesting the war in Vietnam, I read 27
a simple statement that stays with me. I have not in thirty years been able
to find the book again, and I am told that the lines I remember are really
quoted from a speech by Martin Luther King. I remember seeing them in a
poem, but perhaps the book in which I saw them was published only in my
dreams. The lines as I remember them, in any case, are these:

> *When one is guided by conscience only,*
> *there is no other side*
> *to which one can cross.*

There is no other earth to cross to either. There are no new worlds. 28
Paradise will not be our asylum, and our hell will not be anywhere other
than here. The world is one, at the same time that it is plural, inherently
plural, like the mind. The proof of this plurality is the persistence of poetry
in our time. It is extraordinary but true, in the present day, that poetry
survives in the voices of humans, just as it does in the voices of all the other
species in the world.

NOTES

The following notes are editors' notes, except where "Author's note" is indicated in parentheses.

[1] Plato in Book X of *The Republic* banishes the poets from the ideal city because Plato views poetry as imitation and, therefore, removed from reality, or truth.

[2] Altiplano refers to the high plains of South America.

[3] Bringhurst delivered this talk in 1996, shortly after Bosnia and Hercegovina experienced the Bosnian war (1992–1995).

[4] Skaay is a Haida oral poet whom Bringhurst has translated into written English.

[5] The first-person account of this event is in Donald R. Currey, "An Ancient Bristlecone Pine Stand in Eastern Nevada." *Ecology* 46.4 (Durham, North Carolina, 1965): 564-6. Galen Rowell retells the story well in *High and Wild* (San Francisco: Sierra Club, 1979): 99-105. (Author's note)

[6] Ozymandias is the name of an Egyptian Pharaoh made famous in English literature by Percy Bysshe Shelley in a sonnet that warns against the arrogance of powerful individuals desiring immortality.

[7] Jehosaphat was a Biblical figure who was a recorder (historian) of events. He is referenced in 1 Kings 4.3 and elsewhere.

[8] Herod was a Roman leader of the first century BCE in Jerusalem, who is known for ruling by terror.

VOCABULARY

homophonic—music that has a single melodic line

Pangaea—the supercontinent that existed between the Paleozoic and Mesozoic periods, roughly 250 million years ago

polyphonic—music that has multiple melodic lines, often called contrapuntal

QUESTIONS

1. Bringhurst draws on very long views of history and geography in order to make his point. Do you think these kinds of generalizations help or hinder his argument?

2. Bringhurst claims that poetry "does not need us. We are the ones in need of it." Do you think poetry today is as important as Bringhurst suggests it is?

3. Near its conclusion, the essay states that "murder is not the answer." The essay does not specifically state an alternative answer. What do you think Bringhurst might suggest as a solution to humanity's challenges?

SUGGESTION FOR WRITING

Part of the purpose of this essay is to define poetry. Bringhurst utilizes several unusual examples to make his argument, such as trees listening to each other and sea animals diving below the surface of the ocean. Using one of Bringhurst's examples or one of your own choosing, define the inherent poetic qualities of the reality of an area of study. For example, define the poetic qualities of engineering or environmentalism.

My Wood

E. M. Forster

A few years ago I wrote a book which dealt in part with the difficulties   1
of the English in India. Feeling that they would have had no difficulties in India themselves, the Americans read the book freely.
The more they read it the better it made them feel, and a cheque to the
author was the result. I bought a wood with the cheque. It is not a large
wood—it contains scarcely any trees, and it is intersected, blast it, by a public footpath. Still, it is the first property that I have owned, so it is right that
other people should participate in my shame, and should ask themselves, in
accents that will vary in horror, this very important question: What is the
effect of property on the character? Don't let's touch economics; the effect
of private ownership upon the community as a whole is another question—
a more important question, perhaps, but another one. Let's keep to psychology. If you own things, what's their effect on you? What's the effect on
me of my wood?

In the first place, it makes me feel heavy. Property does have this effect.   2
Property produces men of weight, and it was a man of weight who failed
to get into the Kingdom of Heaven. He was not wicked, that unfortunate
millionaire in the parable, he was only stout; he stuck out in front, not
to mention behind, and as he wedged himself this way and that in the
crystalline entrance and bruised his well-fed flanks, he saw beneath him
a comparatively slim camel passing through the eye of a needle and being
woven into the robe of God. The Gospels all through couple stoutness and
slowness. They point out what is per-
fectly obvious, yet seldom realized: that
if you have a lot of things you cannot
move about a lot, that furniture requires
dusting, dusters require servants, servants require insurance stamps,[1] and the
whole tangle of them makes you think
twice before you accept an invitation to
dinner or go for a bathe in the Jordan.[2]
Sometimes the Gospels proceed further
and say with Tolstoy[3] that property is
sinful; they approach the difficult ground
of asceticism here, where I cannot follow
them. But as to the immediate effects of

The opening sentence of "My Wood" refers to
the success of Edward Morgan Forster's most
famous novel, *A Passage to India* (1924). Besides
novels and short stories, Forster (1879–1970)
wrote *Aspects of the Novel* (1927), a work of literary criticism; biography; travel literature; and two
collections of essays: *Abinger Harvest* (1936), from
which "My Wood" is taken, and *Two Cheers for
Democracy* (1951).

"My Wood" is reprinted with permission of the Provost and
Scholars of King's College, Cambridge, and The Society of
Authors as the Literary Representatives of the Estate of
E. M. Forster.

property on people they just show straightforward logic. It produces men of weight. Men of weight cannot, by definition, move like the lightning from the East unto the West, and the ascent of a fourteen-stone[4] bishop into a pulpit is thus the exact antithesis of the coming of the Son of Man. My wood makes me feel heavy.

In the second place, it makes me feel it ought to be larger. 3

The other day I heard a twig snap in it. I was annoyed at first, for I 4 thought that someone was blackberrying, and depreciating the value of the undergrowth. On coming nearer, I saw it was not a man who had trodden on the twig and snapped it, but a bird, and I felt pleased. My bird. The bird was not equally pleased. Ignoring the relation between us, it took fright as soon as it saw the shape of my face, and flew straight over the boundary hedge into a field, the property of Mrs. Henessy, where it sat down with a loud squawk. It had become Mrs. Henessy's bird. Something seemed grossly amiss here, something that would not have occurred had the wood been larger. I could not afford to buy Mrs. Henessy out, I dared not murder her, and limitations of this sort beset me on every side. Ahab[5] did not want that vineyard—he only needed it to round off his property, preparatory to plotting a new curve—and all the land around my wood has become necessary to me in order to round off the wood. A boundary protects. But—poor little thing—the boundary ought in its turn to be protected. Noises on the edge of it. Children throw stones. A little more, and then a little more, until we reach the sea. Happy Canute![6] Happier Alexander![7] And after all, why should even the world be the limit of possession? A rocket containing a Union Jack, will, it is hoped, be shortly fired at the moon. Mars. Sirius. Beyond which . . . But these immensities ended by saddening me. I could not suppose that my wood was the destined nucleus of universal dominion—it is so very small and contains no mineral wealth beyond the blackberries. Nor was I comforted when Mrs. Henessy's bird took alarm for the second time and flew clean away from us all, under the belief that it belonged to itself.

In the third place, property makes its owner feel that he ought to do 5 something to it. Yet he isn't sure what. A restlessness comes over him, a vague sense that he has a personality to express—the same sense which, without any vagueness, leads the artist to an act of creation. Sometimes I think I will cut down such trees as remain in the wood, at other times I want to fill up the gaps between them with new trees. Both impulses are pretentious and empty. They are not honest movements towards money-making or beauty. They spring from a foolish desire to express myself and from an inability to enjoy what I have got. Creation, property, enjoyment form a sinister trinity in the human mind. Creation and enjoyment are both very very good, yet they are often unattainable without a material basis, and at such moments property pushes itself in as a substitute, saying, 'Accept me instead—I'm good enough for all three.' It is not enough. It is, as Shakespeare said of lust, 'The expense of spirit in a waste of shame': it is 'Before, a joy proposed; behind, a dream.'[8] Yet we don't know how to shun it. It is forced on us by our economic system as the alternative to starvation. It is also forced on us by an internal defect in the soul, by the feeling that in property may lie the germs of self-development and of exquisite or heroic deeds. Our life on earth is, and ought to be, material and carnal.[9] But we have not yet learned to manage our materialism and carnality properly; they are still entangled with the desire for ownership, where (in the words of Dante) 'Possession is one with loss.'

And this brings us to our fourth and final point: the blackberries.   6

Blackberries are not plentiful in this meagre grove, but they are easily   7
seen from the public footpath which traverses it, and all too easily gathered. Foxgloves, too—people will pull up the foxgloves, and ladies of an educational tendency even grub for toadstools to show them on the Monday in class. Other ladies, less educated, roll down the bracken in the arms of their gentlemen friends. There is paper, there are tins. Pray, does my wood belong to me or doesn't it? And, if it does, should I not own it best by allowing no one else to walk there? There is a wood near Lyme Regis,[10] also cursed by a public footpath, where the owner has not hesitated on this point. He has built high stone walls each side of the path, and has spanned it by bridges, so that the public circulate like termites while he gorges on the blackberries unseen. He really does own his wood, this able chap. Dives[11] in Hell did pretty well, but the gulf dividing him from Lazarus could be traversed by vision, and nothing traverses it here. And perhaps I shall come to this in time. I shall wall in and fence out until I really taste the sweets of property. Enormously stout, endlessly avaricious, pseudo-creative, intensely selfish, I shall weave upon my forehead the quadruple crown of possession until those nasty Bolshies[12] come and take it off again and thrust me aside into the outer darkness.

NOTES

[1] Insurance stamps: required in the UK to validate health and disability insurance benefits.

[2] The Jordan River flows between the Sea of Galilee and the Dead Sea.

[3] A Russian writer, author of *War and Peace* (1869) and *Anna Karenina* (1877), Leo Tolstoy (1828–1910) believed that possession of private property was an evil and practised severe asceticism.

[4] A stone equals fourteen pounds.

[5] Ahab was the seventh king of Israel from 874 to 853 BC. His wife, Jezebel, coveting a fine vineyard adjoining the palace grounds, arranged that its owner, Naboth, be convicted of blasphemy and executed. Ahab then became legal owner of the vineyard.

6 Canute, or C'nut, was an ambitious conqueror of the eleventh century who was simultaneously King of England (1016–1035), Denmark (1018–1035), and Norway (1028–1035).

7 Alexander the Great, King of Macedonia, sought to conquer the entire world to satisfy his desire for power and glory.

8 The phrases are from Shakespeare's Sonnet 129. The single quotation marks are British usage.

9 In Forster's day the word *carnal* referred to the body as the seat of all appetites. Also, archaically, *carnal* was used as the opposite of *spiritual.*

10 Lyme Regis: a coastal town in England chartered as a royal borough in 1284 that eventually became known, in Forster's time, as a beach resort of some notoriety.

11 Dives and Lazarus figure in a biblical story. Dives, a rich man, takes no notice of Lazarus, a beggar. Dives ends up in Hades and Lazarus in heaven (Luke 16:19–31).

12 The Bolsheviks ("Bolshies") were the majority group of the Russian Social Democratic Party. They favoured revolutionary tactics to achieve socialism and seized power during the Russian Revolution to set up a workers' state.

QUESTIONS

1. In the first paragraph of "My Wood," Forster announces that his essay is concerned with the effects of owning something on a person's character. What does he mean by "character"? Does Forster confine his essay to the effects of ownership on the individual?

2. Does Forster list these effects in an order of increasing importance? In some other order? Explain.

3. Forster introduces the first three effects with similar topic sentences beginning "It [or "property"] makes me [or "its owner"] feel. . . ." Why does he abandon this formula when he introduces the fourth effect?

4. Forster's novel *A Passage to India* (1924) is about the corrupting effects of property and imperialism on the British in India. Thus it is ironic that the proceeds of this novel allowed Forster himself to buy property. Can you find other instances of irony, or an ironic tone, in the essay? Do you think irony, rather than direct statement, makes this essay more persuasive? Explain.

5. Throughout this essay, Forster makes a number of allusions to figures in religion, history, and literature. Why does Forster include these allusions? How do they affect you as a reader?

6. "My Wood" was first published in England in 1936. Does this context illuminate any of the attitudes and concerns in this essay?

SUGGESTION FOR WRITING

Using "My Wood" as a model, write an essay explaining how owning something (a house, a car, a CD collection) corrupted your character. Organize your essay in the same way Forster does, with an introduction and three or four middle paragraphs. Deal with one effect in each paragraph. Like Forster, you can add a separate conclusion. Include allusions if you think they will strengthen your rapport with your reader.

The Right to the City

David Harvey

T he city, the noted urban sociologist Robert Park once wrote, is: 1

> *man's most consistent and on the whole, his most successful attempt*
> *to remake the world he lives in more after his heart's desire. But, if*
> *the city is the world which man created, it is the world in which*
> *he is henceforth condemned to live. Thus, indirectly, and without*
> *any clear sense of the nature of his task, in making the city man has*
> *remade himself.*

The right to the city is not merely a right of access to what already exists,   2
but a right to change it after our heart's desire. We need to be sure we can
live with our own creations (a problem for every planner, architect and utopian thinker). But the right to remake ourselves by creating a qualitatively
different kind of urban sociality is one of the most precious of all human
rights. The sheer pace and chaotic forms of urbanization throughout the
world have made it hard to reflect on the nature of this task. We have been
made and re-made without knowing exactly why, how, wherefore and to
what end. How then, can we better exercise this right to the city?

The city has never been a harmonious place, free of confusions,   3
conflicts, violence. Only read the history of the Paris Commune[1] of 1871,
see Scorsese's fictional depiction of *The Gangs of New York* in the 1850s, and
think how far we have come. But then think of the violence that has divided
Belfast, destroyed Beirut and Sarajevo, rocked Bombay, even touched the "city
of angels." Calmness and civility in urban history are the exception not the rule.
The only interesting question is whether outcomes are creative or destructive.
Usually they are both: the city is the historical site of creative destruction. Yet the
city has also proven a remarkably resilient, enduring and innovative social form.

But whose rights and whose city? The communards of 1871 thought   4
they were right to take back "their" Paris
from the bourgeoisie and imperial lack-
eys. The monarchists who killed them
thought they were right to take back the
city in the name of God and private property. Both Catholics and the Protestants
thought they were right in Belfast, as did
Shiv Sena[2] in Bombay when it violently
attacked Muslims. Were they not all
equally exercising their right to the city?

David Harvey (b. 1935) is a professor of anthropology and geology and is widely known for his work
on Marxism. His books include *Social Justice and
the City* (1973) and *The New Imperialism* (2003).

"Between equal rights," Marx once famously wrote, "force decides." So is this what the right to the city is all about? The right to fight for one's heart's desire and liquidate anyone who gets in the way? It seems a far cry from the universality of the UN Declaration on Human Rights. Or is it?

Marx, like Park, held that we change ourselves by changing our world   5
and vice versa. This dialectical relation lies at the root of all human labor. Imagination and desire play their part. What separates the worst of architects from the best of bees, he argued, is that the architect erects a structure in the imagination before materializing it upon the ground. We are, all of us, architects, of a sort. We individually and collectively make the city through our daily actions and our political, intellectual and economic engagements. But, in return, the city makes us. Can I live in Los Angeles without becoming a frustrated motorist?

We can dream and wonder about alternative urban worlds. With   6
enough perseverance and power we can even hope to build them. But utopias these days get a bad rap because when realized they are often hard to live with. What goes wrong? Do we lack the correct moral and ethical compass to guide our thinking? Could we not construct a socially just city?

But what is social justice? Thrasymachus in Plato's *Republic* argues that   7
"each form of government enacts 'the laws with a view to its own advantage' so that 'the just is the same everywhere, the advantage of the stronger.'" Plato rejected this in favor of justice as an ideal. A plethora of ideal formulations now exist. We could be egalitarian, utilitarian in the manner of Bentham (the greatest good of the greatest number), contractual in the manner of Rousseau (with his ideals of inalienable rights) or John Rawls, cosmopolitan in the manner of Kant (a wrong to one is a wrong to all), or just plain Hobbesian, insisting that the state (Leviathan) impose justice upon reckless private interests to prevent social life being violent, brutal and short. Some even argue for local ideals of justice, sensitive to cultural differences. We stare frustratedly in the mirror asking; "which is the most just theory of justice of all?" In practice, we suspect Thrasymachus was right: justice is simply whatever the ruling class wants it to be.

Yet we cannot do without utopian plans and ideals of justice. They   8
are indispensable for motivation and for action. Outrage at injustice and alternative ideas have long animated the quest for social change. We cannot cynically dismiss either. But we can and must contextualize them. All ideals about rights hide suppositions about social processes. Conversely, social processes incorporate certain conceptions of rights. To challenge those rights is to challenge the social process and vice versa. Let me illustrate.

We live in a society in which the inalienable rights to private property   9
and the profit rate trump any other conception of inalienable rights you can

think of. This is so because our society is dominated by the accumulation of capital through market exchange. That social process depends upon a juridical construction of individual rights. Defenders argue that this encourages "bourgeois virtues" of individual responsibility, independence from state interference, equality of opportunity in the market and before the law, rewards for initiative, and an open marketplace that allows for freedoms of choice. These rights encompass private property in one's own body (to freely sell labor power, to be treated with dignity and respect and to be free from bodily coercions), coupled with freedoms of thought, of expression and of speech. Let us admit it: these derivative rights are appealing. Many of us rely heavily upon them. But we do so much as beggars live off the crumbs from the rich man's table. Let me explain.

To live under capitalism is to accept or submit to that bundle of rights 10 necessary for endless capital accumulation. "We seek," says President Bush as he goes to war, "a just peace where repression, resentment and poverty are replaced with the hope of democracy, development, free markets and free trade." These last two have, he asserts, "proved their ability to lift whole societies out of poverty." The United States will deliver this gift of freedom (of the market) to the world whether it likes it or not. But the inalienable rights of private property and the profit rate (earlier also embedded, at US insistence, in the UN declaration) can have negative, even deadly, consequences.

Free markets are not necessarily fair. "There is," the old saying goes, 11 "nothing more unequal than the equal treatment of unequals." This is what the market does. The rich grow richer and the poor get poorer through the egalitarianism of exchange. No wonder those of wealth and power support such rights. Class divisions widen. Cities become more ghettoized as the rich seal themselves off for protection while the poor become ghettoized by default. And if racial, religious and ethnic divisions cross-cut, as they so often do, with struggles to acquire class and income position, then we quickly find cities divided in the bitter ways we know only too well. Market freedoms inevitably produce monopoly power (as in the media or among developers). Thirty years of neoliberalism teaches us that the freer the market the greater the inequalities and the greater the monopoly power.

Worse still, markets require scarcity to function. If scarcity does not 12 exist then it must be socially created. This is what private property and the profit rate do. The result is much unnecessary deprivation (unemployment, housing shortages, etc.) in the midst of plenty. Hence, the homeless on our streets and the beggars in the subways. Famines can even occur in the midst of food surpluses.

The liberalization of financial markets has unleashed a storm of 13 speculative powers. A few hedge funds, exercising their inalienable right to make a profit by whatever means rage around the world, speculatively destroy whole economies (such as that of Indonesia and Malaysia). They destroy our cities with their speculations, reanimate them with their donations to the opera and the ballet while, like Kenneth Lay[3] of Enron fame, their CEOs strut the global stage and accumulate massive wealth at the expense of millions. Is it worth the crumbs of derivative rights to live with the likes of Kenneth Lay?

If this is where the inalienable rights of private property and the profit 14 rate lead, then I want none of it. This does not produce cities that match my heart's desire, but worlds of inequality, alienation and injustice. I oppose the endless accumulation of capital and the conception of rights embedded therein. A different right to the city must be asserted.

Those that now have the rights will not surrender them willingly: 15 "Between equal rights, force decides." This does not necessarily mean violence (though, sadly, it often comes down to that). But it does mean the mobilization of sufficient power through political organization or in the streets if necessary to change things. But by what strategies do we proceed?

No social order, said Saint-Simon, can change without the lineaments 16 of the new already being latently present within the existing state of things. Revolutions are not total breaks but they do turn things upside down. Derivative rights (like the right to be treated with dignity) should become fundamental and fundamental rights (of private property and the profit rate) should become derivative. Was this not the traditional aim of democratic socialism?

There are, it turns out, contradictions within the capitalist package of 17 rights. These can be exploited. What would have happened to global capitalism and urban life had the UN declaration's clauses on the derivative rights of labor (to a secure job, reasonable living standards and the right to organize) been rigorously enforced?

But new rights can also be defined: like the right to the city which, 18 as I began by saying, is not merely a right of access to what the property speculators and state planners define, but an active right to make the city different, to shape it more in accord with our heart's desire, and to re-make ourselves thereby in a different image.

The creation of a new urban commons, a public sphere of active 19 democratic participation, requires that we roll back that huge wave of privatization that has been the mantra of a destructive neoliberalism. We must imagine a more inclusive, even if continuously fractious, city based not only upon a different ordering of rights but upon different political-economic practices. If our urban world has been imagined and made then it can be re-imagined and re-made. The inalienable right to the city is worth fighting for. "City air makes one free" it used to be said. The air is a bit polluted now. But it can always be cleaned up.

NOTES

[1] Paris Commune is a brief political organization in Paris in 1871, which was revolutionary and socialist in nature.

[2] Shiv Sena is a Hindu political party in India. They have been linked to the 1992–1993 riots in Bombay.

[3] Kenneth Lay (1942–2006) was a leader of the Enron corporation that defrauded millions of dollars from its shareholders.

VOCABULARY

bourgeois—the middle class, sometimes used pejoratively to indicate a materialist, self-absorbed demographic

dialectical—a method for reasoning after truth, often by using contradictory or contrasting terms in order to reach an equilibrium or synthesis of ideas to resolve tension

neoliberalism—a form of liberalism that moves away from traditional liberal principles and toward "new" forms of liberalism such as free-market principles

utopia—usually, the "ideal" society. Thomas More coined this term in English in 1516 from the Greek meaning "no place," ironically to indicate that utopia does not exist

QUESTIONS

1. To what extent do you think you have a right to have meaningful input on the development of your (urban) environment?

2. Harvey distinguishes between fundamental and derivative rights. Do you think current formulations of rights best serve the interests of the people, or do you agree with Harvey that we need to reconfigure the statuses of various rights from one category to the other (fundamental to derivative or vice versa)?

3. Harvey sees the city as a place where resources (financial, material, human) are put to productive use. How, if at all, do you experience the changing dynamics of urban space, from new developments like big-box stores to re-developments like neighbourhood improvements to urban decline like inner-city decay?

SUGGESTION FOR WRITING

Write a proposal to your city council for a change that you think will benefit the inhabitants of your community (whether urban or rural). Try to consider the competing interests for resources, development, and management of this project. It may be a public square, a library, a community centre, a school, or anything else.

Feminist Politics: Where We Stand

bell hooks

S imply put, feminism is a movement to end sexism, sexist exploitation, and oppression. This was a definition of feminism I offered in *Feminist Theory: From Margin to Center* more than 10 years ago. It was my hope at the time that it would become a common definition everyone would use. I liked this definition because it did not imply that men were the enemy. By naming sexism as the problem it went directly to the heart of the matter. Practically, it is a definition which implies that all sexist thinking and action is the problem, whether those who perpetuate it are female or male, child or adult. It is also broad enough to include an understanding of systemic institutionalized sexism. As a definition it is open-ended. To understand feminism it implies one has to necessarily understand sexism.

As all advocates of feminist politics know, most people do not understand sexism, or if they do, they think it is not a problem. Masses of people think that feminism is always and only about women seeking to be equal to men. And a huge majority of these folks think feminism is anti-male. Their misunderstanding of feminist politics reflects the reality that most folks learn about feminism from patriarchal mass media. The feminism they hear about the most is portrayed by women who are primarily committed to gender equality—equal pay for equal work, and sometimes women and men sharing household chores and parenting. They see that these women are usually white and materially privileged. They know from mass media that women's liberation focuses on the freedom to have abortions, to be lesbians, to challenge rape and domestic violence. Among these issues, masses of people agree with the idea of gender equity in the workplace—equal pay for equal work.

bell hooks (b. 1952), born Gloria Jean Watkins, is an American critic, theorist, and feminist, and author of many books. This reading is the first chapter in her book *Feminism Is for Everybody: Passionate Politics* (2000). As the title suggests, hooks's work attempts to overcome class, racial, economic, and gender barriers through her analyses of competing and complementary cultural forces.

Reprinted by permission from *Feminism Politics* "Where We Stand" by bell Hooks, pp. 1–6. © 2000. Distinguished Professor of Appalachian Studies, Berea College.

Since our society continues to be primarily a "Christian" culture, masses of people continue to believe that god has ordained that women be subordinate to men in the domestic household. Even though masses of women have entered the workforce, even though many families are headed by women who are the sole bread-winners, the vision of domestic life which continues to dominate the nation's imagination is one in which the logic of male domination is intact, whether men are present in the home or not. The wrongminded notion of the feminist movement which implied it was anti-male carried with it the wrongminded assumption that all female space would necessarily be an environment where patriarchy and sexist thinking would be absent. Many women, even those involved in feminist politics, chose to believe this as well.

There was indeed a great deal of anti-male sentiment among early 4 feminist activists who were responding to male domination with anger. It was that anger at injustice that was the impetus for creating a women's liberation movement. Early on most feminist activists (a majority of whom were white) had their consciousness raised about the nature of male domination when they were working in anti-classist and anti-racist settings with men who were telling the world about the importance of freedom while subordinating the women in their ranks. Whether it was white women working on behalf of socialism, black women working on behalf of civil rights and black liberation, or Native American women working for indigenous rights, it was clear that men wanted to lead, and they wanted women to follow. Participating in these radical freedom struggles awakened the spirit of rebellion and resistance in progressive females and led them towards contemporary women's liberation.

As contemporary feminism progressed, as women realized that males 5 were not the only group in our society who supported sexist thinking and behavior—that females could be sexist as well—anti-male sentiment no longer shaped the movement's consciousness. The focus shifted to an all-out effort to create gender justice. But women could not band together to further feminism without confronting our sexist thinking. Sisterhood could not be powerful as long as women were competitively at war with one another. Utopian visions of sisterhood based solely on the awareness of the reality that all women were in some way victimized by male domination were disrupted by discussions of class and race. Discussions of class differences occurred early on in contemporary feminism, preceding discussions of race. Diana Press published revolutionary insights about class divisions between women as early as the mid-'70s in their collection of essays *Class and Feminism*. These discussions did not trivialize the feminist insistence that "sisterhood is powerful," they simply emphasized that we could only become sisters in struggle by confronting the ways women—through sex, class, and race—dominated and exploited other women, and created a political platform that would address these differences.

Even though individual black women were active in the contemporary 6 feminist movement from its inception, they were not the individuals who became the "stars" of the movement, who attracted the attention of mass media. Often individual black women active in feminist movement were revolutionary feminists (like many white lesbians). They were already at odds with reformist feminists who resolutely wanted to project a vision of the movement as being solely about women gaining equality with men in the existing system. Even before race became a talked about issue in feminist circles it was clear to black women (and to their revolutionary allies in struggle) that they were never going to have equality within the existing white supremacist capitalist patriarchy.[1]

From its earliest inception feminist movement was polarized. Reformist thinkers chose to emphasize gender equality. Revolutionary thinkers did not want simply to alter the existing system so that women would have more rights. We wanted to transform that system, to bring an end to patriarchy and sexism. Since patriarchal mass media was not interested in the more revolutionary vision, it never received attention in mainstream press. The vision of "women's liberation" which captured and still holds the public imagination was the one representing women as wanting what men had. And this was the vision that was easier to realize. Changes in our nation's economy, economic depression, the loss of jobs, etc., made the climate ripe for our nation's citizens to accept the notion of gender equality in the workforce.

Given the reality of racism, it made sense that white men were more willing to consider women's rights when the granting of those rights could serve the interests of maintaining white supremacy. We can never forget that white women began to assert their need for freedom after civil rights, just at the point when racial discrimination was ending and black people, especially black males, might have attained equality in the workforce with white men. Reformist feminist thinking focusing primarily on equality with men in the workforce overshadowed the original radical foundations of contemporary feminism which called for reform as well as overall restructuring of society so that our nation would be fundamentally anti-sexist.

Most women, especially privileged white women, ceased even to consider revolutionary feminist visions, once they began to gain economic power within the existing social structure. Ironically, revolutionary feminist thinking was most accepted and embraced in academic circles. In those circles the production of revolutionary feminist theory progressed, but more often than not that theory was not made available to the public. It became and remains a privileged discourse available to those among us who are highly literate, well-educated, and usually materially privileged. Works like *Feminist Theory: From Margin to Center* that offer a liberatory vision of feminist transformation never receive mainstream attention. Masses of people have not heard of this book. They have not rejected its message; they do not know what the message is.

While it was in the interest of mainstream white supremacist capitalist 10 patriarchy to suppress visionary feminist thinking which was not anti-male or concerned with getting women the right to be like men, reformist feminists were also eager to silence these forces. Reformist feminism became their route to class mobility. They could break free of male domination in the workforce and be more self-determining in their lifestyles. While sexism did not end, they could maximize their freedom within the existing system. And they could count on there being a lower class of exploited subordinated women to do the dirty work they were refusing to do. By accepting and indeed colluding with the subordination of working-class and poor women, they not only ally themselves with the existing patriarchy and its concomitant sexism, they give themselves the right to lead a double life, one where they are the equals of men in the workforce and at home when they want to be. If they choose lesbianism they have the privilege of being equals with men in the workforce while using class power to create domestic lifestyles where they can choose to have little or no contact with men.

Lifestyle feminism ushered in the notion that there could be as many 11 versions of feminism as there were women. Suddenly the politics was being slowly removed from feminism. And the assumption prevailed that no matter what a woman's politics, be she conservative or liberal, she too could fit feminism into her existing lifestyle. Obviously this way of thinking has made feminism more acceptable because its underlying assumption is that women can be feminists without fundamentally challenging and changing themselves or the culture. For example, let's take the issue of abortion. If feminism is a movement to end sexist oppression, and depriving females of reproductive rights is a form of sexist oppression, then one cannot be anti-choice and be feminist. A woman can insist she would never choose to have an abortion while affirming her support of the right of women to choose and still be an advocate of feminist politics. She cannot be anti-abortion and an advocate of feminism. Concurrently there can be no such thing as "power feminism" if the vision of power evoked is power gained through the exploitation and oppression of others.

Feminist politics is losing momentum because feminist movement 12 has lost clear definitions. We have those definitions. Let's reclaim them. Let's share them. Let's start over. Let's have T-shirts and bumper stickers and postcards and hip-hop music, television and radio commercials, ads everywhere and billboards, and all manner of printed material that tells the world about feminism. We can share the simple yet powerful message that feminism is a movement to end sexist oppression. Let's start there. Let the movement begin again.

NOTES

[1] "White supremacist capitalist patriarchy" is a term hooks uses throughout her writings. She employs it to identify the major forces at work in dominant culture: race, economics (or class), and gender.

VOCABULARY

patriarchal—a system of social organization where males, usually the eldest males, are the privileged or dominant group that controls most of the decision-making power.

QUESTIONS

1. At the end of her essay, hooks calls for the feminist movement to begin again. Do you think the "movement" ever stopped? If so, when did it stop? Why is it necessary for it to begin again?

2. What is lifestyle feminism? What is hooks's view of lifestyle feminism?

3. With gender, what other two categories does hooks place alongside the historical developments of feminism? According to hooks, which one of the two emerged first? Why?

4. Canada is a multicultural society that is supposed to be accepting of cultural differences. Do you think feminism is a cultural issue? How is it similar to or different from other familiar elements of multiculturalism like language, religion, or race?

SUGGESTION FOR WRITING

Before reading this short essay, what, if any, was your definition of *feminism*? Has your understanding of the term changed after reading this essay? Write a paragraph or two outlining how this essay has or has not changed your understanding or definition of *feminism*.

Science Says: Revolt!

Naomi Klein

In December 2012, a pink-haired complex-systems researcher named Brad Werner made his way through the throng of 24,000 earth and space scientists at the Fall Meeting of the American Geophysical Union, held annually in San Francisco. This year's conference had some big-name participants, from Ed Stone of Nasa's Voyager project, explaining a new milestone on the path to interstellar space, to the film-maker James Cameron, discussing his adventures in deep-sea submersibles.

2   But it was Werner's own session that was attracting much of the buzz. It was titled "Is Earth F**ked?" (full title: "Is Earth F**ked? Dynamical Futility of Global Environmental Management and Possibilities for Sustainability via Direct Action Activism").

3   Standing at the front of the conference room, the geophysicist from the University of California, San Diego walked the crowd through the advanced computer model he was using to answer that question. He talked about system boundaries, perturbations, dissipation, attractors, bifurcations and a whole bunch of other stuff largely incomprehensible to those of us uninitiated in complex systems theory. But the bottom line was clear enough: global capitalism has made the depletion of resources so rapid, convenient and barrier-free that "earth-human systems" are becoming dangerously unstable in response. When pressed by a journalist for a clear answer on the "are we f**ked" question, Werner set the jargon aside and replied, "More or less."

4   There was one dynamic in the model, however, that offered some hope. Werner termed it "resistance"—movements of "people or groups of people" who "adopt a certain set of dynamics that does not fit within the capitalist culture." According to the abstract for his presentation, this includes "environmental direct action, resistance taken from outside the dominant culture, as in protests, blockades and sabotage by indigenous peoples, workers, anarchists and other activist groups."

5   Serious scientific gatherings don't usually feature calls for mass political resistance, much less direct action and sabotage. But then again, Werner wasn't exactly calling for those things. He was merely observing that mass uprisings of

Naomi Klein (b. 1970) is a Canadian author and activist best known for her books *No Logo* (1999) and *The Shock Doctrine* (2007). She has published widely on politics, economics, environmentalism, and activism. Her 2014 book *This Changes Everything* won the Hilary Weston Writers' Trust Prize.

people—along the lines of the abolition movement, the civil rights movement or Occupy Wall Street—represent the likeliest source of "friction" to slow down an economic machine that is careening out of control. We know that past social movements have "had tremendous influence on . . . how the dominant culture evolved," he pointed out. So it stands to reason that, "if we're thinking about the future of the earth, and the future of our coupling to the environment, we have to include resistance as part of that dynamics." And that, Werner argued, is not a matter of opinion, but "really a geophysics problem."

6 Plenty of scientists have been moved by their research findings to take action in the streets. Physicists, astronomers, medical doctors and biologists have been at the forefront of movements against nuclear weapons, nuclear power, war, chemical contamination and creationism. And in November 2012, *Nature* published a commentary by the financier and environmental philanthropist Jeremy Grantham urging scientists to join this tradition and "be arrested if necessary," because climate change "is not only the crisis of your lives—it is also the crisis of our species' existence."

7 Some scientists need no convincing. The godfather of modern climate science, James Hansen, is a formidable activist, having been arrested some half-dozen times for resisting mountain-top removal coal mining and tar sands pipelines (he even left his job at NASA this year in part to have more time for campaigning). Two years ago, when I was arrested outside the White House at a mass action against the Keystone XL tar sands pipeline, one of the 166 people in cuffs that day was a glaciologist named Jason Box, a world-renowned expert on Greenland's melting ice sheet.

8 "I couldn't maintain my self-respect if I didn't go," Box said at the time, adding that "just voting doesn't seem to be enough in this case. I need to be a citizen also."

9 This is laudable, but what Werner is doing with his modelling is different. He isn't saying that his research drove him to take action to stop a particular policy; he is saying that his research shows that our entire economic paradigm is a threat to ecological stability. And indeed that challenging this economic paradigm—through mass-movement counter-pressure—is humanity's best shot at avoiding catastrophe.

10 That's heavy stuff. But he's not alone. Werner is part of a small but increasingly influential group of scientists whose research into the destabilisation of natural systems—particularly the climate system—is leading them to similarly transformative, even revolutionary, conclusions. And for any closet revolutionary who has ever dreamed of overthrowing the present economic order in favour of one a little less likely to cause Italian pensioners to hang themselves in their homes, this work should be of particular interest.

Because it makes the ditching of that cruel system in favour of something new (and perhaps, with lots of work, better) no longer a matter of mere ideological preference but rather one of species-wide existential necessity.

Leading the pack of these new scientific revolutionaries is one of Britain's 11 top climate experts, Kevin Anderson, the deputy director of the Tyndall Centre for Climate Change Research, which has quickly established itself as one of the UK's premier climate research institutions. Addressing everyone from the Department for International Development to Manchester City Council, Anderson has spent more than a decade patiently translating the implications of the latest climate science to politicians, economists and campaigners. In clear and understandable language, he lays out a rigorous road map for emissions reduction, one that provides a decent shot at keeping global temperature rise below 2° Celsius, a target that most governments have determined would stave off catastrophe.

But in recent years Anderson's papers and slide shows have become more 12 alarming. Under titles such as "Climate Change: Going Beyond Dangerous . . . Brutal Numbers and Tenuous Hope," he points out that the chances of staying within anything like safe temperature levels are diminishing fast.

With his colleague Alice Bows, a climate mitigation expert at the 13 Tyndall Centre, Anderson points out that we have lost so much time to political stalling and weak climate policies—all while global consumption (and emissions) ballooned—that we are now facing cuts so drastic that they challenge the fundamental logic of prioritising GDP growth above all else.

Anderson and Bows inform us that the often-cited long-term mitigation 14 target—an 80 per cent emissions cut below 1990 levels by 2050—has been selected purely for reasons of political expediency and has "no scientific basis." That's because climate impacts come not just from what we emit today and tomorrow, but from the cumulative emissions that build up in the atmosphere over time. And they warn that by focusing on targets three and a half decades into the future—rather than on what we can do to cut carbon sharply and immediately—there is a serious risk that we will allow our emissions to continue to soar for years to come, thereby blowing through far too much of our 2° "carbon budget" and putting ourselves in an impossible position later in the century.

Which is why Anderson and Bows argue that, if the governments of 15 developed countries are serious about hitting the agreed-upon international target of keeping warming below 2° Celsius, and if reductions are to respect any kind of equity principle (basically that the countries that have been spewing carbon for the better part of two centuries need to cut before the countries where more than a billion people still don't have electricity), then the reductions need to be a lot deeper, and they need to come a lot sooner.

To have even a 50/50 chance of hitting the 2° target (which, they and 16 many others warn, already involves facing an array of hugely damaging climate impacts), the industrialised countries need to start cutting their greenhouse-gas emissions by something like 10 per cent a year—and they need to start right now. But Anderson and Bows go further, pointing out that this target cannot be met with the array of modest carbon-pricing or green-tech solutions usually advocated by big green groups. These measures will certainly help, to be sure, but they are simply not enough: a 10 per cent drop in emissions, year after year, is virtually unprecedented since we started powering our economies with coal. In fact, greenhouse-gas cuts above 1 per cent per year "have historically been associated only with economic recession or upheaval," as the economist Nicholas Stern put it in his 2006 report for the British government.

Even after the Soviet Union collapsed, reductions of this duration and 17 depth did not happen (the former Soviet countries experienced average annual reductions of roughly 5 per cent over a period of ten years). They did not happen after Wall Street crashed in 2008 (wealthy countries experienced about a 7 per cent drop between 2008 and 2009, but their CO_2 emissions rebounded with gusto in 2010 and emissions in China and India had continued to rise). Only in the immediate aftermath of the great market crash of 1929 did the United States, for instance, see emissions drop for several consecutive years by more than 10 per cent annually, according to historical data from the Carbon Dioxide Information Analysis Centre. But that was the worst economic crisis of modern times.

If we are to avoid that kind of carnage while meeting our science-based 18 emissions targets, carbon reduction must be managed carefully through what Anderson and Bows describe as "radical and immediate de-growth strategies in the US, EU and other wealthy nations." Which is fine, except that we happen to have an economic system that fetishises GDP growth above all else, regardless of the human or ecological consequences, and in which the neoliberal political class has utterly abdicated its responsibility to manage anything (since the market is the invisible genius to which every-thing must be entrusted).

So what Anderson and Bows are really saying is that there is still time to 19 avoid catastrophic warming, but not within the rules of capitalism as they are currently constructed. Which may be the best argument we have ever had for changing those rules.

In a 2012 essay that appeared in the influential scientific journal *Nature* 20 *Climate Change*, Anderson and Bows laid down something of a gauntlet, accusing many of their fellow scientists of failing to come clean about the kind of changes that climate change demands of humanity. On this it is worth quoting the pair at length:

> . . . *in developing emission scenarios scientists repeatedly and severely underplay the implications of their analyses. When it comes to avoiding a 2°C rise, "impossible" is translated into "difficult but doable," whereas "urgent and radical" emerge as "challenging"—all to appease the god of economics (or, more precisely, finance). For example, to avoid exceeding the maximum rate of emission reduction dictated by economists, "impossibly" early peaks in emissions are assumed, together with naive notions about "big" engineering and the deployment rates of low-carbon infrastructure. More disturbingly, as emissions budgets dwindle, so geo-engineering is increasingly proposed to ensure that the diktat of economists remains unquestioned.*

In other words, in order to appear reasonable within neoliberal 21 economic circles, scientists have been dramatically soft-peddling the implications of their research. By August 2013, Anderson was willing to be even more blunt, writing that the boat had sailed on gradual change. "Perhaps at the time of the 1992 Earth Summit, or even at the turn of the millennium, 2°C levels of mitigation could have been achieved through significant *evolutionary changes* within *the political and economic hegemony*. But climate change is a cumulative issue! Now, in 2013, we in high-emitting (post-) industrial nations face a very different prospect. Our ongoing and collective carbon profligacy has squandered any opportunity for the 'evolutionary change' afforded by our earlier (and larger) 2°C carbon budget. Today, after two decades of bluff and lies, the remaining 2°C budget demands *revolutionary change* to *the political and economic hegemony*" (his emphasis).

We probably shouldn't be surprised that some climate scientists are a 22 little spooked by the radical implications of even their own research. Most of them were just quietly doing their work measuring ice cores, running global climate models and studying ocean acidification, only to discover, as the Australian climate expert and author Clive Hamilton puts it, that they "were unwittingly destabilising the political and social order."

But there are many people who are well aware of the revolutionary 23 nature of climate science. It's why some of the governments that decided to chuck their climate commitments in favour of digging up more carbon have had to find ever more thuggish ways to silence and intimidate their nations' scientists. In Britain, this strategy is becoming more overt, with Ian Boyd, the chief scientific adviser at the Department for Environment, Food and Rural Affairs, writing recently that scientists should avoid "suggesting that policies are either right or wrong" and should express their views "by working with embedded advisers (such as myself), and by being the voice of reason, rather than dissent, in the public arena."

If you want to know where this leads, check out what's happening in 24 Canada, where I live. The Conservative government of Stephen Harper has done such an effective job of gagging scientists and shutting down critical research projects that, in July 2012, a couple thousand scientists and supporters held a mock-funeral on Parliament Hill in Ottawa, mourning "the death of evidence." Their placards said, "No Science, No Evidence, No Truth."

But the truth is getting out anyway. The fact that the business-as-usual 25 pursuit of profits and growth is destabilising life on earth is no longer something we need to read about in scientific journals. The early signs are unfolding before our eyes. And increasing numbers of us are responding accordingly: blockading fracking activity in Balcombe; interfering with Arctic drilling preparations in Russian waters (at tremendous personal cost); taking tar sands operators to court for violating indigenous sovereignty; and countless other acts of resistance large and small. In Brad Werner's computer model, this is the "friction" needed to slow down the forces of destabilisation; the great climate campaigner Bill McKibben calls it the "antibodies" rising up to fight the planet's "spiking fever."

It's not a revolution, but it's a start. And it might just buy us enough 26 time to figure out a way to live on this planet that is distinctly less f**ked.

VOCABULARY

neoliberal—a form of liberalism that moves away from traditional liberal principles and toward "new" forms of liberalism such as free-market principles

profligacy—extravagant and wasteful use of resources

QUESTIONS

1. Klein's adoption of Brad Werner's use of the word *f**ked* is a direct way of creating urgency in her subject and audience. Does this language stir an emotional response in you as a reader? A logical response? Does it instill feelings of futility for the future or hope for change?

2. Klein's article discusses the role and the authority of scientists to speak on matters of policy, politics, economics, and activism. Given the principles of expertise and authority, where are the boundaries between professionalism and civic duty? In other words, should scientists be activists based on their research findings?

3. According to some commentators on climate change, there is still a debate about the severity of climate change. Do you think there is still debate? What is the evidence for this so-called debate? Does Klein and the people she cites think there is a debate? Who benefits from this supposed debate?

SUGGESTIONS FOR WRITING

1. Write a letter to one of your political leaders (mayor, MP, MLA, or other) regarding the tensions between economics and climate science outlined by Klein in her article. Make an argument and suggest some reforms or changes that you consider would help mitigate the problems posed by climate change.

2. In the vein of Jonathan Swift's "A Modest Proposal," write a satirical essay about solving the problems of climate change.

Globalisation's Time Is Up

James Howard Kunstler

The big yammer these days in the United States is to the effect that 1
globalisation[1] is here to stay: it's wonderful, get used to it. The chief
cheerleader for this point of view is Thomas Friedman, columnist for
the *New York Times* and author of *The World Is Flat*. The seemingly unanimous embrace of this idea in the power circles of America is a marvellous
illustration of the madness of crowds, for nothing could be further from
the truth than the idea that globalisation is now a permanent fixture of the
human condition.

Today's transient global economic relations are a product of very 2
special transient circumstances, namely relative world peace and absolutely
reliable supplies of cheap energy. Subtract either of these elements from
the equation and you will see globalisation evaporate so quickly it will suck
the air out of your lungs. It is significant that none of the cheerleaders for
globalisation takes this equation into account. In fact, the American power
elite is sleepwalking into a crisis so severe that the blowback may put both
major political parties out of business.

The world saw an earlier phase of robust global trade run from the 3
1870s to a dead stop in 1914. This was the boom period of railroad construction and the advent of the ocean-going steamship. The great powers
had existed in relative peace since Napoleon's last stand. The Crimean war
was a minor episode that took place in the backwaters of Eurasia, and the
Franco-Prussian war was a comic opera
that lasted less than a year. The American
civil war hardly affected the rest of the
world.[2]

This first phase of globalisation then 4
took off under coal-and-steam power.
There was no shortage of fuel, the colonial boundaries were stable, and the
pipeline of raw materials from them
to the factories of western Europe ran
smoothly. The rise of a middle class running the many stages of the production
process provided markets for all the new
production. Innovations in finance gave
legitimacy to all kinds of tradable paper.

James Howard Kunstler (b. 1948) lives in
Saratoga Springs, NY, and writes extensively on
environmental issues. *The Geography of Nowhere*
(1993) and *Home from Nowhere* (1996) explore
the American urban landscape and the possibilities for its regeneration. *The Long Emergency:
Surviving the Converging Catastrophes of the
Twenty-First Century* (2005) explores human
possibilities in a future shaped by crises in oil
supply, global climate change, and other world
problems.

"Globalisation's Time Is Up" was originally published in *The
Guardian Weekly*, 12–18 Aug. 2005: 3. Reprinted with permission of the author.

Life was very good for Europe and America, notwithstanding a few sharp cyclical depressions. Trade boomed between the great powers. The belle époque represented the high tide of hopeful expectations. In America it was called the progressive era.[3] The 20th century looked golden.

It all fell apart in 1914, and a new round of globalisation did not ramp   5
up again until the mid-1960s.

It may be significant that the first collapse of globalisation occurred   6
as the coal economy was transitioning into an oil economy, with deep geopolitical implications for those who had oil (America) and those who might seek to control the other major region closest to Europe that possessed it (then the Caspian,[4] since Arabian oil was as yet undiscovered). The first world war was settled by those nations (Britain and France) that were friendly with the greatest producer of oil most readily accessed. Germany was the loser and again in the reprise for its poor access to oil. Japan suffered similarly.

We are now due for another folding up of the periodic global trade   7
fair as the industrial nations enter the tumultuous era beyond the global oil production peak. The economic perversities that have built up in the current era are not hard to see, though our leaders dread to acknowledge them. The dirty secret of the US economy for at least a decade now is that it has come to be based on the ceaseless elaboration of a car-dependent suburban infrastructure—McHousing[5] estates, eight-lane highways, big-box chain stores, hamburger stands—that has no future as a living arrangement in an oil-short future.

The American suburban juggernaut can be described succinctly as the   8
greatest misallocation of resources in the history of the world. The mortgages, bonds, real estate investment trusts and derivative financial instruments associated with this tragic enterprise must make the judicious goggle with wonder and nausea.

Add to this grim economic picture a far-flung military contest, already   9
under way, really, for control of the world's remaining oil, and the scene grows darker. Two-thirds of that oil is in the possession of people who resent the West (America in particular), many of whom have vowed to destroy it. Both America and Britain have felt the sting of freelance asymmetrical warmakers not associated with a particular state but with a transnational religious cause that uses potent small arms and explosives to unravel western societies and confound their defences.

China, a supposed beneficiary of globalisation, will be as desperate for   10
oil as all the other players, and perhaps more ruthless in seeking control of the supplies, some of which they can walk to. Of course, it is hard to imagine the continuation of American chain stores' manufacturing supply lines with

China, given the potential for friction. Even on its own terms, China faces issues of environmental havoc, population overshoot, and political turmoil—orders of magnitude greater than anything known in Europe or America.

Viewed through this lens, the sunset of the current phase of 11 globalisation seems dreadfully close to the horizon. The American public has enjoyed the fiesta, but the blue-light special orgy of easy motoring, limitless air-conditioning, and super-cheap products made by factory slaves far, far away is about to close down. Globalisation is finished. The world is about to become a larger place again.

NOTES

1 "Globalisation" (British spelling) or "globalization" refers to an increased openness of national borders to the movement of trade, products, and money in the last forty years or so.

2 The Crimean War was fought between Russia and Britain and its allies in 1853–1856. The Franco-Prussian War was fought between France and Prussia (the core of present-day Germany) in 1870–1871. The American Civil War was fought between the Union North and the Confederate South, largely over the issue of slavery, between 1861 and 1865.

3 Belle Époque, which could be translated from the French as "the beautiful period," was the period of European history from 1871 to 1914. It was characterized by peace and the development of arts and culture, as was the Progressive era (1890–1913) in the United States.

4 The Caspian is the area surrounding the Caspian Sea, in the territory of the then Soviet Union.

5 McHousing is a reference to McDonald's, the hamburger chain; the implication is that suburban housing has as much originality and value as fast food.

VOCABULARY

blowback—significant reaction

colonial—of the colonies, countries, and areas settled during the period of European expansion from the seventeenth to the nineteenth centuries

geopolitical—concerning the interaction between geography and politics

judicious—well-judged, carefully considered

transient—not lasting for long, passing

QUESTIONS

1. This essay appeared in a British newspaper. Is Kunstler addressing a British audience? How can you tell?

2. Why is the continuing development of suburbs in the United States a "tragic enterprise," according to Kunstler? What standard(s) of evaluation does he base this judgment on?

3. Why are the cycles of history so important to Kunstler? How does using these cycles as evidence link with his thesis?

4. Does Kunstler consider counter-arguments to his case? If not, can you think of any?

SUGGESTION FOR WRITING

Does globalization affect your own life or the life of your community in any way? Do you, for example, get products from distant places, but find that local jobs have gone abroad too? If globalization has effects on your local situation, write an essay analyzing (and, if you like, also evaluating) these effects.

The Loons

Margaret Laurence

Just below Manawaka, where the Wachakwa River ran brown and noisy over the pebbles, the scrub oak and grey-green willow and chokecherry bushes grew in a dense thicket. In a clearing at the centre of the thicket stood the Tonnerre family's shack. The basis of this dwelling was a small square cabin made of poplar poles and chinked with mud, which had been built by Jules Tonnerre some fifty years before, when he came back from Batoche with a bullet in his thigh, the year that Riel was hung and the voices of the Metis entered their long silence.[1] Jules had only intended to stay the winter in the Wachakwa Valley, but the family was still there in the thirties, when I was a child. As the Tonnerres had increased, their settlement had been added to, until the clearing at the foot of the town hill was a chaos of lean-tos, wooden packing cases, warped lumber, discarded car tyres, ramshackle chicken coops, tangled strands of barbed wire and rusty tin cans.

The Tonnerres were French half-breeds, and among themselves they spoke a *patois* that was neither Cree nor French. Their English was broken and full of obscenities. They did not belong among the Cree of the Galloping Mountain reservation, further north, and they did not belong among the Scots-Irish and Ukrainians of Manawaka, either. They were, as my Grandmother MacLeod would have put it, neither flesh, fowl, nor good salt herring. When their men were not working at odd jobs or as section hands on the C.P.R., they lived on relief. In the summers, one of the Tonnerre youngsters, with a face that seemed totally unfamiliar with laughter, would knock at the doors of the town's brick houses and offer for sale a lard-pail full of bruised wild strawberries, and if he got as much as a quarter he would grab the coin and run before the customer had time to change her mind. Sometimes old Jules, or his son Lazarus, would get mixed up in a Saturday-night brawl, and would hit out at whoever was nearest, or howl drunkenly among the offended shoppers on Main Street, and then the Mountie would put them for the night in the barred cell underneath the Court House, and the next morning they would be quiet again.

Margaret Laurence (1926–1987) was born in Neepawa, Manitoba. Much of her writing is set in the fictional town of Manawaka and represents Canadian prairie life. "The Loons" comes from a collection of interconnected Laurence short stories entitled *A Bird in the House* (1970). Laurence twice won the Governor General's Award, for *A Jest of God* (1966) and *The Diviners* (1974).

Piquette Tonnerre, the daughter of Lazarus, was in my class at school. 3
She was older than I, but she had failed several grades, perhaps because her
attendance had always been sporadic and her interest in schoolwork negligible. Part of the reason she had missed a lot of school was that she had had
tuberculosis of the bone, and had once spent many months in hospital. I
knew this because my father was the doctor who had looked after her. Her
sickness was almost the only thing I knew about her, however. Otherwise,
she existed for me only as a vaguely embarrassing presence, with her hoarse
voice and her clumsy limping walk and her grimy cotton dresses that were
always miles too long. I was neither friendly nor unfriendly towards her.
She dwelt and moved somewhere within my scope of vision, but I did not
actually notice her very much until that peculiar summer when I was eleven.

"I don't know what to do about that kid," my father said at dinner one 4
evening. "Piquette Tonnerre, I mean. The damn bone's flared up again.
I've had her in hospital for quite a while now, and it's under control all
right, but I hate like the dickens to send her home again."

"Couldn't you explain to her mother that she has to rest a lot?" my 5
mother said.

"The mother's not there," my father replied. "She took off a few years 6
back. Can't say I blame her. Piquette cooks for them, and she says Lazarus would
never do anything for himself as long as she's there. Anyway, I don't think she'd
take much care of herself, once she got back. She's only thirteen, after all. Beth,
I was thinking—what about taking her up to Diamond Lake with us this summer? A couple of months rest would give that bone a much better chance."

My mother looked stunned. 7

"But Ewen—what about Roddie and Vanessa?" 8

"She's not contagious," my father said. "And it would be company for 9
Vanessa."

"Oh dear," my mother said in distress, "I'll bet anything she has nits in 10
her hair."

"For Pete's sake," my father said crossly, "do you think Matron would 11
let her stay in the hospital for all this time like that? Don't be silly, Beth."

Grandmother MacLeod, her delicately featured face as rigid as a cameo, 12
now brought her mauve-veined hands together as though she were about to
begin a prayer.

"Ewen, if that half-breed youngster comes along to Diamond Lake, I'm 13
not going," she announced. "I'll go to Morag's for the summer."

I had trouble in stifling my urge to laugh, for my mother brightened 14
visibly and quickly tried to hide it. If it came to a choice between
Grandmother MacLeod and Piquette, Piquette would win hands down,
nits or not.

"It might be quite nice for you, at that," she mused. "You haven't seen 15
Morag for over a year, and you might enjoy being in the city for a while.
Well, Ewen dear, you do what you think best. If you think it would do
Piquette some good, then we'll be glad to have her, as long as she behaves
herself."

So it happened that several weeks later, when we all piled into my 16
father's old Nash, surrounded by suitcases and boxes of provisions and toys
for my ten-month-old brother, Piquette was with us and Grandmother
MacLeod, miraculously, was not. My father would only be staying at the
cottage for a couple of weeks, for he had to get back to his practice, but the
rest of us would stay at Diamond Lake until the end of August.

Our cottage was not named, as many were, "Dew Drop Inn" or 17
"Bide-a-Wee," or "Bonnie Doon." The sign on the roadway bore in austere
letters only our name, MacLeod. It was not a large cottage, but it was on the
lakefront. You could look out the windows and see, through the filigree of
the spruce trees, the water glistening greenly as the sun caught it. All around
the cottage were ferns, and sharp-branched raspberry bushes, and moss that
had grown over fallen tree trunks. If you looked carefully among the weeds
and grass, you could find wild strawberry plants which were in white flower
now and in another month would bear fruit, the fragrant globes hanging
like miniature scarlet lanterns on the thin hairy stems. The two grey squirrels were still there, gossiping at us from the tall spruce beside the cottage,
and by the end of the summer they would again be tame enough to take
pieces of crust from my hands. The broad moose antlers that hung above
the back door were a little more bleached and fissured after the winter, but
otherwise everything was the same. I raced joyfully around my kingdom,
greeting all the places I had not seen for a year. My brother, Roderick, who
had not been born when we were here last summer, sat on the car rug in the
sunshine and examined a brown spruce cone, meticulously turning it round
and round in his small and curious hands. My mother and father toted
the luggage from car to cottage, exclaiming over how well the place had
wintered, no broken windows, thank goodness, no apparent damage from
storm-felled branches or snow.

Only after I had finished looking around did I notice Piquette. She 18
was sitting on the swing, her lame leg held stiffly out, and her other foot
scuffing the ground as she swung slowly back and forth. Her long hair hung
black and straight around her shoulders, and her broad coarse-featured face
bore no expression—it was blank, as though she no longer dwelt within
her own skull, as though she had gone elsewhere. I approached her very
hesitantly.

"Want to come and play?" 19

Piquette looked at me with a sudden flash of scorn.   20

"I ain't a kid," she said.   21

Wounded, I stamped angrily away, swearing I would not speak to her   22
for the rest of the summer. In the days that followed, however, Piquette
began to interest me, and I began to want to interest her. My reasons did
not appear bizarre to me. Unlikely as it may seem, I had only just realised
that the Tonnerre family, whom I had always heard called half-breeds,
were actually Indians, or as near as made no difference. My acquaintance
with Indians was not extensive. I did not remember ever having seen a
real Indian, and my new awareness that Piquette sprang from the people
of Big Bear[2] and Poundmaker,[3] of Tecumseh,[4] of the Iroquois[5] who had
eaten Father Brebeuf's heart[6]—all this gave her an instant attraction in my
eyes. I was a devoted reader of Pauline Johnson[7] at this age, and sometimes
would orate aloud and in an exalted voice, *West Wind, blow from your prai-*
rie nest; Blow from the mountains, blow from the west—and so on. It seemed
to me that Piquette must be in some way a daughter of the forest, a kind of
junior prophetess of the wilds, who might impart to me, if I took the right
approach, some of the secrets which she undoubtedly knew—where the
whippoorwill made her nest, how the coyote reared her young, or whatever
it was that it said in Hiawatha.[8]

I set about gaining Piquette's trust. She was not allowed to go swimming,   23
with her bad leg, but I managed to lure her down to the beach—or rather,
she came because there was nothing else to do. The water was always icy,
for the lake was fed by springs, but I swam like a dog, thrashing my arms
and legs around at such speed and with such an output of energy that I
never grew cold. Finally, when I had had enough, I came out and sat beside
Piquette on the sand. When she saw me approaching, her hand squashed
flat the sand castle she had been building, and she looked at me sullenly,
without speaking.

"Do you like this place?" I asked, after a while, intending to lead on   24
from there into the question of forest lore.

Piquette shrugged. "It's okay. Good as anywhere."   25

"I love it," I said. "We come here every summer."   26

"So what?" Her voice was distant, and I glanced at her uncertainly,   27
wondering what I could have said wrong.

"Do you want to come for a walk?" I asked her. "We wouldn't need to   28
go far. If you walk just around the point there, you come to a bay where
great big reeds grow in the water, and all kinds of fish hang around there.
Want to? Come on."

She shook her head.   29

"Your dad said I ain't supposed to do no more walking than I got to."   30

I tried another line.   31

"I bet you know a lot about the woods and all that, eh?" I began   32
respectfully.

Piquette looked at me from her large dark unsmiling eyes.   33

"I don't know what in hell you're talkin' about," she replied. "You nuts   34
or somethin'? If you mean where my old man, and me, and all them live,
you better shut up, by Jesus, you hear?"

I was startled and my feelings were hurt, but I had a kind of dogged   35
perseverance. I ignored her rebuff.

"You know something, Piquette? There's loons here, on this lake. You   36
can see their nests just up the shore there, behind those logs. At night,
you can hear them even from the cottage, but it's better to listen from the
beach. My dad says we should listen and try to remember how they sound,
because in a few years when more cottages are built at Diamond Lake and
more people come in, the loons will go away."

Piquette was picking up stones and snail shells and then dropping   37
them again.

"Who gives a good goddamn?" she said.   38

It became increasingly obvious that, as an Indian, Piquette was a dead   39
loss. That evening I went out by myself, scrambling through the bushes
that overhung the steep path, my feet slipping on the fallen spruce needles
that covered the ground. When I reached the shore, I walked along the firm
damp sand to the small pier that my father had built, and sat down there.
I heard someone else crashing through the undergrowth and the bracken,
and for a moment I thought Piquette had changed her mind, but it turned
out to be my father. He sat beside me on the pier and we waited, without
speaking.

At night the lake was like black glass with a streak of amber which was   40
the path of the moon. All around, the spruce trees grew tall and close-set,
branches blackly sharp against the sky, which was lightened by a cold flick-
ering of stars. Then the loons began their calling. They rose like phantom
birds from the nests on the shore, and flew out onto the dark still surface
of the water.

No one can ever describe that ululating sound, the crying of the loons,   41
and no one who has heard it can ever forget it. Plaintive, and yet with a
quality of chilling mockery, those voices belonged to a world separated by
aeons from our neat world of summer cottages and the lighted lamps of
home.

"They must have sounded just like that," my father remarked, "before   42
any person ever set foot here."

Then he laughed. "You could say the same, of course, about 43
sparrows, or chipmunks, but somehow it only strikes you that way with the
loons."

"I know," I said.   44

Neither of us suspected that this would be the last time we would ever 45
sit here together on the shore, listening. We stayed for perhaps half an
hour, and then we went back to the cottage. My mother was reading beside
the fireplace. Piquette was looking at the burning birch log, and not doing
anything.

"You should have come along," I said, although in fact I was glad she 46
had not.

"Not me," Piquette said. "You wouldn' catch me walkin' way down 47
there jus' for a bunch of squawkin' birds."

Piquette and I remained ill at ease with one another. I felt I had somehow 48
failed my father, but I did not know what was the matter, nor why she
would not or could not respond when I suggested exploring the woods or
playing house. I thought it was probably her slow and difficult walking that
held her back. She stayed most of the time in the cottage with my mother,
helping her with the dishes or with Roddie, but hardly ever talking. Then
the Duncans arrived at their cottage, and I spent my days with Mavis, who
was my best friend. I could not reach Piquette at all, and I soon lost interest in trying. But all that summer she remained as both a reproach and a
mystery to me.

That winter my father died of pneumonia, after less than a week's 49
illness. For some time I saw nothing around me, being completely immersed
in my own pain and my mother's. When I looked outward once more, I
scarcely noticed that Piquette Tonnerre was no longer at school. I do not
remember seeing her at all until four years later, one Saturday night when
Mavis and I were having Cokes in the Regal Café. The jukebox was boom-
ing like tuneful thunder, and beside it, leaning lightly on its chrome and its
rainbow glass, was a girl.

Piquette must have been seventeen then, although she looked about 50
twenty. I stared at her, astounded that anyone could have changed so much.
Her face, so stolid and expressionless before, was animated now with a gai-
ety that was almost violent. She laughed and talked very loudly with the
boys around her. Her lipstick was bright carmine, and her hair was cut
short and frizzily permed. She had not been pretty as a child, and she was
not pretty now, for her features were still heavy and blunt. But her dark
and slightly slanted eyes were beautiful, and her skin-tight skirt and orange
sweater displayed to enviable advantage a soft and slender body.

She saw me, and walked over. She teetered a little, but it was not due to 51
her once-tubercular leg, for her limp was almost gone.

"Hi, Vanessa." Her voice still had the same hoarseness. "Long time no 52
see, eh?"

"Hi," I said. "Where've you been keeping yourself, Piquette?" 53

"Oh, I been around," she said. "I been away almost two years now. 54
Been all over the place—Winnipeg, Regina, Saskatoon. Jesus, what I could
tell you! I come back this summer, but I ain't stayin'. You kids goin' to the
dance?"

"No," I said abruptly, for this was a sore point with me. I was fifteen, 55
and thought I was old enough to go to the Saturday-night dances at the
Flamingo. My mother, however, thought otherwise.

"Y'oughta come," Piquette said. "I never miss one. It's just about the 56
on'y thing in this jerkwater town that's any fun. Boy, you couldn' catch me
stayin' here. I don' give a shit about this place. It stinks."

She sat down beside me, and I caught the harsh over-sweetness of her 57
perfume.

"Listen, you wanna know something, Vanessa?" she confided, her voice 58
only slightly blurred. "Your dad was the only person in Manawaka that ever
done anything good to me."

I nodded speechlessly. I was certain she was speaking the truth. I knew 59
a little more than I had that summer at Diamond Lake, but I could not
reach her now any more than I had then. I was ashamed, ashamed of my
own timidity, the frightened tendency to look the other way. Yet I felt no
real warmth towards her—I only felt that I ought to, because of that distant summer and because my father had hoped she would be company for
me, or perhaps that I would be for her, but it had not happened that way.
At this moment, meeting her again, I had to admit that she repelled and
embarrassed me, and I could not help despising the self-pity in her voice. I
wished she would go away. I did not want to see her. I did not know what
to say to her. It seemed that we had nothing to say to one another.

"I'll tell you something else," Piquette went on. "All the old bitches an' 60
biddies in this town will sure be surprised. I'm gettin' married this fall—my
boyfriend, he's an English fella, works in the stockyards in the city there, a
very tall guy, got blond wavy hair. Gee, is he ever handsome. Got this real
classy name. Alvin Gerald Cummings—some handle, eh? They call him Al."

For the merest instant, then, I saw her. I really did see her, for the first 61
and only time in all the years we had both lived in the same town. Her defiant face, momentarily, became unguarded and unmasked, and in her eyes
there was a terrifying hope.

"Gee, Piquette—" I burst out awkwardly, "that's swell. That's really   62
wonderful. Congratulations—good luck—I hope you'll be happy—"

As I mouthed the conventional phrases, I could only guess how great   63
her need must have been, that she had been forced to seek the very things
she so bitterly rejected.

When I was eighteen, I left Manawaka and went away to college. At the   64
end of my first year, I came back home for the summer. I spent the first few
days in talking non-stop with my mother, as we exchanged all the news that
somehow had not found its way into letters—what had happened in my life
and what had happened here in Manawaka while I was away. My mother
searched her memory for events that concerned people I knew.

"Did I ever write you about Piquette Tonnerre, Vanessa?" she asked   65
one morning.

"No, I don't think so," I replied. "Last I heard of her, she was going to   66
marry some guy in the city. Is she still there?"

My mother looked perturbed, and it was a moment before she spoke,   67
as though she did not know how to express what she had to tell and wished
she did not need to try.

"She's dead," she said at last. Then, as I stared at her, "Oh, Vanessa,   68
when it happened, I couldn't help thinking of her as she was that summer—so sullen and gauche and badly dressed. I couldn't help wondering if
we could have done something more at that time—but what could we do?
She used to be around in the cottage there with me all day, and honestly,
it was all I could do to get a word out of her. She didn't even talk to your
father very much, although I think she liked him, in her way."

"What happened?" I asked.   69

"Either her husband left her, or she left him," my mother said. "I don't   70
know which. Anyway, she came back here with two youngsters, both only
babies—they must have been born very close together. She kept house, I
guess, for Lazarus and her brothers, down in the valley there, in the old
Tonnerre place. I used to see her on the street sometimes, but she never
spoke to me. She'd put on an awful lot of weight, and she looked a mess, to
tell you the truth, a real slattern, dressed any old how. She was up in court
a couple of times—drunk and disorderly, of course. One Saturday night
last winter, during the coldest weather, Piquette was alone in the shack with
the children. The Tonnerres made home brew all the time, so I've heard,
and Lazarus said later she'd been drinking most of the day when he and the
boys went out that evening. They had an old woodstove there—you know
the kind, with exposed pipes. The shack caught fire. Piquette didn't get out,
and neither did the children."

I did not say anything. As so often with Piquette, there did not seem 71
to be anything to say. There was a kind of silence around the image in my
mind of the fire and the snow, and I wished I could put from my memory
the look that I had seen once in Piquette's eyes.

I went up to Diamond Lake for a few days that summer, with Mavis 72
and her family. The MacLeod cottage had been sold after my father's death,
and I did not even go to look at it, not wanting to witness my long-ago
kingdom possessed now by strangers. But one evening I went down to the
shore by myself.

The small pier which my father had built was gone, and in its place 73
there was a large and solid pier built by the government, for Galloping
Mountain was now a national park, and Diamond Lake had been re-named
Lake Wapakata, for it was felt that an Indian name would have a greater
appeal to tourists. The one store had become several dozen, and the settlement had all the attributes of a flourishing resort—hotels, a dance-hall,
cafés with neon signs, the penetrating odours of potato chips and hot dogs.

I sat on the government pier and looked out across the water. At night 74
the lake at least was the same as it had always been, darkly shining and bearing within its black glass the streak of amber that was the path of the moon.
There was no wind that evening, and everything was quiet all around me.
It seemed too quiet, and then I realized that the loons were no longer here.
I listened for some time, to make sure, but never once did I hear that long-
drawn call, half mocking and half plaintive, spearing through the stillness
across the lake.

I did not know what had happened to the birds. Perhaps they had gone 75
away to some far place of belonging. Perhaps they had been unable to find
such a place, and had simply died out, having ceased to care any longer
whether they lived or not.

I remembered how Piquette had scorned to come along, when my 76
father and I sat there and listened to the lake birds. It seemed to me now
that in some unconscious and totally unrecognised way, Piquette might
have been the only one, after all, who had heard the crying of the loons.

NOTES

[1] Louis Riel was the leader of the Métis after founding the province of Manitoba. He led the Red River
Rebellion (1869–1870) and the North-West Rebellion (1885) against the Canadian government to
try to gain rights and independence for the Métis. Riel was defeated at Batoche on May 15, 1885.

[2] Big Bear (1825–1888) was a chief of the Cree First Nation and, like Louis Riel, resisted the expansion of the Canadian government into the West.

[3] Poundmaker (1842–1886) was a chief of the Cree First Nation who participated in the North-West
Rebellion.

[4] Tecumseh (1768–1813), a leader of the Shawnee, helped slow the progress of Americans into Upper Canada during the War of 1812.

[5] The Iroquois Confederacy expanded into much of the Northeastern United States in the late 1600s; its members were largely pushed back into their original homeland in Ontario, Quebec, and upstate New York after the American Revolution (1775–1776).

[6] Jean de Brébeuf (1593–1649) was a Jesuit who worked among the Hurons. He and the Hurons were defeated in 1649 by the Iroquois. Iroquois reportedly ate Brébeuf's heart as they killed him.

[7] Pauline Johnson (1861–1913) was a Canadian writer who celebrated her Aboriginal ancestry. Her most noted work is *Flint and Feather* (1912), a collection of poetry.

[8] *The Song of Hiawatha* is an epic poem by American Henry Wadsworth Longfellow (1807–1882), loosely based on Ojibwe legends. Although widely criticized later for its romanticism, the poem was immensely popular for many years.

VOCABULARY

patois—a regional dialect that is often considered substandard or vulgar

QUESTIONS

1. After a few days at the cottage, Vanessa says, "Piquette began to interest me, and I began to want to interest her" (261). What do you notice about the way Vanessa phrases this statement?

2. At one point, Vanessa says that Piquette and her family "were actually Indians, or as near as made no difference" (261). To what cultural heritage does Piquette belong? What are the effects of Vanessa erasing this cultural difference?

3. Count the number of times Piquette actually speaks in the story. Is this surprising? Why or why not? What does her relative quietness tell us about the story?

4. In describing Piquette's life, Beth says, "Either her husband left her, or she left him. . . . I don't know which" (265). Do you think these details might be important? What does this statement tell us about Beth?

5. Near the end of the story, Vanessa offers two explanations for the disappearance of the loons. What are they, and which is more realistic?

6. At the end of the story, Vanessa thinks that Piquette really heard the loons' cries and that the birds and Piquette have much in common. Do you agree with this connection? Do you see any problems with it?

Time and the Narrative Voice

Margaret Laurence

The treatment of time and the handling of the narrative voice—these two things are of paramount importance to me in the writing of fiction. Oddly enough, although they might seem to be two quite separate aspects of technique, in fact they are inextricably bound together. When I say "time," I don't mean clock-time, in this context, nor do I mean any kind of absolute time—which I don't believe to exist, in any event. I mean historical time, variable and fluctuating. 1

In any work of fiction, the span of time present in the story is not only as long as the time-span of every character's life and memory; it also represents everything acquired and passed on in a kind of memory-heritage from one generation to another. The time which is present in any story, therefore, must—by implication at least—include not only the totality of the characters' lives but also the inherited time of perhaps two or even three past generations, in terms of parents' and grandparents' recollections, and the much much longer past which has become legend, the past of a collective cultural memory. Obviously, not all of this can be conveyed in a single piece of prose. Some of it can only be hinted at; some of it may not be touched on at all. Nevertheless, it is *there* because it exists in the minds of the characters. How can one even begin to convey this sense of time? What parts of the time-span should be conveyed? These are questions which I always find enormously troubling, and before beginning any piece of writing, I tend to brood for quite a long time (clockwise) on these things. Not that the brooding does very much good, usually, or perhaps it bears fruit at some unrecognized subconscious level, because when the writing begins, a process of selection takes place in a way not consciously chosen, and this is where the long time-span implicit in every story or novel is directly and intimately related to the narrative voice. 2

Most of the fiction I have written in recent years has been written in the first person, with the main character assuming the narrative voice. Even when I have written in the third person, as I did in part of my novel *The Fire-Dwellers,* it is really a first-person narrative which happens to be written in the third person, for the narrative voice even here is essentially that of the main character, and the writer does not enter in as 3

For biographic details, see the previous reading, Laurence, Margaret, "The Loons."

Reprinted by permission of AP Watt at United Agents from "Time and the Narrative Voice" by Margaret Laurence from *The Narrative Voice,* ed. John Metcalf.

commentator. Some people hold the erroneous belief that this kind of fiction is an evasion—the writer is hiding behind a mask, namely one of the characters. Untrue. The writer is every bit as vulnerable here as in directly autobiographical fiction. The character is not a mask but an individual, separate from the writer. At the same time, the character is one of the writer's voices and selves, and fiction writers tend to have a mental trunk full of these—in writers, this quality is known as richness of imagination; in certain inmates of mental hospitals it has other names, the only significant difference being that writers are creating their private worlds with the ultimate hope of throwing open the doors to other humans. This means of writing fiction, oriented almost totally towards an individual character, is obviously not the only way, but it appears to be the only way I can write.

Once the narrative voice is truly established—that is, once the writer 4 has listened, really listened, to the speech and idiom and outlook of the character—it is then not the writer but the character who, by some process of transferral, bears the responsibility for the treatment of time within the work. It is the character who chooses which parts of the personal past, the family past and the ancestral past have to be revealed in order for the present to be realized and the future to happen. This is not a morbid dwelling on the past on the part of the writer or the character. It is, rather, an expression of the feeling which I strongly hold about time—that the past and the future are both always present, *present* in both senses of the word, always now and always here with us. It is only through the individual presence of the characters that the writer can hope to convey even a fragment of this sense of time, and this is one reason, among others, why it is so desperately important to discover the true narrative voice—which really means knowing the characters so well that one can take on their past, their thoughts, their responses, can in effect for a while *become* them. It has sometimes occurred to me that I must be a kind of Method[1] writer, in the same way that some actors become the characters they play for the moments when they are portraying these characters. I didn't plan it this way, and possibly it sounds like gibberish, but this is how it appears to take place.

Theorizing, by itself, is meaningless in connection with fiction, just as 5 any concept of form is meaningless in isolation from the flesh and blood of content and personality, just as a skeleton is only dry bone by itself but when it exists inside a living being it provides the support for the whole creature. I'll try to show something of what I mean about time and voice by reference to . . . two stories of mine. . . .

These stories are part of a collection called *A Bird in the House,* eight 6 in all, published separately before they were collected in a single volume, but conceived from the beginning as a related group. Each story is self-contained in the sense that it is definitely a short story and not a chapter from a novel, but the net effect is not unlike that of a novel. Structurally, however, these stories as a group are totally unlike a novel. I think the outlines of a novel (mine, anyway) and those of a group of stories such as these interrelated ones may be approximately represented in visual terms. In a novel, one might perhaps imagine the various themes and experiences and the interaction of characters with one another and with themselves as a series of wavy lines, converging, separating, touching, drawing apart, but moving in a *horizontal* direction. The short stories have flow-lines which are different. They move very close together but parallel and in a *vertical* direction. Each story takes the girl Vanessa along some specific course of her life and each follows that particular thread closely, but the threads are presented separately and not simultaneously. To this extent, the structure of these stories is a good deal simpler than that of a novel. Nevertheless, the relationship of time and the narrative voice can be seen just as plainly in the stories as in a novel.

"To Set Our House in Order" takes place when Vanessa is ten years   7
old. Her age remains constant throughout the story. The actual time-span of the story itself is short, a few days in her life, immediately before, during and after the birth of her brother. The things which happen on the surface are simple, but the things that happen inside Vanessa's head are more complex.

The narrative voice is, of course, that of Vanessa herself, but an older   8
Vanessa, herself grown up, remembering how it was when she was ten. When I was trying to write this story, I felt as I did with all the stories in *A Bird in the House,* that this particular narrative device was a tricky one, and I cannot even now personally judge how well it succeeds. What I tried to do was definitely *not* to tell the story as though it were being narrated by a child. This would have been impossible for me and also would have meant denying the story one of its dimensions, a time-dimension, the viewing from a distance of events which had happened in childhood. The narrative voice had to be that of an older Vanessa, but at the same time the narration had to be done in such a way that the ten-year-old would be conveyed. The narrative voice, therefore, had to speak as though from two points in time, simultaneously.

Given this double sense of time-present, Vanessa herself had to   9
recollect those things which were most meaningful to her, and in doing so, she reveals (at least I hope she does to the reader as she does to me) what the story is really about. It is actually a story about the generations, about the pain and bewilderment of one's knowledge of other people, about the reality of other people which is one way of realizing one's own reality, about the fluctuating and accidental quality of life (God really doesn't love

Order), and perhaps more than anything, about the strangeness and mystery of the very concepts of *past, present and future*. Who is Vanessa's father? The doctor who is struggling to support his family during the depression and who seems a pillar of strength to the little girl? Or the man who has collected dozens of travel books because once he passionately wanted to go far beyond Manawaka and now knows he won't? Or the boy who long ago half-blinded his brother accidentally with an air-rifle? Or the nineteen-year-old soldier who watched his brother die in the First World War? Ewen is all of these, and many many more, and in the story Vanessa has the sudden painful knowledge of his reality and his intricacy as a person, bearing with him the mental baggage of a lifetime, as all people do, and as she will have to do. The events of the story will become (and have become, to the older Vanessa) part of her mental baggage, part of her own spiritual fabric. Similarly, her father passes on to her some actual sense of her grandparents, his parents—the adamant Grandmother MacLeod, whose need it has been to appear a lady in her own image of herself; the dead Grandfather MacLeod, who momentarily lives for his granddaughter when she sees for the first time the loneliness of a man who could read the Greek tragedies in their original language and who never knew anyone in the small prairie town with whom he could communicate.

In "The Loons," the narrative voice is also that of the older Vanessa, 10 but in her portrayal of herself in past years, she ranges in age from eleven to eighteen. This meant, of course, that the tone of the narration had to change as Vanessa recalled herself at different ages, and this meant, for me, trying to feel my way into her mind at each age. Here again, the narrative voice chooses what will be recalled, and here again, the element of time is of great importance in the story. The eleven-year-old Vanessa sees the Métis girl, Piquette Tonnerre, in terms of romanticized notions of Indians, and is hurt when Piquette does not respond in the expected way. That summer lies submerged in Vanessa's mind until she encounters Piquette at a later time, but even then her reaction is one mainly of embarrassment and pity, not any real touching, and Piquette's long experience of hurt precludes anything except self-protectiveness on her part. It is only when Vanessa hears of Piquette's death that she realizes that she, too, like the entire town, is in part responsible. But the harm and alienation started a long way back, longer even than the semimythical figure of Piquette's grandfather, Jules Tonnerre, who fought with Riel at Batoche. The loons, recurring in the story both in their presence and in their absence, are connected to an ancestral past which belongs to Piquette, and the older Vanessa can see the irony of the only way in which Piquette's people are recognized by the community, in the changing of the name Diamond Lake to the more tourist-appealing Lake Wapakata.

What I said earlier may perhaps be more clearly seen now to show a　11
little of the relationship between the narrative voice and the treatment of
time—it is the character who chooses which parts of the personal past, the
family past and the ancestral past have to be revealed in order for the present to be realized and the future to happen.

NOTE

[1] Developed in the 1940s, Method acting is an approach to character where actors draw upon their
own emotions and imagination in order to become the character they are playing. Actors seek to
represent lifelike, realistic emotional responses through the characters.

QUESTIONS

1. Laurence mentions three different types of time in the introduction. Define each of these
   different meanings of time.

2. Many readers and critics consider Laurence's writing to be largely autobiographical. How
   does Laurence respond to this idea in this essay?

3. For Laurence, what distinguishing features separate a novel from a collection of related
   short stories?

4. To what extent are Piquette and Métis history part of Vanessa's personal, family, and
   ancestral pasts? To what extent are Vanessa and white history part of Piquette's personal,
   family, and ancestral pasts?

5. Laurence ends the piece by claiming that both the present and the future require the past
   in order to happen at all. To what extent do you think the past determines the future?

SUGGESTION FOR WRITING

Laurence states that in writing the character of Vanessa, "The tone of the narration had to
change as Vanessa recalled herself at different ages, and this meant, for me, trying to feel my
way into her mind at each age." Select an event or situation from your childhood, and write
two different versions of that event: one from the narrative point of view of your past self as
a child, the other from the narrative point of view of your present self as an adult. Try to use
diction that is appropriate to each age or point of view.

Reconstructing the Canadian Identity

Jocelyn Letourneau

Much has been said about the Harper government's decision to restore certain symbols of the monarchy and to tie them anew to the emblematic figure of Canada. Its decision to transform the War of 1812 into a decisive event in the creation of the country has also been contested. In Quebec, as well as the rest of Canada, many pundits are resisting what they have called a step backward in the production of national symbols and a hijacking of the past for political purposes in the present. How should we interpret the Prime Minister's actions? 1

This "royalization" of the national symbolic landscape and recasting of Canada's historical experience can be linked to the exhaustion of the paradigm that has formed the heart of the Canadian project for the past 40 years: multiculturalism. 2

Multiculturalism has not been abandoned by the Canadian government as the country's official ideology, of course. But at federal headquarters, the limits of defining the country this way are becoming increasingly evident. 3

Some have suggested that the original goal of Canadian multicultural policy was to undermine Quebec nationalism. In reality, Pierre Trudeau wanted to undo the framework in which Canadian identity was evolving at the time—that of two solitudes.[1] He also dreamed of tapping Quebec's momentum for the construction of a country of his own devising, a kind of postmodern society expunged of its separate and, to his mind, pointless ethno-nationalities. 4

In many respects, his plan failed. Rather than disappearing, the two solitudes dwindled into two lassitudes. Now, engaging Quebec and English Canada in a shared, pan-national symbolic project is a pipe dream. 5

What is perhaps more alarming, at least for Canadian thinkers, is that, after 40 years of ascendancy, multiculturalism has somehow sanitized the country's historical identity. Canada's historic roots—and those of English Canada in particular—have been replaced by civic arrangements that sap its strength. As this national identity has spread more widely, it has become shallower. It now seems impractical to maintain Canada, and particularly English Canada, in a crucible that weakens the country as it expands. 6

Jocelyn Letourneau is a professor of history at University of Laval in Quebec. He holds the Canada Research Chair in Contemporary Political History and Economy in Quebec. His books include *A History for the Future* (2004) and *Canadians and Their Pasts* (2013).

Reprinted by permission from "Reconstructing the Canadian Identity" by Jocelyn Letourneau : *The Globe and Mail* [Toronto, Ont] 01 July 2013: A.9.

Stephen Harper may have foreseen the consequences of these perils for   7
Canada. So, given the impossibility of denying Quebec's dissonance within
the country, he granted Quebeckers some recognition, that of a "nation
within a united Canada." His expedience did not, of course, satisfy the sep-
aratists, but it was nonetheless a significant symbolic gesture.

The "rest of Canada" also needed to re-establish its historical authenticity.   8
But around what meaningful symbols and ideas? It appears that reclaim-
ing Canada's elemental Britishness and distancing the country from
Americanization is the option the government has chosen so far.

It is clear in these circumstances that the restoration of royal symbols   9
(central to British heritage in Canada as a constitutional monarchy) and
the importance given to the War of 1812 (presented as a pivotal moment
of resistance to American invasion and the preservation of the country's
distinctiveness) are not the expression of a foolish plan on the part of a disconnected government. These initiatives are contributing to the reconstruc-
tion of Canadian identity at a time when the country is looking for a new
symbolic basis for its current reality.

Over the coming years, under the auspices of Mr. Harper, if his 10
government survives the next election, Canadian identity will be subject
to a process of regeneration to lead to consolidation. This identity will be
built around three pillars: recognition of the Quebec nation as a principal stakeholder in a united country; recognition of British heritage and
roots as distinctive aspects of Canadianness; and insistence on Canada's
desire to stand up as an independent and sovereign nation, particularly
with regard to its powerful southern neighbour, including (defensive) military actions, now considered central to Canada's historical identity. We
can add a fourth pillar—needing strength in light of the Prime Minister's
dealing with the Idle No More movement: symbolic recognition of the
First Nations' contribution to the foundation and actual building of the
country.

At the centre of the identity formed by these four pillars[2] remains the 11
idea of Canada as a nation of immigrants, formed by many cultures that
have created their shared living space in mutual tolerance based on three
complementary platforms: distaste for open violence and respect for the
rule of law; the primacy of politics as the best method of dispute resolution; and the search for complex and even unconventional political arrangements. From this reconstituted history of Canada, Mr. Harper believes, will
flow a reinvigorated nation.

Will this script be adequate to reconstruct Canadian symbols and 12
history? Only the future will tell whether the present can be conjugated in
this particular past tense.

NOTES

[1] *Two Solitudes* is a title of a 1945 novel from Hugh MacLennan. The "solitudes" are the often-tense French and English relations in Canada.

[2] Four pillars is a frequently employed architectural metaphor for stability that is invoked in a variety of contexts. It is often used in politics, specifically democracy, to talk about the founding principles of democratic rule.

VOCABULARY

lassitude—a state of physical or mental exhaustion

QUESTIONS

1. Do you agree with Letourneau's assessment that Stephen Harper has tried to make Canadian history and identity more "British"?

2. Given Harper's attempts to make the War of 1812 a central symbol of Canadian identity, do you identify with this event as a significant part of your history and identity?

3. Charles Taylor's essay "All for One, and One for All" (Readings) suggests a Canadian ethos based on "very different views" (359), yet Letourneau's essay suggests a common "four pillars" for identity construction. On what principles do you think Canadians can agree (distaste for violence, for example), and on what principles must we agree to disagree (religious freedoms, for example)?

4. Letourneau suggests that the quest for defining Canadian Identity is a tired one. Do you agree or disagree? Do we have a reasonable working definition of Canadian identity? Is it so important to have an agreed-upon definition?

SUGGESTION FOR WRITING

Letourneau's article discusses the importance of the interpretation of past events for the future imagining of identity. Describe an historical event that you think is important to Canadian identity and explain why it is an important incident for imagining our future.

Embraced by the Needle

Gabor Maté

Addictions always originate in unhappiness, even if hidden. They are emotional anesthetics; they numb pain. The first question—always—is not "Why the addiction?" but "Why the pain?" The answer, ever the same, is scrawled with crude eloquence on the wall of my patient Anna's room at the Portland Hotel in the heart of Vancouver's Downtown Eastside: "Any place I went to, I wasn't wanted. And that bites large." 1

The Downtown Eastside is considered to be Canada's drug capital, with an addict population of 3,000 to 5,000 individuals. I am a staff physician at the Portland, a non-profit harm-reduction facility where most of the clients are addicted to cocaine, to alcohol, to opiates like heroin, or to tranquilizers—or to any combination of these things. Many also suffer from mental illness. Like Anna, a 32-year-old poet, many are HIV positive or have full-blown AIDS. The methadone[1] I prescribe for their opiate dependence does little for the emotional anguish compressed in every heartbeat of these driven souls. 2

Methadone staves off the torment of opiate withdrawal, but, unlike heroin, it does not create a "high" for regular users. The essence of that high was best expressed by a 27-year-old sex-trade worker. "The first time I did heroin," she said, "it felt like a warm, soft hug." In a phrase, she summed up the psychological and chemical cravings that make some people vulnerable to substance dependence. 3

Gabor Maté is a Vancouver family physician and counsellor with a special interest in counselling adults, parents, and children with attention deficit hyperactivity disorder (ADHD). He is widely known for his expertise on addictions, mental health, and parenting. His most recent book is *In the Realm of Hungry Ghosts: Close Encounters with Addiction* (2009), for which he won the Hubert Evans Non-Fiction Prize. A long-time medical columnist for the *Vancouver Sun* and the *Globe and Mail,* he is also the author of *When the Body Says No: The Cost of Hidden Stress (2004), Hold On to Your Kids: Why Parents Need to Matter More than Peers* (2004), and *Scattered Minds: A New Look at the Origins and Healing of Attention Deficit Disorder* (1999).

"Embraced by the Needle" was first published in the *Globe and Mail,* August 27, 2001. Reprinted with permission.

No drug is, in itself, addictive. Only about 8 per cent to 15 per cent of people who try, say alcohol or marijuana, go on to addictive use. What makes them vulnerable? Neither physiological predispositions nor individual moral failures explain drug addictions. Chemical and emotional vulnerability are the products of life experience, according to current brain research and developmental psychology. 4

Most human brain growth occurs following birth; physical and emotional 5 interactions determine much of our brain development. Each brain's circuitry and chemistry reflects individual life experiences as much as inherited tendencies.

For any drug to work in the brain, the nerve cells have to have 6 receptors—sites where the drug can bind. We have opiate receptors because our brain has natural opiate-like substances, called endorphins, chemicals that participate in many functions, including the regulation of pain and mood. Similarly, tranquilizers of the benzodiazepine[2] class, such as Valium, exert their effect at the brain's natural benzodiazepine receptors.

Infant rats who get less grooming from their mothers have fewer 7 natural benzo receptors in the part of the brain that controls anxiety. Brains of infant monkeys separated from their mothers for only a few days are measurably deficient in the key neuro-chemical dopamine.

It is the same with human beings. Endorphins are released in the 8 infant's brain when there are warm, non-stressed, calm interactions with the parenting figures. Endorphins, in turn, promote the growth of receptors and nerve cells, and the discharge of other important brain chemicals. The fewer endorphin-enhancing experiences in infancy and early childhood, the greater the need for external sources. Hence, the greater vulnerability to addictions.

Distinguishing skid row addicts is the extreme degree of stress they had 9 to endure early in life. Almost all women now inhabiting Canada's addiction capital suffered sexual assaults in childhood, as did many of the males. Childhood memories of serial abandonment or severe physical and psychological abuse are common. The histories of my Portland patients tell of pain upon pain.

Carl, a 36-year-old native, was banished from one foster home after 10 another, had dishwashing liquid poured down his throat for using foul language at age 5, and was tied to a chair in a dark room to control his hyperactivity. When angry at himself—as he was recently, for using cocaine—he gouges his foot with a knife as punishment. His facial expression was that of a terrorized urchin who had just broken some family law and feared draconian retribution. I reassured him I wasn't his foster parent, and that he didn't owe it to me not to screw up.

But what of families where there was not abuse, but love, where parents 11 did their best to provide their children with a secure nurturing home? One also sees addictions arising in such families. The unseen factor here is the stress the parents themselves lived under even if they did not recognize it. That stress could come from relationship problems, or from outside circumstances such as economic pressure or political disruption. The most frequent source of hidden stress is the parents' own childhood histories that saddled them with emotional baggage they had never become conscious of. What we are not aware of in ourselves, we pass on to our children.

Stressed, anxious, or depressed parents have great difficulty initiating 12
enough of those emotionally rewarding, endorphin-liberating interactions
with their children. Later in life such children may experience a hit of heroin as the "warm, soft hug" my patient described: What they didn't get
enough of before, they can now inject.

Feeling alone, feeling there has never been anyone with whom to share 13
their deepest emotions, is universal among drug addicts. That is what Anna
had lamented on her wall. No matter how much love a parent has, the
child does not experience being wanted unless he or she is made absolutely
safe to express exactly how unhappy, or angry, or hate-filled he or she may
feel at times. The sense of unconditional love, of being fully accepted even
when most ornery, is what no addict ever experienced in childhood—often
not because the parents did not have it to give, simply because they did not
know how to transmit it to the child.

Addicts rarely make the connection between troubled childhood 14
experiences and self-harming habits. They blame themselves—and that is
the greatest wound of all, being cut off from their natural self-compassion.
"I was hit a lot," 40-year-old Wayne says, "but I asked for it. Then I made
some stupid decisions." And would he hit a child, no matter how much that
child "asked for it"? Would he blame that child for "stupid decisions"?

Wayne looks away. "I don't want to talk about that crap," says this 15
tough man, who has worked on oil rigs and construction sites and served
15 years in jail for robbery. He looks away and wipes tears from his eyes.

NOTES

[1] Methadone is a synthetic narcotic used in the treatment of drug addictions.

[2] Benzodiazepines (BZDs) are sedative-hypnotic agents widely used to treat conditions like anxiety
and insomnia, and also to induce pre-operative relaxation.

VOCABULARY

hyperactivity—the state of being unusually or excessively active, sometimes identified as a
childhood disorder

neuro-chemical—chemical element found in the brain

opiate—a medicine or substance containing opium

physiological—pertaining to the body

QUESTIONS

1. Maté uses several direct quotations from addicts, some in street language. Does this
technique increase or decrease the credibility of his statements?

2. Maté discusses addicts' feelings, the workings of endorphins and other chemicals in the brain, and the dynamics of stressed and dysfunctional families. Can we assume that he, as a physician, has the authority to speak on these topics? Are there any places in the essay where Maté seems to lack authority for his comments?

3. How does the diction of the essay convey Maté's attitude to the drug addicts he treats? List some key words or phrases that convey his attitude.

4. The essay ends with a story about "40-year-old Wayne" rather than with a conclusion summarizing the development of the thesis. Why do you think Maté chooses to conclude in this way? Is the conclusion effective?

SUGGESTION FOR WRITING

Interview a classmate about his or her experience or views of a current social issue. Then write a one-page essay using direct quotations from the interview that support your thesis or argue against it. For guidelines on using quotations effectively, see Part 3, H2 Quotations.

Unchopping a Tree

W. S. Merwin

S tart with the leaves, the small twigs, and the nests that have been 1
shaken, ripped, or broken off by the fall; these must be gathered and
attached once again to their respective places. It is not arduous work,
unless major limbs have been smashed or mutilated. If the fall was carefully
and correctly planned, the chances of anything of the kind happening will
have been reduced. Again, much depends upon the size, age, shape, and
species of the tree. Still, you will be lucky if you can get through this stage
without having to use machinery. Even in the best of circumstances it is
a labor that will make you wish often that you had won the favor of the
universe of ants, the empire of mice, or at least a local tribe of squirrels, and
could enlist their labors and their talents. But no, they leave you to it. They
have learned, with time. This is men's work. It goes without saying that
if the tree was hollow in whole or in part, and contained old nests of bird
or mammal or insect, or hoards of nuts or such structures as wasps or bees
build for their survival, the contents will have to be repaired where necessary, and reassembled, insofar as possible, in their original order, including
the shells of nuts already opened. With
spiders' webs you must simply do the
best you can. We do not have the spider's
weaving equipment, nor any substitute
for the leaf's living bond with its point of
attachment and nourishment. It is even
harder to simulate the latter when the
leaves have once become dry—as they are
bound to do, for this is not the labor of a
moment. Also it hardly needs saying that
this is the time for repairing any neighboring trees or bushes or other growth
that may have been damaged by the fall.
The same rules apply. Where neighboring
trees were of the same species it is difficult
not to waste time conveying a detached
leaf back to the wrong tree. Practice, practice. Put your hope in that.

Now the tackle must be put into 2
place or the scaffolding, depending on the

W. S. Merwin was born in New York in 1927 and
is principally known for his poetry, though he
won the PEN Translation Prize in 1969 for his
book *Selected Translations 1948–1968*. He won
the Pulitzer Prize in 1971 for his book of poetry
The Carrier of Ladders and gave the Pulitzer Prize
money to the draft resistance movement opposing the Vietnam War. He also won the Pulitzer
Prize in 2009. Recent titles include *The Ends of
the Earth* (2004), *Migration: New & Selected Poems*
(2005), and a memoir of his childhood, *Summer
Doorways* (2006). He has also published numerous books of translation. Merwin was appointed
the seventeenth Poet Laureate Consultant in
Poetry to the Library of Congress for 2010–2011.
He lives and writes in Hawaii.

surroundings and the dimensions of the tree. It is ticklish work. Almost always it involves, in itself, further damage to the area, which will have to be corrected later. But as you've heard, it can't be helped. And care now is likely to save you considerable trouble later. Be careful to grind nothing into the ground.

At last the time comes for the erecting of the trunk. By now it will   3 scarcely be necessary to remind you of the delicacy of this huge skeleton. Every motion of the tackle, every slight upward heave of the trunk, the branches, their elaborately re-assembled panoply of leaves (now dead) will draw from you an involuntary gasp. You will watch for a leaf or a twig to be snapped off yet again. You will listen for the nuts to shift in the hollow limb and you will hear whether they are indeed falling into place or are spilling in disorder—in which case, or in the event of anything else of the kind—operations will have to cease, of course, while you correct the matter. The raising itself is no small enterprise, from the moment when the chains tighten around the old bandages until the bole hangs vertical above the stump, splinter above splinter. Now the final straightening of the splinters themselves can take place (the preliminary work is best done while the wood is still green and soft, but at times when the splinters are not badly twisted most of the straightening is left until now, when the torn ends are face to face with each other). When the splinters are perfectly complementary the appropriate fixative is applied. Again we have no duplicate of the original substance. Ours is extremely strong, but it is rigid. It is limited to surfaces, and there is no play in it. However the core is not the part of the trunk that conducted life from the roots up into the branches and back again. It was relatively inert. The fixative for this part is not the same as the one for the outer layers and the bark, and if either of these is involved in the splintered section they must receive applications of the appropriate adhesives. Apart from being incorrect and probably ineffective, the core fixative would leave a scar on the bark.

When all is ready the splintered trunk is lowered onto the splinters of   4 the stump. This, one might say, is only the skeleton of the resurrection. Now the chips must be gathered, and the sawdust, and returned to their former positions. The fixative for the wood layers will be applied to chips and sawdust consisting only of wood. Chips and sawdust consisting of several substances will receive applications of the correct adhesives. It is as well, where possible, to shelter the materials from the elements while working. Weathering makes it harder to identify the smaller fragments. Bark sawdust in particular the earth lays claim to very quickly. You must find your own ways of coping with this problem. There is a certain beauty, you will notice at moments, in the pattern of the chips as they are fitted back into place.

You will wonder to what extent it should be described as natural, to what extent man-made. It will lead you on to speculations about the parentage of beauty itself, to which you will return.

The adhesive for the chips is translucent, and not so rigid as that for the   5
splinters. That for the bark and its subcutaneous layers is transparent and runs into the fibers on either side, partially dissolving them into each other. It does not set the sap flowing again but it does pay a kind of tribute to the preoccupations of the ancient thoroughfares. You could not roll an egg over the joints but some of the mine-shafts would still be passable, no doubt, for the first exploring insect who raises its head in the tight echoless passages. The day comes when it is all restored, even to the moss (now dead) over the wound. You will sleep badly, thinking of the removal of the scaffolding that must begin the next morning. How you will hope for sun and a still day!

The removal of the scaffolding or tackle is not so dangerous, perhaps,   6
to the surroundings, as its installation, but it presents problems. It should be taken from the spot piece by piece as it is detached, and stored at a distance. You have come to accept it there, around the tree. The sky begins to look naked as the chains and struts one by one vacate their positions. Finally the moment arrives when the last sustaining piece is removed and the tree stands again on its own. It is as though its weight for a moment stood on your heart. You listen for a thud of settlement, a warning creak deep in the intricate joinery. You cannot believe it will hold. How like something dreamed it is, standing there all by itself. How long will it stand there now? The first breeze that touches its dead leaves all seems to flow into your mouth. You are afraid the motion of the clouds will be enough to push it over. What more can you do? What more can you do?

But there is nothing more you can do.   7

Others are waiting.   8

Everything is going to have to be put back.   9

QUESTIONS

1. How well does "Unchopping a Tree" satisfy the requirements for step-by-step instructions and precise, easy-to-visualize detail in the "how-to" process analysis essay?

2. At what point did you first realize that these instructions are, in fact, impossible to carry out? Is process analysis an effective way to make this point? Why?

3. Reread the first paragraph and analyze the rhythm Merwin creates through his use of sentence lengths and sentence patterns. How does this rhythm help to establish the tone of the essay?

4. Note Merwin's use of figurative language throughout this essay (for more on this, see Joyce MacDonald's essay on Merwin and Suzuki in Readings: Sample Essays). How does this language develop and strengthen Merwin's thesis?

5. Throughout the essay, Merwin adopts the persona of a teacher instructing the reader-student. Where is this persona most evident? What purposes does it serve?

6. Merwin creates irony by leaving the obvious unsaid: that it is impossible to unchop a tree. How similar is Merwin's irony to Swift's in "A Modest Proposal" (Readings)? Do you think irony is an effective strategy for persuasion? Is irony ever risky?

SUGGESTION FOR WRITING

Using "Unchopping a Tree" as a model, write an essay in which the impossibility of carrying out your instructions makes a persuasive point. Remember that in an ironic essay, your real thesis is the opposite of what you seem to be saying. You will find this irony easier to create and sustain if, like Merwin, you adopt the persona of the teacher who encourages the students but who provides impossibly complex instructions. Like Merwin, you should develop your essay as a process analysis, so be sure to include transitions that help your readers to follow the steps in your procedure.

Facebook and Coaxed Affordances

Aimée Morrison

I n a 2007 *PMLA* article addressing "the changing profession," Nancy K. 1
Miller (2007) suggests that "[a]utobiography may emerge as a master
form in the twenty-first century" (545). Recognizing both the expansion and explosion of popular forms of published autobiography, and the
strength and durability of what Sidonie Smith and Julia Watson have called
"the memoir boom" (Smith and Watson 2010, 127), Miller points to the
rich variety of texts and contexts animating autobiographical production
and consumption, as well as to the necessity of promoting a similar richness
in scholarly approach. She happily concludes that, in the face of such variety and plenitude, "[a]cademics have risen to the occasion with refreshing
inventiveness" (Miller 2007, 546). Since that publication, popular Internet
life writing forms—among them blogs, vlogs, and social network sites—
have begun to demand a similar inventiveness.

Such invention proceeds in fits and starts, but the challenges presented 2
by digital life writing are arguably more sweeping and various than those
uncovered by the graphic memoirs and print "autobiofictionalography"
Miller considers in her survey. Digital life writing maps a realm with no
gatekeepers, editors, or canons, producing texts to excess on a scale of production and publication that completely overwhelms the boutique reading practices of literary scholarship. Digital life writing develops normative
writing and reading practices that shift with each software upgrade or each
new cultural meme. Digital life writing troubles the hard-won notion of the
artfulness of auto/biographical texts as the basis for their appropriateness as
objects of scholarly attention. Digital life writing, in fact, poses a kind of
limit case of autobiographical theory and criticism, at once terrifying and
compelling in its sheer scale and its wide-
open popular production.

How can we understand the Facebook 3
status update? This is a deceptively modest question, one that will generate further
pointed inquiries into digital life writing
practices in all their variety. Facebook
offers both fertile ground and a terrible
problem to auto/biography scholars. That
the service cries out for autobiographical
analysis seems beyond doubt. That more

Aimée Morrison is an associate professor of
English at the University of Waterloo. Her
research and writing includes the subjects of
social media, film, digital spaces, and other forms
of textuality.

than 1 billion people are enrolled in the network, with more than half of them accessing Facebook daily, renders that analysis as urgent as it is important (Facebook 2012). But fundamental questions confront the analyst, questions that are complicated to formulate, let alone answer: What are the ethics of the interpolation of the stories and voices of others into a user's digital life narrative? What to make of the use of photographs? What social pressures are at play in determining what is written on the site and who can see it? These are serious questions, but insofar as they pertain to the relationality of identity, the ethics of life storytelling, or the role of visual material in autographic narratives, auto/biography studies is well enough equipped already to handle them.

But what if, as Gillian Whitlock and Anna Poletti suggest, social   4
network sites present "auto-assemblages" rather than authored texts as such (Whitlock and Poletti 2008, xiv)? Whitlock and Poletti describe these auto-assemblages as "the result of ongoing selection and appropriation of content across several modes brought together into a constellation for the purpose of self-representation or life narrative" (xv).[1] To account for the "auto" of this "assemblage" would be to acknowledge the necessity of dealing with the technological characteristics of digital media. And so the fact of Facebook poses us yet more questions, perhaps even thornier for auto/ biography scholars to address and for which less groundwork has been laid. We must begin to consider the style sheets that organize display of user-generated materials; the input prompts that coax and restrict user action by turns; the ever-shifting privacy settings that dramatically and continually reset the boundaries between personal narrative and public dissemination; and the automated, algorithm-driven recitation of users' actions across their social graphs. Each shapes the resulting digital life writing "text" as much as do the more traditional authorial practices of a typing subject deliberately arranging her life into a story. Whitlock and Poletti (2008) assert that scholars must consider "how the functionality of the software, in conjunction with the cultures of usage . . . , shape the production of specific autographic performances" (xvi). One way to proceed, they note, is by "asking precise questions about software" (xvi). To do just this, the path forward must be mapped by both auto/biography and new media studies. A conjunction of the methods and insights of these fields offers real explanatory power, a means by which to engage substantively with online texts as instances and genres of digital life writing produced in and through both social practices and technological artifacts.

By opening the status update function of Facebook to analysis here, I   5
delineate a generalizable interpretive methodology that balances key ideas from two scholarly discourse communities: from autobiography studies,

the notion of "coaxing" imbricates with the theory of "affordances," drawn from the social studies of science and technology. Taken together, coaxing and affordances offer a theory and a method by which to read how and why Facebook and its users are mutually implicated in the construction of digital life writing texts on that site.

IS "FACEBOOK" A COERCIVE TECHNOLOGY?

The question of what Facebook *is* seems to be a vexed one. How we understand the service and its relationship to its users necessarily colors our interpretations of the life-writing texts solicited, produced, and consumed through that platform. In February 2004, "Thefacebook" was a hobby project devised by some Harvard students to employ technical wizardry for intramural social purposes. There were no ads; it was a closed network; strong privacy was the default (Kirkpatrick 2010, 29). By February 2012, Facebook had become an enormous media company preparing for an initial public stock offering at a market valuation of $100 billion (Raice 2011). Advertising is its main source of revenue; the network is global and expanding exponentially; "radical transparency" is its new privacy mantra (Kirkpatrick 2010, 200). Depending on your own position relative to this ever-shifting platform, Facebook "is" an advertising medium, a public square, a place to play games, a place to nurture and maintain friendships, a digital photo album, a broadcast medium, and a place to document your daily doings.

* * *

As the service grew and matured, Facebook and its users developed a sometimes-conflictual relationship. Facebook has suffered some well-publicized public outrages—from the introduction of the original News Feed in 2006 to the short-lived Beacon advertising program the following year to the perpetual rewriting of privacy permissions that is currently drawing the attention of legislators and watchdogs around the world (see boyd 2008a; Story and Stone 2007; Zuckerberg 2006). In the face of some of these outrages, Facebook has held steady (e.g., News Feed) and waited for users to accustom themselves to the new interface, and in others it has relented (e.g., Beacon) and cancelled the change outright. This tension is ultimately irremediable: the users of Facebook are not its customers but rather its product. Facebook's current revenue model is built on targeted marketing, where advertising is sold at a premium based on the depth of information the service harvests from its users.

Nevertheless, without engaged (i.e., happy) users, the service cannot survive. A kind of symbiosis necessarily develops, even if the lines of force and power are asymmetrical. The status update enacts both this tension and this symbiosis. A steady stream of status updates is important to Facebook. It provides value to the company in the form of greater consumer profile reporting by which to sell targeted advertising, and also the promise of longer time spent on the site both by the authoring user creating the updates and by that user's friends who become engaged in reading them. Of course, ever-growing user numbers and the increasing amount of time these users spend on the site indicate that these same features are as valuable to users as to Facebook's financial interests. A recent Nielsen report found, tellingly, that Americans spent a collective 53.5 billion minutes on Facebook in May 2011—this was more minutes than the four next-most popular sites (Yahoo, Google, AOL, and MSN) combined (Nielsen 2011).

* * *

AUTOBIOGRAPHICAL COAXING AND THE THEORY OF AFFORDANCES AND CONSTRAINTS

In asking every user "What's on your mind?" Facebook elicits personal disclosure. But how, exactly? The ways that compliant subjects answer the question demonstrate the way their practices are shaped by the coaxing technologies, both discursive and material, afforded by the moment of interaction between status update interface and human user. In constructing our life stories—or assembling the disclosures, facts, and documents that offer the basis for the inference of life story—we are guided not only by the often-implicit discursive precedent of the genre in which we write or speak but also by the material affordances and constraints of the objects through which we structure these stories of ourselves. 9

"Affordance" is a concept first articulated in ecological psychology, then moving through industrial design, and into human-computer interaction, usability, and user-experience design for digital environments. James Gibson (1986) devised the neologism "affordance" to describe the set of possibilities for action an environment presents to its users. Gibson's theory aims to explain the visual processing of the broader physical world by subjects moving through it: elements of the environment as thus perceived, relative to the perceiving subject, as "climb-on-able or fall-off-able or get-underneath-able or bump-into-able" (128). He describes this notion of the action-potentiating affordances of environments and objects as "a radical hypothesis, for it implies that the 'values' and 'meanings' of things in the environment can be directly perceived" (127). Later work by Donald Norman (2002) brought the concept of affordance into the realm of industrial design, famously tackling the problems of baffling car stereos and door handles that required instruction to be operated. Norman's work builds on 10

Gibson's insights into the affordances of man-made objects by proposing ways that a designed object's potential-for-action could be more effectively and easily conveyed to a consumer.

Affordances in the world of manufactured objects should, Norman 11 suggests, guide and structure our uses of these objects in ways that reduce the amount of cognitive friction involved in moving through the world: for example, a chef knife's size and weight indicates to us that we should hold it firmly in one hand, and the shape of the handgrip lets us know that the blade edge should point downward, for example. "Constraints," on the other hand, are features that restrict user action: they are often just as important as affordances. The child's plastic figurine has a head of larger diameter than that of the infant windpipe; the car cannot be shifted out of park unless the brake is depressed; the food processor's blades will not spin until all the components—bowl, lid, blade—are locked into position. Constraints in the object world are often devised to protect us from ourselves: from choking on a toy, from crashing into the garage, from slicing our fingers off or spraying the kitchen in hot soup. So beyond offering a set of potential actions to a perceiving user, designed objects discipline these actions by making some potential actions more obvious than others and even making other actions impossible. Manipulating affordances and constraints, a well-designed object teaches us how to use it without us ever consciously puzzling the matter out: it places "knowledge in the world," in Norman's phrase (Norman 2002, 74). A well-designed object leads us toward an appropriate use (sitting on a chair), and away from an inappropriate use (lying down on a chair) but not entirely away from all nonstandard uses (standing on a chair).

Digital environments require even greater care in their design. In 12 digital environments, "the range of possible actions are limited to typing on a keyboard, pointing with a mouse, and clicking on mouse and keyboard switches. . . . All of these actions are abstract and arbitrary compared to the real, physical manipulation of objects" (Norman 1999, 41). With Jakob Nielsen, Norman further pushed the idea of designed-affordance into the virtual landscape of potential action offered by what appears on a computer screen. The fields concerned are those of usability and human-computer interaction (Nielsen 2012). What's essential to a well-designed, functional web application is that the user can figure out what purpose the application is meant to serve, suss out the range of potential actions relating to that purpose, and easily accomplish a goal. Nielsen and Norman's work demonstrates that as the purely virtual perceptual field of the computer screen is necessarily filled with abstractions, designers must better disburse perceived affordances and constraints consistently and obviously to structure user action.[2]

* * *

THE COAXING AFFORDANCES OF THE STATUS UPDATE INTERFACE

Facebook's status update feature makes use of designed affordances 13 and constraints, as well as emerging cultural convention, in order to coax life narratives from its users. Since the introduction of the feature in 2006, the interface by which a user engages as both an author and consumer of these brief texts has changed in subtle but consequential ways. By examining the status update's shifting composition and display interface, the shaping role of affordances becomes clear as do the kinds of coaxing the feature supports. Of course, some of the problems that bedevil scholarly analysis become apparent as well. To begin with, the primary text is highly individualized and unstable: my Facebook doesn't look like yours, and each might look and act differently tomorrow, in any case. Similarly, there is no archive of Facebook. The site exists in the perpetual present, with all traces of its prior incarnations, interfaces, functions, and displays obliterated at the moment the service is updated, rendering historical work nearly impossible. The simple question of versioning is thus complicated by Facebook's near constant, usually incremental updates: one day, a small shift to how photos are displayed in News Feed; another day, auto-tagging is introduced; all of a sudden, all the privacy options have been reset and reordered; then Timeline is announced, and while it is introduced over the course of a year, the change is massive and the prior forms irrecoverable. These characteristics make well-referenced scholarship based on close reading very difficult to produce.

* * *

The early status update interface comprised a text-input field of a 14 specified length in characters, preceded by a label reading: "[Firstname Lastname] is." The most obvious affordance of the text box is, in Gibsonian language, that it is "click-in-able" and subsequently "type-in-able." This perceived affordance is conventional to text-input boxes provided for in HTML forms, regardless of where they appear on the web, and so would be a familiar element of the digital environment to Facebook's early, college-student users. The HTML specifications allow for the length, size, and capacity of the input field to be customized. For example, it is possible to create a text box that appears to cover twenty characters on screen but which allows an infinite number of characters to be input; it is possible, too, to create an input field that covers multiple lines of screen space. The Facebook status update text box covers one line of text, a visible length of not more than forty to sixty characters. The conventional affordance (click-in-able, type-in-able) of the text-input field leads the user to know that he is meant to type. The small size of the visible typing area indicates that brevity is expected. [. . .]

The text-field label constitutes half a statement; the user is meant to 15 complete it. This requires some deciphering to produce the desired speech in a socially competent way. While grammatically correct, "*Aimée Morrison is* an associate professor of English at the University of Waterloo" or "*Aimée Morrison is* married, and the mother of a seven-year-old girl" are not likely normative status updates, because they convey information already solicited by and visible in the profile. Additionally, these statements convey facts that don't really change and so do not seem to qualify as a status that might need frequent or repeated "updating" in the way this little box, soliciting the user at every login, seems to imply. Further implications might be derived from user experiences of other, similar software: in this case, users might discern a link to the generic precedent of the AIM (AOL Instant Messenger) "away message." These away messages are short statements a user could craft to appear online to indicate the user was away from his computer and thus not available to instant-message. Therefore, a statement like "*Jessica Louise Barber is* on campus, at the library" seems appropriate based on this generic precedent, and its conventional use. A more creative user could bend the norm without quite breaking it and write: "*Jessica Louise Barber is* hoping that the deadline gets extended." The designed affordance, that is, pushes users toward a particular kind of "correct" practice, while allowing for a certain degree of unanticipated, creative deployment of the feature.

As a solicitation of speech, the text-field's label is both subtle and 16 economical; it coaxes the desired speech more implicitly and more briefly than a command to, for example, "Write something about yourself here."[3] In addition to suggesting, with the provided half-statement, what kind of disclosure is sought, the label also acts as a prompt that authorizes a subject to disclose at all. Such authorization is especially important when a user might be insecure about the social norms surrounding a given practice—self-narration on the site might be seen as unreasonably boastful, as it is in real life, for example. John Killoran (2003) notes the cultural constraints against disclosure that digital life writers may face. "In their autobiographical trespass into the public domain," he writes, "the work of these authors . . . must skirt the disrepute typically attending the public airing of the lower class to fashion a legitimate subject position for the ordinary human subject in the canon of public discourse" (70). Coaxing in this sense offers the necessary social precondition for near-continual self-disclosure. [. . .]

Conventional usage is reinforced by the way Facebook published the   17
updates as flowing text constituting usually one sentence, mashing together
the text-field label with the user-generated text. "*Marion Watier is* eating a
sandwich" narrates an activity currently being undertaken. "*Aline Meakin is*
blonde" describes a physical characteristic of the speaking subject but carries an additional potential connotative meaning of "Aline Meakin has done
something dumb" in the tradition of the punchline of jokes whose protago-
nists are fair-haired. "*Ernest Barber is* unhappy" articulates an emotional
state. The resulting status updates, no matter which user creates them, are
uniformly crafted in the third person and, when assembled into the News
Feed by which each user surveys her social universe, present a unified register and point of view, making the whole look more deliberate and more
immediately comprehensible than similar sentiments expressed outside of
the template might appear.

As much as the interface affords certain actions and coaxes or shapes   18
particular kinds of disclosures, it also constrains other actions and disclosures. These constraints are inherent in the enforced "is" statement and
in the shortness of the text-input box, as well as in the format in which
the statements are published. This particular iteration of the status update
does not admit of direct address, for example. The question "Can you tell
me why everyone forgets how to drive when it snows?" would instead need
to be phrased like this: "*George Cole is* wondering why everyone forgets
how to drive when it snows." It's impossible, also, to craft an update in
the first person: to express the statement "I love Justin Bieber," a user's
passion needed the indirect devices of third-person narration and passive
construction, as in "*Hope Desormeau is* in love with Justin Bieber." Thus the
mode by which the published statements are displayed, in addition to the
affordance of the text-input box and the coaxing function of the label text,
constrain user practice, thus making some kinds of statements impossible.[4]

A more recent iteration of the status update removed the verb from the   19
text-box label prompt, resulting in a terser opening to each update, thus:
"[*Firstname Lastname*] [blank field for user generated text]." This reconfig-
uration of input and display removed some of the constraints against variety of sentence construction and point of view, but did not alter the way the
resulting text was displayed. A user could interpret the label as an indicator
of the character who is speaking, like in a screenplay, where the appearance
of the proper name is set on its own, followed by some sort of first-person
speech by the named character. A possible status update in this view could
read: "*Hugh Donn* I want to eat ice cream for breakfast." The formatting of
the published status update as flowing text does not seem to support this
usage, but it was very common nevertheless. It is more orthodox, however,

to interpret the removal of the verb "is" as an indication that another verb is meant to replace it; such a practice was supported by the display interface. In this view, the status update must take the same third-person narrator, but with a wider range of sensible statements One might then see: "*Hugh Donn* wants ice cream for breakfast" or, again, "*George Cole* wonders why everyone forgets how to drive when it snows."

In this iteration of the feature, as in the first one discussed, what 20 appears to be produced more often takes the form of self-biography rather than autobiography; that is, the subject of the (short) life story must be described in the third-person rather than the first. This particular constraint may be motivated by the exigence of display: one main way that status updates are read is in the context of another user's News Feed, where information drawn from all that user's friends is collated into a single stream.[5] This stream, which includes not only status updates but also auto-reported activity like changing a profile picture or joining a group, gains in legibility by this uniformity. The algorithmically generated news items are grammatically parallel to the user-authored ones, creating a news feed text that combines disparate information and actions into a unified narrative, grammatically at least. Thus, the status update "*Thomas Ouya* wishes he were sleeping," authored by that user, meshes neatly with the Facebook-generated "*Thomas Ouya* joined the group 'Insomniacs of Waterloo'" in my News Feed, for example.

The next innovation made first-person status updates possible, by 21 simply shifting the way the text is displayed once "published"—in this case, moving the name of the user onto a separate line, distinct from the user-generated text:

> AIMÉE MORRISON
> *My parents are five minutes away. They had to phone for*
> *directions, and also to ask me to have the cocktails ready.*

The user's proper name now acts as a simple heading, like the title of a blog post or the byline of a (very short) newspaper article. Radical shifts in narration become possible, although, intriguingly, among longtime users of the site it is still not uncommon to see the prior forms of speech survive—third-person narration, with each statement taking the user's name as the opening of a sentence. This points both to the momentum a practice acquires as people become accustomed to it, as well as users' sometimes unwillingness to acquiesce to the new norms a shift in interface demands. [. . .] The News Feed where this information is published becomes more cacophonous, a series of short free-form monologues headed by a proper name. Statuses thus became longer and more various.

As the status update became conventionalized, with users both 22 comfortably accustomed to providing these updates, and seeking out or being offered ever more opportunities to share information of all kinds, the features underwent a fundamental shift, rendering analysis yet more complicated. A 2009 version of the status update brings full multimedia capacity (and automation, too!) to bear on self-expression. Indeed, at this point, the status update interface is renamed "Publisher" to indicate the greater variety of user actions it can support (Eldon 2009). The text-input box is now much larger: it easily affords multiline text and even paragraphs. The prompt has shifted location: the text-input field is pre-filled with grayed-out text reading "What's on your mind?" Making use of new web-programming features, this prompt disappears once the user begins to type into the field, seamlessly making way for the user's own text. Rather than a direct question that labels the text-input field, the grayed-out text of the question seems rather to imply than to ask.

Additionally, the input interface is now tabbed, multiplying the user's 23 possibilities of action. Beyond the textual status update feature, Publisher now affords several other interactions. A user can now use the feature to "share" a link, a video, a poll, or a photo. Currently, a user can "tag" other users in a post, or generate linked location data associated with where a post was composed and on what kind of device. In fact, the act of frequent real-time sharing inaugurated by the status update has become even more diffuse than the tabbed options indicate. Many user actions within and without the Facebook environment now result in an update being automatically generated and published—for example, if a user has checked into a location automatically, or posted to a blog, or "liked" something somewhere on the web, or completed an online yoga class, or earned a badge in a social game. This innovation raises the difficult question of how and if these "updates" are an act of authorship on the part of a life writer, and how we are to understand them as part of the digital life writing practices on Facebook.

FACEBOOK'S EVOLVING USERS, USERS EVOLVING FACEBOOK

. . .

Ever-greater sections of the population engage in digital life writing 24 online, populating dating profiles, personal blogs, or social network sites with their life stories, or otherwise leaving numberless small traces of their ideas and experiences in their daily digital travels: a comment on a news site, a contest form filled out, a shopping basket and personalized recommendations at Amazon, a collection of book marks and interests maintained in the cloud. Digital life writing runs the full length of the field between the exacting, bureaucratic, computerized coercions of life in the database society to an independent, creative, and liberatory "autobiography in real time" (Morrison 2010). Some categories of digital life writing are easier to interpret in proportion to their adherence to the forms, purposes, and content of established print modes. Others, in their deep imbrication of computation and authorship, are much more difficult to fit to our established theories and practices. Blogs, for example, with their long-format, single-authored texts arranged in reverse chronological order—even if they feature hyperlinks and user comments and photographs—are much easier to relate to diary or memoir or auto/biography than are the multivocal, multimediated, social network texts like Facebook that seem as much algorithmically produced as they do authored.

There is no question—particularly since the introduction of the 25 Timeline interface—that Facebook and its users are producing life narratives. The company purports that Timeline will do nothing less than "tell the story of your life with a new kind of profile" (Facebook 2011). The Timeline reconfigures how materials already in its database are displayed on a user's home page: it reorganizes a user's entire social media history (increasingly conflated with that user's entire life) chronologically, attaching all interactions with the site, other users, and the broader web ecosystem to, well, a timeline. Each user's Facebook suddenly attains the classical structure of the biographical text, almost inadvertently.[6] For the first time, users are actively encouraged to go back in time to fill out those parts of their lives that were not logged in real time over the service. Of course, users have for years uploaded unflattering photos of their friends from high-school times—but the new interface allows these photos to be dated according to when they were *taken*, rather than *uploaded*, creating Facebook life stories that aim to account for the past as easily and comprehensively as the present. The impact of this change remains to be examined. [. . .] This paper has dealt with only one aspect of the Facebook platform, and its conclusions are tentative, marred by incomplete or unauthoritative primary textual data. But it begins the work of devising means by which literary scholars trained in close textual reading and broad cultural contextualization can bring these methods to bear on digital life writing texts, by finding points of overlap between auto/biography and new media studies.

NOTES

The notes in this section are original to Morrison's article.

[1] Whitlock and Poletti modify the neologism "autographics" to "online autographics" when describing digital life writing, hinting at the scale of critical creativity that will be needed to meaningfully interpret these texts, even among scholars whose work already pushes the boundaries of auto/biography criticism.

[2] An accessible and engaging introduction to this work can be found at Jakob Nielsen's website, in particular the weekly "Alertbox" columns on specific design issues in virtual environments.

[3] The technology blogs track what kinds of prompts each social network service uses and infer major shifts in corporate strategy or user practice from alterations to these short phrases. One recent Twitter prompt change—from "What are you doing?" to "What's happening?"   was even commented upon by a linguist. See Cutler (2009), Stone (2009), and Tate (2009), for example.

[4] The next major change in the status update was not in the input format but rather in the output: News Feed. The introduction of the news feed offers ample material for an analysis of the role of audience in digital life writing; this feature immediately made status updates much more visible to all of a user's friends, and prompted much hue and cry about privacy, even though the only thing altered was that already-public updates were much easier for Friends to read (see Kirkpatrick 2010, 180–82).

[5] This mode of display made less sense in the "Mini Feed," which brought a dynamic element to a user's profile page by creating a news feed of that one user's interactions. Everyone looked like a narcissist with a whole stream of updates, each headed by "Aimée Morrison is" or "Aimée Morrison [verb]" (see Sanghvi 2006).

[6] Anecdotal reports of cognitive dissonance among users following this change are beginning to trickle out. One newspaper reporter was so discomfited by the "biography" his reconfigured Timeline told of him that he deleted his entire account and started fresh, with the Timeline's display structure in mind (Ladurantye 2011).

REFERENCES

Abram, Carolyn, and Leah Pearlman, 2010. *Facebook for Dummies*. 3rd ed. Hoboken, NJ: Wiley.

Arthur, Paul Longley. 2009. "Digital Biography: Capturing Lives Online." *a/b: Auto/Biography Studies* 24, no.1: 74–92.

boyd, danah. 2008a. "Facebook's Privacy Trainwreck: Exposure, Invasion, and Social Convergence." *Convergence* 14, no.1 (2008): 13–20.

_____. 2008b. "Why Youth (Heart) Social Network Sites: The Role of Networked Publics in Teenage Social Life." In *Youth, Identity, and Digital Media*, edited by David Buckingham, 119–42. Cambridge, MA: MIT Press.

boyd, danah, and Nicole B. Ellison. 2007. "Social Network Sites: Definition, History, and Scholarship." *Journal of Computer-Mediated Communication* 13, no.1. http://jcmc.indiana.edu/vol13/issue1/boyd.ellison.html. Accessed April 8, 2012.

Cohen, Nicole S., and Leslie Regan Shade. 2008. "Gendering Facebook: Privacy and Commodification." *Feminist Media Studies* 8, no.2: 210–14.

Cutler, Kim-Mai. 2009. "Twitter Retools Prompt, Asks 'What's Happening?'" *Venture-Beat*, November 19. http://venturebeat.com/2009/11/19/twitter-retools-prompt-asks-whats-happening/.

Debatin, Bernhard, Jeanette P. Lovejoy, Ann-Kathrin Horn, and Brittany N. Hughes. 2009. "Facebook and Online Privacy: Attitudes, Behaviors, and Unintended Consequences." *Journal of Computer-Mediated Communication* 15, no.1: 83–108.

Eldon, Eric. 2009. "Spoon Feeding: Facebook Redesign Brings Feeds (and Ads) to the Masses." *VentureBeat*, March 12. http://venturebeat.com/2009/03/12/spoon-feeding-facebook-redesign-brings-feeds-and-ads-to-the-masses/. Accessed March 29, 2012.

Facebook. 2011. "Introducing Timeline." http://www.facebook.com/about/timeline. Accessed March 29, 2012.

_____. 2012. "Key Facts" *Facebook Newsroom*. http://newsroom.fb.com/content/default.aspx?NewsAreaId=22. Accessed March 27, 2012.

Fovet, Frédéric. 2009. "Impact of the Use of Facebook Amongst Students of High School Age with Social, Emotional and Behavioral Difficulties." Paper presented at the 39th IEEE Frontiers in Education Conference, October 18–21, San Antonio. http://fieconference.org/fie2009/papers/1081df. Accessed April 18, 2010.

Gibson, James J. 1986. *The Ecological Approach to Visual Perception*. Hillsdale, NJ: Lawrence Erlbaum Associates.

Hutchby, Ian. 2001. "Technologies, Texts and Affordances." *Sociology* 35, no.2: 441–56.

Inside Facebook. 2012. WebMediaBrands. http://www.insidefacebook.com/. Accessed March 27, 2012.

Jolly, Margaretta. 2004. "E-mail in a Global Age: The Ethical Story of 'Women on the Net.'" *Biography* 28, no. 1: 152–65.

Killoran, John B. 2003. "The Gnome in the Front Yard and Other Public Figurations: Genres of Self-Presentation on Personal Home Pages." *Biography* 26, no.1: 66–83.

Kirkpatrick, David. 2010. *The Facebook Effect: The Inside Story of the Company That Is Connecting the World*. New York: Simon and Schuster.

Ladurantaye, Steve. 2011. "Facebook: Deactivated, and Back Again." December 24. http://www.steveladurantaye.ca/facebook-deactivated/. Accessed March 29, 2012.

Mashable.com. 2012. http://mashable.com/. Accessed March 27, 2012.

McLuhan, Marshall.1994. *Understanding Media: The Extensions of Man*. Cambridge, MA: MIT Press.

Mezrich, Ben. 2009. *The Accidental Billionaires: The Founding of Facebook: A Tale of Sex, Money, Genius, and Betrayal*. New York: Anchor Books.

Miller, Nancy K. 2007. "The Entangled Self: Genre Bondage in the Age of the Memoir." *PMLA* 122, no. 2: 537–48.

Morrison, Aimée. 2010. "Autobiography in Real Time: A Genre Analysis of Personal Mommy Blogging." *Cyberpsychology: Journal of Psychosocial Research on Cyberspace* 4, no. 2. http://www.cyberpsychology.eu/view.php?cisloclanku=2010120801&article=5.

_____. 2011. "'Suffused by Feeling and Affect': The Intimate Public of Personal Mommy Blogging." *Biography* 34, no.1: 37–55.

Naghibi, Nima. 2011 "Diasporic Disclosures: Social Networking, Neda, and the 2009 Iranian Presidential Elections." *Biography* 34, no. 1: 56–69.

Nielsen. 2011. *State of the Media: The Social Media Report*. http://blog.nielsen.com/nielsenwire/social/. Accessed March 27, 2012.

Nielsen, Jakob. 2012. *UseIt.com*. http://www.useit.com/. Accessed March 27, 2012.

Nielsen Norman Group. 2012. "About Nielsen Norman Group." http://www.nngroup.com/about/. Accessed March 27, 2012.

Nissenbaum, Helen Fay. 2010. *Privacy in Context: Technology, Policy and the Integrity of Social Life*. Stanford, CA: Stanford University Press.

Norman, Donald A.1999. "Affordances, Conventions, and Design." *Interactions* (June): 38–42.

_____. 2002. *The Design of Everyday Things*. New York: Basic Books.

Nosko, Amanda, Eileen Wood, and Seija Molema. 2010. "All about Me: Disclosure in Online Social Networking Profiles: The Case of Facebook." *Computers in Human Behavior* 26, no. 3: 406–18.

O'Reilly, Tim. 2007. What Is Web 2.0: Design Patterns and Business Models for the Next Generation of Software." *Communications and Strategies* 65:17–37.

O'Riordan, Kate. 2011. "Writing Biodigital Life: Personal Genomes and Digital Media." *Biography* 34, no. 1: 119–31.

Poletti, Anna. 2011. "Coaxing an Intimate Public: Life Narrative in Digital Storytelling." *Continuum: Journal of Media and Cultural Studies* 25, no. 1: 73–83.

Raice, Shayndi. 2011. "Facebook Targets Huge IPO." *Wall Street Journal*, November 29.

Rak, Julie. 2005. "The Digital Queer: Weblogs and Internet Identity." *Biography* 28, no: 1: 66–82.

Sanghvi, Ruchi. 2006. "Facebook Gets a Facelift." The Facebook Blog. Last modified September 5, 2006. http://blog.facebook.com/blog.php?post=2207967130. Accessed March 29, 2012.

Seder, J. Patrick. 2009. "Ethnic/Racial Homogeneity in College Students' Facebook Friendship Networks and Subjective Well-being." *Journal of Research in Personality* 43, no. 3: 438–43.

Skågeby, Jörgen. 2009. "Exploring Qualitative Sharing Practices of Social Metadata Expanding the Attention Economy." *Information Society* 25, no. 1: 60–72.

Smith, Sidonie, and Julia Watson. 1996. "Introduction." In *Getting a Life Everyday Uses of Autobiography*, edited by Sidonie Smith and Julia Watson, 1–24. Minneapolis: University of Minnesota Press.

_____. 2010. *Reading Autobiography: A Guide for Interpreting Life Narratives*. 2nd ed. Minneapolis: University of Minnesota Press.

Stone, Biz. 2009. "What's Happening?" Twitter Blog, November 19. http://blog.twitter.com/2009/11/whats-happening.html. Accessed March 29, 2012.

Story, Louise, and Brad Stone. 2007. "Facebook Retreats on Online Tracking." *New York Times*, November 30.

Tate, Ryan. 2009. "Twitter's New Prompt: A Linguist Weighs In." *Gawker*, November 19. http://gawker.com/5408768/. Accessed March 29, 2012.

Tufekci, Zeynep. 2008. "Can You See Me Now? Audience and Disclosure Regulation in Online Social Network Sites." *Bulletin of Science, Technology and Society* 28, no 1: 20.

Vander Veer, E. A. 2010. *Facebook: The Missing Manual.* 2nd ed. Sebastopol, CA: O'Reilly Media.

Wang, Shaojung Sharon. 2010. "Face Off: Implications of Visual Cues on Initiating Friendship on Facebook." *Computers in Human Behavior* 26, no. 2: 226–34.

Westlake, E. J. 2008. "Friend Me If You Facebook: Generation Y and Performative Surveillance." *TDR/Drama Review* 52, no. 4: 21–40.

Whitlock, Gillian, and Anna Poletti. 2008. "Self-Regarding Art." *Biography* 31, no. 1: v–xxiii.

Young, Debo Dutta. 2009. "Extrapolating Psychological Insights from Facebook Profiles: A Study of Religion and Relationship Status." *CyberPsychology and Behavior* 12, no. 3: 347–50.

Zhao, Shanyang, Sherri Grasmuck, and Jason Martin. 2008. "Identity Construction on Facebook: Digital Empowerment in Anchored Relationships." *Computers in Human Behavior* 24, no. 5: 1816–36.

Zuckerberg, Mark. 2006. "An Open Letter from Mark Zuckerberg." The Facebook Blog. Accessed March 29, 2012.

Zuern, John, ed. 2003. "Online Lives." Special issue, *Biography* 26, no. 1.

VOCABULARY

The authors of this book are leaving this section intentionally blank. If you come across unfamiliar words in research, look them up in an appropriate dictionary. It is a good habit to develop.

QUESTIONS

1. Do you keep, or have you ever kept, a written personal journal (diary)? How is the journal genre different from online genres like Facebook updates, blogs, or discussion boards?

2. If you update your status on Facebook, do you think of it as a piece of data for Facebook to sell to companies? If you think of it this way, does it change how you may approach your status updates?

3. Can you think of any other "affordances" or "constraints" to add to Morrison's analysis of Facebook?

4. On the one hand, Morrison says "there is no archive of Facebook" (301). On the other hand, she says that Facebook's "Timeline reconfigures how materials already in its databases are displayed" (306), which suggests that Facebook saves data in its own database. Public history is extremely limited. Private history is nearly comprehensive. What differences do you think you would see when comparing your public history with your private history?

SUGGESTION FOR WRITING

Keep a log or record of your status updates for a set period of time (a week or a month, depending on frequency of updates). When you have a significant number of updates, write a short autobiographical story that incorporates the status updates. Aim to include the updates word for word, if possible. What challenges do you find working with source materials like status updates? How does it influence your view of yourself?

Shooting an Elephant

George Orwell

In Moulmein, in lower Burma,[1] I was hated by large numbers of people—the only time in my life that I have been important enough for this to happen to me. I was sub-divisional police officer of the town, and in an aimless, petty kind of way anti-European feeling was very bitter. No one had the guts to raise a riot, but if a European woman went through the bazaars alone somebody would probably spit betel juice[2] over her dress. As a police officer[3] I was an obvious target and was baited whenever it seemed safe to do so. When a nimble Burman tripped me up on the football field and the referee (another Burman) looked the other way, the crowd yelled with hideous laughter. This happened more than once. In the end the sneering yellow faces of young men that met me everywhere, the insults hooted after me when I was at a safe distance, got badly on my nerves. The young Buddhist priests were the worst of all. There were several thousands of them in the town and none of them seemed to have anything to do except stand on street corners and jeer at Europeans.

All this was perplexing and upsetting. For at that time I had already made up my mind that imperialism was an evil thing and the sooner I chucked up my job and got out of it the better. Theoretically—and secretly, of course—I was all for the Burmese and all against their oppressors, the British. As for the job I was doing, I hated it more bitterly than I can perhaps make clear. In a job like that you see the dirty work of Empire at close quarters. The wretched prisoners huddling in the stinking cages of the lock-ups, the gray, cowed faces of the long-term convicts, the scarred buttocks of the men who had been flogged with bamboos—all these oppressed me with an intolerable sense of guilt. But I could get nothing into perspective. I was young and ill educated and I had had to think out my problems in the utter silence that is imposed on every Englishman in the East. I did not even know that the British Empire is dying, still less did I know that it is a great deal better than the younger empires that are going to supplant it. All I

George Orwell (1903–1950) was born in India as Eric Arthur Blair. Primarily a journalist, he worked as a police officer for the Indian Imperial Police in Burma from 1922 to 1927. His fiction includes *Animal Farm* (1945) and *Nineteen Eighty-Four* (1949). He also wrote many essays, often exploring his ideas about democracy and socialism; collections include *Inside the Whale and Other Essays* (1940) and *Shooting an Elephant and Other Essays* (1950).

George Orwell, "Shooting an Elephant." First published in the journal *New Writing* in 1936.

knew was that I was stuck between my hatred of the empire I served and my rage against the evil-spirited little beasts who tried to make my job impossible. With one part of my mind I thought of the British Raj[4] as an unbreakable tyranny, as something clamped down, in *saecula saeculorum,*[5] upon the will of prostrate peoples; with another part I thought that the greatest joy in the world would be to drive a bayonet into a Buddhist priest's guts. Feelings like these are the normal by-products of imperialism; ask any Anglo-Indian official, if you can catch him off duty.

One day something happened which in a roundabout way was enlightening. It was a tiny incident in itself; but it gave me a better glimpse than I had had before of the real nature of imperialism—the real motives for which despotic governments act. Early one morning the sub-inspector at a police station the other end of the town rang me up on the 'phone and said that an elephant was ravaging the bazaar. Would I please come and do something about it? I did not know what I could do, but I wanted to see what was happening and I got on to a pony and started out. I took my rifle, an old .44 Winchester and much too small to kill an elephant, but I thought the noise might be useful *in terrorem.*[6] Various Burmans stopped me on the way and told me about the elephant's doings. It was not, of course, a wild elephant, but a tame one which had gone "must."[7] It had been chained up, as tame elephants always are when their attack of "must" is due, but on the previous night it had broken its chain and escaped. Its mahout,[8] the only person who could manage it when it was in that state, had set out in pursuit, but had taken the wrong direction and was now twelve hours' journey away, and in the morning the elephant had suddenly reappeared in the town. The Burmese population had no weapons and were quite helpless against it. It had already destroyed somebody's bamboo hut, killed a cow and raided some fruitstalls and devoured the stock; also it had met the municipal rubbish van and, when the driver jumped out and took to his heels, had turned the van over and inflicted violences upon it. 3

The Burmese sub-inspector and some Indian constables were waiting for me in the quarter where the elephant had been seen. It was a very poor quarter, a labyrinth of squalid bamboo huts, thatched with palm-leaf, winding all over a steep hillside. I remember that it was a cloudy, stuffy morning at the beginning of the rains.[9] We began questioning the people as to where the elephant had gone and, as usual, failed to get any definite information. That is invariably the case in the East; a story always sounds clear enough at a distance, but the nearer you get to the scene of events the vaguer it becomes. Some of the people said that the elephant had gone in one direction, some said that he had gone in another, some professed not even to have heard of any elephant. I had almost made up my mind that the whole 4 story was a pack of lies, when we heard yells a little distance away. There was a loud, scandalized cry of "Go away, child! Go away this instant!" and an old woman with a switch in her hand came round the corner of a hut, violently shooing away a crowd of naked children. Some more women followed, clicking their tongues and exclaiming; evidently there was something that the children ought not to have seen. I rounded the hut and saw a man's dead body sprawling in the mud. He was an Indian, a black Dravidian coolie,[10] almost naked, and he could not have been dead many minutes. The people said that the elephant had come suddenly upon him round the corner of the hut, caught him with its trunk, put its foot on his back and ground him into the earth. This was the rainy season and the ground was soft, and his face had scored a trench a foot deep and a couple of yards long. He was lying on his belly with arms crucified and head sharply twisted to one side. His face was coated with mud, the eyes wide open, the teeth bared and grinning with an expression of unendurable agony. (Never tell me, by the way, that the dead look peaceful. Most of the corpses I have seen looked devilish.) The friction of the great beast's foot had stripped the skin from his back as neatly as one skins a rabbit. As soon as I saw the dead man I sent an orderly to a friend's house nearby to borrow an elephant rifle. I had already sent back the pony, not wanting it to go mad with fright and throw me if it smelt the elephant.

The orderly came back in a few minutes with a rifle and five cartridges, 5 and meanwhile some Burmans had arrived and told us that the elephant was in the paddy fields[11] below, only a few hundred yards away. As I started forward practically the whole population of the quarter flocked out of the houses and followed me. They had seen the rifle and were all shouting excitedly that I was going to shoot the elephant. They had not shown much interest in the elephant when he was merely ravaging their homes, but it was different now that he was going to be shot. It was a bit of fun to them, as it would be to an English crowd; besides they wanted the meat. It made me vaguely uneasy. I had no intention of shooting the elephant—I had merely sent for the rifle to defend myself if necessary—and it is always unnerving to have a crowd following you. I marched down the hill, looking and feeling a fool, with the rifle over my shoulder and an ever-growing army of people jostling at my heels. At the bottom, when you got away from the huts, there was a metalled road and beyond that a miry waste of paddy fields a thousand yards across, not yet ploughed but soggy from the first rains and dotted with coarse grass. The elephant was standing eight yards from the road, his left side toward us. He took not the slightest notice of the crowd's approach. He was tearing up bunches of grass, beating them against his knees to clean them, and stuffing them into his mouth.

I had halted on the road. As soon as I saw the elephant I knew with   6
perfect certainty that I ought not to shoot him. It is a serious matter to
shoot a working elephant—it is comparable to destroying a huge and costly
piece of machinery—and obviously one ought not to do it if it can possibly
be avoided. And at that distance, peacefully eating, the elephant looked no
more dangerous than a cow. I thought then and I think now that his attack
of "must" was already passing off; in which case he would merely wander
harmlessly about until the mahout came back and caught him. Moreover,
I did not in the least want to shoot him. I decided that I would watch him
for a little while to make sure that he did not turn savage again, and then
go home.

But at that moment I glanced round at the crowd that had followed   7
me. It was an immense crowd, two thousand at the least and growing every
minute. It blocked the road for a long distance on either side. I looked at
the sea of yellow faces above the garish clothes—faces all happy and excited
over this bit of fun, all certain that the elephant was going to be shot. They
were watching me as they would watch a conjurer about to perform a trick.
They did not like me, but with the magical rifle in my hands I was momentarily worth watching. And suddenly I realized that I should have to shoot
the elephant after all. The people expected it of me and I had got to do it;
I could feel their two thousand wills pressing me forward, irresistibly. And
it was at this moment, as I stood there with the rifle in my hands, that I
first grasped the hollowness, the futility of the white man's dominion in
the East. Here was I, the white man with his gun, standing in front of the
unarmed native crowd—seemingly the leading actor of the piece; but in
reality I was only an absurd puppet pushed to and fro by the will of those
yellow faces behind. I perceived in this moment that when the white man
turns tyrant it is his own freedom that he destroys. He becomes a sort of
hollow, posing dummy, the conventionalized figure of a sahib.[12] For it is
the condition of his rule that he shall spend his life in trying to impress the
"natives," and so in every crisis he has got to do what the "natives" expect
of him. He wears a mask, and his face grows to fit it. I had got to shoot the
elephant. I had committed myself to doing it when I sent for the rifle. A
sahib has got to act like a sahib; he has got to appear resolute, to know his
own mind and do definite things. To come all that way, rifle in hand, with
two thousand people marching at my heels, and then to trail feebly away,
having done nothing—no, that was impossible. The crowd would laugh
at me. And my whole life, every white man's life in the East, was one long
struggle not to be laughed at.

But I did not want to shoot the elephant. I watched him beating his   8
bunch of grass against his knees with that preoccupied grandmotherly air

that elephants have. It seemed to me that it would be murder to shoot him. At that age I was not squeamish about killing animals, but I had never shot an elephant and never wanted to. (Somehow it always seems worse to kill a *large* animal.) Besides, there was the beast's owner to be considered. Alive, the elephant was worth at least a hundred pounds; dead, he would only be worth the value of his tusks, five pounds, possibly. But I had got to act quickly. I turned to some experienced-looking Burmans who had been there when we arrived, and asked them how the elephant had been behaving. They all said the same thing: he took no notice of you if you left him alone, but he might charge if you went too close to him.

It was perfectly clear to me what I ought to do. I ought to walk up to 9 within, say, twenty-five yards of the elephant and test his behavior. If he charged, I could shoot; if he took no notice of me, it would be safe to leave him until the mahout came back. But also I knew that I was going to do no such thing. I was a poor shot with a rifle and the ground was soft mud into which one would sink at every step. If the elephant charged and I missed him, I should have about as much chance as a toad under a steam-roller. But even then I was not thinking particularly of my own skin, only of the watchful yellow faces behind. For at that moment, with the crowd watching me, I was not afraid in the ordinary sense, as I would have been if I had been alone. A white man mustn't be frightened in front of "natives"; and so, in general, he isn't frightened. The sole thought in my mind was that if anything went wrong those two thousand Burmans would see me pursued, caught, trampled on, and reduced to a grinning corpse like that Indian up the hill. And if that happened it was quite probable that some of them would laugh. That would never do. There was only one alternative. I shoved the cartridges into the magazine and lay down on the road to get a better aim.

The crowd grew very still, and a deep, low, happy sigh, as of people who 10 see the theater curtain go up at last, breathed from innumerable throats. They were going to have their bit of fun after all. The rifle was a beautiful German thing with cross-hair sights. I did not then know that in shooting an elephant one would shoot to cut an imaginary bar running from ear-hole to ear-hole. I ought, therefore, as the elephant was sideways on, to have aimed straight at his ear-hole; actually I aimed several inches in front of this, thinking the brain would be further forward.

When I pulled the trigger I did not hear the bang or feel the kick—one 11 never does when a shot goes home—but I heard the devilish roar of glee that went up from the crowd. In that instant, in too short a time, one would have thought, even for the bullet to get there, a mysterious, terrible change had come over the elephant. He neither stirred, nor fell, but every line of his body had altered. He looked suddenly stricken, shrunken, immensely old, as though the frightful impact of the bullet had paralyzed him without knocking him down. At last, after what seemed a long time—it might have been five seconds, I dare say—he sagged flabbily to his knees. His mouth slobbered. An enormous senility seemed to have settled upon him. One could have imagined him thousands of years old. I fired again into the same spot. At the second shot he did not collapse but climbed with desperate slowness to his feet and stood weakly upright, with legs sagging and head drooping. I fired a third time. That was the shot that did for him. You could see the agony of it jolt his whole body and knock the last remnant of strength from his legs. But in falling he seemed for a moment to rise, for as his hind legs collapsed beneath him he seemed to tower upward like a huge rock toppling, his trunk reaching skyward like a tree. He trumpeted, for the first and only time. And then down he came, his belly toward me, with a crash that seemed to shake the ground even where I lay.

I got up. The Burmans were already racing past me across the mud. 12 It was obvious that the elephant would never rise again, but he was not dead. He was breathing very rhythmically with long rattling gasps, his great mound of a side painfully rising and falling. His mouth was wide open—I could see far down into caverns of pale pink throat. I waited for a long time for him to die, but his breathing did not weaken. Finally I fired my two remaining shots into the spot where I thought his heart must be. The thick blood welled out of him like red velvet, but still he did not die. His body did not even jerk when the shots hit him, the tortured breathing continued without a pause. He was dying, very slowly and in great agony, but in some world remote from me where not even a bullet could damage him further. I felt that I had got to put an end to that dreadful noise. It seemed dreadful to see the great beast lying there, powerless to move and yet powerless to die, and not even to be able to finish him. I sent back for my small rifle and poured shot after shot into his heart and down his throat. They seemed to make no impression. The tortured gasps continued as steadily as the ticking of a clock.

In the end I could not stand it any longer and went away. I heard later 13 that it took him half an hour to die. Burmans were bringing dahs[13] and baskets even before I left, and I was told they had stripped his body almost to the bones by the afternoon.

Afterward, of course, there were endless discussions about the shooting 14 of the elephant. The owner was furious, but he was only an Indian and could do nothing. Besides, legally I had done the right thing, for a mad elephant has to be killed, like a mad dog, if its owner fails to control it. Among the Europeans opinion was divided. The older men said I was right, the younger men said it was a damn shame to shoot an elephant for killing a coolie, because an elephant was worth more than any damn Coringhee coolie.[14] And afterward I was very glad that the coolie had been killed; it put me legally in the right and it gave me a sufficient pretext for shooting the elephant. I often wondered whether any of the others grasped that I had done it solely to avoid looking a fool.

NOTES

[1] Burma (Union of Myanmar) is a country in Southeast Asia, and was part of the British Empire at the time to which Orwell is referring.

[2] Betel juice is produced by chewing the leaf of the betel plant wrapped around parings of the areca nut.

[3] As an officer in the Indian Imperial Police, Orwell was an agent of the Empire, and thus often resented by the local population.

[4] British Raj: British rule in the Indian subcontinent prior to 1947.

[5] For ever and ever.

[6] As a warning.

[7] *Must* is a state of dangerous frenzy to which certain male animals, especially elephants and camels, are subject at infrequent intervals.

[8] A *mahout* is an elephant driver.

[9] The rainy season.

[10] *Coolie* is a European word used to describe natives in India and elsewhere who are hired as labourers or burden carriers. Dravidians, so called because they speak one of the Dravidian family of languages, live in southern India and northern Sri Lanka.

[11] Paddy fields are fields of rice.

[12] *Sahib* is a respectful term of address used by Indians and Asians to Europeans, equivalent to "Sir."

[13] A *dah* is a short heavy sword, also used as a knife.

[14] A Coringhee coolie is from Coringa, a small town in southern India.

VOCABULARY

despotic—oppressive or tyrannical

imperialism—the principle, spirit, or ideology by which the existence of an empire, or the extension of territory in the name of protection of existing trading or economic interests, is justified

QUESTIONS

1. Reread the first two paragraphs of "Shooting an Elephant." What are Orwell's attitudes toward the Burmese, the British, and his own position in Burma? How does Orwell use descriptive details and diction to establish his perspective and create the tone of this essay?

2. Note the description of the man killed by the elephant (fourth paragraph). What purposes does this description serve in the essay as a whole?

3. Make a list of Orwell's reasons for not shooting the elephant. Then make a list of the reasons he gives for shooting the elephant. Are you convinced that Orwell was justified in shooting the elephant? What would you have done if you had been in his situation?

4. Note the detailed and graphic description of the elephant's death. What purposes does this description serve? What does the elephant symbolize?

5. Where does Orwell indicate his subject? What insights into the real motives for which imperialist governments act does Orwell actually gain from his experience? What is his thesis?

6. Do you think Orwell uses narration effectively as a persuasive strategy in this essay?

SUGGESTION FOR WRITING

Like Orwell, most of us have done something we are rather ashamed of but have never forgotten because it taught us something important. Using Orwell's essay as a model, write a narrative essay in which you tell a story about a single incident. Be sure this incident has a definite beginning, middle, and end. Try to begin by establishing the context of the incident (how old you were, where it happened, why it was especially important). Include plenty of vivid, precise descriptive details. You can imitate the structure of "Shooting an Elephant" by leading up to your thesis, which you may choose to imply rather than state explicitly.

Loneliness: The Trouble with Solitude

Elizabeth Renzetti

1 Shaheen Shivji was happier in Kabul. There were bombs going off outside the compound where she worked for a development agency, but she preferred life in the Afghan capital to the one she had at home in Abbotsford, B.C., for one simple reason: She wasn't lonely.

2 "For the first time in my adult life, I didn't feel isolated," she says, "I felt socially connected, I was with like-minded people. I was doing something important to better the world."

3 Afghanistan became too dangerous and, after a year, Ms. Shivji moved back to B.C., where she lives with her parents and works as a communications manager for local government. She has one friend she texts regularly, but otherwise her old university crowd has married and drifted away. She yearns for simple connection in her life, to meet a friend regularly for coffee or a movie, to occasionally feel a kind hand on her arm. Work is her main source of satisfaction.

4 The toll of her loneliness isn't just emotional. At 44, she feels tired, distracted, unable to concentrate. It's an effort to get to the gym. Over the phone, her voice becomes strained. "I just feel sad most of the time."

Ms. Shivji feels like she's on the outside looking in and, in that sense, she's not alone. In the West, we live faster, higher in the air, farther from our workplaces, and more singly than at any time in the past. Social scientists will be struggling to understand the consequences of these transformations for decades to come, but one thing is clear: Loneliness is our baggage, a huge and largely unacknowledged cultural failing.

5 In Vancouver, residents recently listed social isolation as their most pressing concern. More Canadians than ever live alone, and almost one-quarter describe themselves as lonely. In the United States, two studies showed that 40 per cent of people say they're lonely, a figure that has doubled in 30 years. Britain has a registered charity campaigning to end chronic loneliness, and last month, health secretary Jeremy Hunt gave a speech about the isolated many, calling attention to "a forgotten million who live amongst us ignored, to our national shame."

6 It is the great irony of our age that we have never been better connected, or more adrift.

Elizabeth Renzetti (b. 1966) is a Canadian journalist who writes extensively about foreign affairs in *The Globe and Mail*. Her first novel, *Based on a True Story,* appeared in 2014 from House of Anansi Press.

The issue isn't just social, it's a public-health crisis in waiting. If you   7
suffer from chronic loneliness, you run the risk of illness, and premature
death.

"This is a bigger problem than we realize," says Ami Rokach, a   8
psychologist and lecturer at York University in Toronto, who has been
researching the subject for more than three decades.

"Loneliness has been linked to depression, anxiety, interpersonal   9
hostility, increased vulnerability to health problems, and even to suicide."

And yet loneliness is the longing that dare not speak its name.   10
Keenly aware that isolation carries with it the whiff of failure, Ms. Shivji
was reticent to be identified for this story. Inside every lonely adult is a kid
eating lunch by herself on a bench.

Says Prof. Rokach, "There is such a stigma about it. People will talk   11
about having depression or even schizophrenia, but . . . I've been practicing
for more than 30 years, and never has anyone come to me and said, 'I feel
lonely.' But then they start talking and it comes out."

This is why David Sutcliffe has launched a bit of a one-man   12
shame-reduction campaign. Mr. Sutcliffe is no one's idea of a social outcast:
He's a handsome and accomplished actor, once a regular on *Gilmore Girls*
and now the star of CBC-TV's *Cracked*, about a detective with mental-
health issues.

And yet, for his whole life, he has been plagued by a profound sense of   13
isolation. He stayed inside. He self-medicated. When he was in his mid-
twenties, his therapist asked, "Have you always been this lonely?" He burst
into tears.

There was a point when Mr. Sutcliffe, now 44, felt so alone that he   14
would get a massage just to feel another person's touch. He has a friend
in Los Angeles who runs a "hugging practice," offering long embraces to
people who have no one to comfort them. "At first it seemed like a wacky
California idea," he says, "but now it makes complete sense."

It was difficult for Mr. Sutcliffe to watch himself on screen during   15
the first season of *Cracked*: "I saw a very lonely guy, and I know that
pain wasn't the character; it was me. But I was glad to put it out there,
because it's important for people to know they're not alone. We're all
struggling."

We are, indeed, but why? Chronic loneliness has roots that are both   16
internal and external, a combination of genes and social circumstance, but
something is making it worse. Blame the garage-door opener, which keeps
neighbours from seeing each other at the end of the day, or our fetish for
roads over parks, or the bright forest of condo towers that bloom on our
city's skylines.

Or blame an increasingly self-absorbed society, as John Cacioppo does. 17
Prof. Cacioppo, the leading authority on the health effects of loneliness,
is director of the University of Chicago's Center for Cognitive and Social
Neuroscience. "One of the things we've seen is a movement away from a
concern for others," he says in a phone interview. "Economics basically says
you should be concerned about your own short-term interests. There's more
division in society, more segmentation; there's less identity with a national
or global persona, but rather on the family or the individual. People aren't
as loyal to their employers, and employers are certainly not as loyal to their
workers." The research that Prof. Cacioppo has done with colleagues also
adds to the growing body of work that shows how bad loneliness can be for
your health. It shows that loneliness suppresses the immune system and car-
diovascular function, and increases the amount of stress hormone the body
produces. It causes wear and tear on a cellular level, and impairs sleep. As he
writes in his book *Loneliness*, "these changes in physiology are compounded
in ways that may be hastening millions of people to an early grave." His
theory, simply, is that we are social animals who function most successfully
in a collective; the physical pain and degradation caused by loneliness are
a kind of early-warning signal of a failure to connect, the way the pain of a
cut finger tells you to fetch a Band-Aid.

A study last year from the University of California at San Francisco 18
showed a clear link between loneliness and serious heart problems and early
death in the elderly. Seniors in the study who identified themselves as lonely
had a 59-per-cent greater chance of health problems, and a 45-per-cent
greater chance of early death. Carla Perissinotto, the doctor who led the
study, said she once encountered an elderly patient in a hospital emergency
ward who seemed to have nothing wrong with her. She soon realized the
woman was so lonely that she just wanted someone to talk to.

Older people come to mind first when we think about loneliness. 19
As a 78-year-old woman living alone in a small Ontario city puts it, "I
feel like everything is behind me, and that there's nothing to look forward
to." Some 20 per cent of older people in this country report feeling lonely,
according to a 2012 Statistics Canada report. But that's not the whole picture, because a sense of isolation doesn't arrive with grey hair: In a study of
34,000 Canadian university students, almost two-thirds reported feeling
"very lonely" in the past 12 months.

More Canadians are living alone than at any other point in history, and 20
half again as many of them (21 per cent) are more likely to report feeling
lonely than those who are part of a couple (14 per cent).

Being alone is not the same as being lonely, of course. Plenty of people 21
are happy to sit in their studies, play World of Warcraft and not see another

human being for days. The problem arises when the lonely become incapacitated by their situation, losing all sense of how to reconnect, and withdraw even further in a wearying circle. The holiday season, which comes wreathed in idealized depictions of cheery families, is particularly dreaded.

In some cases, isolation is taken to gothic extremes. In Britain, a young 22 woman named Joyce Carol Vincent died and wasn't discovered for three years. Neighbours ignored the strange smell coming from in her apartment and, when her body was finally found, the TV was still on. She became the subject of morbid fascination, and a documentary.

This month the story of Harold Percival, a British veteran of the 23 Second World War, caused a brief sensation. When he died alone in a nursing home at 99, a Twitter campaign drew hundreds to his funeral. More than a few observers wondered whether the mourners might have been better employed visiting Mr. Percival while he was still alive.

Does the wired world make us feel even more cut off? Proponents 24 and detractors of social media can cherry-pick from studies showing that technology makes people feel either more connected, or more isolated. But one this summer from the University of Michigan analyzed subjects' responses to a variety of texted questions during the day, and showed that using Facebook increased feelings of loneliness and alienation: "On the surface," the researchers wrote, "Facebook provides an invaluable resource for fulfilling the basic human need for social connection. Rather than enhancing well-being, however, these findings suggest that Facebook may undermine it."

Talk to enough lonely people and you'll find they have one thing in 25 common: They look at Facebook and Twitter the way a hungry child looks through a window at a family feast and wonders, "Why is everyone having a good time except for me?"

Marci O'Connor, 42, is an anglophone living in the largely 26 French-speaking community of Mont Saint-Hilaire, just south of Montreal, with her husband and two children. She "almost feels guilty" for her feelings of isolation, but years of working alone as a freelance writer have taken their toll, and she's now applying to be a waitress so she'll have more human contact.

She has come to believe that there is no substitute for that contact, 27 even if it's just a smile while delivering a beer. For a while, Ms. O'Connor advised companies on their social-media strategies, but she has become increasingly disenchanted with the online world. "It's so hollow," she says. "You might get a lot of likes or retweets, but it's fragile and meaningless. It's not like I could call any of these people at 3 a.m. and they'd help me with my flooded basement."

Ask Vancouverites what bothers them, and you'd think they might 28
say house prices. Drugs on the street. Not being able to get into the hot new
sushi joint. But when the Vancouver Foundation asked that question, it
received a gobsmacking response.

"The biggest issue people had is that they felt lonely, isolated, and 29
unconnected to their communities," says Kevin McCort, president of the
community-outreach charity. Last year, the foundation conducted a survey
of almost 4,000 Vancouverites and found that one-third of those between
25 and 34 felt "alone more than they would like." Another one-third said
they have trouble making friends. Forty per cent of high-rise dwellers felt
lonely, almost twice the number (22 per cent) living in detached homes.
Crucially, the study found that the loneliest also reported being in poorer
health and lacking trust in others.

"Social isolation just may be the greatest environmental hazard of city 30
living," writes Vancouver-based author Charles Montgomery in his new
book, *Happy City: Transforming Our Lives Through Urban Design*. "Worse
than noise, pollution, or even crowding." And the way we've built cities—
suburbs with no central meeting place, prioritizing the car and the condo
tower, passing restrictive zoning bylaws—has made the problem worse, he
says in an interview. "If we're concerned about happiness, then social disconnection in Canadian cities is an acute problem."

Mr. Montgomery points to cities that have done things right, from 31
Portland, Ore., turning its intersections into urban piazzas to the community gardens built in disused lofts in Berlin. Research has shown that
a varied streetscape will cause people to slow down, and perhaps even
exchange a smile or flirtatious glance, and that even a brief exposure to
nature—cutting through a park—makes us feel more generous, and more
social. The Vancouver Foundation has another answer: It is giving out
grants of $500 to people who will organize a community event that brings
strangers together—a knitting circle, an origami workshop, a pumpkin-
carving jamboree. Mr. McCort attended one gathering recently, and was
struck by an unfamiliar sight: "No one was on their phone, or checking email. There were a hundred people, just talking and making new
friends."

On a personal level, being lonely can seem crippling, and saying 32
"just get out and make friends" is like telling an asthmatic to climb Mount
Everest. Prof. Cacioppo notes that lonely people will either withdraw into
their shells or attempt to soothe their pain by lashing out. The first step, he
says, is to recognize and acknowledge painful feelings, and to try to make
small advances each day—by smiling at a neighbour, or performing an
unexpected kindness for a stranger.

David Sutcliffe says he forces himself to keep a busy social schedule, or 33 he would never leave the house. Group therapy has been a huge help. He also is evangelical about sharing his story, to combat what he calls "society's tranquillity mask" —our tendency to pretend that everything is swell, even when it isn't. He knows he speaks for those who can't or won't.

"There are a lot of people walking around who feel that they don't fit 34 in, they don't belong. That sense of disconnection is really common. But when you realize that you're like everyone else, not only in your dreams and passions but also in your pain and sadness, there's incredible comfort in that."

QUESTIONS

1. What kinds of evidence does Renzetti use to support her argument about loneliness?

2. Much of Renzetti's piece focuses on the mental health of Vancouver residents. What do you think about her opening comparison to Shaheen Shivji's experiences in Afghanistan? Is this an appropriate comparison? Why or why not?

3. Renzetti's article suggests that social media makes people feel more lonely. Do you agree or disagree with this assessment based on your experiences with social media?

SUGGESTION FOR WRITING

Gabor Mate's writing on addiction draws attention to one addict's desire for a warm "hug." Similarly, Renzetti's examples include a hugging group in California. Write a comparison essay that examines the similarities and differences between the causes and symptoms of both addiction and loneliness.

Girl Unprotected

Laura Robinson

It is the winter of 1996–97 and your daughter's boyfriend is a junior hockey player. He lives with a bunch of other players and their coach in a hotel suite in Deseronto, Ontario.[1] The relationship does not venture outside the hockey rink or the hotel but the coach is always there and he has a reputation of ensuring players go to school, do their homework, keep their grades up and observe a curfew.

The coach and the players he brought with him have turned the team around. Once it could never win, now it seems never to lose and everybody loves a winner. Your daughter must be safe.

In 2004 you and the rest of Canada are shocked when Michael Jefferson, one of those star players who had since remade himself into Mike Danton in the NHL, pleads guilty to conspiracy to murder charges in St. Louis, and you learn it was David Frost, his coach back in Deseronto, now his agent, whom he conspired to have murdered. Both Danton and Frost deny a conspiracy or intent of any kind, but at least with a guilty plea there will be no investigation. Danton commences his jail term in New Jersey.

Your daughter and her best friend are now young women, removed from Deseronto and the near zero options small towns offer girls. There were no chances for them to become great junior players, because, like every other small town in Canada, Deseronto did not provide "professional" junior hockey teams for girls. In this highly gendered equation, girls were only allowed to be adjectives that helped describe boys, much as hockey scores do. Shortly after the Danton story broke they went to the police.

With distance and maturity the girls understood that the limited sexual opportunities offered by their ex-boyfriends weren't about loving the female body at all; rather they were twisted relationships that revolved around their all powerful coach. The coach Danton wanted dead.

In a Napanee courtroom this week one young woman said, "I felt uncomfortable with it, but . . . I felt kind of pressured to do it" referring to having to have sex with Mr. Frost. She added that she

Laura Robinson is a freelance journalist who writes primarily about issues in sport. Her book *Crossing the Line: Violence and Sexual Assault in Canada's National Sport* (1998) was one of the earlier examinations of the negative downsides of hockey culture in Canada. She has also written extensively about women in sport, including *She Shoots, She Scores: Canadian Perspectives on Women in Sport* (1997) and *Black Tights: Women, Sport and Sexuality* (2002). She is also a former member of Canada's national cycling team and a former Canadian rowing champion.

"didn't want to do it again, but finally I got persuaded into it" after her boyfriend continued to pressure her to have sex once more with him and Mr. Frost.

Robin Warshaw wrote the groundbreaking book *I Never Called It Rape* in 1988. She went to university campuses across the United States and asked girls and young women if they had ever been raped. Almost exclusively they responded in the negative. Then she asked them if they had ever been pressured to have sex by someone who was much larger, who held power over them, who used intimidating or coercive tactics physically, psychologically or emotionally? Had they ever been brow-beaten into sex; simply worn down by a guy who wouldn't take "no"? Had they ever agreed to have sex because it seemed to be the only way out of the situation? The answers came back in the affirmative.   7

The girls in Deseronto cooperated with police for over two years, but on March 6, 2007, Crown Attorney Adam Zegouras dropped the charges that concerned the alleged assaults against the girls, declaring there was insufficient evidence.   8

It was at this point that one of the girls finally gave the police her diary where she kept her most intimate and embarrassing recollections of what went on in the hotel room. Too late: the charges had been dropped and eventually her name, which I will not use, was disclosed to the media as everyone pretended she was a willing participant in acts that sexually exploited and degraded her in a situation she was coerced into.   9

Somehow, though, the charges involving hockey players who were allegedly abused in the exact same incidents at exactly the same time as the girls moved forward. These were the young men who the girls say colluded with Mr. Frost and persuaded them to have sex with their coach. Obviously Mr. Zegouras does not understand what acquaintance rape is, and how was Judge Geoffrey Griffin understanding it when he lifted the publication ban on the girls' names?   10

These girls are all of our daughters. While writing *Crossing the Line: Violence and Sexual Assault in Canada's National Sport* I found too many cases where the "justice" system propped up the hockey mythology and abandoned girls, blind to the cyclical nature of sexual abuse because such ugliness could not be part of hockey. In a subculture presided over with an iron fist, where garbage and garbage cans were thrown over players who didn't play well, where Frost was convicted of assault after he punched a player in the face, everyone became a victim.   11

Girls' bodies were objectified in the most absolute meaning of the word, becoming the surface on which and in which the real relationship— that between the coach and players—took place. Abusive sex was a stand-in   12 for hockey; the female body a stand-in for ice as Mr. Frost's players did as they were told. Like the Swift Current Broncos, who were paid $50.00 to bring a girl back to their coach Graham James' house so he could videotape them having sex, these allegedly victimized players became victimizers.[2] James pled guilty to 350 counts of sexual assault at the exact same time Frost started his fiefdom in Deseronto. Plus ça change.

Girls, in a subculture where Frost told players they were "pussies" and   13 to put their skirts back on and go home, were not human beings. One ex-girlfriend testified she only came to the hotel when "invited." Determining when she saw her boyfriend and when and with whom she would have sexual activity was not her right; another tragic chapter in a litany of many that the hockey myth continues to deny.

NOTES

[1] Deseronto is a town on the northern shore of Lake Ontario, west of Kingston.

[2] Graham James coached junior hockey and was the subject of controversy when Sheldon Kennedy made allegations of sexual abuse against James. In 1997, James pleaded guilty to sexual assault charges and served jail time until his parole in 2001. In October 2010, James faced a new set of charges for sexual assault against the former NHL player Theoren Fleury. Fleury discusses his abuse by James in his autobiographical book, *Playing with Fire* (2009).

VOCABULARY

acquaintance rape—sexual assault where the victim knows the perpetrator

QUESTIONS

1. After reading what Robinson has to say about the dark side of hockey culture in Canada, do you think hockey should be a national symbol for Canada? Can Canada reconcile its pride in hockey (or should it), when hockey is revealed to be entrenched in such violence?

2. Robinson specifically introduces gender in this essay to highlight the limited opportunities that girls and women have in the hockey world. How do you see gender differences in hockey or in sport as a whole? While star athletes are generally held in high regard, what does this say about female role models for girls?

3. Robinson states that the girls are mere "adjectives that helped describe boys." Can you think of any scenarios where these gender roles might be reversed?

SUGGESTION FOR WRITING

Define the myth of hockey and write about which elements you believe are true and which elements you believe are false.

The Men We Carry in Our Minds

Scott Russell Sanders

"This must be a hard time for women," I say to my friend Anneke. 1
"They have so many paths to choose from, and so many voices calling them."

"I think it's a lot harder for men," she replies. 2

"How do you figure that?" 3

"The women I know feel excited, innocent, like crusaders in a just 4
cause. The men I know are eaten up with guilt."

We are sitting at the kitchen table drinking sassafras tea,[1] our hands 5
wrapped around the mugs because this April morning is cool and drizzly.
"Like a Dutch morning," Anneke told me earlier. She is Dutch herself, a
writer and midwife and peacemaker, with the round face and sad eyes of a
woman in a Vermeer painting[2] who might be waiting for the rain to stop,
for a door to open. She leans over to sniff a sprig of lilac, pale lavender, that
rises from a vase of cobalt blue.

"Women feel such pressure to be everything, do everything," I say. 6
"Career, kids, art, politics. Have their babies and get back to the office a
week later. It's as if they're trying to overcome a million years' worth of
evolution in one lifetime."

"But we help one another. We don't try to lumber on alone, like so 7
many wounded grizzly bears, the way men do." Anneke sips her tea. I gave
her the mug with the owls on it, for wisdom. "And we have this deep-down
sense that we're in the *right*—we've been held back, passed over, used—
while men feel they're in the wrong. Men
are the ones who've been discredited, who
have to search their souls."

I search my soul. I discover guilty 8
feelings aplenty—towards the poor,
the Vietnamese, Native Americans, the
whales, an endless list of debts—a guilt in
each case that is as bright and unambiguous as a neon sign. But toward women I
feel something more confused, a snarl of
shame, envy, wary tenderness, and amazement. This muddle troubles me. To hide
my unease I say, "You're right, it's tough
being a man these days."

Scott Russell Sanders (b. 1945) is a fiction writer,
essayist, critic, and former professor of English at
Indiana University. His publications include *The
Country of Language* (1999), *The Force of Spirit*
(2000), and *A Private History of Awe* (2006). He was
named winner of the Mark Twain Award in 2009,
National Winner of the Eugene and Marilyn Glick
Indiana Authors Award in 2010, and winner of
the Cecil Woods Jr. Award in Nonfiction in 2011.

"Don't laugh." Anneke frowns at me, mournful-eyed, through the 9
sassafras steam. "I wouldn't be a man for anything. It's much easier being
the victim. All the victim has to do is break free. The persecutor has to live
with his past."

How deep is that past? I find myself wondering after Anneke has left. 10
How much of an inheritance do I have to throw off? Is it just the beliefs I
breathed in as a child? Do I have to scour memory back through father and
grandfather? Through St. Paul?[3] Beyond Stonehenge[4] and into the twilit
caves? I'm convinced the past we must contend with is deeper even than
speech. When I think back on my childhood, on how I learned to see men
and women, I have a sense of ancient, dizzying depths. The back roads of
Tennessee and Ohio where I grew up were probably closer, in their sexual
patterns, to the campsites of Stone Age hunters than to the genderless cities
of the future into which we are rushing.

The first men, besides my father, I remember seeing were black 11
convicts and white guards, in the cottonfield across the road from our farm
on the outskirts of Memphis. I must have been three or four. The prisoners wore dingy gray-and-black zebra suits, heavy as canvas, sodden with
sweat. Hatless, stooped, they chopped weeds in the fierce heat, row after
row, breathing the acrid dust of boll-weevil poison.[5] The overseers wore
dazzling white shirts and broad shadowy hats. The oiled barrels of their
shotguns flashed in the sunlight. Their faces in memory are utterly blank.
Of course those men, white and black, have become for me an emblem of
racial hatred. But they have also come to stand for the twin poles of my
early vision of manhood—the brute toiling animal and the boss.

When I was a boy, the men I knew labored with their bodies. They 12
were marginal farmers, just scraping by, or welders, steel-workers, carpen-
ters; they swept floors, dug ditches, mined coal, or drove trucks, their fore-
arms ropy with muscle; they trained horses, stoked furnaces, built tires,
stood on assembly lines wrestling parts onto cars and refrigerators. They got
up before light, worked all day long whatever the weather, and when they
came home at night they looked as though somebody had been whipping
them. In the evenings and on weekends they worked on their own places,
tilling gardens that were lumpy with clay, fixing broken-down cars, ham-
mering on houses that were always too drafty, too leaky, too small.

The bodies of the men I knew were twisted and maimed in ways 13
visible and invisible. The nails of their hands were black and split, the hands
tattooed with scars. Some had lost fingers. Heavy lifting had given many of
them finicky backs and guts weak from hernias. Racing against conveyor
belts had given them ulcers. Their ankles and knees ached from years of
standing on concrete. Anyone who had worked for long around machines

was hard of hearing. They squinted, and the skin of their faces was creased like the leather of old work gloves. There were times, studying them, when I dreaded growing up. Most of them coughed, from dust or cigarettes, and most of them drank cheap wine or whiskey, so their eyes looked bloodshot and bruised. The fathers of my friends always seemed older than the mothers. Men wore out sooner. Only women lived into old age.

As a boy I also knew another sort of men, who did not sweat and break 14 down like mules. They were soldiers, and so far as I could tell they scarcely worked at all. During my early school years we lived on a military base, an arsenal in Ohio, and every day I saw GIs in the guardshacks, on the stoops of barracks, at the wheels of olive drab Chevrolets. The chief fact of their lives was boredom. Long after I left the Arsenal I came to recognize the sour smell the soldiers gave off as that of souls in limbo. They were all waiting—for wars, for transfers, for leaves, for promotions, for the end of their hitch—like so many braves waiting for the hunt to begin. Unlike the warriors of older tribes, however, they would have no say about when the battle would start or how it would be waged. Their waiting was broken only when they practiced for war. They fired guns at targets, drove tanks across the churned-up fields of the military reservation, set off bombs in the wrecks of old fighter planes. I knew this was all play. But I also felt certain that when the hour for killing arrived, they would kill. When the real shooting started, many of them would die. This was what soldiers were *for,* just as a hammer was for driving nails.

Warriors and toilers: those seemed, in my boyhood vision, to be the 15 chief destinies for men. They weren't the only destinies, as I learned from having a few male teachers, from reading books, and from watching television. But the men on television—the politicians, the astronauts, the generals, the savvy lawyers, the philosophical doctors, the bosses who gave orders to both soldiers and laborers—seemed as remote and unreal to me as the figures in tapestries. I could no more imagine growing up to become one of these cool, potent creatures than I could imagine becoming a prince.

A nearer and more hopeful example was that of my father, who had 16 escaped from a red-dirt farm to a tire factory, and from the assembly line to the front office. Eventually he dressed in a white shirt and tie. He carried himself as if he had been born to work with his mind. But his body, remembering the earlier years of slogging work, began to give out on him in his fifties, and it quit on him entirely before he turned sixty-five. Even such a partial escape from man's fate as he had accomplished did not seem possible for most of the boys I knew. They joined the army, stood in line for jobs in the smoky plants, helped build highways. They were bound to work as their fathers had worked, killing themselves or preparing to kill others.

A scholarship enabled me not only to attend college, a rare enough feat   17
in my circle, but even to study in a university meant for the children of the
rich. Here I met for the first time young men who had assumed from birth
that they would lead lives of comfort and power. And for the first time I
met women who told me that men were guilty of having kept all the joys
and privileges of the earth for themselves. I was baffled. What privileges?
What joys? I thought about the maimed, dismal lives of most of the men
back home. What had they stolen from their wives and daughters? The
right to go five days a week, twelve months a year, for thirty or forty years
to a steel mill or a coal mine? The right to drop bombs and die in war? The
right to feel every leak in the roof, every gap in the fence, every cough in
the engine, as a wound they must mend? The right to feel, when the lay-off
comes or the plant shuts down, not only afraid but ashamed?

I was slow to understand the deep grievances of women. This was   18
because, as a boy, I had envied them. Before college, the only people I had
ever known who were interested in art or music or literature, the only ones
who read books, the only ones who ever seemed to enjoy a sense of ease and
grace were the mothers and daughters. Like the menfolk, they fretted about
money, they scrimped and made-do. But, when the pay stopped coming in,
they were not the ones who had failed. Nor did they have to go to war, and
that seemed to me a blessed fact. By comparison with the narrow, ironclad
days of fathers, there was an expansiveness, I thought, in the days of mothers. They went to see neighbors, to shop in town, to run errands at school,
at the library, at church. No doubt, had I looked harder at their lives, I
would have envied them less. It was not my fate to become a woman, so it
was easier for me to see the graces. Few of them held jobs outside the home,
and those who did filled thankless roles as clerks and waitresses. I didn't see,
then, what a prison a house could be, since houses seemed to me brighter,
handsomer places than any factory. I did not realize—because such things
were never spoken of—how often women suffered from men's bullying.
I did learn about the wretchedness of abandoned wives, single mothers,
widows; but I also learned about the wretchedness of lone men. Even then I
could see how exhausting it was for a mother to cater all day to the needs of
young children. But if I had been asked, as a boy, to choose between tending a baby and tending a machine, I think I would have chosen the baby.
(Having now tended both, I know I would choose the baby.)

So I was baffled when the women at college accused me and my sex of   19
having cornered the world's pleasures. I think something like my baffle-
ment has been felt by other boys (and by girls as well) who grew up in
dirt-poor farm country, in mining country, in black ghettos, in Hispanic
barrios,[6] in the shadows of factories, in Third World nations—any place

where the fate of men is as grim and bleak as the fate of women. Toilers and warriors. I realize now how ancient these identities are, how deep the tug they exert on men, the undertone of a thousand generations. The miseries I saw, as a boy, in the lives of nearly all men I continue to see in the lives of many—the body-breaking toil, the tedium, the call to be tough, the humiliating powerlessness, the battle for a living and for territory.

When the women I met at college thought about the joys and privileges   20 of men, they did not carry in their minds the sort of men I had known in my childhood. They thought of their fathers, who were bankers, physicians, architects, stockbrokers, the big wheels of the big cities. These fathers rode the train to work or drove cars that cost more than any of my childhood houses. They were attended from morning to night by female helpers, wives, and nurses and secretaries. They were never laid off, never short of cash at month's end, never lined up for welfare. These fathers made decisions that mattered. They ran the world.

The daughters of such men wanted to share in this power, this glory.   21 So did I. They yearned for a say over their future, for jobs worthy of their abilities, for the right to live at peace, unmolested, whole. Yes, I thought, yes yes. The difference between me and these daughters was that they saw me, because of my sex, as destined from birth to become like their fathers, and therefore as an enemy to their desires. But I knew better. I wasn't an enemy, in fact or in feeling. I was an ally. If I had known, then, how to tell them so, would they have believed me? Would they now?

NOTES

[1] Sassafras tea is made from the root of the sassafras tree, a small tree native to North America.

[2] Jan Vermeer (1632–1675) was a Dutch painter known in particular for his depiction of peaceful domestic scenes.

[3] St. Paul, author of a number of biblical Epistles, is known for his stern views on Christian belief and behaviour.

[4] Stonehenge is a prehistoric circle of stones on Salisbury Plain in England.

[5] The boll weevil is a beetle that attacks the seed vessels of cotton, a major crop in the American South.

[6] Barrios are Spanish-speaking districts of cities or towns in the United States, especially poor neighbourhoods populated by immigrants.

VOCABULARY

arsenal—an arms repository or store

limbo—a place between heaven and hell, where the souls of the unbaptized are supposed to reside

QUESTIONS

1. How does Sanders's account of his conversation with his friend Anneke create a framework for the rest of the essay?

2. What do the men Sanders carries in his mind—convicts and guards, marginal farmers, factory workers, labourers, soldiers—have in common? How have these men shaped Sanders's attitudes toward gender issues?

3. How does Sanders use comparison as a strategy to develop and organize his ideas in this essay?

4. Do you think Sanders makes effective use of descriptive detail?

5. If you are a female reader, did Sanders's essay make you more willing to believe that men have problems? If you are a male reader, can you identify with Sanders's account of men's lives?

SUGGESTION FOR WRITING

What men or women do you carry in your mind? How have they influenced your attitudes toward whether men or women have easier lives? Write an essay in which you describe the appearance of the men or women you grew up with and the work they did. Be sure to include a range of specific sensory details.

Systems: Open or Closed?

Virginia Satir

I want to discuss something that at first you might not think has much to do with your family and peoplemaking.[1] Stay with me. The concept of *systems* was borrowed from the world of industry and commerce. It has become a way of understanding how human beings in groups work.

Any system consists of several individual parts. Each part is essential and related to each other part to attain a certain outcome; each acts as a stimulus to other parts. The system has an order and a sequence which is determined through the actions, reactions, and interactions among the parts. This constant interplay governs how the system manifests itself. A system has life only now, when its component parts are present.

Sounds confusing? It isn't really. You put yeast, flour, water, and sugar together to make bread. The bread isn't like any one of its ingredients, yet it contains all of them.

Steam isn't like any of its parts, but it contains them all.

All human life is part of a system. We hear a lot about beating the system, which would seem to say that all systems are bad. Not so. Some are and some are not. The implications of systems thinking for personal, family, and societal behavior are evident everywhere today. . . .

An operating system consists of the following:

A purpose or goal. Why does this system exist in the first place? In families, the purpose is to grow new people and to further the growth of those already here.

Essential parts. In families, this means adults and children, males and females.

An order to the parts' working. In families, this refers to the various family members' self-esteem, rules, and communication.

Power to maintain energy in the system so the parts can work. In families, this power is derived from food, shelter, air, water, activity, and beliefs about the emotional, intellectual, physical, social, and spiritual lives of the family members and how they work together.

Ways of interacting with the outside. In families, this means relating to changing contents, the new and different.

Virginia Satir (1916–1988) is known for her pioneering work in exploring the way that family systems affect the mental health of family members. She co-founded the Mental Health Research Institute (Menlo Park, California), which, in 1962, offered the first formal training in family therapy. Her key books include *Conjoint Family Therapy* (1964), *Peoplemaking* (1972), and *The New Peoplemaking* (1988). The Avanta network, which she founded in 1977, continues her work today.

Reprinted by permission from *Systems: Open or Closed? The New Peoplemaking* Science and Behavior Books, 1988, pp. 130–140. By Virginia Satir. Science and Behavior Books, Inc.

There are two types of systems: closed and open. The main difference 12 between them is the nature of their reactions to change, both from the inside and from the outside. In a closed system, the parts are rigidly connected or disconnected altogether. In either case, information does not flow between parts or from outside in and inside out. When parts are disconnected, they often appear as if they are operating: information leaks in and out but without any direction. There are no boundaries.

An open system is one in which the parts interconnect, are responsive 13 and sensitive to one another, and allow information to flow between the internal and external environments.

If one were to deliberately design a closed family system, the first step 14 would be to separate it as completely as possible from outside interference, and to rigidly fix all roles for all time. The fact is, I don't believe anyone would deliberately design a closed system. Closed family systems evolve from certain sets of beliefs:

People are basically evil and must be continually controlled to be good.

Relationships have to be regulated by force or by fear of punishment.

There is one right way, and the person with most power has it.

There is always someone who knows what is best for you.

These beliefs are powerful because they reflect the family's perception 15 of reality. And the family then sets rules according to their beliefs. In other words, in closed systems:

Self-worth is secondary to power and performance.

Actions are subject to the whims of the boss.

Change is resisted.

In open systems: 16

Self-worth is primary; power and performance, secondary.

Actions represent one's beliefs.

Change is welcomed and considered normal and desirable.

Communication, the system, and the rules all relate to each other.

Most of our social systems are closed or very nearly so. A little change is 17 allowed, which in my opinion is the reason we have been able to limp along as well as we have.

Now we come to an important philosophical question. Do you believe 18 that all human life deserves the highest priority? *I believe this with all my being.* Therefore I unashamedly admit I will do everything I can to change closed systems into open ones. An open system can choose to be open or closed when it fits. The important word is choice.

I believe that human beings cannot flourish in a closed system; at best, they can only exist. Human beings want more than that. The task of the therapist is to see the light that shines in every person or family, and to uncoil the wrappings that shroud that light.   19

Right now you and I could point to countless examples of closed systems, including dictatorships in current society, schools, prisons, churches, and political groups. What about the system in your family? Is it open or closed? If your communication now is mostly growth-impeding and if your rules are inhuman, covert, and out of date, you probably have a closed family system. If your communication is growth-producing and your rules are human, overt, and up to date, you have an open one. . . .   20

The following chart shows how the closed system applies to troubled families, and the open system to nurturing families: 21

	CLOSED SYSTEM
SELF-ESTEEM	low
COMMUNICATION STYLES	indirect, unclear, unspecific, incongruent, growth-impeding blaming placating computing[2] distracting
RULES	covert, out-of-date, inhuman rules remain fixed; people change their needs to conform to established rules restrictions on commenting
OUTCOME	accidental, chaotic, destructive, inappropriate

Self-worth grows ever more doubtful and depends more and more heavily on other people.   22

	OPEN SYSTEM
SELF-ESTEEM	high
COMMUNICATION STYLE	direct, clear, specific, congruent, growth-producing leveling
RULES	overt, up-to-date, human rules; rules change when need arises full freedom to comment on anything
OUTCOME	related to reality; appropriate, constructive

Self-worth grows ever more reliable, confident, and draws increasingly 23
more from the self.

All right. When three or more people are related in any way and are 24
joined in one common purpose, they will develop into a system. This happens in families, with friends, and at work. Once established, the system
remains very much in operation, even when not in evidence. If it's a closed
system, it will probably operate on a *life-death, right-wrong* basis; fear per-
meates the atmosphere. If open, it probably operates on the basis of *growth,
intimacy,* and *choice.*

Put very simply, your self-worth, your communication, together with your 25
rules and your beliefs, are the ingredients that make up your family system.
Leveling communication and human rules characterize an open system and
allow everyone in that system to flourish. Crippling communication and
inhuman rules make a closed system, retarding and distorting growth.

Becoming aware of their system usually opens the way for family 26
members to become searchers and to stop berating themselves and others
when things go wrong. People can ask "how" questions instead of "why"
questions. Generally speaking, "how" questions lead to information and
understanding, and "whys" imply blame and so produce defensiveness.
Anything contributing to defensiveness contributes to low pot[3] and leads to
potentially unsatisfying outcomes.

Another important part of any system is that it tends to perpetuate 27
itself. Once established, a system will stay the same until it dies or something changes it: a part breaks down from lack of care or because of a defect;
or a catastrophic event affects the system. Sometimes even a minor incident can overwhelm the system, which indicates that the system's designers
behaved as though change would never happen.

Each member in a system is a most significant factor in keeping the 28
system going as it is or changing it. Discovering your part in the system and
seeing others' parts is an exciting, although sometimes painful, experience.
And you can certainly see the importance of systems when you consider the
very life of the family depends on its system to a very large degree. . . .

NOTES

[1] For Satir, "peoplemaking" is the process by which families help or hinder the growth of their members.

[2] In Satir's framework of terms, "computing" denotes a personality style emphasizing super-rationality.

[3] In Satir's work, your "pot" is the place where you store good feelings. "Low pot" means that your good feelings are relatively absent.

QUESTIONS

1. Satir associates human flourishing with open family systems. What's her support for this association? Are you persuaded by her claim?

2. Satir does not offer details of specific open and closed family systems. Does the essay need this detail? Why or why not?

3. This essay analyzes family systems as either open or closed. Is the organization of systems analysis around a simple opposition a weakness or strength (or both) in this essay? Can you imagine a family system being partly open and partly closed?

SUGGESTION FOR WRITING

Satir claims there are many closed or nearly closed systems in "current society" and its institutions. Write an essay on a current social or cultural organization (such as a college department, a church, or a provincial government) or a current belief system (such as neo-conservatism), examining its degree of openness or closure.

In Search of a Modest Proposal

Fred Stenson

My gratitude to the education system for teaching my children to read lasted for many years. Whenever teachers were attacked in my earshot, I rose to defend them. Then my daughter hit Grade 9 and was taught to write the essay. 1

When she told me she had been assigned to write an essay, I felt a thrill. She was about to learn one of the great literary forms, used for hundreds of years to persuade and argue. In the hands of a great writer, the essay could shape society. Part of the thrill was also that she had finally reached a topic about which I knew something. I was eager to help, and she allowed that I could. 2

The essay, as I recall (it's been a few years), was about "why it is good to converse with seniors." I was surprised in that I didn't know my daughter held that opinion, and here she was making it the thesis of a personal essay. 3

When I asked her about the choice, she said, oh no, it was just one of a list that the teacher had given them to choose from. "But yet you chose it?" I countered. "Well, my small group did. We did all the preparation in group." 4

Teacher? Group? The whole point of a personal essay is to be personal. Her personal opinion. Something she wanted to convince others of. She waved this away as immaterial. Time was wasting. The essay was due on Friday. 5

The thesis statement, that it was good to visit with old people, had to be in paragraph one. That was mandatory. Also, the first paragraph had to contain the three arguments, one per sentence. After that, she must devote one paragraph to each argument. Restate the argument; give five points to support that argument. And so on. 6

Her arguments were on a very messy piece of paper, covered in many people's handwriting, the result of a brain-storming session in the small group. 7

"Seniors know a lot." 8

"Seniors get lonely because their families neglect them." 9

"Seniors deserve respect." 10

"Seniors are nice." 11

Albertan Fred Stenson is the author of several books of fiction and nonfiction focusing on the Canadian West. He has also written numerous film scripts. His novels *The Trade* (2000) and *Lightning* (2005) were nominated for the Giller Prize, and both novels won the Grant MacEwan author prize. Stenson was a founding member of the Writers Guild of Alberta. He lives in Calgary with his family and his partner, writer and teacher Pamela Banting.

Reprinted by permission from "In Search of a Modest Proposal" *Alberta Views*, January/February 2004, pp. 14–15 by Fred Stenson.

"A lot of seniors are not neglected by their families," I said. "Some 12
seniors are not even slightly nice. I might turn out to be one of them."

Again, I was waved silent. My daughter and her friends were much 13
better qualified than I to determine how the subject should be approached,
and what should be said about it.

My daughter had already started writing. I read what she had so far. 14

"It's fine," I said, "but you shouldn't use all those words like 'therefore' 15
and 'consequently' at the start of every paragraph. I mean, really.
'Henceforth'?"

My daughter looked at me with pity. She pulled out a sheet, a class 16
handout, and she read: "Each paragraph is to be connected to the next
paragraph by a transitional word or phrase at the beginning of the new
paragraph. Use transitional words within each paragraph as well for greater
unity and cohesion." There was a list. "Henceforth" was on it.

"And you're repeating a lot," I said. "That's not good writing." 17

She pointed to a different place on the handout. 18

"Repeat important words and phrases." 19

"What's with all the adjectives and adverbs?" 20

"Says here: 'Use bright descriptive language.'" 21

"What else does it say?" 22

"Support each of your three arguments with five points, in three 23
separate paragraphs. Then repeat the three arguments in the concluding
paragraph, ending with a strong conclusion statement."

"That's not an essay!" I cried. "That's, that's . . ." 24

"A formula," she said. "A formula I have to stick to, or I will flunk. 25
Now, let's get busy."

* * *

A couple of months later, it was parent/teacher day. I confronted my 26
daughter's Language Arts teacher with my concerns about how the essay
was being taught. I suspect I buttered it on a bit thick about the tradition
of Rousseau and Swift, and the great modern practitioners like Richler and
Fussell.[1] The teacher was a pleasant, able-seeming woman, who instantly
deflated me with agreement. No, theirs was not a creative approach to the
essay. No, that approach probably would not endear the students to the
essay form. Asked why it was so, she shrugged and said, "It's the curriculum, on which they will be tested. The results of the test will determine
their future in high school. So we teach it that way."

I sought out the Grade 9 curriculum for Language Arts. Everything 27
was there. "Bright descriptive language." The mathematical equation: this
many arguments each supported by this many points. Special emphasis on

transitional words and phrases, the more the merrier. I said no more about it. My daughter passed her provincial Language Arts exam and moved on into high school.

Nonetheless, it is sad about the essay. I find myself thinking about 28 Jonathan Swift's "A Modest Proposal," the essay he published in 1729 to address the problem of Irish poverty and starvation. He proposed that the higher classes eat Irish children while they were still young and succulent, thus reducing the number of poor to a more manageable level.

This "modest proposal" is the essay's thesis statement. When I examined 29 the essay with the Alberta Language Arts curriculum in mind, I was disturbed to find that Swift does not actually state his thesis until he has expended over 1,000 words! His use of transitional devices is equally shoddy. Out of 28 paragraphs, he uses transitional words and phrases to begin only eight of them. Of the eight, six are an enumeration of his six strongest points toward the essay's end. This enumeration is good and would get him some important marks. *But,* "finally," "similarly" and "in addition" are absent from the essay, leaving Swift's thoughts sadly unconnected.

However, let us remember that this essay was written almost 300 years 30 ago. On that account, let us be kind to Mr. Swift and give him a "C." It would be a shame to keep him out of Grade 10.

NOTE

[1] Jean Jacques Rousseau (1712–1778) was a Swiss-born French philosopher whose *Confessions* (1770, 1782) was influential in the evolution of the personal essay. Jonathan Swift is one of the authors featured in Readings. Mordecai Richler, who died in 2001, is primarily known as a Canadian novelist, but his journalism and essays are collected in four books, including *Shovelling Trouble* (1972). American Paul Fussell (b. 1924) has written books on war, class, and travel, among other topics.

QUESTIONS

1. Why does Stenson open his essay with comments on his appreciation of teachers and on his love for the essay as "one of the great literary forms"?

2. Stenson is writing a personal essay about the value of personal essays. How far does his own essay embody what he argues for? To help you answer this question, you might find it useful to refer to our discussion of informal and formal essays in Chapter 1.

3. Stenson clearly admires Jonathan Swift's "A Modest Proposal" (Readings), and, like Swift, he writes to criticize cultural and social attitudes and institutions. How does his use of satire and irony compare to Swift's?

SUGGESTIONS FOR WRITING

1. Stenson defends the role of "personal opinion" in the personal essay. Write an essay exploring the role of personal opinion in the essay form in general and referring to several essayists from the Readings.

2. What was your own experience of writing essays in junior high or high school? Was it like that of Stenson's daughter, or quite different? Do you now write essays in the way you were taught then? Write an essay on this topic.

It Always Costs

David Suzuki

I have long believed that we have to have greater scientific literacy at all levels of society if we are to have any hope of affecting the way science and technology are impacting on our lives. That's why I went into broadcasting.   1

But I have only recently realized that my underlying faith in the power of greater awareness is misplaced. First of all, we must understand that there is no such thing as a problem-free technology. However beneficent, technology always has a cost.   2

Think, for example, of DDT[1]—it killed malaria-carrying mosquitoes in huge numbers and without question saved millions of lives in tropical countries. But geneticists could have predicted that DDT would exert incredible selective pressure for mutations that would confer resistance to DDT in the mosquitoes and that within a few years large numbers would return. They did. But once committed to a chemical approach, we had to turn to other more toxic compounds.   3

The ecological damage from massive use of chemical sprays has been enormous because DDT is not specific and kills all insects. Furthermore, the compound is ingested by many organisms, so that initially minute quantities become concentrated up the food chain in a process called *biomagnification*. The final result was that DDT ended up in the shell glands of birds, affecting the thickness of egg shells and eventually causing heavy bird mortality.   4

A third-generation Japanese Canadian born in Vancouver, David Takayoshi Suzuki was interned with his family in interior British Columbia during the Second World War. Suzuki went on to earn a PhD in zoology from the University of Chicago, carry out research on genetic adaptations in fruit flies, and enjoy a thirty-year career as a professor of zoology at the University of British Columbia. His later career has been devoted to the popularization of scientific and urgent environmental issues, notably as the host of *The Nature of Things*, a long-running CBC television show that has been shown worldwide. He is the author of over thirty-two books, including *Genethics* (1990), *Wisdom of the Elders* (1993), *The Sacred Balance* (2002), and *The Legacy* (2010).

"It Always Costs" is taken from *Inventing the Future* by David Suzuki. Reprinted with permission of Stoddart Publishing Co. Limited, North York, Ontario.

There are numerous examples of how technological innovations have had detrimental side effects that eventually outweighed their benefits. It has been my assumption that what we needed was some kind of vehicle, like panels of citizens representing a broad range of interests, to do a cost/benefit analysis of all new technologies. The idea was that by carefully weighing the benefits and bad side effects, we could make a more informed decision on whether to allow a   5 new technology to be used. My belief that this would help us avoid future problems was based on faith in our predictive capabilities. Indeed, much of the testing of environmental and health impacts is made on that faith. But we can't rely on such a system.

For one thing, our assessments are always limited. For example, suppose 6 we do an environmental impact assessment of drilling for oil in the high Arctic. The studies, of necessity, are carried out in a limited time within a restricted area. It is simply assumed that scaling up the observed effects of the two drill holes by a factor of one hundred or more gives a reasonable estimate of the impact of major exploration.

Well, there are effects called *synergistic;* several components interact to 7 give new or greater effects than the sum of their individual impact. Also, during an assessment, you can bet industry will be on its best behaviour, so the results will always be on the conservative side.

It is also true that even if a study is made over ten years (which it won't 8 be) we could never anticipate all the fluctuation of conditions in this sensitive area. I've known colleagues who have studied populations of animals or plants over decades and find nice cycles and patterns that are predictable until suddenly completely unexpected fluctuations occur. They get out more publications that way, but we ought, then, to be a lot more humble about how *little* we know.

Finally, we know that major blowouts, spills or accidents are relatively 9 rare. Suppose one happens an average of once every twenty holes. By studying *two* holes and finding no effect, we are not justified in concluding that drilling one hundred holes will also be accident free. It would be just as invalid were an accident to happen in one of the test holes to conclude that half of all drilling sites will have a bad episode. The numbers are statistically meaningless.

Food additives, pesticides and drugs are extensively tested before they 10 are approved for use. But numerous cases inform us that we can't anticipate all the effects. The DDT example is classic—at the time it was used, we didn't even know about biomagnification, let alone its concentration in bird shell glands.

Remember thalidomide[2] or DES?[3] Or consider the oral contraceptive. 11 It had been extensively tested (in Puerto Rico, of course) and shown to be efficacious without detrimental side effects. It was only after millions of healthy, normal women had taken the pill for years that epidemiologists could see negative effects. No amount of pretesting could have anticipated them.

So we come to a terrible conclusion. Technology has enormous 12 benefits. They are undeniable—that's why we're hooked on it. Once technology is in place, it becomes impossible to do without it and we can't go back to doing things the old way. But the pretesting of any new technology is flawed because it provides only a limited assessment of its impact. The tests are restricted in size, scope and time and are based on what we decide a priori might be a possible effect.

But how can we test for something that we don't know will happen? If 13 every technology has a cost, the more powerful the technology, the greater its potential cost. We have to build into our judgements a large leeway for our ignorance and err on the side of extreme caution. And perhaps it's time to realize we don't have to do everything just because we can.

NOTES

[1] DDT—dichlorodiphenyltrichloroethane—has been used extensively as an insecticide, particularly in combatting malarial mosquitoes. It is a persistent pesticide (it does not break down readily) and is stored in human fat almost indefinitely. Tolerance to DDT is widely variable in humans and its use has led to much controversy. It has been shown, in laboratory experiments, to be an "enzyme inducer" that breaks down estrogen, which in birds mediates calcium metabolism. It is also readily passed through the placenta into the fetus. The use of DDT is now banned in Canada and the United States, though DDT is still manufactured for export.

[2] Thalidomide, or alpha phthaloyl glutarimide, is a close relative of aminopteria, a drug known since 1950 to have teratogenic (causing monstrous genetic defect) properties. Thalidomide was introduced for sale in Britain in April 1958. It was released for sale despite an almost complete lack of chemical and pharmacological testing, and of research into the scientific literature. It was touted as being perfectly safe as a sedative for pregnant women despite testing that indicated that it could completely shut down thyroid function. It caused birth defects such as shortened or absent limbs and flipper-like appendages in more than 450 births as well as nerve damage in more than 400 adults and children. Despite medical evidence of its effects, it continued to be sold until its withdrawal in November 1961.

[3] DES, or diethylstilbestrol, is a synthetic estrogen. It was widely prescribed to women in the United States between 1938 and 1971 to prevent miscarriages and treat other complications of pregnancy. Its use for pregnant women was halted in 1971 when the drug was found to affect the reproductive system of children exposed to it in the womb. Women who took DES while pregnant have a slightly elevated risk of breast cancer. "DES daughters"—daughters exposed to DES in the womb—have an increased risk of a rare cancer of the vagina or cervix, as well as increased risk of reproductive tract abnormalities, complications of pregnancy, and infertility. Sons exposed to DES also have some increased health risks.

VOCABULARY

a priori—*a priori* here means being knowable by reasoning from something that is considered self-evident or presupposed from general experience

epidemiologists—those who study the incidence, distribution, and control of diseases in large populations

QUESTIONS

1. Suzuki's title "It [technology] Always Costs" is also his thesis. How is his essay organized to support this thesis?

2. Why does Suzuki include his reassessments of the value of scientific research in his essay? How do these inclusions affect his tone? Be specific about his attitudes to himself, his readers, and his subject.

3. What does Suzuki's comment that the oral contraceptive was tested "in Puerto Rico, of course" reveal about his attitude to the scientific establishment? Do you think this comment affects Suzuki's credibility?

4. Is this essay written for scientists, for specialists in environmental issues, or for the general public? Does Suzuki's style define the audience he is aiming for?

SUGGESTION FOR WRITING

Do you agree that scientific advances *always* have costs? Write a letter to David Suzuki expressing your views on the costs and/or benefits of recent developments in science and technology, such as cloning, digital television, social networking, voice mail, the internet, and smartphones.

A Modest Proposal

For preventing the Children of Poor People
from being a Burthen to
their Parents, or the Country,
and for making them
Beneficial to the Publick.

Jonathan Swift

I t is a mellancholly Object to those, who walk through this great Town,[1] or travel in the Country, when they see the *Streets,* the *Roads,* and *Cabbin-Doors,* crowded with *Beggars* of the female Sex, followed by three, four, or six Children, *all in Rags,* and importuning every Passenger for an Alms. These *Mothers* instead of being able to work for their honest Livelyhood, are forced to employ all their time in Stroling, to beg Sustenance for their *helpless Infants,* who, as they grow up, either turn *Thieves* for want of work, or leave their *dear native Country to fight for the Pretender in Spain,*[2] or sell themselves to the *Barbadoes.*[3]

I think it is agreed by all Parties, that this prodigious number of Children, in the Arms, or on the Backs, or at the *Heels* of their *Mothers,* and frequently of their *Fathers,* is *in the present deplorable state of the Kingdom,*[4] a very great additional grievance; and therefore whoever could find out a fair, cheap and easy method of making these Children sound and useful Members of the Commonwealth would deserve so well of the publick, as to have his Statue set up for a Preserver of the Nation.

But my Intention is very far from being confined to provide only for the Children of *professed Beggars:* It is of a much greater extent, and shall take in the whole number of Infants at a certain Age, who are born of Parents in effect as little able to support them, as those who demand our Charity in the Streets.

As to my own part, having turned my thoughts, for many Years, upon this important Subject, and maturely weighed

Jonathan Swift (1667–1745) is often regarded as the foremost prose satirist to write in English. Born in Ireland of English parents, he was educated at Trinity College, Dublin, and then attempted a career in writing, politics, and the church in England. Most of his best-known works, including "A Modest Proposal" (1729) and the satiric fiction *Gulliver's Travels* (1726), were written during the thirty years between his appointment in 1714 as Dean of St. Patrick's (Anglican) Cathedral in Dublin and his death in 1745, a period in which he more and more took on the role of defender of Ireland against English absentee landlords and their upper-class Irish collaborators.

the several *Schemes of other Projectors,* I have always found them grossly mistaken in their computation. It is true a Child, *just dropt from its Dam,* may be supported by her Milk, for a Solar year with little other Nourishment, at most not above the Value of two Shillings, which the Mother may certainly get, or the Value in *Scraps,* by her lawful Occupation of begging, and it is exactly at one Year old that I propose to provide for them, in such a manner, as, instead of being a Charge upon their *Parents,* or the *Parish,* or *wanting Food and Raiment* for the rest of their Lives, they shall, on the Contrary, contribute to the Feeding and partly to the Cloathing of many Thousands.

There is likewise another great Advantage in my Scheme, that it will 5 prevent those *voluntary Abortions,* and that horrid practice of *Women murdering their Bastard Children*; alas! too frequent among us; sacrificing the *poor innocent Babes,* I doubt, more to avoid the Expence, than the Shame; which would move Tears and Pity in the most Savage and inhuman breast.

The Number of Souls in this Kingdom being usually reckoned one 6 Million and a half; of these I calculate there may be about two hundred thousand Couple whose Wives are Breeders; from which number I Subtract thirty Thousand Couples, who are able to maintain their own Children, although I apprehend there cannot be so many under *the present distresses of the Kingdom;* but this being granted, there will remain an Hundred and Seventy Thousand Breeders. I again Subtract fifty Thousand for those Women who miscarry, or whose Children dye by accident, or disease within the Year. There only remain an hundred and twenty thousand Children of poor Parents annually born: The question therefore is, how this number shall be reared, and provided for, which, as I have already said, under the present Situation of Affairs, is utterly impossible by all the methods hitherto proposed, for we can *neither employ them in Handicraft,* or *Agriculture;* we neither build Houses, (I mean in the Country) nor cultivate Land: They can very seldom pick up a Livelyhood *by Stealing* till they arrive at six years Old, except where they are of towardly parts, although, I confess they learn the Rudiments much earlier, during which time, they can however be properly looked upon only as *Probationers,* as I have been informed by a principal Gentleman in the County of *Cavan,*[5] who protested to me, that he never knew above one or two Instances under the Age of six, even in a part of the Kingdom *so renowned for the quickest proficiency in that Art.*

I am assured by our Merchants, that a Boy or Girl, before twelve Years 7 old, is no saleable Commodity, and even when they come to this Age, they will not yield above three Pounds, or three Pounds and half a Crown at most on the Exchange, which cannot turn to Account either to the Parents or the Kingdom, the Charge of Nutriment and Rags having been at least four times that Value.

I shall now therefore humbly propose my own thoughts, which I hope 8
will not be liable to the least Objection.

I have been assured by a very knowing *American* of my acquaintance in 9
London, that a young healthy Child well Nursed is at a Year old a most delicious, nourishing, and wholesome Food, whether *Stewed, Roasted, Baked,*
or *Boyled,* and I make no doubt that it will equally serve in a *Fricasie,* or a
Ragoust.

I do therefore humbly offer it to *publick consideration,* that of the 10
hundred and twenty thousand Children, already computed, twenty thousand may be reserved for Breed, whereof only one fourth part to be Males,
which is more than we allow to *Sheep, black Cattle,* or *Swine,* and my reason
is that these Children are seldom the Fruits of Marriage, *a Circumstance not
much regarded by our Savages,* therefore *one Male* will be sufficient to serve
four Females. That the remaining hundred thousand may at a Year old be
offered in Sale to the *persons of Quality,* and *Fortune,* through the Kingdom,
always advising the Mother to let them Suck plentifully in the last Month,
so as to render them Plump, and Fat for a good Table. A Child will make
two Dishes at an Entertainment for Friends, and when the Family dines
alone, the fore or hind Quarter will make a reasonable Dish, and seasoned
with a little Pepper or Salt will be very good Boiled on the fourth Day,[6]
especially in Winter.

I have reckoned upon a Medium, that a Child just born will weigh 11
12 pounds, and in a solar Year if tollerably nursed encreaseth to 28 Pounds.

I grant this food will be somewhat dear, and therefore very *proper for* 12
Landlords, who, as they have already devoured most of the Parents, seem to
have the best Title to the Children.

Infant's flesh will be in Season throughout the Year, but more plentiful 13
in *March,* and a little before and after, for we are told by a grave Author[7]
an eminent *French* Physitian, that *Fish being a prolifick Dyet,* there are more
Children born in *Roman Catholick Countries* about nine Months after *Lent,*
than at any other Season: Therefore reckoning a Year after *Lent,* the Markets
will be more glutted than usual, because the number of *Popish Infants,* is at
least three to one in this Kingdom, and therefore it will have one other
Collateral advantage by lessening the Number of *Papists*[8] among us.

I have already computed the Charge of nursing a Beggars Child (in 14
which list I reckon all *Cottagers, Labourers,* and four fifths of the *Farmers*)
to be about two Shillings *per Annum,* Rags included, and I believe no
Gentleman would repine to give Ten Shillings for the *Carcass of a good fat
Child,* which, as I have said will make four Dishes of excellent Nutritive
Meat, when he hath only some particular friend, or his own Family to Dine
with him. Thus the Squire will learn to be a good Landlord, and grow

popular among his Tenants, the Mother will have Eight Shillings net profit, and be fit for Work till she produceth another Child.

Those who are more thrifty (*as I must confess the Times require*) may flay the Carcass; the Skin of which, artificially dressed, will make admirable *Gloves for Ladies,* and *Summer Boots for fine Gentlemen.* 15

As to our City of *Dublin,* Shambles may be appointed for this purpose, in the most convenient parts of it, and Butchers we may be assured will not be wanting, although I rather recommend buying the Children alive, and dressing them hot from the Knife, as we do *roasting Pigs.* 16

A very worthy Person, *a true Lover of his Country,*[9] and whose Virtues I highly esteem, was lately pleased, in discoursing on this matter, to offer a Refinement upon my Scheme. He said, that many Gentlemen of this Kingdom, having of late destroyed their Deer, he conceived that the want of Venison might be well supplied by the Bodies of young Lads and Maidens, not exceeding fourteen Years of Age, nor under twelve, so great a Number of both Sexes in every Country being now ready to Starve, for want of Work and Service: And these to be disposed of by their Parents if alive, or otherwise by their nearest Relations. But with due deference to so excellent a friend, and so deserving a Patriot, I cannot be altogether in his Sentiments, for as to the Males, my *American* acquaintance assured me from frequent Experience, that their flesh was generally Tough and Lean, like that of our Schoolboys, by continual exercise, and their Taste disagreeable, and to Fatten them would not answer the Charge. Then as to the Females, it would, I think with humble Submission, *be a loss to the Publick,* because they soon would become Breeders themselves: And besides it is not improbable that some scrupulous People might be apt to Censure such a Practice, (although indeed very unjustly) as a little bordering upon Cruelty, which, I confess, hath always been with me the strongest objection against any Project, however so well intended. 17

But in order to justify my friend, he confessed, that this expedient was put into his head by the famous *Sallmanaazor,* a Native of the Island *Formosa,*[10] who came from thence to *London,* above twenty Years ago, and in Conversation told my friend, that in his Country when any young Person happened to be put to Death, the Executioner sold the Carcass to *Persons of Quality,* as a prime Dainty, and that, in his Time, the Body of a plump Girl of fifteen, who was crucified for an attempt to Poison the Emperor, was sold to his Imperial *Majesty's prime Minister of State,* and other great *Mandarins* of the Court, *in Joints from the Gibbet,* at four hundred Crowns. Neither indeed can I deny, that if the same use were made of several plump young Girls in this Town, who, without one single Groat[11] to their Fortunes, cannot stir abroad without a Chair, and appear at the 18

Play-House, and *Assemblies* in Foreign fineries, which they never will Pay for; the Kingdom would not be the worse.

Some Persons of a desponding Spirit are in great Concern about that 19 vast Number of poor People, who are aged, diseased, or maimed, and I have been desired to imploy my thoughts what Course may be taken, to ease the Nation of so grievous an Incumbrance. But I am not in the least pain about the matter, because it is very well known, that they are every Day *dying,* and *rotting,* by *cold,* and *famine,* and *filth,* and *vermin,* as fast as can be reasonably expected. And as to the younger Labourers they are now in almost as hopeful a Condition. They cannot get Work, and consequently pine away for want of Nourishment, to a degree, that if at any time they are accidentally hired to common Labour, they have not strength to perform it, and thus the Country and themselves are happily delivered from the Evils to come.

I have too long digressed, and therefore shall return to my subject. I 20 think the advantages by the Proposal which I have made, are obvious, and many, as well as of the highest importance.

For, *First,* as I have already observed, it would greatly lessen *the Number* 21 *of Papists,* with whom we are Yearly over-run, being the principal Breeders of the Nation, as well as our most dangerous Enemies, and who stay at home on purpose with a design *to deliver the Kingdom to the Pretender,* hoping to take their Advantage by the absence *of so many good Protestants,* who have chosen rather to leave their Country, than stay at home, and pay Tithes against their Conscience, to an *Episcopal Curate.*

Secondly, the poorer Tenants will have something valuable of their 22 own, which by Law may be made liable to Distress,[12] and help to pay their Landlord's Rent, their Corn and Cattle being already seazed, and *Money a thing unknown.*

Thirdly, Whereas the Maintenance of an Hundred Thousand Children, 23 from two Years old, and upwards, cannot be computed at less than Ten Shillings a piece *per Annum,* the Nation's Stock will be thereby encreased fifty thousand pounds *per Annum,* besides the profit of a new Dish, introduced to the Tables of all *Gentlemen of Fortune* in the Kingdom, who have any refinement in Taste, and the Money will circulate among ourselves, the Goods being entirely of our own Growth and Manufacture.

Fourthly, The constant Breeders, besides the gain of Eight Shillings *per* 24 *Annum,* by the Sale of their Children, will be rid of the Charge of maintaining them after the first Year.

Fifthly, This food would likewise bring great *Custom to Taverns,* where 25 the Vintners will certainly be so prudent as to procure the best receipts for dressing it to perfection, and consequently have their Houses frequented by all the *fine Gentlemen,* who justly value themselves upon their Knowledge in good *Eating,* and a skillful Cook, who understands how to oblige his Guests, will contrive to make it as expensive as they please.

Sixthly, This would be a great Inducement to Marriage, which all wise 26 Nations have either encouraged by Rewards, or enforced by Laws and Penalties. It would encrease the care and tenderness of Mothers towards their Children, when they were sure of a Settlement for Life, to the poor Babes, provided in some sort by the Publick to their annual Profit instead of Expence. We should soon see an honest Emulation among the married Women, *which of them could bring the fattest Child to the Market.* Men would become as fond of their *Wives,* during the Time of their Pregnancy, as they are now of their *Mares* in Foal, their *Cows* in Calf, or *Sows* when they are ready to Farrow, nor offer to Beat or Kick them (as it is too frequent a practice) for fear of a Miscarriage.

Many other advantages might be enumerated. For Instance, the 27 addition of some thousand Carcases in our exportation of Barreled Beef: The Propagation of *Swines Flesh,* and Improvement in the Art of making good *Bacon,* so much wanted among us by the great destruction of *Pigs,* too frequent at our Tables, which are no way comparable in Taste, or Magnificence to a well grown, fat Yearling Child, which Roasted whole will make a considerable Figure at a *Lord Mayor's Feast,* or any other Publick Entertainment. But this, and many others I omit, being studious of Brevity.

Supposing that one thousand Families in this City, would be constant 28 Customers for Infants Flesh, besides others who might have it at *Merrymeetings,* particularly *Weddings* and *Christenings,* I compute that *Dublin* would take off annually about Twenty Thousand Carcases, and the rest of the Kingdom (where probably they will be sold somewhat cheaper) the remaining Eighty Thousand.

I can think of no one Objection, that will possibly be raised against 29 this Proposal, unless it should be urged that the Number of People will be thereby much lessened in the Kingdom. This I freely own, and it was indeed one principal Design in offering it to the World. I desire the Reader will observe, that I Calculate my Remedy *for this one individual Kingdom of IRELAND, and for no other that ever was, is, or, I think, ever can be upon Earth.* Therefore let no Man talk to me of other Expedients: *Of taxing our Absentees at five Shillings a pound: Of using neither Cloaths, nor household Furniture, except what is of our own Growth and Manufacture: Of utterly rejecting the Materials and Instruments that promote Foreign Luxury: Of curing the Expensiveness of Pride, Vanity, Idleness, and Gaming in our Women: Of introducing a Vein of Parsimony, Prudence and Temperance: Of learning to Love our Country, wherein we differ even from LAPLANDERS, and the Inhabitants of TOPINAMBOO:*[13] *Of quitting our Animosities, and Factions, nor Act any longer like the Jews, who were Murdering one another at the very moment their City was taken:*[14] *Of being a little Cautious not to Sell our Country and Consciences for nothing: Of teaching Landlords to have at least one degree of Mercy towards their Tenants. Lastly of putting a Spirit of Honesty, Industry and Skill into our Shopkeepers, who, if a Resolution could now be taken to Buy only our Native Goods, would immediately unite to Cheat and Exact upon us in the Price, the Measure, and the Goodness, nor could ever yet be brought to make one fair Proposal of just dealing, though often and earnestly invited to it.*

Therefore I repeat, let no Man talk to me of these and the like 30 Expedients, till he hath at least some Glimpse of Hope, that there will ever be some hearty and sincere Attempt to put them in Practice.

But as to my self, having been wearied out for many Years with offering 31 vain, idle, visionary thoughts, and at length utterly despairing of Success, I fortunately fell upon this Proposal, which as it is wholly new, so it hath something Solid and Real, of no Expence and little Trouble, full in our own Power, and whereby we can incur no Danger in *disobliging* England. For this kind of Commodity will not bear Exportation, the Flesh being of too tender a Consistance, to admit a long continuance in Salt, *although perhaps I could name a Country, which would be glad to Eat up our whole Nation without it.*

After all, I am not so violently bent upon my own Opinion, as to reject 32 any Offer, proposed by wise Men, which shall be found equally innocent, cheap, easy and effectual. But before something of that kind shall be advanced in Contradiction to my Scheme, and offering a better, I desire the Author, or Authors will be pleased maturely to consider two points. *First,* as things now stand, how they will be able to find Food and Raiment for an hundred thousand useless Mouths and Backs. And *Secondly,* there being a round Million of Creatures in human Figure, throughout this Kingdom, whose whole Subsistance put into a common Stock, would leave them in Debt of two Million of Pounds *Sterling,* adding those, who are Beggars by Profession, to the Bulk of Farmers, Cottagers and Labourers with their Wives and Children, who are Beggars in Effect; I desire those *Politicians,* who dislike my Overture, and may perhaps be so bold to attempt an Answer, that they will first ask the Parents of these Mortals, whether they would not at this Day think it a great Happiness to have been sold for Food at a year Old, in the manner I prescribe, and thereby have avoided such a perpetual Scene of Misfortunes, as they have since gone through, by the *oppression of Landlords,* the Impossibility of paying Rent without Money or Trade, the want of common Sustenance, with neither House nor Cloaths to cover them from Inclemencies of Weather, and the most inevitable Prospect of intailing the like, or greater Miseries upon their Breed for ever.

I Profess in the sincerity of my Heart that I have not the least personal 33
Interest, in endeavouring to promote this necessary Work; having no other
Motive than the *publick Good of my Country,* by *advancing our Trade, providing for Infants, relieving the Poor, and giving some Pleasure to the Rich.* I
have no Children, by which I can propose to get a single Penny; the young-
est being nine Years old, and my Wife past Childbearing.

NOTES

1 Dublin, Ireland.

2 The Pretender is James Edward Stuart, who claimed (or "pretended" to) the throne lost by his father, James II, in 1688. (Because of his Catholic sympathies, James II had been overthrown by support- ers of his Protestant daughter and son-in-law, Mary II and William II.) The French upheld James Stuart's claim because of his Roman Catholicism, and, by the Limerick Treaty of 1691, Irish Roman Catholics were granted the right to bear arms in the service of France, and thus, by affiliation, in the service of the Pretender.

3 Because of the poverty in Ireland, many Irish immigrated to British colonies in America and the West Indies, indenturing themselves to plantation owners for their passage.

4 Ireland had just suffered three successive bad harvests.

5 Soil conditions in county Cavan are particularly unsuited to tillage and require a great deal of capital to manage. Cavan also had a long history of high rents and exploitation.

6 Boiling was a way to render meat edible if it was beginning to turn bad.

7 François Rabelais (1494–1553) was a French humorist and satirist and anything but "grave."

8 "Papist" is a hostile name for a Roman Catholic. Swift, as an Anglican (Protestant) clergyman, might be expected to be hostile to Catholicism, but the hostility here is, of course, ironic.

9 It is not clear whether the "true Lover of his Country" refers to an actual person or not.

10 George Psalmanazar was a Frenchman who posed as a Formosan (modern Taiwanese). His fictitious accounts, *Historical and Geographical History of Formosa* (1704) and *A Dialogue between a Japanese and a Formosan about some points of the religion of the time* (1707), contained passages describing human sacrifice and cannibalism. The remainder of this paragraph is a paraphrase of one of the sto- ries told by Psalmanazar.

11 A groat was a small British coin worth four pence.

12 Distress or distraint is the act of distraining or legally forcing a person to give up personal goods to be used as payment against debts.

13 The Tupinamba were a group of tribes, now extinct, that lived on the coast of Brazil from the mouth of the Amazon to the southern part of the state of São Paulo. Swift says that even those who live in places of extreme cold and heat love their countries better than the Anglo-Irish.

14 In AD 70, the Roman Emperor Titus laid siege to, captured, and destroyed Jerusalem. Throughout the period of siege and capture, the city was being torn apart internally by warring religious factions.

VOCABULARY

alms—anything given freely to relieve want

artificially—with skill or artifice

burthen—burden

crown—a coin worth five shillings, a shilling being worth 1/20 of a pound or five pence. Half a crown is, therefore, a coin worth 12½ pence.

dressing—preparing meat for the market, usually by bleeding and cleaning it

emulation—an attempt to equal or excel, here perhaps each other

gibbet—a gallows

importuning—pressing or urging with unreasonable requests

intailing (or usually, entailing)—settling something (for example, land, title, obligation) on a number of persons in succession so that it cannot be bequeathed to another person

joints—a large section of meat usually including a large bone or joint

probationers—those whose fitness is being tested

repine—to complain or fret

shambles—a slaughterhouse

squire—a country gentleman, particularly the principal landowner of a district

towardly—dutiful, tractable

vintner—not only the maker but also the seller of wines

QUESTIONS

1. In this essay, Swift speaks through a persona (a mask, or second self, created by the author). Give three or four examples that show that Swift is not speaking in his own voice.

2. List the main interests and characteristics of Swift's persona.

3. How does Swift use the gap between his own feelings and opinions and those of his persona to create and sustain the irony throughout the essay? What standard(s) of evaluation does the persona employ as he presents his solution to the terrible poverty in Ireland? What standards does Swift imply?

4. Can you identify any places where Swift steps out from behind his mask?

5. For what reasons, literary or otherwise, do you think Swift chose irony, rather than direct statement, as a strategy to persuade his audience to alleviate poverty in Ireland?

6. In a satiric essay, writers achieve their purpose by undermining the apparent thesis rather than by supporting it. What is the apparent thesis of "A Modest Proposal"? How does Swift undermine it?

7. Matters like spelling, punctuation, capitalization, and the use of italics were far less standardized in Swift's day than in ours. Do these or other features of Swift's style affect your reading of this essay? If so, how?

SUGGESTION FOR WRITING

Using Swift's essay as a model, write a "modest proposal" in which you present an outrageous solution to a current social problem. Follow the structure of "A Modest Proposal" and feel free to include verbal echoes from it. Remember that you will need to adopt a persona whose attitudes and values present to your readers an exaggerated version of their own. Like Swift, you want to shock your readers into a recognition of their moral inadequacies in not responding to a social need.

All for One, and One for All

Charles Taylor

Solidarity is essential to democratic societies; otherwise, they fall apart. 1
They cannot function beyond a certain level of mutual distrust or a
sense on the part of some members that other members have abandoned them. Many view the development of an individualistic outlook as
the greatest threat to solidarity. But this is closely linked to a diminishing
sense of common identity.

It's no accident, for example, that Europe's most successful welfare 2
states were created in ethnically homogeneous Scandinavia. People in those
countries had the sense that they could understand their neighbours and
fellow citizens, and that they shared a close link with them.

The challenge nowadays is to maintain that sense of intense solidarity 3
amid diversifying populations. There are two ways to do this. One is to hark
back to older modes of solidarity. French identity, for example, is based on
the country's unique brand of republican secularism, known as *laïcité*. But
France's efforts to shore up solidarity by insisting on *laïcité* and erecting a
dam against Muslim immigrants are both ineffective and counterproduc-
tive, because they exclude from a sense of
fully belonging to the nation many people
who are already in France.[1]

The other way to preserve solidarity 4
is to redefine identity. All democratic
societies are faced with the challenge of
redefining their identity in dialogue with
some elements that are external, and some
that are internal. Consider the influence
of feminist movements throughout the
West. These are not people who came
from outside their countries. They are
people who, in some ways, lacked full citi-
zenship, who demanded it, and who redefined the political order by obtaining it.

The great task is to calm the fears that 5
our traditions are being undermined;
to reach out to people who are coming

Charles Taylor (b. 1931) is a Canadian philosopher who has held professorships at Oxford
University in England and McGill University in
Montreal. He has been active in politics and is a
defender of Canadian nationalism. In 1991, he
delivered the Massey Lecture that was published
as *The Malaise of Modernity*. He has published
*Reconciling the Solitudes: Essays on Canadian
Federalism and Nationalism* (1993) and is most
famous for his book *Multiculturalism: Examining
the Politics of Recognition* (1994), which has been
translated into several languages. He follows in
the philosophical tradition of Martin Heidegger,
Hans-Georg Gadamer, and Ludwig Wittgenstein.

Reprinted by permission from Charles Taylor, "All for One
and One for All." From *The Globe and Mail*, September 20,
2010, p. A21.

to our lands from other countries; and to find a way of recreating our political ethic around the kernel of human rights, equality, non-discrimination and democracy. If we succeed, we can create a sense that we belong together, even though our reasons for believing so may be different.

But increasing individualism—a focus on one's own ambitions and 6 economic prosperity—in many countries poses a stubborn obstacle to realizing this vision. Indeed, the utter lack of a sense of solidarity among so many people—horrifyingly evident in the U.S. health-care debate—is undermining the very basis of what a modern democratic society is.

A society's sense of solidarity can be sustained only if all of its different 7 spiritual groups recreate their sense of dedication to it: if Christians see it as central to their Christianity, if Muslims see it as central to their Islam, and if the various kinds of lay philosophies see it as central to their philosophies.

Religion provides a profound and powerful base of solidarity, and to 8 marginalize it would be a big mistake, just as marginalizing atheistic philosophies would be a mistake. Democratic societies, in their tremendous diversity, are powered by many different engines of commitment to a common ethic. They cannot afford to switch off any of these engines and hope to maintain a political community.

Historically, the political ethic of confessional societies has been 9 grounded in a single, basic foundation. In Europe, various kinds of *laïque* societies have tried to invent themselves out of the ruins of the Christian foundation, but they have made the same mistake in another way, with a kind of Jacobin insistence on the civil religion of the Enlightenment.

Well, we can no longer have a civil religion—not one based on God, or 10 on *laïcité* and the rights of man, or, indeed, on any particular view. We live in uncharted territory. We face a challenge that is unprecedented in human history: creation of a powerful political ethic of solidarity self-consciously grounded on the presence and acceptance of very different views.

This can succeed only if we engage in vigorous exchange with each 11 other in order to create a kind of mutual respect for these different views. The advancing force of Islamophobia in Europe and the U.S., with its attempt to reduce Islam's complex and varied history to a few demagogic slogans, is the kind of utterly ignorant stupidity—there's no better description of it—on which democratic societies founder.

But that's true of any kind of dismissive view of the "other." Our 12 societies will hold together only if we talk to each other with openness and frankness, and, in doing so, recreate a certain sense of solidarity from all our different roots.

NOTE

[1] In February 2011, French President Nikolas Sarkozy claimed that multiculturalism had failed in France. This statement followed German Chancellor Angela Merkel's claim in October 2010 that multiculturalism had failed in Germany and British Prime Minister David Cameron's claim in February 2011 that multiculturalism had also failed in England.

VOCABULARY

laïcité—often transcribed as secularism, it is basically the separation of church and state

laïque—the adjectival form of *laïcité*

Enlightenment—a general term for Western intellectual history and development since the eighteenth century. Key thinkers include René Descartes and Immanuel Kant.

QUESTIONS

1. What are the two ways that Taylor suggests to help maintain solidarity among people?

2. Canada has a significant population of immigrants. How do you think Canada should address difficulties that arise when immigrants bring principles that conflict with Canadian laws and customs? For example, what should happen when an immigrant comes from a country that does not prohibit polygamy or multiple spouses? What are the political and ethical values at stake?

3. Part of Taylor's essay involves the separation of church and state. If religion is no longer the primary common ground for community solidarity, what principles are the grounds for political solidarity today?

SUGGESTION FOR WRITING

Charles Taylor ends with a caution against a "dismissive view of the 'other.'" Write an essay that explains an encounter you have had with an "other" and how you engaged with and gained an understanding of that "other."

Summer of Our Discontent Revisited[1]

Drew Hayden Taylor

It seems that opinions about the treatment of the all-too-frequent Native crisis are being voiced more openly. Or more accurately, there appears to be a double standard in relation to blockades: a belief that perhaps Natives are getting preferential treatment, and getting handled with kid gloves.

Tell that to Dudley George,[2] the Ojibway man killed at Ipperwash.

Many critics outside and within the government have commented that there seems to be two sets of laws in Canada: one for the Native people and one for Whites. As I've often heard said, "You get White people blockading a road or doing what the Indians are doing and the police would be in there breaking things up faster than Mike Harris[3] can hit a golf ball. They should treat them Indians like they would White people."

Equal rights—what a concept. That would be nice. Very nice in fact, but in reality, unlikely. It does seem there is a double standard. Chief Tom Bressette of the Stony-Kettle Reserve agrees with these irate voices, saying that there are "two separate laws" for Indians and Whites, and that Indians "get the lower end of the stick."

Anyone who is even slightly familiar with the Native community is well aware of the incredibly high levels of Aboriginal people incarcerated in the provincial and federal jails. While Native people make up less than five percent of the general population, they sometimes exceed forty percent of those in jail.

You don't have to work for Revenue Canada to know that something is wrong with these numbers. Especially when you take into consideration that Native culture, as a whole, never had jails nor a real need for them. There was no institutionalized punishment, no witness relocation, no prison riots.

To go from a culture with no use for jails, to an obscenely high incarceration rate should tell these politicians and nay sayers something is dreadfully wrong. Either, in a scant few years, we as a people

Drew Hayden Taylor (b. 1962) is an Ojibway author who has written plays, stories, and essays. He served as the Artistic Director of the Native Earth Performing Arts theatre from 1994 to 1997. Within the traditions of the storyteller, Taylor's frequent use of humour allows him to raise and address contemporary issues that Aboriginal people face. "Summer of Our Discontent Revisited" is included in *Funny, You Don't Look Like One: Observations of a Blue-Eyed Ojibway*, a collection of essays and articles, many of which were published in *Windspeaker*, *The Globe and Mail*, and *The Toronto Star*, and aired on CBC Radio.

"Summer of Our Discontent Revisited" is reprinted from *Funny, You Don't Look Like One: Observations of a Blue-Eyed Ojibway*. Written by Drew Hayden Taylor. Reprinted by permission.

have become an anarchic gang of hoodlums with no appreciation of law or government, bent on overcrowding prisons for the hell of it, or there *is* a double standard. The justice system's famous inflexibility or inability to take into account different perceptions of what is right and what is wrong is legendary. For instance, White society reveres the nuclear family principle, while the Native community is structured around the extended family concept. Such misunderstanding led to incidents like "the scoop up"[4] when thousands of Native kids were forcibly removed from communities and put up for adoptions, and moved into residential schools.

Centuries of alienation, dispossession and insensitivity have also had their effect. When you take away from Native people their culture, their language and their land, it creates a vacuum. And as White scientists love to quote, nature hates a vacuum. 8

Logically, something has to fill this gaping black hole. Anger and frustration at what has been lost or taken rushes into that vacuum. Simple physics. And while I and the vast majority of Native people across this country do not condone violence, I challenge any people with this history not to be overcome by emotions such as these. 9

Hugh MacLennan was incredibly naive when he wrote his book *Two Solitudes*.[5] He couldn't even begin to understand how many solitudes there really are. 10

NOTES

[1] The title of this piece is a literary allusion to William Shakespeare's play *Richard III* that begins "Now is the winter of our discontent / Made glorious summer by this sun of York" (1.1.1-2).

[2] Dudley George was protesting the Canadian government's refusal to return land at Ipperwash to the people in 1995. George was shot on September 6, 1995, and later died in hospital.

[3] Mike Harris was the premier of Ontario from 1995 to 2002, including the time of the protest at Ipperwash.

[4] The "scoop up" includes the forced adoption policies for Aboriginal children in several Canadian provinces, as well as the residential school system where children were removed from their communities and placed in boarding schools for education.

[5] Hugh MacLennan's 1945 novel *Two Solitudes* is about the relations between the French and English in Canada. Taylor is obviously suggesting that there are many more historical conflicts between different groups in Canada.

QUESTIONS

1. Taylor suggests that there are "two sets of laws in Canada: one for the Native people and one for Whites." Do you agree with his assessment?

2. Taylor's reference to Dudley George is very brief. Have you ever heard of Dudley George before? Is Taylor's use of this reference effective in his argument?

3. Taylor claims that the justice system is unable "to take into account different perceptions of what is right and what is wrong." Given that different communities may have different ethical standards and practices, what do you make of this argument? Is this a valid form of reasoning? How would "different perceptions" be understood in terms of the law?

4. What is Taylor doing when he refers to white scientists, physics, and vacuums?

SUGGESTIONS FOR WRITING

1. Write an essay about the importance of cross-cultural understanding between those of Aboriginal ancestry and those of settler ancestry in Canada. How can we understand our history—the intertwinement of Aboriginal and settler histories—and respond to it politically and ethically?

2. Write a comparison essay in which you consider Drew Hayden Taylor's discussion of Aboriginal/settler-descendant relations in "Summer of Our Discontent Revisited" and Margaret Laurence's discussion of Aboriginal/settler-descendant relations in "The Loons" (Readings).

[Shakespeare's Sister]

Virginia Woolf

What I find deplorable . . . is that nothing is known about women before the eighteenth century. I have no model in my mind to turn about this way and that. Here am I asking why women did not write poetry in the Elizabethan age,[1] and I am not sure how they were educated; whether they were taught to write; whether they had sitting-rooms to themselves; how many women had children before they were twenty-one; what, in short, they did from eight in the morning till eight at night. They had no money evidently; according to Professor Trevelyan[2] they were married whether they liked it or not before they were out of the nursery, at fifteen or sixteen very likely. It would have been extremely odd, even upon this showing, had one of them suddenly written the plays of Shakespeare, I concluded, and I thought of that old gentleman, who is dead now, but was a bishop, I think, who declared that it was impossible for any woman, past, present, or to come, to have the genius of Shakespeare. He wrote to the papers about it. He also told a lady who applied to him for information that cats do not as a matter of fact go to heaven, though they have, he added, souls of a sort. How much thinking those old gentlemen used to save one! How the borders of ignorance shrank back at their approach! Cats do not go to heaven. Women cannot write the plays of Shakespeare.

Be that as it may, I could not help thinking, as I looked at the works of Shakespeare on the shelf, that the bishop was right at least in this; it would have been impossible, completely and entirely, for any woman to have written the plays of Shakespeare in the age of Shakespeare. Let me imagine, since facts are so hard to come by, what would have happened had Shakespeare had a wonderfully gifted sister, called Judith, let us say. Shakespeare himself went, very probably—his mother was an heiress—to the grammar school, where he may have learnt Latin—Ovid, Virgil and Horace[3]—and the elements of grammar and logic. He was, it is well known, a wild boy who poached rabbits, perhaps shot a deer, and had, rather sooner than he should have done, to marry a woman in the neighbourhood, who bore him a child

1

2

Virginia Woolf (1882–1941) is widely regarded as one of the most important English writers of the twentieth century. She wrote experimental fiction, often using the technique called stream-of-consciousness, and nonfiction exploring the situation of women both in history and in her own lifetime. Her novels include *Mrs. Dalloway* (1925), *To the Lighthouse* (1927), and *The Waves* (1931). Her extended essay *A Room of One's Own* (1929) is a key feminist text.

"[Shakespeare's Sister]" is excerpted from Virginia Woolf's *A Room of One's Own* (New York: Harvest/HBJ, 1957).

rather quicker than was right. That escapade sent him to seek his fortune in London. He had, it seemed, a taste for the theatre; he began by holding horses at the stage door. Very soon he got work in the theatre, became a successful actor, and lived at the hub of the universe, meeting everybody, knowing everybody, practising his art on the boards, exercising his wits in the streets, and even getting access to the palace of the queen. Meanwhile his extraordinarily gifted sister, let us suppose, remained at home. She was as adventurous, as imaginative, as agog to see the world as he was. But she was not sent to school. She had no chance of learning grammar and logic, let alone of reading Horace and Virgil. She picked up a book now and then, one of her brother's perhaps, and read a few pages. But then her parents came in and told her to mend the stockings or mind the stew and not moon about with books and papers. They would have spoken sharply but kindly, for they were substantial people who knew the conditions of life for a woman and loved their daughter—indeed, more likely than not she was the apple of her father's eye. Perhaps she scribbled some pages up in an apple loft on the sly, but was careful to hide them or set fire to them. Soon, however, before she was out of her teens, she was to be betrothed to the son of a neighbouring wool-stapler.[4] She cried out that marriage was hateful to her, and for that she was severely beaten by her father. Then he ceased to scold her. He begged her instead not to hurt him, not to shame him in this matter of her marriage. He would give her a chain of beads or a fine petticoat, he said; and there were tears in his eyes. How could she disobey him? How could she break his heart? The force of her own gift alone drove her to it. She made up a small parcel of her belongings, let herself down by a rope one summer's night and took the road to London. She was not seventeen. The birds that sang in the hedge were not more musical than she was. She had the quickest fancy, a gift like her brother's, for the tune of words. Like him, she had a taste for the theatre. She stood at the stage door; she wanted to act, she said. Men laughed in her face. The manager—a fat, loose-lipped man—guffawed. He bellowed something about poodles dancing and women acting—no woman, he said, could possibly be an actress. He hinted—you can imagine what. She could get no training in her craft. Could she even seek her dinner in a tavern or roam the streets at midnight? Yet her genius was for fiction and lusted to feed abundantly upon the lives of men and women and the study of their ways. At last—for she was very young, oddly like Shakespeare the poet in her face, with the same grey eyes and rounded brows—at last Nick Greene the actor-manager took pity on her; she found herself with child by that gentleman and so—who shall measure the heat and violence of the poet's heart when caught and tangled in a woman's body?—killed herself one winter's night and lies buried at some cross-roads where the omnibuses now stop outside the Elephant and Castle.[5]

That, more or less, is how the story would run, I think, if a woman in Shakespeare's day had had Shakespeare's genius. But for my part, I agree with the deceased bishop, if such he was—it is unthinkable that any woman in Shakespeare's day should have had Shakespeare's genius. For genius like Shakespeare's is not born among labouring, uneducated, servile people. It was not born in England among the Saxons and the Britons. It is not born today among the working classes. How, then, could it have been born among women whose work began, according to Professor Trevelyan, almost before they were out of the nursery, who were forced to it by their parents and held to it by all the power of law and custom? Yet genius of a sort must have existed among women as it must have existed among the working classes. Now and again an Emily Brontë or a Robert Burns[6] blazes out and proves its presence. But certainly it never got itself on to paper. When, however, one reads of a witch being ducked, of a woman possessed by devils, of a wise woman selling herbs, or even of a very remarkable man who had a mother, then I think we are on the track of a lost novelist, a suppressed poet, of some mute and inglorious Jane Austen,[7] some Emily Brontë who dashed her brains out on the moor or mopped and mowed about the highways crazed with the torture that her gift had put her to. Indeed, I would venture to guess that Anon, who wrote so many poems without signing them, was often a woman. It was a woman Edward Fitzgerald,[8] I think, suggested who made the ballads and the folk-songs, crooning them to her children, beguiling her spinning with them, on the length of the winter's night.

This may be true or it may be false—who can say?—but what is true in it, so it seemed to me, reviewing the story of Shakespeare's sister as I had made it, is that any woman born with a great gift in the sixteenth century would certainly have gone crazed, shot herself, or ended her days in some lonely cottage outside the village, half witch, half wizard, feared and mocked at. For it needs little skill in psychology to be sure that a highly gifted girl who had tried to use her gift for poetry would have been so thwarted and hindered by other people, so tortured and pulled asunder by her own contrary instincts, that she must have lost her health and sanity to a certainty. No girl could have walked to London and stood at a stage door and forced her way into the presence of actor-managers without doing herself a violence and suffering an anguish which may have been irrational— for chastity may be a fetish invented by certain societies for unknown reasons—but were none the less inevitable. Chastity had then, it has even now, a religious importance in a woman's life, and has so wrapped itself round with nerves and instincts that to cut it free and bring it to the light

3

4

of day demands courage of the rarest. To have lived a free life in London in the sixteenth century would have meant for a woman who was poet and playwright a nervous stress and dilemma which might well have killed her. Had she survived, whatever she had written would have been twisted and deformed, issuing from a strained and morbid imagination. And undoubtedly, I thought, looking at the shelf where there are no plays by women, her work would have gone unsigned. That refuge she would have sought certainly. It was the relic of the sense of chastity that dictated anonymity to women even so late as the nineteenth century. Currer Bell, George Eliot, George Sand,[9] all the victims of inner strife as their writings prove, sought ineffectively to veil themselves by using the name of a man. Thus they did homage to the convention, which if not implanted by the other sex was liberally encouraged by them (the chief glory of a woman is not to be talked of, said Pericles,[10] himself a much-talked-of man), that publicity in women is detestable. Anonymity runs in their blood. The desire to be veiled still possesses them. . . .

That woman, then, who was born with a gift of poetry in the sixteenth   5
century, was an unhappy woman, a woman at strife against herself. All the conditions of her life, all her own instincts, were hostile to the state of mind which is needed to set free whatever is in the brain. . . .

NOTES

[1] The Elizabethan age is roughly the period during which Elizabeth I was queen of England (1558–1603). This was the period during which Shakespeare and many other writers and artists produced a significant body of work.

[2] George Macaulay Trevelyan (1876–1962), born six years before Woolf, was an influential English historian.

[3] Ovid (43 BC–AD 17?), Virgil (70–19 BC), author of *The Aeneid,* and Horace (65–8 BC), inventor of the Horatian Ode, were Roman poets.

[4] The staple is the fibre of the wool. A wool-stapler would likely be a dealer in wool, not a common labourer.

[5] The Elephant and Castle pub in inner south London dates from 1765 and gives its name (unofficially) to the surrounding area.

[6] Emily Brontë (1818–1848) was notably the author of *Wuthering Heights,* a powerful novel of doomed romance set on the Yorkshire Moors. Robert Burns (1759–1796) was a poet of working-class origins who wrote extensively in the Scots dialect.

[7] Jane Austen (1775–1817) was the author of *Emma, Pride and Prejudice,* and other novels dealing with moral choice and social hierarchy.

[8] Edward Fitzgerald (1809–1883) was an English poet known particularly for his translations from the writings of Persian poet and mathematician Omar Khayyám.

[9] Currer Bell was the pen name of Charlotte Brontë (1816–1855), Emily Brontë's sister. George Eliot was the pen name of Mary Ann Evans (1819–1880), author of *Middlemarch* and other novels.

George Sand was the pen name of the French novelist Lucile Aurore Dupin, later Baroness Dudevant (1804–1876), who dressed in men's clothes and smoked a pipe.

[10] Pericles (c. 495–429 BC) was an Athenian statesman. The Periclean age is the period when Athens dominated Greek political and cultural life.

QUESTIONS

1. Does Virginia Woolf use irony in this essay? If so, where and with what effect?

2. In *A Room of One's Own* (originally two lectures given to audiences interested in the arts and scholarship), Woolf invents a hypothetical example, a sister of Shakespeare's with the same creative drives as he had, but provides real examples of historical and contemporary views on women. It is generally assumed that it is the examples that make this section of *Room* nonfictional rather than fictional. Do you agree? Why or why not?

3. Why does Woolf agree with an unnamed bishop that "it is unthinkable that any woman in Shakespeare's day should have had Shakespeare's genius"? Is it for the same reasons that the bishop held this belief, or for some other reasons?

4. Woolf is making a case about women in the Elizabethan age. Does anything in the essay tell you whether she thinks her points apply to women in her own time as well?

SUGGESTIONS FOR WRITING

1. How much do the conditions that inhibited women's expression in the sixteenth century still apply today? Write an essay exploring this issue.

2. Can men and women write about issues of gender inequality in the same way? Write an essay comparing Virginia Woolf's approach to these issues with that taken by Scott Russell Sanders (also in Readings).

African National Identities Can't Be Built on Soccer Fever

Jonathan Zimmerman

Can sports make a nation? 1

That's a strange question. Americans love high-profile athletic 2
events, as the current buildup to Super Bowl XLII illustrates. But
nobody hangs America's future upon sports.

In Africa, though, it's quite common to do so. In a continent ravaged 3
by political and ethnic violence, people often invoke sports—especially soccer—as [a] force for national unity. And nobody does so more than the
Ghanaians, who are hosts of the 16-country Africa Cup of Nations tournament at four sites around the country.

"We all speak football," one headline announced this week. 4
"Football—A real source of unity," declared another. When Ghana celebrated
a last-minute defeat over Guinea in the tournament's opening match, one
commentator wrote, "There were no distinctions as to who belonged to which
political party, religious sect, or ethnic division." Another editorialist compared Ghana's stability to the ethnic violence plaguing Kenya. "Is it because
Kenya does not have an accomplished, unifying football team?" he asked.

As a rabid supporter of Ghana's "Black Stars" soccer team, I can appreciate 5
the sentiment. But as a historian, I am also deeply worried by it. Over the
last century, sports have rarely spawned true national harmony and recon-
ciliation. Instead, they provide a convenient tool for one part of a nation—
or, even, for one leader—to oppress the
rest of it.

To take the most notorious example: 6
Adolf Hitler used the 1936 Olympic
Games in Berlin to "unify" Germany—
around the idea of Aryan superiority.

With the next Olympics slated for 7
Beijing this summer, China has been jail-
ing dissidents and pushing poor people
from their homes to build stadiums.

Here in Africa, tyrants have often 8
seized upon sports to bolster their power.
Zaire's Mobutu,[1] Nigeria's Sani Abacha,[2]
and especially Uganda's Idi Amin[3] all

Jonathan Zimmerman is Professor of Education
and History, and Director of the History of
Education Program at New York University's
Steinhardt School of Culture, Education, and
Human Development. His books include *Whose
America? Culture Wars in the Public Schools* (2002),
*Innocents Abroad: American Teachers in the
American Century* (2006), and *Small Wonder: The
Little Red Schoolhouse in History and Memory* (2009).

"African National Identities Can't Be Built on Soccer Fever"
is reprinted with permission of the author, Jonathan
Zimmerman, Professor of Education and History, NYU
Steinhardt.

poured vast resources into national sports programs. A former boxing and swimming champion, the 6-foot-4-inch Amin lavished cash upon the country's star athletes. He also competed with them personally, knocking out one of the country's leading boxers and offering 10,000 shillings to anyone who could defeat him in the breast stroke. (Amin lost to a brave challenger, in 1976, and promptly paid up.)

Did these antics help Amin "unify" Uganda? Perhaps. More than 9 anything else, however, they helped him solidify his dictatorial regime. When a Voice of Uganda sports reporter criticized the national football team, Amin promptly fired him; and when two players were rumoured to have links to a Tanzania-based opposition group, he threw them both in prison. Only a last-minute appeal from their teammates on the eve of a big match saved them from likely torture and death.

Here in Ghana, the independence leader Kwame Nkrumah[4] promoted 10 soccer to demonstrate the new nation's freedom from its former colonial masters. Nkrumah helped start the Africa Cup of Nations tournament, which would "earn for our dear continent a greater respectability and recognition at the universal level," he predicted.

But as a force for national unity and stability, soccer's record is pretty 11 poor. Three years after Ghana's victory in the inaugural Africa Cup tourney, Nkrumah himself would be deposed.

Even worse, some governments use sports to divert attention from their 12 own misdeeds. "It is good to see people talking about football in Sudan, and not about Darfur," said the coach of the Sudanese national team, which is competing in the Africa Cup for the first time in 32 years. Good for the butchers in Khartoum, perhaps; but not for the victims in Darfur, where an estimated 200,000 people have perished and 2.5 million have lost their homes.

Most of all, sports are unpredictable: Even the best team has to lose, 13 now and then. And that's a slender reed for national identity, as was demonstrated by a recent editorial in the Accra Daily Graphic. The soccer team's first-round victory against Guinea had created a "national euphoria," the editorial noted, which "transcended ethnic, gender, age, political, and social barriers." But the Black Stars' lacklustre second match against a much weaker Namibian team squad gave the paper pause.

"The Daily Graphic believes that this nationalistic feeling will last for 14 as long as the Black Stars continue to win their matches," the editorial explained. "The moment they are out, we will lose that feeling and our hearts will be broken."

My heart will break, too, if Ghana fails to win the Africa Cup. But my 15 biggest hope is for the country, not for its soccer team.

NOTES

[1] Mobutu Sese Seko (1930–1997) was the president of Zaire (the Democratic Republic of the Congo) from 1965 to 1997.

[2] Sani Abacha (1943–1998) was the president of Nigeria from 1993 to 1998.

[3] Idi Amin (1925–2003) was the president of Uganda from 1971 to 1979.

[4] Kwame Nkrumah (1909–1972) was the president of Ghana from 1952 to 1966.

QUESTIONS

1. Zimmerman claims that "nobody hangs America's future upon sports." Do you agree or disagree with this claim?

2. Which dynamic do you think is stronger: sport as a unifier through common interest or sport as a divider through competition and team rivalry?

3. Zimmerman claims sport is a fragile basis for a nation. What other kinds of things contribute to nationhood or national unity?

SUGGESTION FOR WRITING

Write a comparison essay that analyzes the strengths and weaknesses of both Jonathan Zimmerman's and Kofi Annan's (Readings) arguments about sport and its relationship to politics.

Sample Essays

Perspectives on Addictions*

C. Jones

Like many Western nations, Canada has a long-standing problem with addictions. Mothers against Drunk Driving is a group formed to fight the consequences of alcoholism; Vancouver's Downtown Eastside is one of the drug capitals of the world. Since addiction is widespread and growing, it is important to understand its causes. Two recent essays—both originating from the Vancouver area—address this issue in interesting ways. In "Embraced by the Needle," Dr. Gabor Maté, an Eastside physician, claims that addiction has its roots in emotional deprivation. In "Reframing Canada's 'Drug Problem,'" Bruce K. Alexander, a professor emeritus of Simon Fraser University, argues that addiction rises from social dislocation. Seemingly very different in their detail, development, points, and perspectives, these essays finally seem to offer complementary rather than contradictory explanations of the causes of addiction.

The most obvious difference between "Embraced by the Needle" and "Reframing Canada's 'Drug Problem'" is in the kind of detail they use. "Embraced" includes references to theories of brain chemistry and dysfunctional parenting. However, the details we remember from the essay are the stories about individuals: Anna, who "wasn't wanted" (288); Carl, who "had dishwashing liquid poured down his throat . . . at age 5" (289); Wayne, who was "hit a lot" and, at the end of the essay, "looks away and wipes tears from his eyes" (290). In "Reframing," in contrast, the details are general rather than specific. The authors describe the world where "[j]obs disappear on short notice; communities are weak and unstable; people routinely change spouses, occupations, technical skills, languages, nationalities and ideologies as their lives progress" (228). The specific examples of dislocation that eventually turn up are still large-scale: "19th century England, as much by Whig theoreticians . . . as by socialists" (227); "the settlers and

1

2

---

* Sample comparison essay

natives in English colonies and to the rest of western Europe" (227). Detail in the two essays, then, reflects a dramatic contrast between focus on the individual and focus on the general.

The same contrast is reflected in the way the essays are organized. Both 3 essays present a straightforward causal sequence. According to Maté, the lack of "warm, non-stressed, calm interactions with the parenting figures" (289) actually changes brain functioning, causing a greater need for external calming and pleasure enhancing, a need which, in later life, can be temporarily satisfied by drugs. In Alexander, the sequence can be summarized even more simply: free market societies create social dislocation, and then social dislocation creates addiction. If both these sequences are straightforward, the way the essays are organized differs significantly. We remember the detail about addicts' lives in "Embraced" because it appears at the beginning, middle, and end of the essay, wrapping the causal sequence in a narrative framework. In "Reframing" the sequence is presented in a linear, analytic way. The essay discusses and defines addiction and dislocation; it then gives extensive examples of the connections between the two before finally arguing that understanding and reversing dislocation is necessary if mass addiction is to be cured.

The roots of these differences between "Embraced by the Needle" and 4 "Reframing Canada's 'Drug Problem'" lie in the different points Maté and Alexander are making, and the different perspectives that lie behind these points. Maté's essay opens with his thesis: "Addictions always originate in unhappiness, even if hidden. They are emotional anesthetics; they numb pain" (288). "Unhappiness," "emotional," "numb": these terms indicate a psychological perspective on the causes of addiction. Alexander's thesis, implied most clearly at the end of the essay, is that "it is time to reframe the problem. For decades there has been a futile debate about whether self-destructive drug use is a 'criminal problem' or a 'medical problem.' I hope that it can now be clear that it is neither—it is a political problem" (229). Alexander's use of terms like "the common good," "war on drugs," "globalization," and "prolonged dislocation" point to the more collective perspective of sociology.

Are these essays as different as they seem? Psychological and sociological 5 perspectives on the causes of addiction are different, but they are not mutually exclusive. One significant similarity between the essays is that Maté and Alexander have a similar sense of whom they are arguing against. Maté insists that "[n]either physiological predispositions nor individual moral failures explain drug addictions" (288). Alexander sees their antagonists as the addiction professionals and politicians who continue to promote and follow demonstrably failing strategies to counteract addiction, strategies that rely on "some manipulation of the drug-using person" (228). Furthermore, Maté acknowledges that parental stress could come "from outside circumstances such as economic pressure or political disruption" (289), whereas Alexander refers to the "painful dislocation" that social and economic globalization creates (227).

The different ways that "Embraced by the Needle" and "Reframing   6 Canada's 'Drug Problem'" handle detail and development, their different points and perspectives, ensure that each essay charts a different area of causal explanation. However, the similarity in antagonists and the acknowledgment of the other perspective reflect an important truth: while physiological and ethical explanations of addiction are incompatible with psychological and sociological ones, these psychological and sociological explanations of cause are not incompatible with each other. Judging from the material in these two essays, it would be perfectly possible to show that free markets cause social dislocations and that social dislocations, in turn, affect parental functioning and thus, via brain and emotions, increase the likelihood of addiction in individuals. Neither essay presents this whole causal sequence, but when compared, they provide strong evidence that both sociological and psychological factors are at work in causing addiction.

The Complexity of Power and Gender Relations: An Evaluative Essay on Scott Russell Sanders's "The Men We Carry in Our Minds"*

D. Jones

Scott Russell Sanders's essay "The Men We Carry in Our Minds" 1
addresses a common misperception: that men have historically been
more privileged than women. Sanders suggests that this assumption,
held by some white middle-class feminists, needs to be questioned and
critiqued. For Sanders, this misguided notion has personal and emotional
impact. While "The Men We Carry in Our Minds" uses only examples
and appeals to emotion as evidence to support the overall argument, the
examples are many and varied and directly support Sanders's claim, and the
appeals to emotion are powerful and convincing. Sanders's essay, which he
develops through storytelling and references to his own life, is an entertaining and logical piece that conveys an important argument about the complexity of gender. Power and privilege, Sanders argues, depend not only on
relations of gender but also on relations of race and class.

At first it might seem as though Sanders's argument is weak, since he 2
draws only upon narrative examples for evidence and since he draws heavily on personal experience. Sanders begins his essay, for instance, with a
conversation he had with his friend Anneke about the history of gender and
power relations, and, after this conversation, he says that he does not feel
guilt regarding a sense of so-called privilege he has supposedly had in relation to women. Rather, toward women he feels "something more confused,
a snarl of shame, envy, wary tenderness, and amazement" (329). Not only
does Sanders fail to express his argument here, but also he draws only upon
his own feelings—"confusion, shame, and envy"—to suggest a disagreement with Anneke's point of view. Sanders relies on narration, or storytelling, as a method to develop his argument. In order to strengthen his essay,
Sanders might draw upon cause and effect, analyzing the causes and effects
of the perception of male privilege. Or, he might engage in an analysis of
the system of patriarchy in American history. But he does not. Sanders's

---

* Sample evaluative essay

argument, one might argue, is limited because he uses only examples and relies solely on a storytelling method of development.

The strengths of Sanders's essay, though, clearly outweigh its weaknesses. 3 The examples Sanders uses to prove his argument are varied and convincing. In order to show that men are not always more powerful than women, Sanders describes the men he knew in childhood. He states, "The first men, besides my father, I remember seeing were black convicts and white guards, in the cottonfield across the road from our farm on the outskirts of Memphis. I must have been three or four" (330). This statement is powerful, since Sanders immediately gives the reader an image of jailed, disempowered men, and also indicates that these men were "black" in opposition to the "white guards." Already, Sanders has indicated that men's positions in American society can be determined by gender, by race, or by sociohistorical factors. Soldiers are another example of men Sanders "[carries] in his mind." Sanders calls the soldiers he knew "souls in limbo" (331). "They were all waiting," he explains, "for transfers, for leaves, for promotions" (331); and "unlike the warriors of older tribes . . . they would have no say about when the battle would start or how it would be waged" (331). Like the "black convicts," soldiers, contrary to what we might expect, are also disempowered, with no say over where or when or for what they fight. Seemingly the keepers of order and hierarchy, soldiers themselves, Sanders demonstrates, are disadvantaged. Here, Sanders shows that power is as dependent upon class as it is on gender and race.

Upon a first reading of this essay, one might argue that storytelling 4 is not a good method of development to argue a point, or at least that one should combine that method of development with another. In "The Men We Carry in Our Minds," though, we can perceive Sanders's narrative method of development positively: it is the vitality of the essay. This is because Sanders engages in vivid descriptive details in order to move his narrative forward and appeal to the readers' emotions. The "black convicts" Sanders sees as a child, "wore dingy gray-and-black zebra suits, heavy as canvas, sodden with sweat. Hatless, stooped, they chopped weeds in the fierce heat, row after row, breathing the acrid dust of boll-weevil poison" (330). The "bodies" of the labourers that Sanders knew "were twisted and maimed" (330). Furthermore, "The nails of their hands were black and split, the hands tattooed with scars. Some had lost fingers. Heavy lifting had given many of them finicky back and guts weak from hernias" (330). These descriptions are convincing, since it is hard to argue that men are more privileged than women when some men labour so hard that they lose fingers, or "[breathe] poison" as they work (330). Such descriptions, moreover, appeal to the readers' emotions: Sanders draws his readers into his world by the vivid and disturbing pictures he paints. The reader feels that no person should suffer as have the ones Sanders describes.

Clearly, "The Men We Carry in Our Minds" is a convincing essay in   5 which the author encourages his readers to think about—and re-assess—a common misperception, that men have historically been more privileged than women. While readers might deduce that the essay is weak, since it relies almost solely on a storytelling method, and since Sanders does not state his thesis explicitly at the beginning of the essay, the essay is strong: it systematically provides varied examples that support the overall argument; and, through description, it couples these examples with appeals to emotion. Sanders never explicitly states his thesis. However, his thesis—that power and privilege depend on class, race, and socio-historical conditions, as much as they do on gender—is evident and clear by the end of the essay. Therefore, Sanders strategically writes an inductively structured essay. What is more, Sanders supports his thesis with concrete, descriptive details and personal anecdotes about the men and women he has known. Overall, then, Sanders's essay is one worth reading, one in which readers find themselves rethinking long-held assumptions about the dynamics of power and privilege in our historical and contemporary world.

Canadian National Identity*

E. Jones

Should the federal government of Canada actively promote and foster   1
a Canadian national identity? What are the benefits and drawbacks of
creating and assuming such an identity for the nation of Canada and
for individual citizens? While these questions might appear to be nebulous
or unimportant, Canadian national identity has been a central concern for
the federal government since Confederation. Early Canadian settlers worried that Canada would be annexed by the United States, and so Canada's
first Prime Minister, John A. Macdonald, envisioned and initiated the
construction of the Canadian Pacific Railway, which unified Canada from
coast to coast. In the 1950s, the federal government funded the Massey
Commission, which supported Canadian artists in an effort to articulate a
distinct Canadian national identity through art and culture. In the 1970s,
Prime Minister Pierre Elliott Trudeau introduced state-implemented multiculturalism. Thereafter, Canada's national identity shifted from a focus
on its character in relation to Britain and the United States to a focus on
its character as a nation of immigrants. Currently, Prime Minister Stephen
Harper is working to shift the national identity of the country once again:
he speaks of claiming the North by invoking early explorer–settler conceptions of Canadian national identity. Historically and presently, then,
Canada has invested and continues to invest in a national identity. Though
some might argue that Canadian citizens and the Canadian government
need not be interested in creating and promoting a Canadian national identity, there are ethical, logical, and practical reasons to suggest that Canadian
identity is important—both for individual citizens and for the nation-state.

An ethical reason against creating and promoting a Canadian national   2
identity for citizens is that immigrants might not see themselves included
in or represented by that identity. If, for example, the nation promotes its
identity by funding Canadian content writing or art, then where does that
leave the immigrant artist or writer who writes about places and cultures
outside of the country? Moreover, what do immigrants from other countries
have to do with doughnuts, ice-hockey, and the cold, white North—images
that invoke the Canadian nation—if they have immigrated from Southern
climes? In addition, Aboriginals and French Canadians might have a different vision for the nation than English Canadians do. Such arguments

---

* Sample persuasive essay

have some merit. However, by the same ethical reasoning, a shared national identity, if dynamic, might not alienate immigrants but rather encourage cross-cultural understanding and the promotion of multiculturalism. A Canadian national identity open to flux could enable those from diverse cultural and ethnic backgrounds to come together, continually reimagining the nation and enhancing cross-cultural understanding within a flexible national framework.

Using logical persuasion, some have argued that we cannot have a 3 shared national identity in a country that is as vast and diverse as Canada. Northrop Frye believes that geographic identity is not national but regional: "What can there be in common between an imagination nurtured on the prairies, where it is a centre of consciousness diffusing itself over a vast flat expanse stretching to the remote horizon, and one nurtured in British Columbia, where it is in the midst of gigantic trees and mountains leaping into the sky all around it, and obliterating the horizon everywhere?" However, while Frye grounds the notion of identity in region, he simultaneously speaks of "unity" as important for Canada, and he defines "unity" as "national in reference, international in perspective, and rooted in a political feeling". Frye's notion of "unity" articulates a kind of flexible, dynamic sense of national identity. While individual citizens may identify with their region or their community, that geographical identity might relate to a larger, imaginative sense of belonging—a national identity. Critics such as Northrop Frye, in "Preface to the Bush Garden," and Benedict Anderson, in *Imagined Communities,* point out that any sense of national identity that is forged across vast landscapes and shared among diverse peoples is necessarily imagined. Therefore, many critics refer to a "national imaginary" rather than a "national identity." Most, however, logically acknowledge a relationship between a local or regional identity and a larger, national one. The constant back-and-forth between locale and nation, region and country, in all of these critics' accounts, demonstrates a need for a national identity. This national identity must be understood in broad terms, as flexible and changing, and it must make room for people of various regions, backgrounds, and cultures.

What about Canadian citizens who wish not to identify in terms of 4 nation, but rather, in terms of a personal or gendered identity? Many might wish to focus on creating and asserting an identity focused on their individualities—to understand themselves in relation to their own experiences throughout their lifetimes. Others might wish to focus on their gender or sexual identity, perceiving themselves as a woman or a man, as heterosexual, homosexual, bisexual, or transgendered. Using ethical reasoning, some may believe that working on women's rights in a global or international context is more important than fostering a national identity of any sort. I argue, however, that personal and gendered identities are intimately intertwined with national identities: one kind of identity cannot be entirely separated from another. In "Feminist Politics: Where We Stand" (Readings), bell hooks discusses feminist identities, but she also discusses class and race in an American context. She is writing from the perspective of an African-American woman who is aware of historical and current oppression in relation to gender, class, and race in her country. Moreover, nations have clear federal policies that impede or enable citizens to proclaim kinds of individual or gendered identities. In Canada, for instance, same-sex marriages are legal, and so the nation legitimizes gay and lesbian identities within a national framework. While personal and gender identities are important, they cannot be seen as separate from or competing with national identities. A dynamic and flexible Canadian national identity, in fact, is important in order to include and enable the expression of various individual identities.

Clearly, there are logical and ethical reasons to support the creation and   5
promotion of a Canadian national identity for Canada's citizens. But there are also important practical reasons to do so, not only for citizens, but for the government itself. The Canadian Multiculturalism Act, implemented by Prime Minister Brian Mulroney in 1988 but introduced by Prime Minister Pierre Elliott Trudeau in 1971, emphasizes Canada as a nation of immigrants. The national identity promoted at this time was one of inclusivity and plurality. The push for this multicultural identity was practical for the federal government, not only to solicit support from Canadian citizens, including immigrants, but also for economic reasons. The promotion and implementation of multiculturalism are related to changing immigration policies, including those that enable Canada to admit immigrants for skilled labour and professional expertise in the workforce. Therefore, the promulgation of a national identity has political force and affects the lives of individuals.

Prime Minister Stephen Harper's more recent push for Canada's   6
sovereignty over the North exemplifies another practical reason, on the part of the federal government, to create and promote a Canadian national identity. The practical reason for Harper's emphasis on national identity for Canada is to attain natural resources in the North. Interestingly, Harper has turned away from imagining a Canadian national identity rooted in multiculturalism and toward one rooted in an older version of Canadian nationhood—a version espoused by early explorers and settlers in Canada. In a 2014 interview with *The Globe and Mail*, Harper states, "I've always been fascinated by d'Iberville fighting the Hudson's Bay Company and Henry Hudson and Frobisher and all the great explorers." In the same interview, Harper fur-

ther explains that in order to revive a sense of Canadian nationalism that he sees as slipping away, he promotes "a renewed emphasis on Canada's fundamental northern nature." To this effect, Harper encourages research with regard to Anglo-settlers' history of early exploration in the Northwest Passage, while simultaneously emphasizing the prominence of Anglo-settler history in Canada. Take note, for instance, of his emphasis on Britain's royal family, the Franklin expedition, and the bicentennial of the war of 1812. At the same time, Harper actively discourages, even shuts down research that counters evidence to Anglo-settler-Canadian claims on the North. This discouragement is evident in in the firing of Patricia Sutherland, who was featured in CBC's *The Fifth Estate* in the documentary *Silence of the Labs.* Sutherland is a Canadian archeologist who worked at the Canadian Museum of History and was on the brink of proving that the Norse had settled on Baffin Island as early as 1300 AD, when her job was terminated. Whether or not you agree with Harper's politics, the Prime Minister's focus on promoting Canadian nationalism by hearkening back to older visions of the nation exemplifies the power that a persuasive Canadian national identity can have. Essentially, Harper invokes a national identity for practical purposes, in order to stake a claim on the resource-rich North, and in order to legitimate that claim.

Some may believe that fostering a national identity by and for Canadian citizens and the Canadian government is unimportant, difficult, or impractical. There are many ethical, logical, and practical reasons, however, to believe that fostering such an identity is essential to both citizens and the nation-state. Ethical reasons include the cross-cultural understanding that a national identity provides within a multicultural framework, and the personal and gender identities that a national identity can legitimate. Logical reasons include the fact that local or regional identities are necessarily tied to national ones, and that the two kinds of identity work in tandem with one another. Practical reasons include the economic advancement that Canada could attain by fostering a national identity. There are two recent and current examples of this potential for advancement: first, a multicultural national identity facilitates the admittance of foreign workers and experts to aid the economy; and second, a national identity focused on the legitimacy of early Anglo-explorers and settlers in Canada's northern regions enables the potential claim on natural resources in the North. It should be noted that the examples of practical reasons explained here could conflict with ethical reasons against promoting a national identity. For instance, the ethical argument that foreign workers means cheap workers, and that bringing immigrants here to work could result in exploitation of those immigrants, is valid. In addition, the argument that staking a claim to the North is problematic because it does not take into consideration the presence of Inuit peoples and environmental issues is also valid. What I hope I have made clear in this essay is that the creation and promotion of a Canadian national identity has real effects on citizens' lives, for the better or for the worse. A national identity can enable or impede certain personal or gender identities, and it can affect economic change for the country. As such, it is essential for Canadian citizens and the federal government to think about and take action in the creation of an always changing and dynamic national identity. Ultimately, it is the responsibility of both the citizens and the nation-state to ensure that such an identity continues to serve the public good.

Works Cited

Anderson, Benedict. *Imagined Communities*. London: Verso, 1983 (reprinted in 2006). Print.

Frye, Northrop. *The Bush Garden: Essays on the Canadian Imagination*. Concord, ON: Anansi, 1971 (reprinted in 1995). Print.

hooks, bell. *Feminism Is for Everybody*. Cambridge, MA: South End Press, 2000. Print.

"Silence of the Labs." *The Fifth Estate*. Canadian Broadcasting Corporation (CBC), Season 39, Episode 10. January 10, 2014. Television.

Chase, Steven. "Nationalism, Northern Style." *Globe and Mail* 18 January 2014: A12-13. Print.

Laurence's "The Loons": Insight or Stereotype?*

F. Smith

F ollowing the main character Vanessa MacLeod's development from 1
the age of eleven to eighteen, Margaret Laurence's short story "The
Loons" focuses on the white girl's relationship with a Métis girl named
Piquette Tonnerre. Vanessa's attitudes change during the story—from
naive romanticism to "embarrassment and pity" (Laurence, "Time" 283)
to accepting her share of collective responsibility for Piquette's death. This
final change allows the reader to think that Vanessa gains insight into her
would-be friend's life, what Laurence herself called "the pain and bewilderment of one's knowledge of other people" (282). But does Laurence
actually portray Vanessa as achieving a mature understanding of Piquette
and of their relationship by the end of the story? Laurence critics provide a
range of answers to this question. Critics Jon Kertzer and Peter Easingwood
agree that Vanessa MacLeod grows in understanding, whereas critics Janice
Acoose and Tracy Ware lay more emphasis on the persistence of destructive
racial stereotypes in Vanessa's views and in the story as a whole. An analysis
of characterization, narrative structure, figurative language, and point of
view in "The Loons" suggests that, while Laurence shows Vanessa struggling with her conceptions of Piquette and maturing in certain ways, she
also demonstrates Vanessa's inability to escape the historical and social limits of her understanding.

Narrative structure and characterization combine to show Vanessa's 2
changing attitudes toward Piquette. Laurence presents the story of the girls'
relationship in three key summer incidents separated by four-year intervals. At the beginning of the story, Vanessa is eleven, the white, healthy,
well-educated, imaginative daughter of a doctor; Piquette is older, having
"failed several grades" ("The Loons" 271), partly because, Vanessa tells us,
she spent months in hospital under Dr. MacLeod's care for treatment of
tuberculosis of the bone. Piquette is Métis, daughter and granddaughter of
"French half-breeds" (270) who live in a ramshackle dwelling and periodically end up in jail for being drunk and disorderly. Although the girls are
classmates, they are not friends: to Vanessa, Piquette is little more than "a
vaguely embarrassing presence" (271).

---

* Sample research essay

When Dr. MacLeod arranges for Piquette to accompany the family to   3
their summer cottage at Diamond Lake for health reasons, Vanessa tries
to assimilate Piquette into the worlds she knows, the world of the summer cottage and the world of books. She is too immature to understand
why Piquette refuses to play house (in her mother's absence, Piquette cooks
for the family) or to enter into the romantic fantasies that Vanessa con-
cocts when she discovers that the Tonnerres are actually "Indians, or as
near as made no difference" (273). Laurence underscores Vanessa's inability
to understand Piquette's reality by having Vanessa accept at face value the
excuse Piquette offers: "I thought it was probably her slow and difficult
walking that held her back" (275). When Piquette refuses to be assimilated,
Vanessa retreats first into the cottage world she knows, and then into the
pain of her father's death.

In the next stage of the narrative, Laurence shows Vanessa achieving a   4
more mature understanding of Piquette. When Piquette, now seventeen,
with beautiful eyes and a "soft and slender body" (275), approaches her in
the Regal Café, Vanessa, who knows "a little more than I had that summer
at Diamond Lake" (276), feels at first a mixture of shame, guilt, embarrassment, and contempt. Her observation that Piquette is teetering, but
not because of her tubercular leg, suggests that Piquette has been drinking,
though this may be a product of Vanessa's naive and stereotypical thinking
rather than a fact. Then Piquette reveals that she is about to marry a tall,
handsome, blond guy with a classy name who works in the stockyards in
the city. For a moment Piquette's "defiant face" becomes "unguarded and
unmasked," and in her eyes Vanessa sees a "terrifying hope" (276). For
a moment, Vanessa claims, "I really did see her" (276), without the pre-
conceptions and stereotypes that had clouded their earlier encounter. This
moment of empathy and recognition brings with it this insight: "I could
only guess how great her need must have been, that she had been forced to
seek the very things she so bitterly rejected" (277).

This moment of empathy does not bring the two girls into closer   5
relation, however. Piquette again drops out of Vanessa's consciousness
until, returning from her first year of college, she hears among her mother's
bits of dredged-up gossip that Piquette and her two young children were
killed when the Tonnerre shack caught fire in the winter. Vanessa, receiving this news with "a kind of silence around the image in my mind of the
fire and the snow," wishes "I could put from my memory the look that
I had once seen in Piquette's eyes" (278). Having seen that look, however, Vanessa cannot blank out Piquette's death as she had blanked out
so much of the young Métis woman's life. While revisiting the lake (now
renamed Lake Wapakata for greater tourist appeal) one evening, Vanessa

becomes aware that the loons have vanished under the pressure of human development, as her father had long ago predicted. In Vanessa's mind, as Laurence's language makes clear, the disappearance of the birds is linked with Piquette's death:

> I did not know what had happened to the birds. Perhaps they   6
> had gone away to some far place of belonging. Perhaps they had
> been unable to find such a place, and had simply died out, hav-
> ing ceased to care any longer whether they lived or not.
>
> I remembered how Piquette had scorned to come along,   7
> when my father and I sat there and listened to the lake birds. It
> seemed to me now that in some unconscious and totally unrec-
> ognised way, Piquette might have been the only one, after all,
> who had heard the crying of the loons. (278)

This is the progression, then, that leads Jon Kertzer to claim in his book   8
That House in Manawaka that Vanessa arrives at "understanding and feeling compassion for Piquette's plight" (68). In his article on "The Realism
of Laurence's Semi-Autobiographical Fiction," Peter Easingwood makes a
similar claim, arguing that Vanessa's maturing understanding is evident in
the growth of her "psychological compulsion to question reality" (126). In
other words, Easingwood identifies Vanessa's need to question her preju-
dices, although she has yet to find ways of answering the questions. Read
in this way, the story addresses Vanessa's struggle to overcome what she
realizes to be unfounded and destructive preconceived ideas about Piquette.
Where Kertzer suggests Vanessa has developed compassion, Easingwood
claims that she recognizes the need for compassion but has not yet found
a way to achieve it. Janice Acoose is not convinced; she maintains that
Vanessa's "understanding of reality is filtered through a racist, classist, and
male-privileged ideological value system" (79).

Critical debate about Vanessa's perspective centres around the   9
metaphor of the loons. Vanessa's fascination with the loons is introduced in
the first stage of the story, when, unable to interest Piquette in joining her,
she sits on the pier with her father to watch the birds rise from their nests
and to hear their cry: "Plaintive, and yet with a quality of chilling mockery,
those voices belonged to a world separated by aeons from our neat world
of summer cottages and the lighted lamps of home" ("The Loons" 274).
Dr. MacLeod immediately echoes the narrative comment: "They must
have sounded just like that . . . before any person ever set foot here" (274).
When Vanessa tries to make Piquette feel sorry that she hadn't come along,
Piquette again refuses the role of "junior prophetess of the wilds" (273),
referring to the loons as "a bunch of squawkin' birds" (275). It is this incident Vanessa remembers at the end of the story when she reflects "that in

some unconscious and totally unrecognised way, Piquette might have been the only one, after all, who had heard the crying of the loons" (278).

This image identifying Piquette with the loons, it can be argued, 10 encapsulates Vanessa's awareness that Piquette's fate, like that of the loons, is a consequence of the destruction both of nature and of Aboriginal peoples brought about by white settlement, of which she is a part. A number of critics claim that this is a mature vision, a valid moment of powerful empathy. Michelle Gadpaille, for instance, sees this image as "a lament for the passing of an entire way of life among the Indians, epitomized by the haunting call of the loons" (qtd. in Ware 79). However, Tracy Ware, who summarizes the comments of a number of critics on the loons, argues that this symbolism "is a misrecognition because it ignores the historical struggles of both Natives and Metis while assigning both to 'a world separated by aeons from our neat world of summer cottages'" (79), along with the loons. Ware's position is shared by Acoose, who claims that indigenous women "have been variously portrayed as creatures of nature . . . or suffering, helpless victims" (74) by non-indigenous writers.

These seem to be valid critiques of the maturity of Vanessa's 11 understanding. While Vanessa's vision at the end of the story certainly shows more genuine empathy for Piquette than she demonstrated earlier, it does seem to identify the loons as helpless victims of white expansion and modernization and Aboriginal people as "suffering, helpless victims." The implications of this view for actions against Aboriginal people are outlined in Acoose's accounts of the beating, rape and murder of young Aboriginal women (69-70, 85-88); they are also evident in *Stolen from Our Embrace,* Suzanne Fournier and Ernie Crey's chilling account of the abduction of children from Aboriginal communities. Thus Vanessa's final image is not mature in the sense of offering us a vision of Métis and Indian people that moves beyond destructive stereotypes.

Whether Laurence shares this limitation, or "misrecognition" (79), as 12 Ware claims, remains the question. Acoose argues that despite her sympathies for the Métis, Laurence does indeed perpetuate destructive stereotypes. Piquette, according to Acoose, is "represented as a victim who is consistently victimized" (79). Laurence, that is, characterizes Piquette as the victim of every possible disadvantage: she is not only racially mixed, socially underprivileged, marginalized from town, and subjected to the kind of racial stereotyping so freely voiced by Vanessa's mother and grandmother but has also suffered from tuberculosis and has been abandoned by her mother to the care of a father and grandfather with drinking problems. This negative stereotyping, Acoose argues, ignores the many positive role models among indigenous people (88).

Assessing the validity of this argument requires an examination of 13
Laurence's use of point of view in the story and a closer look at the images
and language of the ending.

In "The Loons," as in the other stories in *A Bird in the House,* the point 14
of view is first person. It is tempting to assume that the story is narrated by
eighteen-year-old Vanessa, since she is the focus of its third and final narrative stage. There is also an older narrative voice, however, the voice that
in the first paragraph situates both Jules Tonnerre and Vanessa in historical
time as it describes the shack built by Jules "some fifty years before, when
he came back from Batoche with a bullet in his thigh, the year that Riel was
hung and the voices of the Metis entered their long silence" and the shack
as it appeared in the thirties, "when I was a child" (270). The presence of
this narrative voice contradicts Ware's claim that Laurence shares Vanessa's
"misrecognition": Laurence does not "ignore the historical struggles of both
Natives and Metis" (Ware 79) but locates the story in relation to them.

This narrative voice recurs at various points in the story, most noticeably 15
in the final episode. This narrator introduces the crucial moment in this
episode by saying, "I went up to Diamond Lake for a few days that summer" (278): "that summer," like the phrase "when I was a child" in the
first paragraph, tells us that this narrator is older than the Vanessa who
acts in the scene. The language of the final sentence reinforces this distance
between older and younger self through its emphasis on the provisional,
time-bound quality of this insight: "It *seemed* to me *now* that . . . Piquette
might have been the only one, after all, who had heard the crying of the
loons" (278; italics mine).

This claim that there is critical distance between Laurence and the 16
Vanessa who identifies Piquette with the loons is further supported by a
second look at figurative language at the end of the story. On her visit to the
lake, Vanessa has avoided the family cottage, sold after her father's death,
"not wanting to witness my long-ago kingdom possessed now by strangers"
(278). Her "kingdom" has suffered other changes: a "large and solid pier
built by the government" (278) has replaced the pier built by her father;
stores have proliferated; and the settlement, with its "hotels, a dance hall,
cafés with neon signs, the penetrating odours of potato chips and hot dogs"
(278), now seems like "a flourishing resort" (278).

It is not only the loons that have disappeared but also the world of 17
Vanessa's childhood and the father who shared that world with her. But
just as Vanessa's "distance from her youthful excesses is the source of most
of the [story's] irony" (Ware 76), so Laurence's irony marks the distance
between the older narrative voice and the younger Vanessa. The loons' call
is twice described as both mocking and plaintive ("The Loons" 274, 278).

The elegiac tone of the ending suggests that Vanessa at eighteen hears only the plaintive tones. She does not hear the other half, the half that mocks any idea of permanence, whether of people, of places, or of the creatures that predated them both. Given who Vanessa is and the social world she inhabits, Laurence seems to be saying, this is as much understanding as she is capable of at this moment. Laurence's framing of the loon metaphor thus makes it into a social and historical critique of Vanessa's understanding, not an endorsement of it.

This reading of "The Loons" is reinforced by the comments about time 18 that Laurence makes in her essay "Time and the Narrative Voice." What she means by time in fiction, Laurence says, is not "absolute time—which I don't believe to exist," but "historical time, variable and fluctuating" (280). This conception of time is at odds with Easingwood's claim that the story is "an evocation of atmospheric stillness, a momentary glimpse of a way of life belonging to the past which has almost completely disappeared" (124). Although Easingwood demonstrates that Vanessa's romantic vision of Piquette "is spoiled by [her] confrontation with known reality" (124), he nonetheless desires to retain a romantic vision of the past where the "momentary glimpse" fixes the Métis in a misrepresented history. The way of life may belong to the past, but "the pain and bewilderment of one's knowledge of other people" (Laurence, "Time" 282) are like time itself, "variable and fluctuating" (280).

In Laurence's "The Loons," then, point of view and figurative language 19 convey a more critical perspective on the question of the maturity of narrator Vanessa's understanding than initial responses to characterization and narrative structure might suggest. There is good reason to raise issues of destructive stereotyping in relation to the story, as critics Janice Acoose and Tracy Ware do. However, it finally becomes clear that through the story Laurence herself critiques the successive stereotypes that Vanessa employs in trying to understand Piquette. Acoose suggests that instead of presenting negative stereotypes of indigenous people, non-indigenous writers and the media should present strong indigenous role models and the full range of indigenous personalities. It is also possible to do what Laurence does in "The Loons" and critique stereotyping by showing how it operates in a basically sympathetic character who achieves some maturity and awareness, but not enough to overcome the blinkers of family, social status, and relative privilege.

Works Cited

Acoose, Janice. "Fenced In and Forced to Give Up: Images of Indigenous Women in Selected Non-Indigenous Writers' Fiction." *Iskwewak—Kah' Ki Yaw Ni Wahkomakanak: Neither Indian Princesses nor Easy Squaws.* Toronto: Women's Press, 1995. 69–88. Print.

Easingwood, Peter. "The Realism of Laurence's Semi-Autobiographical Fiction." *Critical Approaches to the Fiction of Margaret Laurence.* Ed. Colin Nicholson. Vancouver: U of British Columbia P, 1990. 119–32. Print.

Fournier, Suzanne, and Ernie Crey. *Stolen from Our Embrace: The Abduction of First Nations Children and the Restoration of Aboriginal Communities.* Vancouver: Douglas & McIntyre, 1997. Print.

Kertzer, Jon. *"That House in Manawaka": Margaret Laurence's* A Bird In the House. Toronto: ECW P, 1992. Print.

Laurence, Margaret. "The Loons." *A Bird in the House: Stories.* Toronto: McClelland & Stewart, 1970. 114–27. Print. [Reprinted in Readings 270–79. Page references are to this text.]

————. "Time and the Narrative Voice." *The Narrative Voice.* Ed. John Metcalf. Toronto: McGraw-Hill Ryerson, 1972. 156–60. Print. [Reprinted in Readings 280–84. Page references are to this text.]

Ware, Tracy. "Race and Conflict in Garner's 'One-Two-Three Little Indians' and Laurence's 'The Loons.'" *Studies in Canadian Literature* 23.2 (1998): 71–84. Print.

Like Me on Facebook: Identity Construction in Social Media*

B. Jones

Facebook has become a global phenomenon that engages hundreds of millions of people on a daily basis. The Social Network Site (SNS) purports to give people a way to express their unique, individual identities. Yet, the site simultaneously limits the user's capabilities for self-expression through its own structure in collecting information and its own reasons or ends for offering the service in the first place. As most users may agree, the general function of Facebook is to connect people to friends, which would seem to be a relatively good-natured or beneficial service where people can chat with current friends, keep in touch with old friends, and potentially meet new friends. However, as some research indicates, Facebook can have many negative consequences. As autobiography researchers Aimée Morrison and Laurie McNeill indicate, the profiles or identities that Facebook constructs are not authentic or accurate representations of real individuals but are inaccurate and highly constructed. Moreover, other researchers like Hui-Tzu Grace Chou and Nicholas Edge have shown that Facebook users frequently misread or misunderstand Facebook posts, leading them to have faulty perceptions of their friends and their world. While Facebook initially appears to be about expressing yourself and keeping in touch with friends, the site can overemphasize the happiness of others and, thereby, lower a user's self-esteem. With Facebook's dynamic ability to respond to user actions and tailor its content accordingly, the site contributes less to self-expression and autobiography than it does to the data-mining and commercial interests of Facebook and its customers. Therefore, while Facebook may be a commonplace tool in our daily lives, it is important to realize that the apparently benign or banal participation on the site simultaneously constructs and defines users more as customers than as people.

The internet era, in general, and Facebook, in particular, have ushered in the possibility for online friendships, ones that may or may not be grounded in real, face-to-face contact. Whether or not we approve of the diverse types of online relationships, it is certain that the online age has created new possibilities for interpersonal communications. We must be aware that we create our identities online in ways that are both similar to and

1

2

---

* Sample research essay

different from our identities in real time and space. We may create friend-ships online, but we must remain attentive that an online identity may be partially or completely false when compared to the actual user on the other point on the network. The personae we both construct and meet online represent new parameters for evaluating our interactions with others, with authenticity as a central concern.

There are two key terms for this discussion of Facebook: *friend* and *profile*. Facebook is based on the existence of friends. Generally speaking, Facebook friends may include real-life friends, family members, sports teammates, people with similar hobbies or tastes, and just about any other basis for forming a friendship. One central factor for friendship is trust. In other words, a friend is someone I can believe in, or rely on, to be true or genuine. Yet, I may concurrently realize that there are certain characteristics that I like and dislike about a person. I may enjoy playing hockey or making music with a particular person, but I may not enjoy that person's company off the ice or outside of the music studio. In the same way, we may assume one persona for work and another for home life. We have friends that fit within certain areas of our lives: we may have one set of friends at school, another set of friends from work, and yet another set of friends for playing hockey. Friends can fulfill many roles and needs just as all of us have dif-ferent aspects of our personalities. For some users, a Facebook profile is a space where many of these different aspects of our lives can intersect in a single site.

Facebook allows its users to formulate their identities through a profile page. As Sidonie Smith and Julia Watson have noted, the very word *profile* implies a particular approach to identity formation: "the medical history, the work history, the credit history" (qtd. in McNeill 75) of the individual. That is, a profile is based on a set of selection criteria, such as a racial profile (race) or a medical profile (health). As users set up accounts on Facebook, the site asks them for their name, gender, birthday, and email address. It additionally asks for optional information of religious views, political views, occupation, musical tastes, and relationship status, among others. Facebook allows its users to establish certain facts about their identities while it ignores or actively prohibits other types of information such as whether or not a potential user has ever defied the laws of gravity or has a criminal record. While on the surface it may appear that Facebook is asking fairly standard questions about a person's identity to formulate a profile, it nonetheless has a set of criteria for selection. Therefore, while people may manage a host of different and possibly competing variables in their real lives, a Facebook profile reveals a generally standardized set of traits of any individual on the network. People's ongoing complaints about Facebook's privacy settings demonstrate an uneasiness with the visibility of certain information, such as relationship status or political views, and they desire a means to control the publication of their information.

Borrowing a term from James Gibson, Aimée Morrison calls this selection process an "affordance" (299), which is "the set of possibilities for action an environment presents to its users" (299). So, for example, a new user must select a gender of either male or female when signing up for Facebook. It excludes the possibility of being non-human, like a Klingon or a unicorn or, more realistically, differently gendered such as transgendered or intersexed. You must be one or the other, not something else. Therefore, Morrison's adoption of an "affordance" demonstrates how Facebook's terminology of *profile* over *person* or *self* privileges certain types of information about an individual at the expense of other information. To put it in terms of friendship, you can be my friend if you are "male" or "female" but not if you are "transgendered," and, suddenly, it doesn't seem so friendly anymore, as you aren't allowed to be transgendered in your Facebook *profile*. You are not allowed to be yourself. Morrison uses the term "constraint" (300) to identify this kind of limitation or prohibition in systems like Facebook.

Morrison points out that this purpose behind these affordances and constraints is to generate "the depth of information the service harvests from its users" (298), and this is the primary motivation for Facebook: to sell user data. This is the point where Facebook and the user part ways in their motivations for using the site. A user would want to maximize the affordances for finding friends while Facebook would want to maximize the affordances for mining data. Morrison's article discusses how the status update and its linguistic constraints force the user to perform certain types of identity formation actions, such as stating daily activities or life events. By collecting this information, Facebook and its client companies can begin to profile people and their activities in order to target them for marketing. If a user claims she went hiking that day, perhaps an advertisement for hiking equipment will appear in her sidebar or she will receive an invitation to a hiking group on Facebook.

The commercial data enterprise underlies almost all Facebook activities. While there is a host of activities available on Facebook—status updates, news articles, games, assorted groups, fan pages, chat—the data collection is always present. Using Facebook is like being at a mall; you can do a lot of things at the mall—shop, eat, meet friends, skateboard—but you are always at the mall, always in a commercialized space. If enough skateboarders show up at the mall, perhaps a skateboard shop will open, or perhaps the police presence will increase to deter skateboarders from going to the mall. It depends on what the mall thinks of skateboarders. Almost anything you do is in the physical context of the mall; the same applies to Facebook. Facebook, like the mall, has most of the control over its affordances and constraints.

Therefore, when we choose to construct a profile on Facebook, it is worth considering the terms and conditions under which we create the representation of the "self." In her article, "There Is No 'I' in Network: Social Networking Sites and Posthuman Auto/Biography," Laurie McNeill argues that Facebook and other SNSs offer a new potential for online identity construction. She argues that the historical notion of identity construction was based on a stable and evolving discreet individual, yet the digital era introduces a self that is positioned within a network of interests. McNeill explains that "it isn't enough to produce material, posting media and status updates on your *own* page, you must consume and, more importantly, *respond* to the acts, and perceived desires, of others" (77). This process is epitomized in liking status, sharing statuses, inviting others to groups, planning events, playing games, and other such activities. I can suggest friends for other people or like certain updates and pages, and advertisers target me with their products because of the things I have done on Facebook. My profile page is not simply an expression of my "self" but a collection of results generated from my previous history of actions and clicks on Facebook. It is not "me," but a virtual commercial rendition of a networked "me." 8

Given these differences between the flesh-and-blood user and the digital construction of the online self, it is important to realize that the historically comfortable realm of friendship is not so trustworthy, accurate, or caring in an online environment where commercial interests underlie most interactions. According to research, increased usage of Facebook tends to instill in users the idea that other people are happier and more interesting as individuals, perhaps leading people to feel badly for or about themselves. As Hui-Tzu Grace Chou and Nicholas Edge point out, people who use Facebook regularly are more likely to perceive that other people on their friends list have better lives than their own and that life is unfair (118). They write, "In contrast to their own life events, which might not always be happy and positive, frequent Facebook users might perceive that life is not fair" (118). This indicates that people post information or events that portray their lives as happy, productive, and meaningful, or, at least, other people perceive their posts in this way. Of course, there are people who post events of misery, breakup, complaint, and death, yet Chou and Edge's research indicates that the positive posts outweigh the negative, leading to an inaccurate representation of the individual in the Facebook profile. Their research finds that the more online users interact with Facebook 9 friends, the more boring or inadequate they feel. This does not appear to be a healthy kind of friendship. Yet, the logical contradiction is apparent: if similar types of users generally perceive that others are happier, then those who are perceived to be happy are simultaneously perceiving others to be still happier, when, in reality, people may be equally happy or equally miserable. The point is that the perception of happiness is skewed toward the positive when this may or may not be true.

While users can benefit from the affordances offered by Facebook and other SNSs by connecting us to other people, the constraints of the conditions of use of SNSs create an environment where an individual's profile is highly influenced and constructed by the underlying commercial and data interests of the hosting site. While users are free in their choice to engage with the site, their construction of online identities must conform to predetermined criteria for participation, such as the profile criteria cited by Morrison as well as the behavioural practices cited by McNeill. Therefore, although people are probably generally aware that Facebook has competing interests in offering its services to users, it is important to realize, as Chou and Edge point out, that significant use of and belief in the representations of other people's Facebook lives can be destructive to self-esteem and self-perception. My conclusion is that, while I am a user of Facebook, I don't have to "like" everything about it.

Works Cited

Chou, Hui-Tzu Grace, and Nicholas Edge. "'They Are Happier and Having Better Lives than I Am': The Impact of Using Facebook on Perceptions of Others' Lives." CyberPsychology, Behavior & Social Networking 15.2 (2012): 117–121. Print.

McNeill, Laurie. "There Is No 'I' in Network: Social Networking Sites and Posthuman Auto/Biography." Biography: An Interdisciplinary Quarterly 35.1 (2012): 65–82. Print.

Morrison, Aimee. "Facebook and Coaxed Affordances." Identity Technologies: Constructing the Self Online. Eds. Anna Poletti and Julie Rak. Madison: U of Wisconsin P, 2013. 112–131. Print.

Nostalgia in Tim Bowling's "Na Na Na Na, Hey Hey Hey, Goodbye"*

C. Stonehouse

Tim Bowling's entertaining essay about NHL hockey, "Na Na Na Na, Hey Hey Hey, Goodbye," is an exploration of the author's own ambivalent attitude toward that sport in Canada. On the one hand, Bowling demonstrates his love and appreciation for the game. On the other hand, however, Bowling recognizes the many real problems that have become inseparable from the culture of hockey in Canada, including corporate ownership and violence. Bowling never really resolves his dilemma about hockey, remaining in a "love/hate" relationship with the game throughout the essay. Interestingly, though, while cataloguing his reasons for and against supporting the game, Bowling generates a feeling of nostalgia. *The Oxford English Dictionary* explains that nostalgia derives from the Greek roots "nostos," meaning "home," and "algia," meaning "pain." M. H. Abrams's *A Glossary of Literary Terms* explains that "nostalgia" is a longing for a past that is pristine and idyllic—like the garden of Eden before the Fall of Adam and Eve. Thus, nostalgia is a painful separation from and longing for one's home, a home that is also construed as one's personal or ancestral past. Bowling's nostalgia for hockey as it was in the past is evident in his references to his own childhood, his linking of hockey to distinctly Canadian icons, and his understanding of hockey as narrative.

Bowling's childhood memories of hockey are tinged with a fondness and a longing that are characteristic of nostalgia. For instance, speaking of his childhood in the early 1960s, Bowling says, "I'd play with hockey cards on the linoleum floor of the kitchen, passing a marble back and forth and re-enacting great goals and saves as my mother clattered dishes in the sink nearby" (235). Bowling's first hockey memory is in his kitchen, the domestic space of home, and Bowling is alongside his mother, a symbol, perhaps, of love, comfort, and belonging. Furthermore, Bowling states, "When I was a boy, the boards, ice and score clock were free of advertising; goals and assists meant more than salaries; and players and teams had distinct characters" (239). Here, hockey in Bowling's childhood is understood as pristine, untouched, and not yet corrupted by corporate culture. This vision of hockey in Bowling's past is contrasted with a present day hockey game

* Sample analysis essay

at which "you're . . . bombarded with supersonic noise and flashing lights and company logos" (239). Bowling's recollection of playing hockey with marbles on his kitchen floor is nostalgic in that it exemplifies a longing for home, domesticity, and love; his recollection of the blank "boards, ice and score clock" (239) is nostalgic in its description as pure and idyllic: hockey has not yet fallen into the corruption of corporate takeover and violence.

Bowling's nostalgia for the old-fashioned game of hockey is not only   3
evident in the description of his childhood but also in his linking of hockey to Canadian icons. For example, Bowling mentions the instance in which Canadian icemakers placed a loonie under the ice at the 2002 Winter Olympic Games in Salt Lake City, and he notes that Team Canada won the gold medal that year (238). Here, the loonie—the Canadian one-dollar coin—stands for Canada, the home to which the players will bring back the gold medal. Team Canada is away from and yet linked to the nation to which it belongs. Moreover, Bowling states that his absence from watching NHL hockey is "like fasting after binging on double-doubles and maple creams down at the local Tim Hortons" (239). Bowling compares watching hockey to eating Tim Hortons' doughnuts, and so links one Canadian reference (hockey) with another (Tim Hortons' doughnuts). In this case, Bowling longs to watch hockey just as he longs to binge on maple creams. His separation from both hockey and doughnuts is pained.

Bowling's nostalgia can be noted in the way he associates hockey with   4
narrative or story. Bowling states that he is compelled to watch NHL hockey because of "the primal pull of narrative" (236). Like the constructed and idyllic story of one's nostalgic past, this narrative is "primal"—the first or original story—and "pull[s]" one into it, seemingly against one's own will. Bowling says that the NHL is "the Great Canadian Novel, a tale replete with villains and heroes, prima donnas and blue collar types, triumph and failure, hope and revenge" (236). He gives examples of moments in that narrative: "six out of seven Sutter brothers from Viking, Alberta, made the big time and Bobby Clarke overcame diabetes to realize his professional dreams" (237). Thus, Canadian hockey is a soap opera, a page-turner that Bowling cannot put down. Like nostalgia, the author has a fondness for it and feels pain at his separation from it. When Bowling goes to a theatre to watch the film *Howards End* instead of watching game seven of the Stanley Cup, what he really wants to do is come home and watch the narrative of his own home-grown Canadian hockey. Bowling finally notices the extremity of his obsession with the Canadian hockey story. Upon leaving the theatre, he pulls a group of teenagers aside, only to find that they do not know the results of the game (236). Bowling must wrench himself away from his nostalgia to "begin the process of cultural de-programming that would find

[him], a decade later, completely indifferent to the labour dispute between the NHL team owners and players" (236).

At the end of his essay, Bowling asks, "Can I resist the lure of *nostalgia* and the pull of narrative?" (239, my emphasis). This statement is the only one in which Bowling mentions the word "nostalgia," but the notion of nostalgia is prevalent throughout his essay. From his recollection of childhood memories of hockey, which include domestic and motherly images, to his linking of hockey to Canadian national icons, to his connection of hockey to narrative, Bowling wishes to come back to a past in which hockey was free from corruption, a past which was also supposedly idyllic, innocent, and comforting. Perhaps Bowling's desire is typical of twenty-first century Canadians who remember or have heard about their ancestor pioneers. Bowling's "Na Na Na Na, Hey Hey Hey, Goodbye" is not just an exploration of the author's reasons for liking or disliking the game of hockey: it is an engagement with the fond memories of his past, an engagement that might apply, in one way or another, to many Canadians.

Works Cited

Abrams, M. H. *A Glossary of Literary Terms*. 8th ed. Boston: Thomson, 2005. Print.

Bowling, Tim. "Na Na Na Na, Hey Hey Hey, Goodbye." *Alberta Views* Dec. 2005–Jan. 2006: 46–49. Print. [Reprinted in Readings 235–40. Page references are to this text.]

Paperback Oxford English Dictionary. 6th ed. Oxford: Oxford UP, 2006. Print.

Tone in William Carlos Williams's "This Is Just to Say"*

L. Strong

William Carlos Williams presents his poem "This Is Just to Say" (Rhetoric 84–85) as a casual note of apology most likely written from one lover to another. Although the poem is deceptively simple, Williams leaves it open to different signifying possibilities that complicate the tone. If we read the poem on a simplistic level, we can perceive the speaker's tone as casual yet honest—in an informal manner, the speaker shows his honesty by admitting his wrong. If we read the poem with scrutiny, we can perceive the speaker's tone as vengeful and haughty—the speaker teases his lover by acknowledging not only that he can freely eat the plums but also that he can skilfully use rhetoric to justify the act and earn forgiveness. 1

The word "this," in the title of the poem, is open to more than one possible meaning. It can refer either to the note of apology or to the act of eating the plums. If we read "this" as a reference to the note, then the speaker's tone is either honest or haughty: he either leaves the note because he wants to admit his wrong or because he wants to declare his action and thus tease his lover. If we read "this" as a reference to the act of eating the plums, then the speaker's tone is vengeful: he eats the plums as a statement of vengeance toward his lover. Similarly, the word "just," also in the title, is open to more than one possibility. It can mean *merely*, or it can mean *legally valid* or *fair*. If we read "just" as a synonym for *merely*, then the speaker takes a casual tone: he implies that his act and the note are not very important. If we read "just" as *legally valid*, then the speaker is saying "this is fair to say"—the tone is then one of retribution. Hence, the tone of the title alters between honest, haughty, casual, and vengeful according to the way in which we read the words "this" and "just." 2

The phrase "forgive me," in the final stanza of the poem, is also open to a number of signifying possibilities: we can read the phrase in a simplistic way as an honest plea; we can read it ironically, as though the speaker taunts his lover by temporarily taking a formal tone rather than a casual one; or we can read it as an appeal for forgiveness that is cuttingly undermined because it is juxtaposed with the lines "they were delicious / so sweet / and 3

---

* Sample essay on literature

so cold" (10–12). The latter reading is perhaps the most interesting. The phrase "forgive me" momentarily privileges obligation over temptation; by following it with a description of the taste and feel of the plums, however, the speaker ultimately takes a snide tone—he cleverly nullifies his wrong by justifying the sensual. Thus, like the words "this" and "just" in the title of the poem, the tone of the phrase "forgive me" varies. We can read it as honest, ironic, or snide.

Although Williams presents his poem as a note of apology, he also   4 presents it as a poem that appears in his collection of poems. What is Williams's purpose in presenting this poem as a piece of literature? In order to answer this question, we may view the poet in the same way that we view the speaker. Like the speaker, the poet creates a seemingly simple work that relays a casual and honest tone, as if the poem can precisely depict and justify the meaning of a particular incident. Essentially, however, he creates a complex piece of literature in which the tone is dependent upon the way we read the words. Williams thus comments on the power of language. We accept words as justifications for action, even though "just saying" is only saying. Perhaps "this" poem then, is "just to say" that there is no single truth or ideal justice that language can express.

Handbook for Final Editing

A Final Editing: The Process

A1 Strategies for Final Editing

Final editing is the last stage of the writing process, your last chance to eliminate the kinds of errors that can distract and annoy your reader. Here are some tips.

1. Wait at least a day after you have finished writing your essay. If you try to edit immediately, you will miss errors.

2. Use a spell-checker and other editing software to pick up errors. Then print out a hard copy and edit it. You will notice errors that you missed onscreen.

3. Read your essay aloud. You or your listener will notice awkward sentences, lack of transitions, and other problems that you might overlook on the page.

4. Make a list of the kinds of errors you frequently make (such as problems with pronoun agreement, apostrophes, and commas) and watch particularly for them.

5. Begin editing with the last sentence in your conclusion. Read each sentence separately and work your way back to the first sentence in your introduction. This procedure will help you to see what you have actually written, not what you have memorized.

The chart on the following pages lists in alphabetical order the most common errors in sentence structure, grammar, mechanics, and format. This chart also includes common marking symbols, an example of each error, and page references to explanations and exercises in the handbook. When you get an essay back, note your errors on the chart and keep the chart handy when you edit your next essay.

A2 Identifying Common Problems

Term	Marking Symbol	Example of Common Error (bold indicates error to be corrected)	Page Reference
abbreviation	Abbrev	The **pres.** of the company will visit **AB & SK** this **yr.**	464
adjective form	Adj	Skirmish was the **most ugliest** dog.	397
adverb form	Adv	Skirmish barked **real** loud.	397
apostrophe	⌣ Apos	We offer exciting **childrens'** programs.	444
capitalization	Caps	My **Mother** and I lived in the **north.**	463
colon	⨀/⋀	The camp offered activities such **as:** canoeing, swimming, and tennis.	453
comma	⨀/⋀	Bill enjoys **tennis,** and football.	447
comma splice, comma fault	CS, CF	Loons are an endangered **species, pollution** is destroying their habitat.	415
dangling modifier	DM	**After running a marathon,** exhaustion is inevitable.	399
dash	⊝\⌣/	The storm ripped and scattered all the shingles— **on the new roof.**	454
diction	Dic	Alison decided **to partake** in the game.	436
documentation	Doc	Macbeth echoes the witches' opening words when he says, "So foul and fair a day I have not seen." **(No in-text citation)**	478
essay format	EF	**Gender stereotypes in *Macbeth*.**	466
faulty coordination	F Coord	Adam was terrified **and** he burst into laughter.	405
faulty subordination	F Subord	**Although** Irene wanted to stop smoking, **however,** she lacked the willpower.	406
fragment	SF, Frag	**Which is the main reason for Allan's success.**	414
fused sentence	FS	The baby is **hot she** must have a fever.	417
hyphen	⊝\⌣/	The **well^prepared** athlete must be mentally and physically fit.	461
italics	Ital.	This summer I read Tolstoy's **War and Peace.**	458
misplaced modifier	MM	I **hardly** have any money.	399
mixed construction	Mix	One reason he is often late **is because** his car has chronic battery problems.	418
numbers	Num	**15** employees were fired; **three hundred and forty seven** went on strike.	463
parallelism	llism	Our servers must be hard-working, intelligent, **and they can't insult the customers.**	402
parentheses	⨀⟋⟍	During the second period, **(the** fans were holding their **breath,)** our team scored.	455

Term	Marking Symbol	Example of Common Error (bold indicates error to be corrected)	Page Reference
passive voice	Passive	After **the ghost was seen by Hamlet,** he hated his uncle more intensely.	395
possessive pronouns	P Poss	The jury made **it's** decision.	384
pronoun agreement	P Agr	**Every student** must check **their** bag at the door.	385
pronouns of address	P Add P Shift	By the end of the movie, **you** could see that the hero had matured.	433
pronoun case	P Case	**Her** and I have been married almost twelve years.	382
pronoun reference	P Ref	Fred doesn't know whether to get married or join the navy **which** makes him uneasy.	387
quotation format	Quot F	Hamlet's despair is clear when he says, **"O that this . . . into a dew."**	474
quotation introduction	Quot	^ "The woods are lovely, dark and deep." The speaker wants to rest.	471
quotation marks	("") ⌄/	Mio liked Munro's story **Boys and Girls.**	456
semicolon	(;) /;\	When the movie **ended;** the audience burst into applause.	451
sentence length and structure	S Var	**Hamlet misses his father. He is angry at his mother. He hates his uncle.**	423
spelling	Sp ◯	Elizabeth was **to** angry to speak.	460
split infinitive	Split	The rebels struggled **to strongly resist** the government forces.	399
subject–verb agreement	S/V Agr	The director's **use** of gimmicky special effects **were attacked** by the critics.	393
transitions	Trans	Peter wants to lose **weight.** ^ **He** refuses to diet.	426
usage/wrong word	WW	Houdini was a master of **allusion.**	438
verb forms	VF	After Sophy **had drank** the last beer, she **laid** on the couch and fell asleep.	389
verb tenses	T, Tense	Hamlet **grieves** for his father, but he **concealed** his feelings.	392
wordiness	Wordy	**Due to the fact that** the tickets sold out in the first half hour, many fans were disappointed.	423

B Grammar: Parts of Speech

A language is a system of communication in which the parts work together to produce messages understood by both sender(s) and receiver(s). In traditional approaches to grammar, English words are divided into eight categories according to their function in sentences. These categories are referred to as **parts of speech**. In this chapter we discuss the eight parts of speech in five sections: Nouns; Pronouns; Verbs; Adjectives and Adverbs; and Conjunctions, Prepositions, and Interjections.

Just as you can drive a car without being able to describe all its parts and how they operate, so you can speak and write English without knowing all about parts of speech. When your car breaks down or starts running rough, however, you need at least a little knowledge to get it fixed. That's also the case with language. Some basic understanding of the parts of speech will help you to avoid or correct problems with grammar, sentence structure, and punctuation. Without these distractions, you and your reader can focus on the act of communication.

B1 Nouns

A **noun** is a word that names a person, place, or thing.

1a Common Nouns and Proper Nouns

Common nouns, which are not capitalized except in special circumstances, refer to objects as members of a class. **Proper nouns**, which are always capitalized, refer to a specific person, place, or thing.

COMMON NOUNS	PROPER NOUNS
baby	Suzie
park	Elk Island Park
toy	Lego

For more on capitalization, see G3b Capitalization.

1b Concrete Nouns and Abstract Nouns

Concrete nouns, such as those in the lists on the previous page, refer to objects with an external physical existence. **Abstract nouns** refer to ideas, feelings, and concepts, such as justice, frustration, and Einstein's theory of relativity. The terms *abstract* and *concrete* are not pigeonholes into which every word must fit; they are end points on a continuum, as the example below illustrates.

MOST CONCRETE	MOST ABSTRACT
Barkley, beagle, dog, pet	animal, living thing

Both concrete and abstract nouns have their place in good writing. Concrete nouns will anchor your writing in the everyday world your readers share. Much of the power of W. S. Merwin's essay "Unchopping a Tree" (Readings), for example, comes from his use of concrete nouns: *leaves, twigs, nests.* He doesn't make vague statements about the destruction of the environment; he makes us *see* the impact of our actions. If your writing tends to be vague, check whether you can make your language more concrete.

Abstract nouns, on the other hand, allow us to put concrete experience within a broader framework. In "Shooting an Elephant" (Readings), for instance, George Orwell places his encounter with a rogue elephant within the context of imperialism. Without the context provided by this abstract idea, the essay would lack the depth that has kept it relevant for more than seventy years. In the sections on gathering material in this text, you will find suggestions for how to arrive at the categories—the abstract level of thinking—that will give your writing a broader meaning.

1c Singular Nouns, Plural Nouns, and Collective Nouns

Singular nouns refer to one person, place, or thing. **Plural nouns** refer to more than one person, place, or thing.

SINGULAR	PLURAL
deer	deer
girl	girls
box	boxes
baby	babies
man	men

These examples illustrate the most common ways of making singular nouns into plural nouns. If you are unsure of the plural form of a noun, check a dictionary.

Note: It is important to understand the difference between the singular and plural form of nouns and the possessive form, which indicates *belonging to*.

Singular	*Singular Possessive*	*Plural*	*Plural Possessive*
society	society's	societies	societies'

For guidelines on forming possessives, see F1b Using Apostrophes to Show Possession.

Collective nouns are words that refer to a group, such as *band, committee, company, herd, team*. If the collective noun refers to the group acting as a unit, it is considered singular (*The band plays every night*). If the collective noun refers to the group members acting as individuals, it is considered plural (*The band disagree about getting a new manager*). Collective nouns also have plural forms that refer to more than one group: *bands, committees, companies, herds, teams*.

Being able to recognize singular, plural, and possessive forms of nouns will help you with spelling, subject–verb agreement (see B3c), and pronoun agreement (see B2b).

1d Uses of Nouns

Understanding the two basic uses of nouns will help you to identify and correct errors in sentence structure and grammar.

Nouns as subjects A sentence must have two basic components: a **verb**, which names the action or state of being (see B3), and a **subject**, which tells who or what performs the action or manifests the state of being. The subject will be a noun or pronoun (for pronouns as subjects, see B2a). In the most common sentence pattern in English, the subject comes before the verb.

> Rain [subject noun] fell [verb].
>
> The committee [subject noun] is meeting [verb].

In some cases the subject will appear after the verb.

> Here (there) are [verb] three books [subject noun].
>
> Through the open window came [verb] the wail [subject noun] of a siren.

Two or more nouns joined by a conjunction (see B5a) may function as the subject of a verb.

> Sunil and Misha [subject nouns] are [verb] angry.
>
> Neither reward nor punishment [subject nouns] improved [verb] the dog's behaviour.

To find the subject of a sentence, first locate the verb or verbs. Then ask yourself who or what performed the action or manifested the state of being.

Note: When the verb is in the passive voice, the subject is the thing acted upon rather than the agent of the action or state of being.

> Active voice: The dog [subject] bit the letter carrier.
>
> Passive voice: The letter carrier [subject] was bitten by the dog.

For more on active and passive voice, see B3d Active and Passive Voice.

Nouns as objects Nouns also function as **objects** in various grammatical constructions. While you are unlikely to make mistakes in using nouns as objects, understanding the difference between subjects and objects will help you with subject–verb agreement (see B3c) and with pronouns (see B2b).

Direct object A direct object is defined as one or more nouns or pronouns that follow the verb and receive its action.

> Subject-verb-direct object
>
> [who or what] did [who or what]
>
> Jamal [subject] hit [verb] the puck [direct object].
>
> His line [subject] scored [verb] three goals [direct object] and killed off [verb] two penalties [direct object].

Indirect object An indirect object answers the question "to whom or what?" about the direct object, without the use of *to*. The indirect object comes before the direct object.

> The father [subject] gave [verb] the baby [indirect object] a cookie [direct object].
>
> The librarian [subject] sent [verb] the interlibrary loan service [indirect object] a request [direct object] for four books.

Object of a preposition The noun or pronoun that ends a prepositional phrase and completes its meaning is called the object of the preposition. (For more on prepositions, see B5b.)

> The woman with the <u>sunglasses</u> [object of the preposition *with*] is my aunt.
>
> The soldiers fought for their <u>country</u> and their <u>lives</u> [objects of the preposition *for*].

Note: Do not confuse the object of a preposition with the subject of a sentence. The subject of a sentence never appears in a prepositional phrase. Make sure the verb agrees with the subject.

> The team [subject] with the best scores [object of the preposition] wins [not *win*] the tournament.

B2 Pronouns

A **pronoun** is a word that takes the place of a noun, usually when the noun has already been mentioned and repeating it would be awkward.

> Scientists created a megavirus.
>
> *They* [pronoun] accidentally let *it* [pronoun] escape from the lab.

2a Uses of Pronouns: Pronoun Case

Personal pronouns Since pronouns take the place of nouns, they serve the same primary functions in sentences: as subjects and as objects. As you can see from the following chart, however, most subject pronouns have different forms from the equivalent object pronouns.

	SUBJECT PRONOUNS		OBJECT PRONOUNS		POSSESSIVE FORM
	Singular	*Plural*	*Singular*	*Plural*	
First person	I	we	me	us	my, mine/ our, ours
Second person	you	you	you	you	your, yours
Third person	he, she, it	they	him, her, it	them	his, her, hers, its/their, theirs

If you use a subject pronoun where you should use an object pronoun, or vice versa, you have made an error in **pronoun case**.

Uses of subject pronouns

1. To replace nouns in the subject position of the sentence.

> NOT   Her and me went to a movie.
>
> BUT   She and I went to a movie.

Note: Errors in pronoun case often occur when only one subject noun is replaced by a pronoun.

> NOT   My brother and me bought a car together.
>
> BUT   My brother and I bought a car together.

2. When the subject pronoun is followed by an explanatory noun.

> NOT   Us students were enraged by the exam.
>
> BUT   We students were enraged by the exam.

3. After comparisons using *than* and *as*.

> NOT   The other team is weaker than us.
>
> BUT   The other team is weaker than we [are].

4. As the subject of a subordinate clause beginning with *that*.

> NOT   Mr. Ramsay said that him and his sister had rented the house on the corner.
>
> BUT   Mr. Ramsay said that he and his sister had rented the house on the corner.

Uses of object pronouns

1. As the object of a verb.

> NOT   The coach told Rajiv and he to come early.
>
> BUT   The coach told Rajiv and him to come early.

2. After a preposition.

> NOT   The manager left a message for my roommate and I.
>
> BUT   The manager left a message for my roommate and me.

Notes: (1) *Me* is not an informal form of *I*. *Me* is a perfectly acceptable object pronoun. (2) Don't substitute *myself* for *me* when you need an object pronoun.

> NOT   Please contact either the supervisor or myself if you have problems.
>
> BUT   Please contact either the supervisor or me if you have problems.

Relative pronouns In addition to the personal pronouns, there are six **relative pronouns**: *that, which, who, whoever, whom, whomever*. These pronouns can link a subordinate clause (see C1d) to the preceding noun or pronoun.

That and *which* can be used as either subject or object pronouns.

> The hand that rocks the cradle rules the world.
>
> Toshimi bought a pound of tea, which she gave to a friend.

Who and *whoever* are subject pronouns. Use them to replace or refer to a subject noun.

> Dr. Wong is the distinguished biologist. She will give the opening address.
>
> Dr. Wong is the distinguished biologist who will give the opening address.
>
> Someone has the best cards. That person will win the poker game.
>
> Whoever has the best cards will win the poker game.

Whom and *whomever* are object pronouns. Use them to refer to an object noun.

> Claudius is a smooth politician. Hamlet distrusts him.
>
> Claudius is a smooth politician whom Hamlet distrusts.
>
> You may invite the people you wish to invite.
>
> You may invite whomever you wish to invite.

As these examples suggest, you can check your usage of *who/whoever* and *whom/whomever* by substituting an appropriate personal pronoun.

> You may invite [they/them] if you wish to invite [they/them].

If you would use *them* rather than *they,* then you should choose the object pronoun *whomever* rather than the subject pronoun *whoever.*

You will find guidelines for punctuating clauses beginning with a relative pronoun in F2e Non-restrictive and Restrictive Modifiers.

Possessive pronouns When you want to show ownership, use these possessive pronouns: *my/mine, our/ours, your/yours, his, her/hers, its, their/theirs, whose.* Remember that possessive pronouns do not take apostrophes.

1. Don't confuse the possessive pronoun *its* with the contraction *it's* (it is).

   POSSESSIVE The board has made its ruling.

   CONTRACTION It's obvious that no one was listening.

2. Don't confuse the possessive pronoun *whose* with the contraction *who's* (who is).

   POSSESSIVE We must decide whose responsibility this is.

   CONTRACTION Who's responsible for this?

3. Don't confuse the possessive pronoun *their* with the dummy subject *there* or the contraction *they're.*

   POSSESSIVE The Inuit in the region are close to settling their land claim.

   DUMMY SUBJECT There are still a few issues to be resolved.

   CONTRACTION They're close to signing a treaty.

4. Don't confuse the possessive pronoun *your* with the contraction *you're*.

POSSESSIVE Don't forget to put your signature on the expense claim.

CONTRACTION If you don't hurry, you're going to be late.

2b Pronoun Agreement

Pronouns must agree in number with the nouns to which they refer. Singular pronouns must replace or refer back to a singular noun; plural pronouns must replace or refer back to plural nouns. This rule applies to possessive pronouns as well as to subject and object pronouns. If nouns and pronouns do not agree in number, there is an error in **pronoun agreement**.

Most pronoun agreement errors occur in these contexts:

1. When the noun refers to a type of person: *the patient, the student, the player*. You can correct this error by making the subject plural.

NOT The first-year student may have problems adjusting to their new freedom.

BUT First-year students may have problems adjusting to their new freedom.

2. When a singular noun is followed by a prepositional phrase ending with a plural noun (*of the workers, of the children*).

NOT One of the children left their lunch on the kitchen table.

BUT One of the children left his lunch on the kitchen table.

OR One of the children left her lunch on the kitchen table.

3. When the writer is trying to avoid gender bias. If you don't want to imply that a singular subject (*the single parent, the nurse, the engineer*) is always male or female, you may make errors in pronoun agreement.

Every doctor these days complains that paperwork encroaches on the time *they* can spend with their patients.

Although this error in pronoun agreement is gradually becoming more acceptable, you may want to avoid it with these strategies.

a. Make the subject plural (*single parents, nurses, engineers*).

b. Use *him or her, he or she* (never *he/she* or *s/he*) to refer to a singular subject.

Typically, a two-year-old will insist that he or she be the focus of all attention.

This strategy works well in a single sentence but becomes cumbersome in a longer piece of writing.

    c.   Rewrite the sentence to avoid pronouns.

       Typically, a two-year-old insists on being the focus of all attention.

    d.   Refer to the subject with masculine pronouns in one paragraph and feminine pronouns in the next.

4. When the subject is an indefinite pronoun. In formal writing, use singular pronouns to refer to *each* and to words that end with *–body, –one,* and *–thing: anybody, everybody, nobody; anyone, everyone, no one; anything, everything, nothing.*

      INFORMAL SPOKEN Everyone wanted to have their picture taken.

      FORMAL WRITTEN Everyone at the convention wanted his or her vote on this issue recorded.

5. When the subject is a collective noun (see B1c). If the sentence indicates unanimous action, the collective noun takes a singular verb and singular pronouns. If the sentence indicates members of the group acting individually, the collective noun takes a plural verb and plural pronouns.

      The committee is circulating the minutes of its [not *their*] last meeting.

      The committee were fighting over the size of their [not *its*] bonuses.

2c Pronoun Reference

Errors in pronoun reference occur whenever a pronoun does not clearly refer to a specific noun. Here are some ways to correct ambiguous pronouns.

1. Keep the pronoun close to the noun to which it refers.

      NOT   Luigi told George that he was a terrible baseball player. He was furious.

      BUT   George was furious because Luigi called him a terrible baseball player.

      OR   Because Luigi was furious, he called George a terrible baseball player.

2. Use pronouns to refer only to nouns or pronouns, not to possessive adjectives such as *his, her, Shakespeare's.*

      James snapped the guitar's neck that belonged to his mother.

In this sentence, *that* refers to the guitar's neck, an error suggesting that only the guitar's neck belonged to James's mother. The next sentence shows how you could make clear that the whole guitar belonged to James's mother.

      James snapped the neck of his mother's guitar.

3. Make sure *that, this,* and *which* refer to a specific noun or pronoun, not to the idea in the preceding sentence or clause. Clarify vague pronoun references by rewriting the sentence or supplying the missing noun or pronoun.

> NOT He did not know whether she would leave or wait for him. This made him anxious.
>
> BUT He did not know whether she would leave or wait for him. This uncertainty made him anxious.
>
> OR He was anxious because he did not know whether she would leave or wait for him.

4. Do not use *they* to refer to people in general or to the author of a text.

> NOT They said hurricanes are affected by the rain cycles in Africa.
>
> BUT Meteorologists say hurricanes are affected by the rain cycles in Africa.
>
> NOT They say in Shaw's play *Major Barbara* that the only crime is poverty.
>
> BUT In Shaw's play *Major Barbara,* Undershaft says that the only crime is poverty.

5. Do not use *it* or *they* to refer to an implied subject. Supply the missing noun or rewrite the sentence.

> NOT I spent two weeks studying for the exam, but it didn't improve my grade.
>
> BUT I spent two weeks studying for the exam, but this effort did not improve my grade.
>
> OR Two weeks of studying for the exam did not improve my grade.
>
> NOT I wrote to the Canada Revenue Agency about my income tax assessment, but they have not yet replied.
>
> BUT I wrote to the Canada Revenue Agency about my income tax assessment, but the taxation officials have not yet replied.
>
> OR I have not yet received a reply to my letter to the Canada Revenue Agency about my income tax assessment.

B3 Verbs

A **verb** is a word that expresses action, existence, possession, or sensation.

> He *plays* hockey. (Action)
>
> I *am* here. (Existence)
>
> You *have* the measles. (Possession)
>
> The bread *smells* mouldy. (Sensation)

A **verb phrase** is made up of the main verb plus one or more **auxiliary (helping) verbs** that indicate time or condition.

> He *is playing/has been playing* hockey.
>
> I *may be/might have been* here.
>
> Do you have the measles? Soon we will have the measles.
>
> The bread *should* not *smell* mouldy.

Here is a list of the most common auxiliary verbs:

1. forms of *to be: am, is, are, was, were, be, been, being*
2. forms of *to have: have, has, had, having*
3. forms of *to do: do, does, did, done*
4. others: *can, could, may, might, must, shall, will, should, would, ought to, have to, supposed to, used to*

To name a verb, give its infinitive form, as in the list of auxiliary verbs above: *to run, to listen*.

3a Principal Parts of Verbs

Principal parts of regular verbs Regular verbs, as their name suggests, form their principal parts in a regular, predictable way. The four main parts of a verb are the present tense, the past tense (formed by adding –*ed* to the present tense), the present participle (formed by adding –*ing* to the present tense), and the past participle (formed by adding the appropriate form of the auxiliary verb *to have* to the past tense).

The present tense usually expresses habitual action (Every day I *walk* to school), whereas the present participle is used with an auxiliary to express ongoing action (I *am walking* to school now). The simple past expresses action that began and ended in the past (I *lived* in Toronto for five years). The past participle expresses action that began in the past and continues to the present (I *have lived* in Canada for twenty years) or action that ended before a subsequent event (I *had lived* in Germany before I came to Canada).

PRESENT	PAST	PRESENT PARTICIPLE	PAST PARTICIPLE
walk	walked	walking	walked
fill	filled	filling	filled

Principal parts of irregular verbs Irregular verbs form their principal parts in various unpredictable ways. Here are three different patterns of irregular verbs.

VERBS

PRESENT	PAST	PRESENT PARTICIPLE	PAST PARTICIPLE
drink	drank	drinking	drunk
burst	burst	bursting	burst
steal	stole	stealing	stolen

The present participle of irregular verbs is always formed by adding –*ing* to the present tense. It's the past tense and the past participle that may cause problems. You need either to memorize these forms or to check your dictionary. Here are some of the most troublesome irregular verbs to watch for in your writing.

Principal parts of troublesome verbs

INFINITIVE	PAST TENSE	PAST PARTICIPLE
to be	was	been
to break	broke	broken
to choose	chose	chosen
to come	came	come
to cost	cost	cost
to go	went	gone
to lay (place)	laid	laid
to lie (recline)	lay	lain
to hang (a person)	hanged	hanged
to hang (a picture)	hung	hung
to lead	led	led
to rise	rose	risen

Note 1: Don't confuse *lose* and *loose*.

NOT   She is afraid that she will loose her mind.

BUT   She is afraid that she will lose her mind.

Note 2: Be sure to add the past tense ending to *use* and *suppose* when they are followed by an infinitive.

NOT   Rosa use to play soccer.

BUT   Rosa used to play soccer.

NOT   Alix is suppose to make dinner.

BUT   Alix is supposed to make dinner.

Note 3: In speech, the contractions for "would have" (*would've*) and "should have" (*should've*) sound like "would of" and "should of." These forms are never correct.

NOT   You should of seen *The Lord of the Rings.*

BUT   You should have seen *The Lord of the Rings.*

3b Verb Tenses

Verb tenses indicate the *time* of existence, action, possession, or sensation. The basic tenses in English are the present, past, and future. The tenses used in a sentence or series of sentences must accurately indicate the time relationships involved.

She walks to the door. She opens her umbrella. She leaves. (All verbs in the present tense)

She walked to the door. She opened her umbrella. She left. (All verbs in the past tense)

When she finishes her meal [present tense], she will walk to the door, open her umbrella, and leave [future tense]. (Change in tense necessary to indicate time relationships)

Unnecessary shifts in tense Unnecessary shifts in tense occur when the verb forms do not correspond to the time relationships. In the following sentence, the tense shifts are confusing.

When she finished her meal, she walks to the door, opens her umbrella, and will leave.

If you are caught up in the ideas you are trying to convey, you may switch from present to past or vice versa without noticing. These suggestions will help you keep your tenses consistent.

1. When you are writing about literary works, keep your analysis and your account of events in the present tense:

    NOT   The small-town setting of William Faulkner's "A Rose for Emily" *explains* the attitude of the townspeople toward Emily because people in small communities traditionally *rejected* and *excluded* those who *were* different from them. Faulkner's description of the setting *emphasizes* Emily's isolation. Most of the action *took place* in and around the house where Emily *lived* all her life.

    BUT   The small-town setting of William Faulkner's "A Rose for Emily" *explains* the attitude of the townspeople toward Emily because people in small communities traditionally *reject* and *exclude* those who *are* different. Faulkner's description of the setting *emphasizes* Emily's isolation. Most of the action *takes place* in and around the house where Emily *has lived* all her life.

VERBS

2. Use the simple present or past tense in preference to –*ing* verbs.

> NOT   Freud *is discussing* the relationships among the id, ego, and superego.

> BUT   Freud *discusses* the relationships among the id, ego, and superego.

3. If you sometimes omit verb endings, writing "he learn" instead of "he learns" or "he learned," check each verb.

4. If you know you have a problem with verb tenses, proofread your final draft a paragraph at a time, checking all verbs to make sure that (a) they are in the same tense or (b) changes in tense are justified by the time relationships.

3c Subject–Verb Agreement

Verbs must agree with their subjects in number: if the subject of the sentence is singular, the verb must be singular; if the subject is plural, the verb must be plural.

> The engine is hot. (Singular subject, singular verb)

> The engines are hot. (Plural subject, plural verb)

By the time you reach college or university, you probably won't make subject–verb errors very often. When you do, you may have lost track of the subject, as in the following cases.

1. Prepositional phrase between the subject and the verb. Remember that the noun in the prepositional phrase (of the *children,* between the *hedges,* beneath the *sheets*) is never the subject of the sentence.

> NOT   The reaction to these incidents were quick and angry.

> BUT   The reaction to these incidents was quick and angry.

2. Phrases that imply a plural subject when the actual subject is singular: *as well as*, *in addition to*, *along with*, *including*.

> NOT   The cost, including parts and labour, were far more than the estimate.

> BUT   The cost, including parts and labour, was far more than the estimate.

3. Indefinite pronouns that may seem plural but take a singular verb:

anybody	anyone	anything	each (of)
everybody	everyone	everything	either (of)
nobody	no one	nothing	neither (of)
somebody	someone	something	

NOT	Each of the passengers have a headphone.
BUT	<u>Each</u> of the passengers <u>has</u> a headphone.
NOT	Neither of the soldiers were wounded.
BUT	<u>Neither</u> [one] of the soldiers <u>was</u> wounded.

4. *There is/are* constructions. In these constructions, the subject comes after the verb. *There* is never the subject of the sentence.

NOT	There is three important issues to consider.
BUT	There <u>are</u> three important <u>issues</u> [subject] to consider.

5. Singular subjects joined with *or.*

NOT	John or Carol are meeting you at the airport.
BUT	<u>John</u> or <u>Carol</u> <u>is meeting</u> you at the airport.

6. A combination of singular and plural subjects joined with *either . . . or, neither . . . nor, not only . . . but also.* With these constructions, the verb agrees with the subject closer to it.

NOT	Neither the students nor the teacher were satisfied with the test results.
BUT	Neither the students nor the <u>teacher</u> <u>was</u> satisfied with the test results.

Note: In these constructions, it is best to put the plural subject second. Neither the teacher nor <u>the students</u> <u>were</u> satisfied with the test results.

3d Active and Passive Voice

Verbs have two voices: active and passive. In the **active voice**, the subject of the sentence performs the action. In the **passive voice**, the subject is acted upon.

ACTIVE Jasmine drove the car.

PASSIVE The car was driven by Jasmine.

Uses of the passive voice Usually the active voice is preferable because it is more direct and concise. Sometimes, however, the passive voice is necessary, as in the following instances.

1. When the agent of the action is understood, unimportant, or unknown:

I was born in Saskatoon.

The roads were sanded regularly.

2. When you want to focus attention on the procedure and the results rather than on the agent.

> Ten milligrams of sodium chloride were placed in a beaker.

Passive constructions are often used in scientific writing to suggest that the steps and outcome will be the same no matter who performs the experiment. Researchers who place more emphasis on their own role in the experiments use the active voice more often.

Misuses of the passive voice

1. Avoid the passive voice when the active voice would be more concise, more direct, or more emphatic.

> NOT   It was reported to the president by the vice-president that an agreement was reached between the workers and the management.
>
> BUT   The vice-president reported to the president that the workers and the management had reached an agreement.

2. Avoid mixing the active and passive voices in the same sentence.

> NOT   Psychologists have found that more realistic estimates of control over future events are made by mildly depressed people.
>
> BUT   Psychologists have found that mildly depressed people make more realistic estimates of their control over future events.

B4 Adjectives and Adverbs

4a Adjectives

An **adjective** is a word that describes (or *modifies*) a noun or pronoun. Single-word adjectives may appear before a noun, after a noun, or after a state-of-being verb (*appears, is, feels, looks, sounds, tastes,* and so forth).

> The *old, bent* man hobbled down the street.
>
> The man, *old* and *bent,* hobbled down the street.
>
> He was *old* and *bent.*

Phrases and clauses can also be used as adjectives.

> An hour *of exercise* will give you more energy.
>
> The woman *dancing the lead role* is Karen Kain.
>
> People *who live in glass houses* shouldn't throw stones.

For more information on phrases and clauses, see C Writing Better Sentences.

Comparative forms of adjectives Most adjectives have comparative forms. The comparative and superlative forms of short adjectives are most often made by adding *–er* or *–est: full, fuller, fullest.* Longer adjectives add *more* or *most: beautiful, more beautiful, most beautiful.* In a few cases, the word changes completely: *good, better, best.*

The **comparative form** is used for comparing two things:

> A peacock is more beautiful than a turkey.

The **superlative form** is used for comparing something with all the other members of its class.

> The peacock is the most beautiful bird in the world.
>
> [The peacock is the most beautiful of all the birds in the world.]

A few adjectives, such as *unique* and *perfect,* are considered absolutes. They have no comparative or superlative form.

4b Adverbs

An **adverb** is a word that describes (modifies) a verb, adjective, or another adverb. Many adverbs end in *–ly.*

> Keisha ran *quickly.*
>
> She ran *very* fast.
>
> Keisha ran *more* quickly.

Phrases and clauses can also be used as adverbs modifying a verb.

> Keisha ran *into the street.*
>
> Keisha ran *until she came to the river.*

For more information on phrases and clauses, see C Writing Better Sentences.

Comparative forms of adverbs Adverbs that end in *–ly* form the comparative and superlative by adding *more* or *most: fashionably, more fashionably, most fashionably.*

Most adverbs that do not end in *–ly* change form in the comparative and superlative: *well, better, best.*

4c Troublesome Adjectives and Adverbs

Careful writers make sure they use the following adjectives and adverbs appropriately.

Farther* and *Further Although these words are often used interchangeably, the current trend is to use *farther* to indicate distance (*farther into the cave*) and *further* to indicate "to a greater degree" (*his argument went further*).

Good* and *Well *Good* is an adjective: a good book, a good cookie.

Well is usually an adverb: to draw well, to swim well. (Exception: in regard to health, *well* is an adjective. *She is not well.*)

Hopefully *Hopefully* is often used as a sentence modifier meaning "I hope" or "perhaps," as in "Hopefully, the construction work will be finished by May." But *hopefully* is really an adverb meaning "full of hope," as in this example:

> Dressed in Halloween costumes, the children shouted hopefully at the door.

Real* and *Really *Real* is an adjective: a real job, a real diamond. *Really* is an adverb: a really good job, a really expensive diamond.

Than* and *Then *Then* is an adverb meaning "at that time": Then he went home.

Than is a preposition or conjunction that introduces the second term of a comparison: faster than a speeding bullet.

Do not use *then* when you are making a comparison.

> NOT   faster *then* a speeding bullet

4d Misplaced and Dangling Modifiers

Adjectives and adverbs, as we suggested above, are modifiers. A modifier is a word, phrase, or clause that supplies further information about another word in the sentence. For clarity, a modifier must be as close as possible to the word it modifies, and there must be a word in the sentence for it to describe. If these conditions are not met, the modifier is either **misplaced** or **dangling**.

Misplaced modifiers Misplaced modifiers are single words (such as the adverbs *especially, almost, even, hardly, just, merely, nearly, only, scarcely*) or phrases that are too far away from the word they describe to be clear.

> This film *only* runs fifty-eight minutes. (Is this the only film that runs fifty-eight minutes, or does it run only fifty-eight minutes?)
>
> She told him *on Friday* she was quitting. (Did she tell him on Friday, or is she quitting on Friday?)

You can easily correct a misplaced modifier by moving it as close as possible to the word it describes.

> Only this film runs fifty-eight minutes. **OR** This film runs only fifty-eight minutes.
>
> On Friday she told him she was quitting. **OR** She told him she was quitting on Friday.

A special type of misplaced modifier is a **split infinitive.** An infinitive is *to* + a verb: *to walk, to think, to breathe.* An infinitive is split when an adverb is placed between *to* and the verb: *to seriously think.* Try to avoid splitting an infinitive when the resulting construction is awkward.

> SPLIT INFINITIVE Alex tried to carefully prepare for the exam.
>
> REVISED Alex tried to prepare carefully for the exam.

Dangling modifiers The implied subject of an introductory adverbial phrase must be the same as the subject of the main clause. If the two subjects are not the same, the phrase is called a **dangling modifier**. The phrase dangles because there is no word for it to modify.

> Bitterly regretting his misspent youth, his days in jail seemed endless.
>
> [implied subject of *regretting: he;* subject of *seemed: his days*]
>
> When empty, return them to the store.
>
> [implied subject and verb: *they are;* understood subject of *return: you*]

You can correct a misplaced modifier by moving it closer to the word it modifies. To correct a dangling modifier, you have to revise the sentence. You can do this in two ways:

1. Expand the dangling modifier into a subordinate clause.

   > Because he bitterly regretted his misspent youth, his days in jail seemed endless.
   >
   > When the bottles are empty, return them to the store.

2. Revise the main clause to give it the same subject as the implied subject of the phrase.

   > Bitterly regretting his misspent youth, the prisoner endured seemingly endless days in jail.
   >
   > When empty, the bottles should be returned to the store.

ADJECTIVES/
ADVERBS

B5 Conjunctions, Prepositions, and Interjections

5a Conjunctions

A **conjunction** is a word that joins words, phrases, clauses, or sentences. Conjunctions are of two main types: **coordinating conjunctions** and **subordinating conjunctions**.

Coordinating conjunctions The coordinating conjunctions are *and, but, or, nor,* and sometimes *for, so, yet.* (*For* can also be used as a preposition; *so* and *yet* can also be used as adverbs. These words are conjunctions only when they introduce clauses.) Remember the acronym BOYSFAN: But, Or, Yet, So, For, And, Nor. Coordinating conjunctions join words, phrases, clauses, or sentences that are equal in importance, as in these examples.

> richer *or* poorer
>
> in through the window *and* out through the door
>
> They hadn't seen the movie, *nor* had they read the book.
>
> The strikers offered to reopen negotiations. *But* the company refused.*

Correlative conjunctions (*either–or, neither–nor, not only–but also*) are two-part conjunctions that connect closely related words, phrases, or clauses of equal importance.

> *Neither* Toshimi *nor* Tariq has missed a day of work.
>
> The military *not only* closed the airports *but also* barricaded the roads.

Parallelism When sentence elements are joined by a coordinating conjunction or correlative conjunction and have the same grammatical construction, they are referred to as parallel. Use parallel structure to give equal weight to words, phrases, and clauses of equal importance; to help your reader follow the steps in a process; or to make comparisons more vivid.

> She was lucky, intelligent, and brave. (Adjectives of equal importance)
>
> Before you leave, close the windows, turn off the lights, and lock the doors. (Steps in a process)
>
> The cowardly fail because of their fear, but the courageous succeed in spite of their fear. (Comparison in parallel clauses)

---

* While it is grammatically permissible to use coordinating conjunctions at the beginning of sentences, some readers object, especially in formal academic writing. Check with your instructor.

Faulty parallelism As its name suggests, faulty parallelism occurs whenever sentence elements are not parallel. You can correct faulty parallelism by balancing words with words, phrases with phrases, and clauses with clauses.

> NOT PARALLEL To write an effective conclusion, restate your thesis, summarize your main points, and the broader context of your subject should be suggested.

> PARALLEL To write an effective conclusion, restate your thesis, summarize your main points, and suggest the broader context of your subject.

> NOT PARALLEL As a winner you will achieve success, and respect will also come your way.

> PARALLEL As a winner, you will achieve both success and respect.

Subordinating conjunctions Subordinating conjunctions join clauses of less importance to main clauses. Here is a list of the words most commonly used as subordinating conjunctions.

Note: These words can also be used as other parts of speech, such as prepositions and adverbs. They are called subordinating conjunctions *only* when followed by a clause.

after	because	in order that	until
although	before	provided that	when
as	even though	since	where
as long as	if	unless	while

Relative pronouns (*that, which, who, whoever, whom, whomever*) also function as subordinating conjunctions (see B2a).

Conjunctive adverbs Subordinating conjunctions are sometimes confused with conjunctive adverbs. Conjunctive adverbs are words that express logical relationships between clauses; they include words such as *accordingly, besides, consequently, furthermore, hence, however, likewise, moreover, nevertheless, otherwise, still, therefore, thus*. Here is an easy way to remember the difference: subordinating conjunctions must come at the beginning of a clause, whereas conjunctive adverbs can be moved to different positions.

> The Prime Minister called an election even though [subordinating conjunction] his party clearly could not win.

> The Prime Minister called an election; however [conjunctive adverb], his party clearly could not win.

CONJUNCTIONS

> The Prime Minister called an election; his party clearly could not win, however [conjunctive adverb].

Clauses beginning with subordinating conjunctions are punctuated differently from clauses with conjunctive adverbs, so it is important to know the difference. For more on punctuating clauses, see C Writing Better Sentences; F2 Comma; and F3 Semicolon.

Coordination and subordination Coordination and subordination help you to use the structure of the sentence to emphasize your main point. Use **coordination** to join points of equal importance. To create coordination, join words, phrases, and clauses with coordinating or correlative conjunctions.

Use **subordination** to join points of unequal importance. To create subordination, put your main point in the main clause and your less important point in a subordinate clause or phrase.

> Although everyone was aware of the problem, no one knew what to do about it.
>
> Marta had her car serviced before she set out on her journey.

The clause or phrase at the end of the sentence always gets more emphasis. Thus, for maximum emphasis, put your main idea in a main clause and put that clause at the end of the sentence. Notice the difference in the emphasis given to the main clause in these two sentences.

> Although the meeting was well publicized, it attracted little interest. (Putting the main clause last gives it maximum emphasis)
>
> The meeting attracted little interest even though it was well publicized. (Putting the subordinate clause last evens the emphasis given to both clauses)

Faulty coordination Faulty coordination occurs if you join ideas that are unrelated or not of equal importance.

> UNRELATED IDEAS The movie was boring and pretentious and hundreds of people lined up for hours to see it.
>
> REVISED Although the movie was boring and pretentious, hundreds of people lined up for hours to see it.
>
> UNEQUAL IDEAS Hamlet is Prince of Denmark and he is disillusioned by his mother's hasty remarriage.
>
> REVISED Hamlet, Prince of Denmark, is disillusioned by his mother's hasty remarriage.

Don't use *and* as an all-purpose conjunction. Although *and* can sometimes be a weak signal of causal connection (I was late and I missed the bus), it's best to use *and* only when you want to signal that what follows is a coordinate fact or idea.

> NOT   Dan was chronically tired and he had anemia.
>
> BUT   Dan was chronically tired because he had anemia.

Faulty subordination Faulty subordination occurs when subordinating conjunctions are used inappropriately. Here are the most common causes of this error.

1. Attaching the subordinating conjunction to the wrong clause.

    > FAULTY Although they missed the plane, they left in plenty of time to reach the airport.
    >
    > REVISED They missed the plane although they left in plenty of time to reach the airport.

2. Using an imprecise subordinating conjunction, especially *since* and *as*. *Since* can mean "because," but *since* can also mean "from the time that." If these two meanings might be confused, use *because* to indicate a causal connection.

    > CONFUSING Since she broke her ankle, she has been housebound.
    >
    > CLEAR Because she broke her ankle, she has been housebound.
    >
    > CLEAR From the time she broke her ankle, she has been housebound.

    As can be used to mean *because,* but it's best to use *as* to mean "while."

    > CLEAR As Felicity struggled to listen to the lecture, her mind began to wander.
    >
    > CONFUSING As Raul is the manager, he thinks he should make all the decisions.
    >
    > CLEAR Raul thinks he should make all the decisions because he is the manager.

3. Using two conjunctions that mean the same thing.

    > MIXED Because he did not want to pay a late penalty for his income tax, so he rushed to the post office just before midnight.
    >
    > REVISED Because he did not want to pay a late penalty for his income tax, he rushed to the post office just before midnight.
    >
    > OR He did not want to pay a late penalty for his income tax, so he rushed to the post office just before midnight.

4. Using too many subordinate clauses in a sentence. Avoid beginning and ending a sentence with similar subordinate clauses. Also avoid piling up clauses beginning with relative pronouns, such as *that, which,* and *who.*

EXCESSIVE SUBORDINATION Because she was afraid of a hailstorm, she covered all the windows because the force of the hail might break them.

REVISED Fearing a hailstorm, she covered all the windows to protect them.

EXCESSIVE SUBORDINATION The novelist who wins this contest which is sponsored by a major publisher will be taken on a cross-country tour that begins July 1.

REVISED The novelist who wins this contest, sponsored by a major publisher, will be taken on a cross-country tour beginning July 1.

5b Prepositions

Prepositions are those little words you probably learned from *Sesame Street* that indicate relationships in time, space, manner, and so forth. Here is a partial list of prepositions.

against	by	into	through	upon
around	down	of	to	with
at	for	on	toward	within
before	from	onto	under	without

The noun or pronoun that follows the preposition is called the **object of the preposition**. If you speak English as a first language, you are not likely to make mistakes with prepositions. You may, however, make errors in subject–verb agreement because you confuse the object of the preposition with the subject of the sentence (see B3c).

5c Interjections

An **interjection** is a word "thrown into" a sentence to express emotion, such as *hurray, oh, well,* and less polite words. An interjection at the beginning of a sentence is set off with a comma. An interjection in the middle of a sentence is set off with a pair of commas.

Oops, I dropped my wallet in a puddle.

It must have been, oh, ten years since I saw you last.

Interjections are seldom used in formal academic writing.

C Writing Better Sentences

In academic writing, as in most business and professional writing, the basic unit of *thought* is the paragraph, which generally states a point and then develops that point through details and examples. Within each paragraph, the basic unit of *expression* is the sentence. The boundaries of the sentence are clearly marked by a capital at the beginning and a period at the end, and the words, as you no doubt learned in grade school, express a complete idea. Your readers will expect sentences that are well structured and correctly punctuated. The aim is not correctness for its own sake, but correctness as an aid to meaning. Poorly constructed, badly punctuated sentences are hard to understand.

Consider an extreme example. In the following paragraph, we have removed all internal punctuation and introduced problems in sentence structure.

> John A. Macdonald was a colourful prime minister before Confederation he had proved his skill as a politician by clinging to power for over thirty years it showed he was bold shrewd and stubborn although he drank heavily still he maintained a firm grip on his party and the country because he helped to bring about the birth of a nation and was serving his country in its infancy he is known as the Father of Confederation a man with great historical importance and also who had many weaknesses Macdonald continues to fascinate historians and biographers.

Notice that without periods or other punctuation to mark sentence boundaries, it is hard to tell how ideas fit together. Was Macdonald a colourful prime minister before Confederation? Of course not—there was no prime minister before Confederation. Was he bold, shrewd, and stubborn although he drank heavily? No, he possessed those character traits regardless of his alcohol consumption.

This paragraph illustrates the difficulties caused by the absence of sentence boundaries. Sentences that run together like this are called *fused sentences*. The wrong punctuation, resulting in *sentence fragments* and *comma splices,* may create similar problems for your reader. We discuss these problems in detail below, along with other errors in sentence structure. First, however, we will discuss clauses and phrases, the building blocks from which sentences are constructed. Understanding these building blocks will help you to write better sentences.

C1 Recognizing Complete Sentences: Clauses and Phrases

1a Main Clauses

In formal academic writing, any words punctuated as a sentence must contain a **main clause**. A main clause (also known as an *independent clause*) consists of one or more subjects and one or more verbs that together express a complete idea. A main clause may take the form of a statement, a question, or a command.

> The boy [subject] hit [verb] the ball. (Statement: declarative sentence)
>
> Did [verb] the boy [subject] hit [verb] the ball? (Question: interrogative sentence)
>
> Hit [verb] the ball [*you* is the understood subject]. (Command: imperative sentence)

A main clause may contain more than one subject and/or more than one verb.

> Jack and Jill ran.
>
> Jack and Jill ran and played.

It may also contain adjectives that *modify* (describe or give additional information about) the subject or adverbs that modify the verb (see B4).

> The ramshackle [adjective] cabin [subject] burned [verb]
>
> quickly [adverb].

Remember this definition: a main clause is a group of words with a subject–verb core that can stand alone as a complete sentence.

1b Phrases

A main clause may also contain one or more **phrases**. A phrase is a group of words that does not contain a subject–verb core. The three most common types of phrases are prepositional, participial, and infinitive phrases.

Prepositional phrases **Prepositional phrases** begin with a preposition (see B5b) and end with a noun (see B1) or pronoun (see B2).

> The referee on the sideline is waving a flag. (*On the sideline:* prepositional phrase modifying *referee*)

Participial phrases **Participial phrases** all begin with a participle (the *-ing* or past tense form of a verb) and end with a noun or pronoun (see B3a and F2e).

The player lying on the ground has broken her ankle. (*Lying on the ground:* participial phrase modifying *player*)

She will be carried to the ambulance parked just off the field. (*Parked just off the field:* participial phrase modifying *ambulance*)

Infinitive phrases **Infinitive phrases** begin with an infinitive (*to* + a verb) and end with a noun or pronoun.

Jill wanted to help Jack. (*To help Jack:* infinitive phrase modifying *wanted*)

1c Simple and Compound Sentences

A sentence that consists of one main clause and its modifiers is called a **simple sentence.** A sentence that contains two or more main clauses is called a **compound sentence.** The main clauses may be joined with a semicolon, a comma and a coordinating conjunction (*and, but, or, nor, for, so, yet*), or a semicolon and a conjunctive adverb (such as *therefore, thus, however, consequently*).

SIMPLE SENTENCES	Civil unrest has increased. Many people have fled the country.
COMPOUND SENTENCES	Civil unrest has increased; many people have fled the country.
	Civil unrest has increased, so many people have fled the country.
	Civil unrest has increased; consequently, many people have fled the country.

1d Subordinate Clauses

Like main clauses, **subordinate clauses** contain a subject and verb. Unlike main clauses, however, subordinate clauses (also known as dependent clauses) cannot stand alone as complete sentences. As its name suggests, a subordinate clause is *subordinate to* or *dependent upon* the main clause. Subordinate clauses may, for example, add extra information or qualify the statement made in the main clause. The precise relationship is signalled by the subordinating conjunction or relative pronoun that introduces the subordinate clause (for lists of the most common subordinating conjunctions and relative pronouns, see B5a Conjunctions).

> *When we finished dinner,* we went to a movie.
>
> The movie, *which starred Colin Firth and Keira Knightley,* was entertaining.

If the ideas are not logically related (as in *Although I like chicken, I went to the store*), the error is called **faulty subordination** (see B5a).

Subordinate clauses that begin with a relative pronoun (see B2a) describe the preceding noun or pronoun.

> The next car *that I buy* will be an energy-efficient hybrid.

The relative pronoun may also function as the subject of the subordinate clause.

> The car *that hit the lamppost* was a total writeoff.

Note: Often *that* is omitted when it is not the subject. Don't overlook subordinate clauses of this type.

> The horse he picks [*that he picks*] never wins.

1e Complex and Compound-Complex Sentences

A sentence that contains one main clause and one or more subordinate clauses is called a **complex sentence**. A sentence that contains two or more main clauses and one or more subordinate clauses is called a **compound-complex sentence**.

The subordinate clause may come before or after the main clause, or it may come between the subject and verb of the main clause. If the subordinate clause comes before the main clause, put a comma after it. This use of the comma is covered in F2b.

COMPLEX SENTENCES

If you are cold, then put on a sweater.

Everyone left *as soon as the meeting ended.*

The candidate *who gets* the most votes will become the next mayor.

COMPOUND-COMPLEX SENTENCE

Although the oil industry reported record profits, one company laid off five thousand workers, and another company closed two plants.

You should now have a better grasp of what makes a complete sentence. A grammatically complete sentence must contain at least one main clause. It may contain more than one main clause; it may also contain one or more subordinate clauses and any number of phrases. But without a main clause, it is not a complete sentence.

C2 Correcting Errors in Sentence Structure

Understanding the difference between main clauses, subordinate clauses, and phrases will help you to identify and correct common errors in sentence structure. Here we will discuss four common problems: sentence fragments, comma splices, fused sentences, and mixed constructions. The first three problems result from failing to punctuate sentences correctly. Mixed constructions occur when grammatically incompatible elements are linked together.

2a Sentence Fragments

As its name implies, a **sentence fragment** is a grammatically incomplete sentence. The sentence may be incomplete because the subject or verb has accidentally been omitted. More often, a subordinate clause or phrase has been punctuated as a sentence.

In advertising, personal essays, and fiction, sentence fragments may be used intentionally for emphasis.

> No more war.

In academic writing, sentence fragments are less acceptable because they seem too informal. They may also be confusing, especially if they are accidental.

To correct sentence fragments, supply the missing word(s) or attach the fragment to the appropriate sentence.

> FRAGMENT The president given the choice of resigning or being impeached.
>
> COMPLETE SENTENCE The president was given the choice of resigning or being impeached. (Auxilliary verb added)
>
> FRAGMENT Even though students had been warned that they would be expected to write an in-class essay. Many of them arrived late.
>
> COMPLETE SENTENCE Even though students had been warned that they would be expected to write an in-class essay, many of them arrived late. (Subordinate clause attached to the main clause)

FRAGMENT Shakespeare's play *Richard III* deals with fundamental human problems. Such as the conflict between good and evil.

COMPLETE SENTENCE Shakespeare's play *Richard III* deals with fundamental human problems, such as the conflict between good and evil. (Phrase attached to main clause)

2b Comma Splices

The **comma splice** (sometimes called the *comma fault*) occurs when two main clauses are joined only by a comma, with no conjunction to show how the clauses are related. Each of the following sentences contains a comma splice.

1. Women become addicted to working out at the gym, they look a little too healthy in their skin-tight pants and bra-tops.

2. She wanted to win the prize, she practised hours every day.

3. If you expect too much you are sure to be disappointed, if you expect too little you may be pleasantly surprised.

4. Many transit users make the mistake of boarding the bus empty-handed, they have nothing with which to mark off their territory.

5. The causeway brings more tourists to Prince Edward Island, they don't stay as long.

Whenever you join two separate ideas, you need more than a comma to show how they are related. There are five ways to correct comma splices. Choose the method that best expresses the relationship between the clauses.

CORRECTING COMMA SPLICES

1. If the clauses are long or the ideas are not closely related, separate the clauses with a period.

   Women become addicted to working out at the gym. They look a little too healthy in their skin-tight pants and bra-tops.

2. If the ideas are of equal importance, join the clauses with a comma and the appropriate coordinating conjunction (*and, but, or, nor, for, so, yet*).

   She wanted to win the prize, so she practised hours every day.

3. If the ideas are closely related and parallel in structure, join the clauses with a semicolon.

   If you expect too much, you are sure to be disappointed; if you expect too little, you may be pleasantly surprised.

   (Continued)

(Continued)

4. If the ideas are closely related and the second clause expresses a contrast, qualification, or addition to the first, join the clauses with a semicolon and the appropriate conjunctive adverb (for a list of conjunctive adverbs, see B5a). If the conjunctive adverb is a word of more than one syllable, set it off with a comma.

   Many transit users make the mistake of boarding the bus empty-handed; consequently, they have nothing with which to mark off their territory.

5. If the clauses are not of equal importance, put the less important idea into a subordinate clause. Notice that when the subordinate clause comes first, it is separated from the main clause by a comma.

   Although the causeway brings more tourists to Prince Edward Island, they don't stay as long.

Note: If you join two independent clauses with only a comma and a conjunctive adverb, you will have created a comma splice. Make sure that you use a semicolon to join the clauses.

2c Fused Sentences

Fused sentences (sometimes called *run-on sentences*) contain two or more main clauses, but there is no punctuation to show how the clauses are related.

> Television networks make money by selling advertising time therefore programs must appeal to people who can afford the products advertised.
>
> Cell phones are not a status symbol anymore most people have them.

Fused sentences can be corrected in the same way as comma splices. Be sure not to create a comma splice by merely putting a comma between main clauses.

2d Mixed Constructions

A **mixed construction** will occur if you begin a sentence with one grammatical construction and complete it with one that is different and incompatible. Any of the errors listed below will produce a mixed construction.

Putting a subordinate clause before or after a linking verb Readers expect linking verbs, such as *is* and *was,* to be followed by a noun or noun clause, not by a subordinate clause that modifies the verb. Formulations like

SENTENCES

an example of this is when and *the reason for this is because* are typical of this sort of mixed construction.

> MIXED *An example* of his hostility *is when* he turns his homicidal bull loose on the mushroom pickers.

> MIXED *One reason* she dropped out of school *is because* she was in constant conflict with authority.

You can revise these sentences by supplying the missing noun or noun clause.

> REVISED An example of his hostility is his decision to turn his homicidal bull loose on the mushroom pickers.

> REVISED One reason she dropped out of school is her constant conflict with authority.

Another way to revise these sentences is to replace the linking verb.

> REVISED He shows his hostility when he turns his homicidal bull loose on the mushroom pickers.

> REVISED She dropped out of school because she was in constant conflict with authority.

Omitting the subject Leaving out the subject typically produces sentences like this:

> MIXED In this documentary makes the point that gorillas are a seriously endangered species.

This sentence is confusing because the prepositional phrase *In this documentary,* which normally introduces a grammatically complete sentence, seems to be the subject of the sentence. You could revise by omitting the preposition.

> REVISED This documentary makes the point that gorillas are a seriously endangered species.

Or you could keep the prepositional phrase and add a subject to the main clause.

> REVISED In this documentary, the filmmaker shows that gorillas are a seriously endangered species.

Leaving out part of a comparison Sentences that begin with phrases such as *the more, the less, the worse, and the further* suggest a comparison. You will confuse your reader if you fail to complete the comparison.

> MIXED The less time I have, I have a lot to do.

You could revise this sentence by pairing *less* with *more.*

> REVISED The less time I have, the more I have to do.

Mixing a question and a statement Be clear about whether or not you are posing a question or making a statement. You will confuse your readers if you mix a question with a statement.

> MIXED The little boy plaintively asked his mother when will she finish writing her essay?

You could revise this sentence by rephrasing the question as direct speech.

> REVISED The little boy plaintively asked his mother, "When will you finish writing your essay?"

You could also make the question a statement.

> REVISED The little boy plaintively asked his mother when she would finish writing her essay.

D Writing Better Paragraphs

In Part 1 (Rhetoric) we stress the importance of writing paragraphs with a main point developed through reasons, examples, and other relevant details. In Part 3 (Handbook), C Writing Better Sentences, we show how to correct errors in sentence structure. This chapter will give you tips on polishing your writing: using sentence structure to create emphasis and to signal movement from point to detail; using transitions to indicate relationships in space, time, and logic; and making every word count. This kind of polishing will help your reader move surely and easily from point to detail and back again.

Without this kind of polishing, your ideas may be hard to follow. Consider this paragraph analyzing symbolism in Margaret Atwood's novel *Cat's Eye:*

> The most important symbol in Margaret Atwood's novel is the cat's eye. *Cat's Eye* is the title. *The Dictionary of Symbols and Imagery* by Ad de Vries gives several meanings of both cats and eyes. Cats have several symbolic interpretations, both good and evil. The eye also has both good and evil interpretations. Cats are beautiful and cuddly on the outside. They are highly independent. They are thought to be the most cunning and untrustworthy of all animals. The duality of their nature is most apparent in their "inverted playfulness" (de Vries 86). Cats turn the act of killing a mouse into a game. The eye can be either evil or protecting. De Vries says that "the divinity can be malevolent: the evil eye, one that scorches" (171). The eye can also be a charm against evil. The Eye of Horus in folklore protects against the Evil Eye of envy, malice, and the like (de Vries 172). The main character of the novel is Elaine. As a child Elaine carries her cat's eye marble everywhere. It is a charm that she hopes will protect her from the cruelty of the girls at school. She finally realizes that she has become like the glass marble. Glass eyes are unmoving and unfeeling.

This paragraph is hard to understand for three main reasons:

1. **Lack of sentence variety** All the sentences have the same basic structure and are about the same length. As a result, it's hard to distinguish the ideas from the examples that support them.

2. **Lack of transitions** There are no words, phrases, or clauses that establish relationships between sentences. As a result, it is hard to tell

whether the writer intended a particular statement to reinforce, qualify, or contradict another statement or to suggest a cause-and-effect relationship.

3. **Wordiness** Because sentence structure and transitions are not used effectively, the writing is wordy. Readers get bogged down in unnecessary repetition.

If you compare the paragraph opposite with the revised version below, you can see just how big a difference these simple changes make.

> The most important symbol in Margaret Atwood's novel is the image of the cat's eye that gives the book its title. According to Ad de Vries in the *Dictionary of Symbols and Imagery,* both the cat and the eye have several symbolic meanings, good and evil. Cats have a dual nature: beautiful and cuddly on the outside, they are nevertheless highly independent and thought to be the most cunning and untrustworthy of all animals. The duality of their nature is most apparent in their "inverted playfulness" (de Vries 86): they turn the act of killing a mouse into a game. Similarly, the eye can be either an Evil Eye, "one that scorches" (de Vries 171), or a protecting presence, like the Eye of Horus that serves as a charm against the Evil Eye of envy and malice (de Vries 172). As a child Elaine, the main character of the novel, uses her cat's eye marble as a charm to protect herself against the cruelty of the girls at her school. By the end of the novel Elaine realizes that she has become like the glass marble, unmoving and unfeeling.

D1 Creating Sentence Variety

1a Sentence Length

Your main points will be clearer and more emphatic if you express them in short sentences. Use longer sentences to gather details, reasons, and examples that support and develop your main points.

> In constructing the Imperial Hotel in Tokyo, Frank Lloyd Wright had to solve several architectural problems [main point: 16 words]. He had to deal with difficulties created by earthquake tremors, correct the weak soil base of the hotel site, and keep the building from cracking [series of explanations: 25 words].

1b Sentence Patterns

The basic sentence pattern in English is subject + verb + object (*Jennifer hit the ball*). If all of your sentences follow this pattern, however, your writing will soon become as monotonous as a Grade 1 reader. You will also make it more difficult for your reader to distinguish major and minor points.

1c Common Sentence Patterns

Here are the most common sentence patterns:

The loose sentence: subject + verb + modifier

> The team lost money, despite better players and an improved stadium.

This is the most common sentence pattern and is thus the easiest for most readers to understand. The modifier gains emphasis because it is placed at the end of the sentence. Readers would expect the sentence that follows it to focus on the improvement in players and the stadium.

The periodic sentence: modifier + subject + verb

> Despite better players and an improved stadium, the team lost money.

Because we have to wait for the subject and the verb, this sentence pattern creates suspense and interest. It puts maximum emphasis on the fact that the team lost money, so readers would expect the next sentence to deal with this issue.

The embedded sentence: subject + modifier + verb

> The team, despite better players and an improved stadium, lost money.

This sentence pattern slows the reader down because the subject and the verb are separated by a lengthy modifier. It is useful if you want to imitate the process of thinking through a problem. It also leads readers to expect that the next sentence will begin to explore the real reasons for the team's inability to make a profit.

The balanced construction: parallel main clauses

> The team gained good players and a better stadium; it still lost money.

The balanced construction creates a compound sentence in which two closely related main clauses with the same structure are joined with a semicolon; a comma and a coordinate conjunction; or a semicolon and a conjunctive adverb. It is especially useful when you want to create a contrast or to suggest a choice between two equal possibilities.

In the following example, notice how emphatic the balanced construction seems after the longer sentences that precede it.

> It would seem from watching CNN that crime has reached epidemic proportions. The truth is that crime statistics are declining. Crime has not grown; fear has.

Sentences with other parallel elements For maximum effect, arrange parallel words, phrases, or clauses in an order of ascending interest, with the most important detail last.

> Although the team is still losing money, it has better players, an improved stadium, and fiercely loyal fans.

For more on parallelism, see B5a Conjunctions.

Rhetorical questions Asking a question actively engages your reader in the process of reading and thinking about your subject. You may give your essay an inductive pattern of organization by asking a question that the essay will explicitly answer.

> The team has better players and an improved stadium. So why is it still losing money?

Or you may pose a question ironically, creating a bond with your reader by assuming that you would both agree on the answer:

> *Ever After* glitters with the predictable Hollywood sparkle.
> Would Prince Henry really have looked twice if this beautiful brain belonged to a homely peasant girl rather than Drew Barrymore?

Questions of this type backfire if your reader disagrees with you. Consequently, some instructors ban questions altogether. If you do use questions, use them sparingly and make sure your answer is clear. Peppering your work with questions will create a tone that seems hectoring or indecisive (for more on tone, see E Creating an Appropriate Tone).

Varying the structure of your sentences will help you to avoid monotony and to clarify the relationships among ideas, explanations, and details. On the other hand, if every sentence follows a different pattern, your reader will find your paragraph confusing. Here are some guidelines for varying sentence structure effectively.

1. Keep the structure of topic sentences fairly simple. When you are making major points, you don't want to lose your reader in elaborate sentence patterns.
2. Change your sentence structure when you introduce an explanation. If your explanation takes more than one sentence, keep the sentences in similar patterns.
3. When you shift from explanation to details, change your sentence pattern.
4. Keep similar sentence patterns for all your details.

D2 Making Transitions

Transitional words and phrases are important for two reasons. They increase your reader's understanding of how your ideas are related. They also create a sense of continuity, both within and between paragraphs, because one idea leads smoothly to the next.

2a Sentence and Paragraph Hooks

Sentence hooks are words and phrases used to create continuity. You can hook sentences together with pronouns, demonstrative pronouns, synonyms, and repeated words and phrases.

Pronouns After the first reference by name, use pronouns and possessive pronouns to indicate a continuity of subject. Make sure that the reference is clear (see B2c).

> Margaret Atwood has written several novels. *Her* most recent is . . . *She* has also written . . .

Demonstrative pronouns To avoid repeating your last point, refer to it with a demonstrative pronoun (*this, that, these, those*) and a noun that identifies the subject to which you are referring.

> During the Depression, prairie farmers suffered because of the severe drought. *This problem* . . .

> Macbeth murders Duncan and is responsible for the murder of Banquo and several others. *These acts* of violence . . .

Synonyms and repeated words and phrases Keep your reader's attention on your subject by repeating key words and phrases or by using synonyms. Notice the continuity created by the repetition of "race" and "racism" in the following paragraph.

> So what is racism? Racism is the idea, whether in the back of your mind or deep in your heart, that there are large groupings within humanity that can be distinguished as separate races, and that the race you belong to is superior to other races in mind, body, and character. The problem with this concept, outside of the monstrous behaviour that such a belief justifies, is that the very notion of race has no scientific value. It is true that there are differences as to how people from different parts of the planet look. That much is obvious. But most of us are unaware that we differ in only 5% of our bodily features. This hardly seems like enough to classify us as separate "races." And even though some of these differences are dramatic, we also note that there is as much variation *within* a so-called race as *between* the

so-called races. And how do we deal with people of mixed "race" parentage? How do we describe them? And what about those sub "race" nationalities that look significantly like peoples of other "races," such as the African Kalahari Desert dwellers who appear to be Asians, or the Australian and Dravidian Aborigines who appear to be straight-haired Africans?

Paragraph hooks are words and phrases that recall key ideas to create continuity between paragraphs.

1. Repeat single words or phrases or use synonyms to link the last sentence of one paragraph to the first sentence of the next.

   > LAST SENTENCE OF PARAGRAPH 1 His pride thus leads him to reject his friends' offers of help.

   > FIRST SENTENCE OF PARAGRAPH 2 His pride also prevents him from helping himself.

2. Use phrases, clauses, or occasionally whole sentences that briefly recall the ideas of one paragraph at the beginning of the next.

   > FIRST TOPIC SENTENCE Mackenzie King, Diefenbaker, and Pearson . . .

   > SECOND TOPIC SENTENCE These three prime ministers were not the only ones to favour such a policy. . . .

2b Transitional Words and Phrases

Transitional words and phrases are means of indicating relationships in time, space, and logic.

RELATIONSHIP		SAMPLE TRANSITIONAL WORDS AND PHRASES
time		before, after, meanwhile, as soon as, during, until, then
space		on the right, near, farther away
logic	1. addition	and, another, a second, also, too, furthermore, moreover, not only . . . but also, first, second, etc.
	2. contrast	but, in contrast, yet, however, on the other hand, nevertheless, otherwise
	3. similarity	just as, like, likewise, similarly, in the same way

(Continued)

PARAGRAPHS

(Continued)

4. examples	for example, for instance, to be specific, in particular, to illustrate
5. cause and effect	therefore, thus, so, for, hence, because, consequently, as a result, accordingly
6. concession and qualification	although, despite, while it is true that . . .
7. emphasis	most important, a crucial point, significantly, of overwhelming importance

You can use these transitional words and phrases to provide continuity both within paragraphs and between paragraphs.

D3 Being Concise

When you write a draft, you may find yourself making false starts on sentences and using inexact, wordy language because you are still working out your ideas. Or you may repeat ideas instead of giving evidence to support them.

You can see both problems in the following draft paragraph from an essay comparing homeless people and nomads.

> There is a difference between being a homeless person and being a nomad. Being homeless is a state of mind; being a nomad is a way of life. Although homeless people have no place to live, many of them do not want a home. When they are placed in shelters or housing, they leave because they do not want ties with family or society. Homeless people have very few possessions, and because they really have no permanent place to stay, they somewhat tend to carry their rather few possessions around with them. Nomads, on the other hand, move from place to place, usually seasonally. Although they have no fixed residence, they tend to stay in different spots within a certain territory. It is a feature of traditional nomads that they live in family groups or small communities. When they move, the whole group moves together. Modern nomads don't have a permanent residence. At different times they may travel to different family members. When they arrive, they may stay with different family members for a few months at a time. When they travel, they take most of the things they own and put them in a storage facility. They take only the most essential things with them when they move. They leave things that are not essential behind. In these ways nomads are different from homeless people.

When you revise, try to be more concise. Here are some suggestions:

1. Choose exact nouns, verbs, and modifiers.

> NOT   When they travel, they take most of the things they own and put them in a storage facility. (18 words)
>
> BUT   When they travel, they store most of their belongings. (9 words)

2. Replace vague words, such as *very, somewhat, really,* and *rather,* with more exact words.

> NOT   Homeless people have very few possessions, and because they really have no permanent place to stay, they somewhat tend to carry their rather few possessions around with them. (28 words)
>
> BUT   Because homeless people have no permanent place to stay, they tend to carry their few possessions around with them. (19 words)

3. Avoid carelessly repeating words and ideas.

> NOT   They take only the most essential things with them when they move. They leave things that are not essential behind.
>
> BUT   They take only the most essential things with them.

4. Don't overuse *there is/are* and *it is . . . that* to introduce sentences.

> NOT   There is a difference between being a homeless person and being a nomad.
>
> BUT   Being a homeless person is different from being a nomad.
>
> NOT   It is a feature of traditional nomads that they live in family groups or small communities.
>
> BUT   Traditional nomads live in family groups or small communities.

5. Reduce sentences to clauses, clauses to phrases, and phrases to single words.

> NOT   At different times they may travel to different family members. When they arrive, they may stay with different family members for a few months at a time. (27 words)
>
> BUT   They may travel to different family members, staying for a few months with each one. (15 words)

E Creating an Appropriate Tone

Formal academic writing does not have to be stuffy or difficult to read. Indeed, you want to create a sense of yourself as a friendly, reasonable person writing for equally friendly, reasonable readers who may be less well informed or hold a different opinion. You create this tone by choosing appropriate pronouns of address, by using an appropriate level of diction, and by using words that accurately convey your meaning.

E1 You and Your Reader: Pronouns of Address

The **pronouns of address** you choose for a piece of writing set up a particular relationship among writer, reader, and subject. First-person pronouns suggest a conversation between friends. If you were writing about a personal experience, you would naturally use first-person pronouns (*I, me, my/ mine, we, us, our/ours*), as George Orwell does in "Shooting an Elephant" (Readings). Second-person pronouns, on the other hand, suggest a conversation between teacher and learner. Thus if you were giving directions on how to carry out a process, you would use second-person pronouns, as W. S. Merwin does in "Unchopping a Tree" (Readings). You might also use second-person pronouns to draw your reader into a hypothetical situation: "What would you do if you encountered a bear?"

Third-person pronouns suggest a more detached, objective point of view. Most often in college and university essays, you will want to keep your reader's attention focused on your subject, so you will use third-person pronouns (*he, she, it, they*). Most of the essays in the Readings, you will notice, are in the third person.

Some instructors forbid the use of first-person pronouns in academic writing. Others permit limited use of first-person pronouns when you clearly need to indicate your agreement or disagreement with a position or to express consensus with your readers. Follow these guidelines to ensure that you use the first person only when necessary and that you do so as unobtrusively as possible.

USING FIRST-PERSON REFERENCES

1. Avoid using "I" when you can rewrite the sentence to give a more general application.

   NOT   I had a hard time figuring out what these two lines mean. (Implies it's your fault)

   BUT   The meaning of these two lines is hard to grasp. (Implies that others would have the same difficulty)

2. Avoid apologetic expressions such as "this is only my opinion" and "I hope I will be able to show."

3. Avoid stilted expressions such as "one" and "this writer."

4. Use "I" as necessary when giving a personal example to support a point.

5. Use "I would argue" or similar wording when necessary to make a clear distinction between your position and the position you are arguing against.

6. Use "we" sparingly to refer to people in general. Be careful not to overgeneralize.

   NOT   We all remember our high school teachers with affection.

   BUT   Many of us remember our high school teachers with affection.

7. Keep expressions such as "I think" or "we have seen" inconspicuous by putting them inside the sentence.

   NOT   We have seen that oil is a major factor in the politics of the Middle East.

   BUT   Oil, as we have seen, is a major factor in the politics of the Middle East.

8. Avoid using "you" to refer to people in general (see E1b).

   NOT   By the end of the play, you can see that Macbeth is desperate.

   BUT   By the end of the play, Macbeth is obviously desperate.

1a Using Third-Person Pronouns: *He, She, They*

Although *he* and other masculine singular pronouns have traditionally been used to refer to both men and women, as in the example "The driver is responsible for the safety of all passengers in *his* vehicle," many people feel that this usage contributes to gender stereotyping. To avoid alienating your reader, try to use more inclusive language, but be careful not to introduce errors in pronoun agreement, as in "The driver is responsible for the safety of all passengers in *their* vehicle." Here are some suggestions for avoiding both sexist language and pronoun agreement errors. For more on the latter, see B2b Pronoun Agreement.

DICTION

USING INCLUSIVE LANGUAGE

1. Reword the sentence to eliminate unnecessary gender pronouns.

   NOT   The average commuter drives his car fifty kilometres a day.

   BUT   The average commuter drives fifty kilometres a day.

2. Make the noun and pronouns plural.

   NOT   The enterprising executive sends his managers to study foreign business practices.

   BUT   Enterprising executives send their managers to study foreign business practices.

3. Alternate references to boys and girls, men and women in examples.

   NOT   Teachers sometimes complain about their students: "He never does his homework," "He constantly disrupts the class," "He never listens."

   BUT   Teachers sometimes complain about their students: "She never does her homework," "He constantly disrupts the class," "She never listens."

1b Avoiding Shifts in Pronouns of Address

Once you have decided on first-, second-, or third-person pronouns as your basic mode, be consistent in using them. If you shift pronouns without good reason, you will confuse or jar your reader.

The most common problem is the inappropriate use of first- or second-person pronouns in a piece of writing that is primarily in the third person, as in the following example:

> The student board governing the residence hall recently approved the installation of a security system designed to curb theft and vandalism by outsiders. With this system, you have locked doors, identification cards, security guards, and an obligatory sign-in procedure for visitors. Unfortunately, the system is ineffective because most of the damage is done by students who live in the residence.

You could eliminate the inappropriate shift to "you" in this paragraph by beginning the second sentence with "This system includes."

E2 Choosing Appropriate Diction

One important element in creating an appropriate tone, as we have seen, is choosing the right pronouns of address. Equally important is your choice of **diction**: the individual words that make up your sentences. If you rely too heavily on formal, abstract language, your writing will seem stuffy and hard to understand. If, however, your writing is too informal, your reader may not take your opinions seriously.

Here are some guidelines for achieving a balance.

1. **Eliminate very informal language and slang; they suggest you do not take your subject seriously.**

    NOT   Bolivia has a lot of social and economic problems.

    BUT   Bolivia has many [a great many] social and economic problems.

    NOT   Hamlet was cheesed off by his mom's hasty marriage to his uncle.

    BUT   Hamlet was infuriated by his mother's hasty marriage to his uncle.

2. **While the presence of some contractions (*don't, can't*) will give your writing a friendlier tone, too many contractions will make your writing seem too casual for a formal essay.**

    NOT   Hamlet decides he'll feign madness while he's gathering proof that the ghost's telling the truth.

    BUT   Hamlet decides he will feign madness while he is gathering proof that the ghost is telling the truth.

3. **Eliminate or define specialized vocabulary that may be unfamiliar to your reader.**

    NOT   Self-worth is affirmed when one's self-image is validated by one's significant others.

    BUT   People like themselves better when their ideas and feelings about themselves are confirmed by those they care about.

4. **Rewrite sentences that are too abstract or too grandiose.**

    NOT   The interpersonal interaction between volunteer counsellors and clients can provide the opportunity for both parties to gain a sense of self-worth and significance in the midst of our institutionalized society. (Too abstract)

    BUT   Meetings between volunteer counsellors and clients can help both to feel more worthwhile.

    NOT   Throughout history man has struggled to understand his place in the ever-changing world in which he was only one infinitesimal link in the infinite chain of being. (Too grandiose and sexist)

    BUT   Men and women often struggle to understand their place in the world.

5. **Eliminate expressions that are too apologetic or argumentative.**

    NOT   I hope I will be able to show that some doctors over-prescribe medications because they want to meet their patients' expectations. (Too apologetic)

BUT   Some doctors over-prescribe medications because they want to meet their patients' expectations.

NOT   Any fool can see that the emission of greenhouse gases is a world-wide problem.

BUT   The emission of greenhouse gases is a worldwide problem.

E3 Choosing the Right Word: Usage

Some diction problems are not a matter of being too formal or too informal, but of confusing the meanings of similar words. Mistakes in **usage** may confuse your reader; they also undermine your credibility. To ensure that such mistakes don't mar your writing, check definitions in a dictionary whenever you are uncertain about the meanings of words. The following list will give you an idea of the kinds of words that are commonly misused.

1. *Affect* and *Effect*

    a.   *Affect* is usually a verb.

        The early frost affected the tomatoes.

    b.   *Effect* is usually a noun.

        The effect of the early frost on the tomatoes was obvious.

2. *Allude* and *Elude*

    a.   Use *allude* when you mean "to refer to," as in an allusion to the Bible or the Quran.

        Forster frequently alludes to the Bible in his essay "My Wood."

    b.   Use *elude* when you mean "to avoid" or "escape."

        The clever thief eluded the police for seven years.

3. *Allusion* and *Illusion*

    a.   An *allusion* is a reference to a piece of literature, a historical event or figure, or a popular movie or television show.

        The speaker's frequent allusions to characters in popular television shows entertained the audience.

    b.   An *illusion* is something that deceives by creating a false impression. An *illusion* can also refer to the state of mind in the person who is deceived.

        The use of perspective in the painting created the illusion of depth.

        Alison clung to the illusion that Juan would never forget her.

4. *Ambiguous* and *Ambivalent*

a. Use *ambiguous* when you mean "having different possible interpretations."

Jean-Paul left an ambiguous message on my answering machine.

b. Use *ambivalent* when you refer to a person's having opposing emotional attitudes toward a single object.

Taylor is ambivalent about attending law school: one moment she's keen, the next she can't stand the idea.

5. *Among* and *Between*

a. Use *among* when you refer to more than two things.

Divide the candy canes evenly among all the Christmas hampers.

b. Use *between* when you refer to two things.

Divide the prize money between the two winners.

6. *Amount* and *Number* (See also 16. *Less* and *Fewer*)

a. Use *amount* to refer to things considered as a mass.

Melt a small amount of butter in a pan.

b. Use *number* to refer to things that can be counted as individual units.

A small number of delegates attended the convention.

7. *Compare with* and *Compare to*

a. Use *compare with* when you examine the similarities and differences in things.

A comparison of the American Senate with the Canadian Senate strengthens the argument for electing senators.

b. Use *compare to* when you want to point out the similarities in two things.

I would compare her eating habits to those of a pig.

8. *Complement* and *Compliment*

a. Use *complement* when you want to indicate something that completes or rounds out (noun) or the act of completing or rounding out (verb).

He was born without a full complement of toes.

This purse will complement your outfit.

b. Use *compliment* to indicate an expression of praise or flattery (noun) or the act of praising or flattering (verb).

Serena was embarrassed by her boss's compliments.

I must compliment our server; he kept all the orders straight despite the changes.

9. *Continually* and *Continuously*

a. Use *continually* when you mean "persistently."

Our conversation was continually interrupted by the ringing of the telephone.

b. Use *continuously* when you mean "without ceasing."

The kitchen tap dripped continuously for two weeks.

10. *Differ from* and *Differ with*

a. Use *differ from* to indicate that two things are unalike.

The stage version of the play differs enormously from the film version.

b. Use *differ with* to express disagreement with a person.

I wish to differ with your assessment of the mayor's voting record.

11. *Different from* (not *different than*)

The effects of an expectorant cough syrup are different from the effects of a cough suppressant.

12. *Elusive* and *Illusory*

a. Use *elusive* when you want to describe something that is good at escaping or difficult to define or express.

The elusive mouse disappeared through a crack in the wall.

The specific implications of the new immigration policy remained elusive.

b. Use *illusory* when you want to describe something that is false or unreal.

The benefits of the proposed tax reduction are illusory.

13. *Eminent* and *Imminent*

a. Use *eminent* when you mean "prominent" or "notable."

He married into an eminent Quebec family.

b. Use *imminent* to refer to a danger or threat near at hand.

Flooding was imminent after the heavy rains.

14. *Flaunt* and *Flout*

    a. Use *flaunt* to refer to a conspicuous display of a person's attributes or possessions.

        Only the newly rich flaunt their wealth.

    b. Use *flout* to mean "to treat with scorn or contempt."

        Rebellious teens often flout authority.

15. *Imply* and *Infer*

    a. Use *imply* to mean "hint at."

        His lack of response to her entreaties implied his refusal to grant her wish.

    b. Use *infer* to mean "make an educated guess" or "draw a conclusion."

        The detective inferred from the blood on the sheets that the victim had been murdered in his sleep.

16. *Less* and *Fewer*

    a. Use *less* to refer to things considered as a mass.

        Although I am earning more, I seem to have less spending money.

    b. Use *fewer* to refer to things that can be counted.

        Fewer students than expected signed up for this course.

17. *Like* and *As*

    a. Use *like* when you are not introducing a clause.

        He looks like his father.

    b. Use *as* to introduce a clause.

        That night she dressed as she did when she was a girl.

18. *Partake of* and *Take part in*

    a. Use *partake of* when you mean "to have a share of something" (usually a meal).

        The guests were invited to partake of the enormous turkey.

    b. Use *take part in* when you mean "to join or participate."

        Will you take part in our volleyball game?

19. *Principle* and *Principal*

    a. *Principle* means "a fundamental belief."

        Most Canadians accept the principle of universal medical coverage.

b. *Principal* means "most important," "first in rank."

My principal objection is that cuts in services will inflict the most damage on the most vulnerable members of the community.

He is the principal dancer with the Royal Winnipeg Ballet company.

20. *Realize*

a. Realize can mean "to make real," as in "to realize a profit."

b. *Realize* can also mean "to understand fully," as in "to realize that he was wrong." You can avoid confusing these two meanings of realize if you use "realize that" when you mean "understand fully."

NOT   He realized his mother's unhappiness.

BUT   He realized that his mother was unhappy.

21. *Simple* and *Simplistic*

a. Use *simple* when you mean "plain, easy to understand."

Follow these simple directions.

b. Use *simplistic* when you want to indicate something has been oversimplified. *Simplistic* always conveys a negative judgment.

The premier offered only simplistic solutions to complex problems.

22. *Uninterested* and *Disinterested*

a. Use *uninterested* to mean "not interested in."

I am uninterested in politics.

b. Use *disinterested* to mean "impartial."

We need a disinterested third person to settle our dispute.

F Punctuation

F1 Apostrophe

The **apostrophe** is used to indicate missing letters in *contractions* and to show *possession*.

1a Recognizing Plurals, Contractions, and Possessives

Plurals, contractions, and possessives are often confused because they sound the same.

> PLURAL Three bikes have been stolen in the last week.
>
> CONTRACTION This bike's for sale. (*Bike's* = bike is)
>
> POSSESSIVE The bike's front wheel is warped. (Front wheel belonging to the bike)

In order to use apostrophes correctly, you need to be able to distinguish among these three forms. The following points will help you.

1. Only nouns and indefinite pronouns (such as *everybody, someone, anything*) take an apostrophe to show possession.

2. Be careful, especially with proper nouns, not to add an apostrophe when you want to indicate a plural.

   > PLURAL All the Lees [plural of *Lee*] want to invite you to their reunion.
   >
   > POSSESSIVE The Lees' garage burned down last year. (The apostrophe shows that the garage belonged to the Lees.)

3. Do not use an apostrophe with possessive pronouns (*yours, hers, its, ours, theirs*).

   > NOT   This problem is your's to solve.
   >
   > BUT   This problem is yours to solve.
   >
   > NOT   The dog pressed it's nose against the window.
   >
   > BUT   The dog pressed its nose against the window.

1b Using Apostrophes to Show Possession

Making indefinite pronouns and singular nouns possessive

1. To make an indefinite pronoun possessive, add *'s*.

    > Everybody's salary will be affected by the budget cutbacks.

2. To make a singular noun possessive, add *'s*.

    > This little boy's epilepsy is getting worse.

3. To make a singular noun that ends with *s* possessive, add *'s*. Do not add only an apostrophe.

    > Charles's car is in the shop again.

    > The albatross's death haunted the Ancient Mariner.

Making plural nouns possessive

1. If the plural noun ends in *s*, add only an apostrophe.

    > Both boys' bathing suits were lost.

    > All the students' marks were excellent.

2. If the plural noun does not end in *s*, add *'s*.

    > All children's toys, men's coats, and women's shoes are on sale.

Showing joint possession and separate possession

1. Joint possession: to indicate that two or more people possess something together, add *'s* to the last name.

    > Tom and Brenda's house is for sale.

2. Separate possession: to indicate that two or more people possess things separately, add *'s* to each name.

    > Tom's and Brenda's cars are for sale.

1c Other Uses of the Apostrophe

1. Expressions of time can be used as possessives. Be sure that the placement of the apostrophe indicates whether the noun naming the time period is singular or plural.

    > I'll contact you in a month's time. (One month)

    > We wasted two weeks' work.

2. To make letters plural, italicize the letter and add *'s*.

    > Have you dotted your *i*'s and crossed your *t*'s?

3. To put a word referred to as a word in the plural, italicize the word and add *'s*.

> There are too many *however*'s in this sentence.

4. To make an abbreviation plural, you can add either *s* or *'s*.

> All the SPCAs in this province are running out of money.
>
> All the YMCA's in the city offer day camps.

5. To make a date plural, add *s* or *'s*.

> Throughout most of the 1980s Canada faced a constitutional crisis.

Note: Forming plurals without the apostrophe is becoming the preferred usage for both abbreviations and dates.

F2 Comma

2a Main Clauses

Use a **comma** to separate main clauses joined by a coordinating conjunction (*and, but, or, nor, for, so, yet*).

> Inflation is under control, but unemployment is still a problem.
>
> No one has succeeded in proving the existence of UFOs, yet many have tried.

2b Subordinate Clauses

Use a comma to set off a subordinate clause at the beginning of a sentence.

> When economic conditions are poor, the incidence of family violence increases.
>
> Because the highways were icy, we postponed our trip.

2c Introductory Phrases

Use a comma to set off long (more than five words) or potentially confusing phrases at the beginning of a sentence.

> In his search for the meaning of life, he examined many religions. (Long phrase)
>
> In winter, darkness comes early. (Could be misread)

2d Items in a Series

Use a comma to separate more than two items joined by *and* or *or*. Include a comma before the conjunction so that the last two items are not read as a unit.

> We watched the children slide, swing, and climb.

The horses galloped over the field, across the stream, and down the road.

He ordered toast, eggs, coffee, and milk for breakfast. (Comma indicates that four items were ordered.)

2e Non-restrictive and Restrictive Modifiers

Non-restrictive modifiers are clauses, phrases, and single words that add information about the preceding noun or pronoun but are not necessary to specify its meaning. Non-restrictive modifiers can be omitted without changing the basic meaning of the sentence.

My dog[, who barks a lot,] sometimes disturbs the neighbours.

In this sentence, "my dog" identifies what disturbs the neighbours. The non-restrictive modifier "who barks a lot" adds the why or how.

Restrictive modifiers, in contrast, cannot be omitted because they help define the preceding noun or pronoun.

Dogs [that bark a lot] disturb the neighbours.

Without the modifier, this sentence would suggest that all dogs are a neighbourhood nuisance; the modifier restricts the meaning to "dogs that bark a lot."

Use a pair of commas to set off non-restrictive modifiers. Do *not* set off restrictive modifiers.

Punctuating non-restrictive and restrictive modifiers

Clauses beginning with relative pronouns

a. *Which* clauses are almost always **non-restrictive**, and so should be set off with commas.

The latest James Bond film, which opens Friday, is sure to be a hit.

b. *That* clauses are almost always **restrictive** and therefore do not take commas.

The hand that rocks the cradle rules the world.

c. Clauses beginning with *who, whom,* or *whose* may be either non-restrictive or restrictive.

NON-RESTRICTIVE Sutton, who injured his knees in a skiing accident, is slowly recovering.

RESTRICTIVE Athletes who injure their knees often recover slowly.

Participial phrases These are phrases beginning with the past participle or *–ing* form of a verb. Participial phrases are condensed clauses. When they come after nouns, they follow the same rules as they would if expanded into clauses.

> NON-RESTRICTIVE Jennifer Aniston, starring in this summer's block-buster, made her name in television.

> RESTRICTIVE The window broken by vandals will have to be replaced.

Appositives These are nouns or noun phrases that rename the preceding noun or pronoun. They may be either non-restrictive or restrictive. Set off non-restrictive appositives with commas.

> NON-RESTRICTIVE The Beatles, the most important rock group of the sixties, sold millions of records.

> RESTRICTIVE The film *The Compleat Beatles* is a history of the group's rise and fall.

Adjectives following nouns These are always **non-restrictive** and are therefore set off with commas.

> NON-RESTRICTIVE The dialogue, [which was] witty and fast-paced, made the play memorable.

> NON-RESTRICTIVE Lear, angry at his fate, railed against the heavens.

2f Parenthetical Expressions

Use commas to set off transitional words and phrases and other expressions that break the flow of the sentence.

> Developing countries, in contrast, may be resource-rich but capital-poor.

> This situation, I believe, leads to economic instability.

> Well, I'd better be going.

> There were, amazingly enough, thirty thousand people at the demonstration.

2g Dates and Place Names

Use a comma with dates and place names when more than one item of information is given.

> The centre of the Canadian automobile industry is Windsor, Ontario.

> Canada officially entered World War II on September 10, 1939.

2h Quotations

Use a comma to set brief quotations off from introductory material.

> One minister said, "This policy should never have been adopted."

> "This policy," said one minister, "should never have been adopted."

COMMA

F3 Semicolon

The **semicolon** is used in two ways: to join main clauses and to join a series of phrases or clauses that is too complicated for commas alone to clarify.

3a When to Use a Semicolon

1. Use a semicolon to join main clauses.

   a. When the ideas are closely related and there is no coordinating conjunction (*and, but, or, nor, for, so, yet*) to join the clauses.

   Mary was an idealist; Martha was a pragmatist.

   b. With a coordinating conjunction when the clauses are long or contain commas.

   The hard-boiled detective, as we have seen in the works of Dashiell Hammett, Raymond Chandler, and Ross MacDonald, is a distinctively American creation; but the amateur sleuth, popularized by British writers such as Dorothy Sayers, Agatha Christie, and Michael Innes, also appears in American fiction.

   c. When the second clause begins with a conjunctive adverb (*accordingly, besides, consequently, furthermore, hence, however, likewise, moreover, nevertheless, otherwise, still, therefore, thus*). Put a comma after a conjunctive adverb of more than one syllable. (See Note in F3b.)

   Byron's poetry soon eclipsed Scott's; therefore, Scott turned to writing novels.

   Few members of the legislature thought an election was necessary; nevertheless, the premier called one.

2. Use a semicolon to separate items within a series that contains commas.

   The defence attorney called three witnesses: her client's brother, who testified that his sister was with him the night of the crime; the brother's caretaker, who testified that he saw the defendant arrive at 10:15 p.m.; and the brother's neighbour, who glimpsed the sister as she left at 11:30 p.m.

3b When Not to Use a Semicolon

1. Do not use a semicolon to join a main clause and a subordinate clause.

   NOT   The restaurant switched to Fair Trade coffee; because the manager knew that customers would support the change.

   BUT   The restaurant switched to Fair Trade coffee because the manager knew that customers would support the change.

OR   The restaurant switched to Fair Trade coffee; the manager knew
that customers would support the change.

Note: Some writers misuse semicolons because they confuse subordinating conjunctions and conjunctive adverbs. Here is an easy way to remember the difference: conjunctive adverbs can be moved to different positions in a clause, whereas subordinating conjunctions cannot.

The premier called an election; however [conjunctive adverb], few members of the party thought an election was necessary.

The premier called an election; few members of the party thought an election was necessary, however.

The premier called an election even though [subordinating conjunction] few members of the party thought an election was necessary.

2. Do not overuse semicolons. Too many semicolons will make your writing seem stuffy, as in the following passage.

NOT   A good opera for beginners is *Carmen*. It is always a hit; it is packed full of recognizable tunes. The lead mezzo-soprano has to ooze with sex and burn with a fiery bitchiness; she has to be the consummate gypsy. In this story love is not the conqueror or sustainer; it is a colourful bird, rebellious and inconsistent. No one knows where it will perch; worse, no one knows when it will fly away. The key to *Carmen* is not heartbreaking emotion; it is passionate drama. If done well *Carmen* becomes absolutely thrilling; if done poorly the music is still great.

Notice how the passage is improved when some ideas are joined through subordination rather than coordination.

BUT   A good opera for beginners is *Carmen*. Packed full of recognizable tunes, it is always a hit. The lead mezzo-soprano has to be the consummate gypsy, oozing with sex and burning with a fiery bitchiness. In this story love is not the conqueror or sustainer but a colourful bird, rebellious and inconsistent. No one knows where it will perch; worse, no one knows when it will fly away. Passionate drama, not heartbreaking emotion, is the key to *Carmen*. Done well, the opera is absolutely thrilling; done poorly, the music is still great.

F4 Colon

Usually the **colon** indicates that what follows is an expansion of what has already been said. Use a colon for the following purposes:

COLON

1. To introduce a list that follows a complete clause. The items following the colon should be grammatically parallel.

   > Car manufacturers have introduced several improvements: better restraint systems, better pollution control devices, and better rust-proofing.

   Note: Do not use a colon when the list begins with *such as* or *for example*.

   > Car manufacturers have introduced several improvements, such as better restraint systems, better pollution control devices, and better rust-proofing.

2. To introduce a phrase or clause that explains the preceding statement.

   > He wanted only one thing out of life: to make money. (Explanatory phrase)

   > My new car is a real lemon: it has broken down for the third time this month. (Explanatory clause)

3. To introduce a quotation. Both the quotation and the sentence that introduces it must be grammatically complete.

   > Goldberg dismissed the arguments against changes in the Fisheries Act: "Contrary to the opinions expressed by packers and the fisheries unions, the proposed changes are not designed to increase federal control over the fishing industry."

   Note: Do not use a colon when the sentence introducing the quotation ends with *that*.

   > In his essay "African National Identities Can't Be Built on Soccer Fever," Jonathan Zimmerman states that "Americans love high-profile athletic events" (369 Readings).

F5 Dash

A **dash** (or pair of dashes) indicates an interruption in a train of thought or in the structure of the sentence. It creates an air of informality and so should be used sparingly in formal writing. Use the dash for the following purposes:

1. To set off abrupt shifts in thought.

   > My Aunt Sadie—you remember her, don't you?—lived to be a hundred.

2. To set off a list when it comes in the middle of a sentence.

   > She had established her goals in life—to travel, to have an interesting career, to develop close relationships—before she was sixteen.

Note: When the list comes at the end of the sentence, use a colon unless you want to indicate special emphasis, for which you use a dash.

> COLON Before she was sixteen, she had established her goals in life: to travel, to have an interesting career, to develop close relationships.

> DASH Early on, she had established her life goals to travel, to have an interesting career, and to develop close relationships—she was not yet sixteen.

DASH

F6 Parentheses

Use **parentheses** in these ways:

1. To enclose bibliographical information in the body of your essay.

   > Tim Bowling's "Na Na Na Na, Hey Hey Hey, Goodbye" (2006) is a discussion of the author's ambivalent attitude toward NHL hockey.

2. To enclose explanatory material, such as brief definitions and historical information.

   > British drivers open the bonnet (hood), put luggage in the boot (trunk), and fill their tank with petrol (gas).

   > Mozart (1756–1791) was an accomplished musician by the time he was six.

3. To indicate that explanatory material is relatively unimportant.

   > The mayor (who was re-elected by a slim majority) promised to improve transportation in the city.

   If you want to emphasize explanatory material, set it off with dashes. If you don't want either to emphasize or to minimize its importance, set it off with commas.

Note: Don't use parentheses to enclose essential information.

> NOT   At a council meeting this morning, the mayor (who holds stock in several land development companies) disqualified herself from voting on the proposal to annex areas north and west of the city.

> BUT   At a council meeting this morning, the mayor—who holds stock in several land development companies—disqualified herself from voting on the proposal to annex areas north and west of the city.

6a Punctuating Material in Parentheses

1. If a complete sentence in parentheses is contained within another sentence, do not begin the parenthetical sentence with a capital letter or end it with a period.

   > When spring finally arrived (winter had seemed endless), children suddenly appeared on the street.

2. If the phrase, clause, or sentence within parentheses requires a question mark or an exclamation mark, put the appropriate punctuation mark inside the closing parenthesis.

   > Although credit cards sometimes lead people disastrously into debt (and who hasn't been appalled by a monthly statement?), they are essential for many business transactions.

F7 Quotation Marks

This section covers the appropriate use of quotation marks as punctuation. For information on the format of quotations, the use of ellipses, and the integration of quotations into your writing, see H2 Quotations.

Use **quotation marks** to indicate direct speech, quotations from other writers, and titles of short works.

1. Put quotation marks around direct speech.

    DIRECT SPEECH Marie said, "I should get more exercise."

    INDIRECT SPEECH Marie said that she should get more exercise.

2. Put quotation marks around three or more consecutive words from any printed material.

    Virginia Woolf imagines what life would have been like for an equally talented sister of Shakespeare's, a sister who had "a taste for the theatre" and "a gift like her brother's, for the tune of words" (365 Readings).

3. Use single quotation marks for quotations within quotations.

    In her essay "Time and the Narrative Voice," Margaret Laurence states that "[i]n 'The Loons,' the narrative voice is also that of the older Vanessa" (283 Readings).

4. Use quotation marks to enclose titles of brief works (essays, magazine and newspaper articles, poems, short stories, songs, single episodes of a television series) that are part of larger works.

    Margaret Laurence's short story "The Loons" is a story in her collection of interconnected short stories, *A Bird in the House.*

5. You can put quotation marks around words referred to as words, but it's often clearer to italicize them (see F8 Italics).

    You use "because" three times in this sentence.

    Do not put quotation marks around slightly informal expressions.

    NOT   Michaela needs to learn to "stand up" for herself.

7a Using Other Punctuation with Quotation Marks

1. Place commas and periods inside quotation marks.

    "Many plant species," he said, "are in danger of extinction."

2. Place colons and semicolons outside quoted material.

    Bruce K. Alexander claims "it would be naïve to suppose that we can return to any real or imagined golden age"; however, he does argue that we must hold to one idea: "the common good" (229 Readings).

3. a. Place other punctuation marks (question marks, exclamation marks, dashes) inside the quotation marks if they punctuate only the quoted words.

> The first lines of Keats's poem "La Belle Dame sans Merci" are "O, what can ail thee, knight-at-arms, / Alone and palely loitering?"

b. Place these punctuation marks outside the quotation marks if they punctuate the sentence containing the quotation.

> Do you agree with Keats's statement that "Beauty is truth, truth beauty"?

F8 Italics

Slanted writing indicates italics in typeset and word-processed material. In typed and handwritten work, indicate by underlining. Use **italics** in the following ways.

1. For the titles of works published separately (books, plays, magazines, newspapers, CDs, films, television series). Titles of works that have been published separately are italicized even when these works are included in anthologies.

> The students referred to *Hamlet* in their copies of the *Norton Introduction to Literature*.

2. For the names of ships and airplanes, works of art, and long musical compositions.

> The choir practised three months for the performance of Handel's *Messiah*.

3. For words and letters referred to as words or letters.

> The word *truly* does not contain an *e*.

4. For foreign words and phrases that have not been incorporated into English.

> The setting epitomized what the Germans would call *Gemütlichkeit*.

5. For emphasis.

> Library materials *must* be returned by the end of term.

Be careful not to overuse italics for emphasis, especially in formal academic writing.

G Spelling and Mechanics

G1 Spelling

Here are some tips that will help you to proofread for spelling errors more efficiently.

1. Check the spelling of the subjects you are writing about, including titles, authors' names, place names, technical terms, and so on. If you put your instructor's name on your title page, check the spelling of that too.

2. Use the spell-checker on your word processor. If you are a weak speller, pay attention to the spell-checker in your word processing program, and if your word processor lacks this feature, consider buying one. You might also consider buying a current dictionary. Spell-checkers will pick up most typos and commonly misspelled words. They will not, however, consistently pick up homonyms: *to/too, there/their/they're, your/you're, it's/its, compliment/complement.* Nor will they pick up typos that would be legitimate words in a different context, such as insurance "clams" (for "claims").

3. Spell-checkers may show Canadian spellings (*labour/defence/centre*) as errors. If you find this irritating, you can add Canadian spellings to the spell-checker or select Canadian English from the language options of your word-processing software.

4. Be consistent in your use of either Canadian or American spellings. Don't write *theatre* in one sentence and *theater* in the next.

5. Some instructors regard errors in the use of apostrophes as spelling mistakes, whereas others see them as punctuation errors. Either way, apostrophe errors can significantly undermine the quality and the credibility of your writing. If you are not sure how to use apostrophes, check F1, Apostrophes, and try to memorize the rules.

6. If you are not sure how to spell a word, don't guess. Consult a dictionary.

7. Don't rely on spell-checkers to find all your spelling errors. Print out a hard copy and read it carefully, sentence by sentence. Make a list of the words you often misspell and check your work for them.

Headliners on the list of commonly misspelled words include the following. It's worthwhile to memorize them:

COMMON SPELLING ERRORS

a lot, acquire, among, argument, conscience, conscious, definitely, dependant (n.)/dependent (adj.), develop, embarrass, environment, even though, existence, interest, occurred, occurrence, prejudiced, privilege, rhyme, rhythm, separate, similar, subtly, tragedy, unnecessary, weird

G2 Hyphens

Use a **hyphen** in these ways:

1. With some compound words: *brother-in-law, major-general, buy-in.*

Note: Other compound words are written as a single word (*textbook, stepmother, railway*) or as two words (*income tax, down payment, gallows humour*). There is no set pattern for forming compound words, so check your dictionary.

2. With two-word numbers (from twenty-one to ninety-nine) and with fractions used as adjectives. Do *not* hyphenate when the fraction functions as a noun.

   The gas tank was one-third full. (*One-third* as adjective)

   One third of the students withdrew from the course. (*One third* as noun)

3. To join two words that function as a single adjective and convey a single idea. If this construction comes after the noun, do *not* hyphenate unless the construction is conventionally spelled with a hyphen. Do *not* hyphenate if the construction contains an *–ly* adjective.

   a well-organized essay

   The essay is well organized.

   a poorly organized essay

4. With the prefixes *self* (*self-sufficient*), *ex* (*ex-wife*); with prefixes that come before proper nouns (*anti-Catholic*); with the suffix *elect* (*president-elect*).

5. To prevent confusion: *re-mark* (mark again), *ten-year-old* children/ten *year-old* children.

6. To show that two or more prefixes share a common root.

   The results of both the pre- and the post-test were excellent.

HYPHENS

2a How to Hyphenate Words at the End of a Line

Avoid dividing a word at the end of a line whenever possible.

Do not hyphenate

1. One-syllable words. (*Dragged*, for example, should not be hyphenated.)
2. Words of six or fewer letters even if they contain two or more syllables. (Do not hyphenate *diet, beauty, elegy*.)
3. Words in more than two consecutive lines in a paragraph, the last word in a paragraph, or the last word on a page.

To hyphenate a word If you occasionally need to hyphenate a word, follow these rules:

1. Try to divide it into two approximately equal parts that convey the sense of the whole word.
2. Divide the word between syllables, making sure that the first part of the word contains at least three letters: *com-fort, impor-tance*.
3. If a double consonant appears at the end of a word because you have added a suffix (*running, committed*), divide the word between the double consonants (*run-ning, commit-ted*). If the double consonant is part of the root word, divide between the root word and the suffix (*drill-ing*).
4. Include a one-letter syllable with the first part of the word (*tabu-late* not *tab-ulate*).

G3 Numbers, Capitalization, and Abbreviations

3a Numbers

Use numerals (1, 2, 3, . . .):

1. To express numbers in scientific and technical writing.
2. For a series of numbers.
3. For numbers that cannot be expressed in two words.
4. For dates.
5. For page, verse, act, scene, and line numbers.

NUMBERS

Use words:

1. For numbers that can be expressed in one or two words.
2. When you begin a sentence with a number.

3b Capitalization

All proper nouns are capitalized. A proper noun names a specific person, place, or thing.

> We'll meet this afternoon for a picnic in the *park*. (Common noun)

> We'll meet this afternoon for a picnic in *Central Park*. (Proper noun)

Use capitalization in the following ways.

1. Capitalize titles of family members when the title substitutes for a name.

   > I asked Mother for a ride downtown.

   Do *not* capitalize titles of family members if they are preceded by a possessive pronoun: my father, your aunt, their brother.

2. Capitalize the names of languages, nationalities, and religions: English, Canadian, Buddhism.

3. Do *not* capitalize the name of an academic discipline unless it's the name of a language: chemistry, psychology, French.

4. Capitalize the names of specific courses: Chemistry 101, Psychology 260.

5. Capitalize the names of faculties: the Arts Faculty, the Faculty of Education.

6. Capitalize the words *college* and *university* when used with the name of an institution (Camrose Lutheran College). Do *not* capitalize these words when used alone: "The drama department at the university has an excellent reputation."

7. Capitalize the days of the week and the months, but not the seasons: Tuesday, January, spring.

8. Capitalize *Native* and *First Nations* when referring to Aboriginal peoples. Do *not* capitalize colour words used to refer to ethnic groups: black, white.

NUMBERS

9. Do *not* capitalize the names of directions unless they are used as place names.

> Turn north after you cross the bridge.

> The old priest had lived in the North for twenty years.

10. Do *not* capitalize to create emphasis.

3c Abbreviations

1. Use abbreviations sparingly in most essays. If it's desirable to abbreviate a term you repeat frequently, give the term in full the first time; then give the abbreviation.

> Sudden infant death syndrome (SIDS) is not fully understood. It seems, however, that SIDS occurs more frequently in the winter months.

2. Do *not* abbreviate days of the week or months of the year.

3. Put *BC* (before Christ) after the year to refer to dates before the birth of Christ.

> Socrates committed suicide in 399 BC.

Use *AD* (in the year of our Lord) before the year to refer to dates after the birth of Christ up to AD 500.

> Venice was founded by refugees from Attila's Huns in AD 452.

Some writers prefer to use *BCE* (before the common era) and *CE* (common era). Both these abbreviations appear after the year.

4. Do not abbreviate *and* with an ampersand (&) unless you are copying the name of an organization (McClelland & Stewart) or following a particular style of documentation, such as APA.

5. Avoid abbreviations for Latin terms, such as e.g. (*exempli gratia*) or i.e. (*id est*). Instead, write out their English equivalents.

> NOT From then on he was considered a coward; e.g., no one forgot that he had saved himself first when the hotel caught fire.

> BUT From then on he was considered a coward; for example, no one forgot that he had saved himself first when the hotel caught fire.

> NOT Susan gradually came to understand the erosion of self-esteem caused by racism: i.e., the assumption that a person's worth could be reliably assessed by the colour of his or her skin.

> BUT Susan gradually came to understand the erosion of self-esteem caused by racism: that is, the assumption that a person's worth could be reliably assessed by the colour of his or her skin.

6. Avoid using *etc.* Use a phrase such as "and so on" or "and similar items" at the end of the list, or use "such as" or "for example" at the beginning of the list.

NOT   Unemployment in this region has increased because of plant closures, the decline in tourism, the decreased demand for agricultural produce, etc.

BUT   Unemployment in this region has increased because of factors such as plant closures, the decline in tourism, and the decreased demand for agricultural produce.

H Format

H1 Essay Format

Here are the most common conventions for the **format** of the essay and the title page. Be sure to confirm your choice of format with your instructor. For information on documenting the sources you use, see H3 Documentation.

1a Manuscript Conventions

Most students use a word processor to write their papers. Familiarize yourself with the formatting functions of your word-processing program for optimum efficiency. Either your instructor or the technical support staff at your college or university can help you with special items such as page or section breaks, hanging indents for bibliographical lists, and so forth.

If you are handing in a hard copy of your paper, staple or clip the pages in the top left corner. Do not use any other method to secure the pages. If you are submitting your paper electronically, follow all manuscript conventions and give your document a concise file name that clearly identifies you and the assignment. Always keep a copy of your essay.

Manuscript conventions for word-processed essays

1. Choose a standard font and size such as Times New Roman and 12 point for all parts of your essay and title page. Make sure you have a spare black ink cartridge for your printer.

2. Use white, 8½ × 11 inch paper in your printer. For drafts, you can save paper by printing on both sides, but your final copy should be printed only on one side of the page.

3. Double space all parts of your essay. Indent each paragraph with one tab and do not leave extra lines between indented paragraphs.

4. The default margins are sufficient; they are usually set at 2.5 cm or 1 inch all around a page of text.

5. Insert automatic page numbers according to the system of documentation you are using. All pages, including the first or title page and the

Works Cited or References list, can be numbered. Using an automatic header saves space and effort.

Conventions for handwritten essays

1. Use blue or black ink and make sure your writing is legible.

2. Use white, 8½ × 11 inch ruled paper but not loose-leaf, notepaper, or other kinds of punched paper. Write only on one side of the page.

3. To double space, skip every other line. Indent each paragraph 1 inch and do not leave extra lines between indented paragraphs.

4. Leave generous margins of at least 2.5 cm or 1 inch all around a page.

5. Number your pages consecutively, including the first or title page and the Works Cited or References list.

1b Title Page

A title page or cover sheet creates a first impression and provides necessary information. Take the time to present your work effectively. Do not scribble a title page at the last minute before handing in your essay.

Title The title is important. At a minimum, it should make clear which topic you are addressing. Never simply label your paper "Essay 1." If you pay attention to the titles in essays and articles that you read, you will see that good titles are usually a short form of the thesis.

In all styles of title page format, present the title in regular font and size. Capitalize the first word and all other words except articles (*a, an, the*), coordinating conjunctions (*and, but, or, . . .*), short prepositions (*on, at, in, of, for*), and the *to* in infinitives. Do not underline the title of your essay or put quotation marks around it. Do not put a period after it.

If your title includes the name of a work you are analyzing, put the title in quotation marks or use italics, following the rules outlined in the sections on Quotation Marks and Italics (F7 and F8).

For the format of your title page, follow the system of documentation you are using in your essay. Two of the most widely accepted styles of documentation are those of the Modern Language Association (MLA), used primarily in the humanities, and the American Psychological Association (APA), used in the sciences and social sciences. Some instructors, however, will want you to prepare a generic title page with the title in the middle and your name, the date, and class information in the bottom right corner.

Title page format—MLA According to the *MLA Handbook*, you do not need a separate title page. Instead, your information and title appear double-spaced on the first page of your essay. With the automatic page numbering in place (as discussed earlier), put the following information in separate lines at the top left-hand corner in regular font and size: your name, your instructor's name, the course number, and the date. Next comes your title, centred, immediately above the beginning of your text. Here is a scaled-down sample in the MLA style:

Strong 1

L. Strong

Professor Loverso

English 101 (20)

28 June 2014

Tone in William Carlos Williams's "This Is Just to Say"

In "This Is Just to Say," one of William Carlos Williams's subjects is the complexity of language.

Title page format—APA The *APA Publication Manual* prescribes a separate title page with three distinct parts. First is the running head (not to exceed fifty characters) with essay title (or abbreviated title) in uppercase and the page number. The page number should be about 2.5 cm or 1 inch from the right-hand margin. Next is the title, in uppercase and lowercase, centred and positioned in the upper part of the page. Below the title, APA format requires your name and institutional affiliation; however, for most academic papers, you should also include the instructor's name, the date, and your course number. Third is an author note, which sets out the author's departmental affiliation, acknowledgments, disclaimers, and contact information. An author's note is usually required only for publishable material, not student assignments, theses, or dissertations. Here is a scaled-down sample in the APA style:

Running head: THE PROBLEM OF ENVIRONMENTAL COSTS   1

The Problem of Environmental Costs:

Suzuki vs. Merwin

Joyce MacDonald

3 March 2014

Sociology 101

Professor Smith

Red Deer College

H2 Quotations

Quotations can be very effective tools to improve your writing. Quotations should not be thought of as a mere requirement for an assignment, however; rather, they should serve a specific purpose. For example, in essays on literature, it is usually essential that you quote the text you are analyzing. In research writing, you often will support your position by drawing upon secondary sources such as experts or authorities in relevant fields. When used for these purposes, quotations can strengthen or clarify your writing.

There is no set standard for how many quotations you should use in an essay. You will need to use your own judgment to decide if a quotation is necessary. Remember, however, that an essay should be about *your* ideas. If the essay includes too many quotations, your own voice and ideas may get lost. If the quotations begin to dominate an essay, the reader may wonder what you, and not the quotations, are saying.

These guidelines will help you decide when quotations are most effective.

2a When to Quote

1. When the precise wording of a short passage of prose, such as the definition of a key term, is the starting point for your analysis or evaluation of a concept, theory, proposal, or text. For example, you may find that a particular writer makes good distinctions between the different meanings for the terms *female, feminine,* and *feminist.*

2. When you are integrating research from an authority in a subject. For example, if you were writing about technology and its social effects, you would want to include statements from authorities who hold both positive and negative opinions of technology.

3. When you offer your own interpretation. Essays on literature often require that you present your opinion of a text. You need to explain why you reach your conclusions, and you can do this by quoting specific passages from the text. For example, you might make the following argument:

> Tim Bowling overstates his argument about hockey when he suggests that boys are "sexually abused by their coaches" (237) because not all boys are subjected to such abuse, such abuse is not limited to hockey culture, and not all coaches abuse boys.

2b When Not to Quote

1. When you can paraphrase or summarize information without loss of meaning or impact. Both paraphrasing and summarizing demonstrate that you understand what you have read because you are able to put the material into your own words. You may paraphrase a writer's ideas to make the language more accessible to your reader. For example, scholarly writing can often employ very complicated terminology, and you may want to state an idea using plain language. You should summarize material when you wish to emphasize major ideas or concepts from a text. For example, academic studies will often include extensive data, examples, or analyses. You may find that you wish to focus on the conclusions a researcher draws rather than on specific examples in his or her study (for more on summarizing, see Chapter 2). Whenever you paraphrase or summarize materials, you must include appropriate bibliographic information (see Chapter 11 and H3 Documentation).

2. When you state statistics or well-known facts. For example, you need not quote the fact that World War II lasted from 1939 to 1945. Usually you should refrain from quoting passages that consist mostly of statistics, numbers, examples, technical jargon, and similar material.

3. When writing a thesis statement. Do not rely on other people's ideas or cliché phrases to make your thesis.

4. When the quotation merely repeats your point. You can generally integrate the two (see H2c, number 3).

5. When you have already used a particular passage. Do not repeat quotations of significant length.

2c How to Use Quotations

1. Introduce the source. If the quotation comes from a previously unmentioned person, identify the person by first and last names; otherwise, use only the last name. For sources other than people (such as reference books, institutions, or governments), state the official title of the source.

   NOT   Jonathan Swift's "use of transitional devices is equally shoddy."

   BUT   When Fred Stenson measures Jonathan Swift's writing against the criteria of Alberta education standards, he finds Swift's "use of transitional devices . . . shoddy" (342).

2. Make sure you give readers enough context to understand the quotation. There are two important contexts to consider: the context of the original material and the context of your own writing. It is commonly understood that you should not take something out of context. For example, consider the following sentence:

   Jonathan Swift argues that children are "a most delicious, nourishing, and wholesome Food" (350).

   This statement seems to indicate that Swift supports cannibalism. The sentence fails to communicate Swift's irony. When quoting, you must represent the original materials in their appropriate context.

   Similarly, you should indicate why or how a quotation is relevant to your purpose. Do not include a quotation for no purpose or to appear important. Instead, when you quote something, you must explain the point it illustrates or supports. Notice that the following statement not only acknowledges the irony in the quotation from Swift but also gives the writer's interpretation of the purpose of Swift's irony:

> When he claims that children are "a most delicious, nourishing, and wholesome Food" (350), Jonathan Swift is using irony to critique the English and the Anglo-Irish for the political and economic policies that are consuming the Irish people.

3. Ensure that your point about the quotation is clear. Do not use rhetorical questions to make your point. Do not assume that the meaning of the quotation or how you are using the quotation is self-evident.

> NOT   Regarding Canadian identity, we need to realize that "We live in uncharted territory," and who wouldn't agree that the world is complex and complicated?

> BUT   Regarding Canadian identity, Charles Taylor claims that "We live in uncharted territory" (359) because Canada tries to base its solidarity and continuity on difference and change, something he believes "is unprecedented in human history" (359).

4. Instead of introducing quotations (or paraphrases and summaries) with "he/she says/writes," use verbs that reveal the degree of certainty with which the author makes statements. You can convey how the author uses ideas and information (or how you perceive the author to be using ideas and information) by using verbs such as these: *acknowledges, argues, articulates, avoids, claims, concludes, confirms, demonstrates, denies, disproves, engages, estimates, evades, expands, hopes, hypothesizes, ignores, illustrates, proves, recognizes, reveals, speculates, states, theorizes.* Consider the following examples:

> John Smith *says* that "95% of people disagree with smoking bylaws."
>
> John Smith *confirms* that "95% of people disagree with smoking bylaws."
>
> John Smith *speculates* that "95% of people disagree with smoking bylaws."
>
> John Smith *estimates* that "95% of people disagree with smoking bylaws."

In each example, the meaning of the quotation changes substantially, even though the quotation is the same.

5. Ensure that your point is related to the quoted material. Students will sometimes make a statement about a text that is either unsupported by the quotation or inaccurate to the text.

> NOT   Laura Robinson cites an expert who says that, when university women were asked if they were ever raped, "they responded in the negative" (327).

> BUT   Laura Robinson cites Robin Warshaw's study that demonstrates that when women are asked about "rape," most "responded in

the negative" (327), yet, when asked about other definitions of sexual coercion, "The answers came back in the affirmative" (327).

6. **Integrate quotations into your own writing. Do not merely insert a sentence-length quotation between two of your own sentences. Do not string quotations together.**

NOT   Silence is important in the novel *Obasan*. Naomi's silence "is a discourse that cures precisely because it simultaneously mimics and resists" (Kamboureli 209).

BUT   Smaro Kamboureli asserts that in *Obasan*, Naomi paradoxically "practices the talking cure but does so in silence." Often, Naomi's silence "is a discourse that cures precisely because it simultaneously mimics and resists" (209).

NOT   The anthropologist Louis Leakey situated Jane Goodall in Gombe to study chimpanzees. "Gradually I was able to move nearer the chimpanzees, until at last I sat among them, enjoying a degree of acceptance that I had hardly dreamed possible." "I was to discover as much as possible about the way of life of the chimpanzee before it is too late—before encroachments of civilization crowd out, forever, all nonhuman competitors (Goodall 275–76)."

BUT   Jane Goodall was situated in Gombe to study chimpanzees, where she "sat among them, enjoying a degree of acceptance that [she] had hardly dreamed possible." Goodall states that she "was to discover as much as possible about the way of life of the chimpanzee before it is too late—before encroachments of civilization crowd out, forever, all nonhuman competitors" (275–76).

7. **Use the correct terminology.** Usually, it is not advisable to refer to a quotation as a quotation in your writing. Quotation marks ("") or indented lines (for long quotations) indicate that something is a quotation. Therefore, you need not write, "The following quote shows that . . . " or "As the previous quotation demonstrates . . . " If you find you must draw attention to a quotation as such, use the correct terminology. *Quote* is a verb; *quotation* is a noun. I may *quote* an authority in my writing, but I am using a *quotation* to support my point.

2d How to Format Quotations

Quotations are most often used for support, clarification, or analysis. They should be as short as possible. Avoid quoting materials that are irrelevant to your writing and its purpose. Try to isolate key words, phrases, or clauses that best articulate the point you want to make.

Quotations almost always require **in-text citations**: parenthetical references indicating their source. The format for in-text citations varies according to the style guide used in specific disciplines. You will find guidelines for MLA style (commonly used in literary studies) and APA style (commonly used in the social sciences) in H3 Documentation.

Integrating quotations Since quotations should be as short as possible, you will most often integrate quotations directly into your own sentence by using quotation marks.

The format for short prose quotations (from an article, a book, a short story, or a play written in prose, for example) differs slightly from the format for short poetry quotations.

- **Prose:** A quotation of four lines of text or less (MLA style) or of fewer than forty words (APA style) should be integrated into your own sentence. Put the in-text citation in parentheses after the closing quotation mark, followed by the end punctuation for the sentence.

  In his article on globalization, James Howard Kunstler argues that American suburbs filled with box stores are "the greatest misallocation of resources in the history of the world" (267).

- **Poetry:** When quoting a poetry passage of fewer than four lines, use a slash (/) to indicate line breaks in the verse. The parenthetical reference follows the closing quotation mark and includes line numbers (act.scene.line numbers for verse plays divided into acts and scenes, such as the plays of Shakespeare: *Macbeth* 1.1.5–7).

  In the poem "This Is Just to Say," we can read the phrase "forgive me" as an appeal for forgiveness that is cuttingly undermined because it is juxtaposed with the lines "they were delicious / so sweet / so cold" (10–12).

There are three principal ways to introduce integrated quotations: with a colon; with an active verb and a comma; with no punctuation.

- **Colon:** Ensure that the writing before the colon is a complete sentence.

  David Suzuki offers an important insight into the impact of technology: "If every technology has a cost, the more powerful the technology, the greater its potential cost" ("It Always Costs" 345–346).

- **Active verb with a comma:** Use the author's name with an active verb (such as *writes, states, claims, argues*). The quotation must be a complete sentence.

  Speaking about Africa in his article on sport and nation, Jonathan Zimmerman writes, "In a continent ravaged by political and ethnic violence, people often invoke sports—especially soccer—as [a] force for national unity" (369).

Note that the comma can be replaced with *that:*

Speaking about Africa in his article on sport and nation, Jonathan Zimmerman writes that "[i]n a continent ravaged by political and ethnic violence, people often invoke sports—especially soccer—as [a] force for national unity" (369).

- **No punctuation:** If possible, try to quote key phrases or clauses within the grammatical structure of your own writing.

  Reflecting upon the allure of hockey to Canadians, Tim Bowling concludes that "the primal pull of narrative" (236) is what most strongly links almost every Canadian to the national sport.

Indenting quotations Occasionally you may need to quote a longer passage. In essays on literature, you may want to offer a detailed analysis of numerous literary qualities of the text. In research writing, you may want to quote a particularly convincing argument or an intricate line of reasoning. Quotations too long to integrate smoothly into your own writing should be indented.

Because of their length, indented quotations must be able to stand alone as independent and complete thoughts. Therefore, indented quotations will usually have a more definite grammatical separation from preceding materials. The most common way to introduce an indented quotation is to use a colon, as in the following examples. Do not put quotation marks around the quotation unless you are quoting dialogue that contains quotation marks.

- **Prose:** In MLA style, if a quotation exceeds four text lines, then you need to indent the quotation. If you are using APA style, the cut-off point for indented quotations is forty or more words of text. An indented quotation is signalled by a break in the paragraph. The quoted text is indented from the left-hand margin of the page: 2.5 cm or 1 inch in MLA style and 1.25 cm or ½ inch in APA style. Font size and spacing remain consistent with the rest of the text in the essay. The parenthetical reference follows the final punctuation of the quotation.

  In "Reframing Canada's 'Drug Problem,'" Bruce K. Alexander claims current analyses of addiction and its solutions lack the correct focus:

  > The solution to the so-called "drug problem" is nothing less than rejecting single-minded neoliberalism and exercising sensible,

humane controls over environments, corporations and public institutions for the common good. This cannot be accomplished piecemeal, but requires a broadly framed policy that at times supersedes the pursuit of wealth and ever-freer markets. (229)

- **Poetry:** When you are quoting poetry that exceeds three lines of verse, the quotation must start on a new line and be indented 2.5 cm or 1 inch from the left-hand margin. Any formal or stylistic features, such as capitalization and length and placement of lines, must be retained in the formatting.

In the final stanza of "This Is Just to Say" (Rhetoric 84–85), Williams's speaker describes the plums in sensuous language:

> Forgive me
>
> they were delicious
>
> so sweet
>
> and so cold (9–12)

2e How to Indicate Deletions, Insertions, and Errors

Quotations are subject to the basic grammatical rules of clarity and coherence. As a general rule, they should be consistent with the rest of the writing in terms of tense, number, and agreement. Sometimes it is necessary to change a quotation for clarity, correctness, or brevity. Three special cases occur.

Deletions Use an ellipsis (. . .) to indicate an omission within a quotation. In this example, the specific items have been deleted since they were not relevant to the writer's purpose.

ORIGINAL Five items—a purse, a watch, a wallet, a ring, a necklace—were stolen.

QUOTATION WITH DELETION "Five items . . . were stolen."

When you quote only part of a sentence within the grammatical structure of your own writing, as in the example from Tim Bowling on page 481, it is generally not necessary to use an ellipsis to indicate that you have omitted material that came before or after the quotation.

Insertions Put square brackets around words added to clarify something in the quotation or to make the quotation fit into the grammatical structure of your sentence.

ADDITION "Unlike the warriors of older tribes, however," Sanders points out, "they [the soldiers of his youth] would have no say about when the battle would start or how it would be waged" (331).

CHANGE Sanders points out that modern soldiers "have no say about when the battle [will] start or how it [will] be waged" (331).

Error in the text Put [*sic*] (Latin for "so," "thus") after the error to indicate typographical errors, deviant spellings, grammatical mistakes, or confused wording in the original.

According to one study, "Each of the provinces are [*sic*] contributing to the problem of acid rain."

H3 Documentation

Research writing, scholarly writing, and academic writing usually require you to cite—that is, to indicate the origin of—any materials or ideas you have taken from books, scholarly articles, internet sources, online databases, or other sources. The main purposes of documentation are to acknowledge your use of secondary sources and to differentiate within your writing between your own ideas and the ideas of other people. Additionally, good documentation practices allow your readers to find interesting or relevant materials quickly and easily, which helps the research process for everyone involved. When using secondary sources, you need to document both direct quotations and paraphrased ideas. Failure to acknowledge secondary sources constitutes plagiarism. For more detailed information on plagiarism, see Chapter 11.

With the increasing ease of access to online information and the consequent debates about intellectual property rights, file sharing and copyright issues, open source materials, and many other questions related to information and technology, it is arguable that information is becoming free for the taking. Similarly, information on many websites appears to have no author, implying that it does not belong to anyone and therefore does not need to be documented. This is not the case in formal writing. For academic writing such as research papers, it is essential that you document any secondary materials in your essay, even if it is a simple web page.

This section focuses on two documentation styles introduced earlier in the chapter: Modern Language Association (MLA) and American Psychological Association (APA). The two main requirements for documentation are in-text citations and a list of secondary sources at the end of the essay. An in-text citation is usually a parenthetical reference in the body of the essay. The list of sources, entitled Works Cited (MLA) or References

(APA), consists of a complete itemization of sources alphabetized by the author's last name. Each in-text citation must correspond to an entry in the Works Cited or References list. Similarly, each entry in the Works Cited or References list should correspond to an in-text citation. One always requires the other.

3a Direct Quotations, Paraphrase, and Ideas

Most students understand that any direct quotation of three or more words needs to be documented. However, a direct quotation is not the only situation where documentation is necessary. When you paraphrase someone else's work—often phrased as "putting the idea into your own words"—the idea still originates from someone else and needs to be documented. Therefore, when you are conducting research, it is important to keep track of what you read so that you have a clear understanding of where ideas or quotations originate. A good strategy is to take detailed notes as you read research materials. You also need to document any ideas from secondary sources that you have put into your own words or incorporated into your argument. In each case, you must have an in-text citation and an entry in the Works Cited or References list. For more information on summarizing other people's ideas, see Chapter 2.

Primary and secondary sources A primary source is usually the main text under discussion. For example, if you were studying William Shakespeare's *The Tempest,* the play itself would be the primary source. Any research materials you gathered—such as scholarly criticism on Shakespeare—would be secondary sources. Secondary sources, as the name implies, often address the primary source or an idea, concept, or theme relevant to the primary source. A Works Cited or References list includes both primary and secondary sources.

3b Systems of Documentation: MLA and APA

This section outlines the basic documentation guidelines for the two systems we have been discussing: Modern Language Association (MLA) and American Psychological Association (APA). While other systems exist (such as *The Chicago Manual of Style*), MLA and APA are commonly used for literary studies and social sciences, respectively. If you are unsure about which system to use, ask your instructor.

Documentation is not difficult; it merely requires careful attention to details of style and punctuation that may seem arbitrary. However, these styles have evolved to give order to a diverse realm of information. As grammar gives shape and coherence to language, documentation gives shape and coherence to research. Failure to adhere to rules of documentation results in a scattered, confusing research essay that can be difficult and frustrating to follow.

Below you will find examples of the most common types of documentation for books, articles, and online sources. Because of the diverse range of materials available to researchers, this section cannot cover every type of secondary source. If you need more information, consult a style manual: the *MLA Handbook for Writers of Research Papers* (MLA) or the *Publication Manual of the American Psychological Association* (APA). These manuals are very detailed and thorough. They are available in most school libraries.

When writing a Works Cited or References entry for a print source, you should always take the bibliographic information from the title page of the work. Do not take information from the cover of the book. The title page is most often identified by the small-print information (such as copyright and publisher details) on the reverse side of the page.

3c MLA Style

Literature courses usually ask that you document sources in MLA style. MLA style requires in-text citations and a Works Cited list.

In-text citations An in-text citation is necessary when you include a direct quotation, paraphrase, or idea from a primary or secondary source. Include enough information to identify the source of the material. Most frequently, you will need to include the author's name and the page number (line number for poetry; act.scene.line number for plays so divided). If you use more than one work by an author, you will need to include a short form of the title. Because online sources often do not have page numbers, you should cite the paragraph number, if given. The in-text citation should point the reader to the relevant entry in the Works Cited list. An in-text citation usually follows the closing quotation mark of a quotation.

- Author identified in sentence

  In Margaret Laurence's "The Loons," narrator Vanessa MacLeod reveals that she did not want "to witness [her] long-ago kingdom possessed now by strangers" (278).

- Author not identified in sentence

  One critic argues that in Africa "tyrants have often seized upon sports to bolster their power" (Zimmerman 369).

- Paraphrased idea, more than one work by the same author

  Margaret Laurence claims that the distinction between first- and third-person narration does not meaningfully apply to her work because her focus is on the main character, not the narrative perspective ("Time" 280–284).

- An online source with paragraph numbers

  John Smith claims that Margaret Laurence's short story "The Loons" creates a "problematic parallel between Piquette and the loons" (par. 22).

- An online source with no page number, paragraph numbers, or other identifying markers

  Near the end of his article, John Smith claims that Margaret Laurence's short story "The Loons" creates a "problematic parallel between Piquette and the loons."

- Quotations within quotations

  Secondary materials often contain references to or direct quotations from both primary and secondary sources. Try to avoid significant use of such quotations: references, not to mention readers, can easily become confused. If you find it necessary to use a quotation within a quotation, follow these examples. Note that the quotation within the quotation is indicated by single quotation marks.

1. A quotation from a primary source within a quotation from a secondary source. The parenthetical reference is to the secondary source, which will appear in the Works Cited list.

   In "The Persistence of Poetry and the Destruction of the World," Robert Bringhurst notes that "The Haida poet Skaay refers to human beings as *xhaaydla xitiit ghidaay*: 'plain, ordinary surface birds'" (242).

2. A quotation from a secondary source within a secondary source. Within the parenthetical reference, begin with *qtd. in* (quoted in) followed by the author of the secondary source in which you found the quotation and the page number of the quotation. You need to include only the secondary source in which you found the quotation in your Works Cited list.

   Karl Polanyi demonstrates how free-markets changed the nature of populations: "the most obvious effect of the new institutional system was the destruction of the traditional character of settled populations and their transmutation into a new type of people, migratory, nomadic, lacking in self-respect and discipline" (qtd. in Alexander 227).

Works Cited A Works Cited list is a bibliography of all primary and secondary sources used in an essay. It starts on a separate page at the end of the essay. Every entry in a Works Cited list should refer to one or more in-text citations of that work in the body of the essay.

The following examples give representative entries for a Works Cited list in MLA style. The most common sources in a Works Cited list include books, articles, and online sources.

Books A standard Works Cited entry for a book includes the author's name (last, first), the title of the book (including subtitle, if any), the city of publication, the publisher, the year of publication, and the medium of publication consulted (for example, *Print* or *Web*). Follow the punctuation and formatting as outlined in the examples. You should also cite any other relevant information about the text, including translations, editions, series, and so on. If you are unsure of what information to include, ask your instructor for clarification.

- **A work by a single author:** Many books have a single author. This is perhaps the most basic entry. Note that the title of the book is italicized and the main words capitalized.

  Solie, Karen. *Short Haul Engine*. London: Brick, 2001. Print.

- **A work by two or more authors:** When citing a book with two or three authors, alphabetize the entry by the name that appears first in the list of authors on the title page. Do not alphabetize the remaining names. Invert only the name of the first author in the list; leave the other authors' names in normal order. This book with two authors is also a translation:

  Horkheimer, Max, and Theodor W. Adorno. *Dialectic of Enlightenment*. Trans. John Cumming. New York: Continuum, 1972. Print.

  When citing a book with four or more authors, either present all names in the order in which they appear in the book (with the first author's name inverted) or present the first author's name (inverted) and add *et al.*

- **An anthology or a compilation:** An anthology or a compilation is a collection of works by different people, selected and arranged by an editor or editors. To cite an entire collection, alphabetize the entry by the last name of the editor, followed by a comma and "ed." If there is more than one editor, follow the format for books by two or more authors and add "eds." (For individual entries in an anthology or compilation, see below.)

Mitchell, Allyson, Lisa Bryn Rundle, and Lara Karaian, eds. *Turbo Chicks: Talking Young Feminisms*. Toronto: Sumach, 2001. Print.

- **An individual work in an anthology or a compilation:** To cite a selection from an anthology or a compilation, alphabetize the entry by the last name of the author, not the editor. Put quotation marks around the titles of short works, such as essays, poems, and short stories. However, italicize the titles of works previously published in independent form, such as novels and plays, as well as the title of the anthology or compilation. Give the edition, if any, after the title of the anthology or compilation. Then add *Ed.* (for "Edited by") and list the name(s) of the editor(s), in normal order. Follow with the city of publication, the publisher, and the year of publication. Include the page numbers for the complete selection, not just the pages you have cited. Conclude with the medium of publication.

  Vanderhaeghe, Guy. "Cages." *The Harbrace Anthology of Literature*. 4th ed. Ed. Jon C. Stott, Raymond E. Jones, and Rick Bowers. Toronto: Thomson Nelson, 2006. 1204-17. Print.

- **Two or more works by the same author(s):** When you cite more than one text by same author, abbreviate the author's name in second and any subsequent references with three hyphens in a row, followed by a period. Alphabetize the author's name as usual in the Works Cited list, and order the author's works alphabetically, ignoring any initial *A*, *An*, or *The*.

  Zwicky, Jan. *Robinson's Crossing*. London: Brick, 2004. Print.

  ____. *Wisdom & Metaphor*. Kentville: Gaspereau, 2003. Print.

Articles Scholarly journals or periodicals are extremely common research sources. You may also draw upon magazine articles, newspaper articles, or encyclopedia entries. Most journal entries for a Works Cited list will be for a specific essay in a particular journal. The entry will include the author's name, the title of the article, the journal's title, the volume (and issue) of the journal, the year of publication, the page numbers, and the medium of publication (for example, *Print* or *Web*).

- **A scholarly article in a scholarly journal:** Note that no period follows the title of the journal. The volume and issue numbers of the journal are separated with a period; when no issue number exists, the volume number stands alone without a period.

  Brooks, Peter. "Aesthetics and Ideology: What Happened to Poetics?" *Critical Inquiry* 20.3 (1994): 509-23. Print.

- **A scholarly article in a collection:** These sources are cited in the same way as individual works in an anthology (see above) if they have not been previously published.

  Kilgour, Maggie. "The Function of Cannibalism at the Present Time." *Cannibalism and the Colonial World*. Ed. Francis Barker, Peter Hulme, and Margaret Iversen. New York: Cambridge UP, 1998. 238-59. Print.

- If the article appeared first in a journal and has been reprinted in a collection, give the complete information for the journal publication. Then add *Rpt. in* and the information for the collection.

  Windle, Phyllis. "The Ecology of Grief." *Bioscience* 42 (May 1992): 363-66. Rpt. in *Ecopsychology: Restoring the Earth, Healing the Mind*. Ed. Theodore Roszak, Mary E. Gomes, and Allen D. Kanner. San Francisco: Sierra Club, 1995. 136-45. Print.

- **A magazine article:** For magazines that are published weekly or biweekly, the date reference should include the day, month, and year of publication. For magazines that are published monthly or bimonthly, the date reference should include the month and year of publication. Do not include the volume and issue numbers of magazines.

  Stenson, Fred. "In Search of a Modest Proposal." *Alberta Views* Jan.-Feb. 2004: 14-15. Print.

- **A newspaper article:** When citing a newspaper article, include the author and title of the article as well as the title of the newspaper (omit any leading *A, An,* or *The*), the date, edition, section, and page number(s). If the article spans more than one page or appears on non-consecutive pages, this should be noted with the first page followed by a plus sign (for example, C41).

  Curry, Bill. "Ottawa Wants Kyoto Softened." *Globe and Mail* 12 May 2006, Alberta ed.: A1+. Print.

- **An encyclopedia entry:** Encyclopedia entries may or may not include author information. If the author is named, alphabetize the entry by the author's last name. If the author is unnamed, alphabetize the entry by the first significant word of the title. You do not need to cite page numbers for encyclopedia entries. Do not list the entry by the encyclopedia editor's name.

  "David Suzuki." *The Canadian Encyclopedia: Year 2000 Edition*. 2000 ed. Ed. James H. Marsh. Toronto: McClelland & Stewart, 1999. Print.

Electronic and online sources Electronic and online sources are much more recent developments than book technologies, and they are still developing and changing more rapidly than print culture. Therefore, the standards for documenting online sources are not as well established, though the principles are the same. The main objective is to identify the source of the information as completely as possible. Essentially, citations of electronic materials contain the same information as print sources as well as relevant electronic details. Include the author's name (if given), title of the work, information about print publication (if any), information about electronic publication (title of the work, name of overall website in italics, and publisher or sponsor of the site), date of publication (day, month, year, as available), the medium of publication (*Web*), and the date of access (day, month, year). Because electronic and online information can change so rapidly, it is very important to include the date of access for any citation. It is not necessary to include the URL of the website in the citation. Much online information is unpaginated; sometimes paragraph numbers are given, other times not. Cite what information is available to you.

- **A web page:** Authors of web pages are often not listed. If no author is listed, alphabetize the entry by the first significant word in the title of the work.

  "No Agreement on Role of Abortion Pill in Fatal Infections." CNN. com. Cable News Network, 11 May 2006. Web. 12 May 2011.

- **An article in an online database:** Full-text articles are increasingly becoming available through online databases. When citing an article from an online database, you cannot simply cut and paste the entry from the search results into your Works Cited list. Rather, follow the same rules for citing a print article and add the title of the database (in italics), the medium of publication consulted (*Web*), and the date of access (day, month, year). Refer to the section on citing journal articles for help on citing online journal articles.

  Scanlan, Margaret. "*Anil's Ghost* and Terrorism's Time." *Studies in the Novel* 36.3 (2004): 302-17. *Academic Search Premier.* Web. 12 May 2011.

3d APA Style

Social science disciplines such as psychology and sociology most frequently use APA style for research papers in college and university courses. APA style requires in-text citations and a References list at the end of research papers.

In-text citations An in-text citation is necessary when you include a direct quotation, paraphrase, or idea from a primary or secondary source. Include enough information to identify the source of the material. Most frequently, you will need to include only the author's name and the year of publication; for direct quotations, you will need to include the page number as well. For online sources that have no pagination, you should include the paragraph number by using *para.* followed by the number. The in-text citation should point the reader to the relevant entry in the References list.

- Author identified in sentence

  Smith (2005) analyzes the effects of behavioural drugs on children.

- Author not identified in sentence

  Recent research (Smith, 2005) analyzes the effects of behavioural drugs on children.

- In-text citation for a single work with two authors

  Smith and Liu (2004) found that behavioural drugs had few side effects.

- In-text citation for a single work with three to five authors

  First in-text citation: Smith, Liu, and Johnson (2004) found that behavioural drugs had few side effects.
  Subsequent in-text citations: Smith et al. (2004) also found that the number of people taking such drugs had risen significantly over the past five years.

- In-text citation for a single work with six or more authors

  Cox et al. (2008) found that the prevalence of chronic medication use in children increased from 2002 to 2005.

- Direct quotation using the author's name

  Taylor (2006) concludes that behavioural drugs have "significant side effects" (p. 288).

- Direct quotation not using the author's name

  One researcher concludes that behavioural drugs have "significant side effects" (Taylor, 2006, p. 288).

- Citation of another work within a secondary source

  Johnson's study (as cited in Smith & Jones, 2004) confirms that behavioural drugs can have negative side effects.

- Direct quotation from an online source with paragraph numbers

  Taylor's study (2003) finds "negligible side effects" (para. 3) in all but
  one type of drug.

- Direct quotation from an online source that does not include page
  numbers or paragraph numbers, but has headings

  Taylor's study (2003) finds "negligible side effects" (Results section, para. 1) in all
  but one type of drug. [In this case, *para. 1* indicates the first paragraph following
  the section heading.]

References list A References list is a bibliography of all primary and secondary sources used in an essay. It starts on a separate page entitled References at the end of the essay. Every entry in the References list should refer
to one or more in-text citations of that work in the body of the essay.

The following examples give representative entries for a References list
in APA style. The most common entries include books, articles, and online
sources.

Books A standard References list entry for a book includes the author's
name (last name and initials), the year of publication (in parentheses),
the title of the work in italics, the city (and state or province, or if outside
the United States and Canada, city and country) of publication, and the
publisher. Follow the punctuation and format as outlined in the examples.
You should also cite any other relevant information about the text, including translations, editions, and series. If you are unsure of what information
to include, ask your instructor for clarification.

- **A work by a single author:** Many books have a single author. This
  is perhaps the most basic entry. Note that the title of the book is
  italicized and only the first word is capitalized (the first word in a
  subtitle and any proper nouns are also capitalized).

  Solie, K. (2001). *Short haul engine*. London, ON: Brick Books.

- **A work by two or more authors:** When citing a book with up
  to seven authors, alphabetize the entry by the name that appears
  first in the list of authors on the title page; do not alphabetize the
  remaining names. Invert all the names in the list. Use an ampersand (&) between the last two names in the list. This book with
  two authors is also a translation. Note that no period follows the
  closing parenthesis of the original date of publication.

  Horkheimer, M., & Adorno, T. W. (1972). *Dialectic of enlightenment*
  (Cumming, J., Trans.). New York, NY: Continuum. (Original work published 1944)

When citing a book with eight or more authors, list the first six names in the order in which they appear in the book, insert an ellipsis (. . .), and add the last author's name.

- **An anthology or a compilation:** An anthology or a compilation is a collection of works by different people, selected and arranged by an editor or editors. To cite an entire collection, alphabetize the entry by the last name of the editor, followed by a comma and *(Ed.)*. If there is more than one editor, follow the format for books by two or more authors and add *(Eds.)*. (For individual entries in an anthology or compilation, see below.)

Mitchell, A., Rundle, L. B., & Karaian, L. (Eds.). (2001). *Turbo chicks: Talking young feminisms*. Toronto, ON: Sumach Press.

- **An individual work in an anthology or a compilation:** To cite a selection from an anthology or a compilation, alphabetize the entry by the last name of the author, not the editor. Do not put quotation marks around the titles of short works, such as essays, poems, and short stories. Capitalize only the first word of the title and the subtitle (if any), and any proper nouns. Add *In* and then list the names of the editors, in normal order. Then, add *(Ed.)* or *(Eds.)* (depending on the number of editors) after the last editor's name. After the title of the anthology or compilation, give the edition of the anthology or compilation (if any) in parentheses, along with the page numbers for the complete selection (not just the pages you have cited). Conclude with the place of publication followed by the publisher.

Vanderhaeghe, G. (2006). Cages. In J. C. Storr, R. E. Jones, & R. Bowers (Eds.), *The Harbrace anthology of literature* (4th ed., pp. 1204– 1217). Toronto, ON: Thomson Nelson.

- **Two or more works by the same author(s):** When you cite more than one text by the same author, include the name of the author in each entry. Entries are ordered chronologically by date, citing the earliest work first.

Zwicky, J. (2003). *Wisdom & metaphor*. Kentville, NS: Gaspereau Press.
Zwicky, J. (2004). *Robinson's crossing*. London, ON: Brick Books.

Articles Scholarly journals or periodicals are extremely common research sources. You may also draw upon magazine articles, newspaper articles, or encyclopedia entries. Most journal entries for a References list will be for a specific essay in a particular journal. The entry will include the author's name, the year of publication, the title of the article, the title of the journal, the volume (and issue) of the journal, and the page numbers of the article.

- **A scholarly article in a scholarly journal:** Note that a comma separates the journal title and the volume number. The volume number is italicized, but the issue number is not italicized. Note that the journal title retains its capitalization.

  Brooks, P. (1994). Aesthetics and ideology: What happened to poetics? *Critical Inquiry, 20*(3), 509–523.

- **A scholarly article in a collection:** These sources are cited in the same way as individual works in an anthology (see above) if they have not been previously published.

  Kilgour, M. (1998). The function of cannibalism at the present time. In F. Barker, P. Hulme, & M. Iversen (Eds.), *Cannibalism and the colonial world* (pp. 238–259). New York, NY: Cambridge University Press.

- If the article appeared first in a journal and has been reprinted in a collection, give the information for the journal publication at the end of the entry in parentheses, preceded by *Reprinted from*.

  Windle, P. (1995). The ecology of grief. In T. Roszak, M. Gomes, & A. Kanner (Eds.), *Ecopsychology: Restoring the earth, healing the mind* (pp. 136–145). San Francisco, CA: Sierra Club Books. (Reprinted from *Bioscience, 42* (1992, May), 363–366)

- **A magazine article:** When citing magazine articles, give the date as it is published on the magazine (month for monthly publications, day and month for weekly publications). Also, include any volume numbers.

  Wells, P. (2006, April 10). Spring break summit. *Maclean's, 119*(15), 16–18.

- **A newspaper article:** When citing newspaper articles, include the author, the date of the article, the title of the article, the name of the newspaper, and page number(s). Sometimes newspaper articles are discontinuous: cite all pages on which the article appears (as follows). If no author is given, alphabetize the article by the first significant word in the title and put the date in parentheses after the title.

  Freeman, A. (2006, May 15). Bush ready to deploy guardsmen to Mexican border. *The Globe and Mail*, pp. A1, A11.

- **An encyclopedia entry:** Encyclopedia entries may or may not include author information. If the author is named, alphabetize the entry by the author's last name. If the author is unnamed, alphabetize the entry by the first significant word of the title. After the title, list the edition, volume and page numbers, if available, in parentheses. List publisher information. Do not list the entry by the encyclopedia editor's name.

David Suzuki. (1999). In J. H. Marsh (Ed.), *The Canadian encyclopedia: Year 2000 edition* (2000 ed., p. 2277). Toronto, ON: McClelland & Stewart.

Electronic and online sources References for online sources should accomplish two objectives: to tell readers where to access a document and to provide an internet address or reference that works. A reference to an online resource should include a document title, a date, an address, and, if possible, an author. Many scholarly articles include a digital object identifier (DOI), which provides an ongoing link to the article on the web. If an article includes a DOI (which appears as doi: xxxxxx), add it to the end of an entry instead of a URL. It is not necessary to include a date of access in an entry unless the online resource might change (for example, a Wiki).

- **A web page:** Authors of web pages are often not listed, or the author may be an institution or corporation. If no author is listed, alphabetize the entry by the first significant word of the title of the document. If the author is an institution, alphabetize the entry using the institution's name.

  Cable News Network. (2006, May 11). No agreement on role of abortion pill in fatal infections. Retrieved from http://www.cnn.com/2006/HEALTH/05/11/abortion.pill.hearing.ap/index.html

- **An article in an online database:** Full-text articles are increasingly becoming available through online databases. When citing an article from an online database, it is not necessary to include the database information. Rather, follow the same rules for citing a print article and add the electronic source of the article.

  Pitt, L., Kilbride, M., Nothard, S., Welford, M., & Morrison, A. P. (2006). Researching recovery from psychosis: A user-led project. *The Psychiatrist, 31*, 55–60. doi:10.1192/pb.bp.105.008532

3e Format of Works Cited or References List

Several basic formatting conventions are common to both MLA and APA styles:

1. The title Works Cited (MLA) or References (APA) is centred at the top of the page without any special formatting (that is, no bold, no italics, no quotation marks, no change in font size).

DOCUMENTATION

2. Entries are alphabetized by the author's last name, as explained earlier.

3. Entries authored by institutions are alphabetized in the same manner as authored texts.

4. Entries with no identifiable author are alphabetized by the first significant word in the title (that is, not *The, A,* or *An*). This can be particularly relevant for internet sources.

5. Entries are double-spaced with no extra spaces between entries.

6. Entries longer than one line are formatted with a hanging indent; that is, subsequent text lines are indented 1.25 cm or ½ inch (one tab). Most word processors have an automatic function for formatting text to hanging indent.

Glossary of Rhetorical Terms

Analyze To divide something into parts in order to understand both the parts and the whole. This can be done by *systems analysis* (where the object is divided into its interconnected parts), *process analysis* (where the object is divided into stages of development), and *cause/effect analysis* (where the object is divided into the reasons that brought it into being, or into its consequences). The main purpose of analysis is to explain something, such as a concept, a text, an event, or a set of data, by examining its parts in detail.

Cause/effect analysis *See* Analyze.

Compare To show the similarities and differences between two things, or among more than two things, in order to reveal the qualities of each more clearly.

Comparison, basis of The common element in terms of which two or more things are compared. Topics that can be put in the form "Compare X and Y in terms of Z" specify the basis of comparison, Z. The basis of comparison tells you which features of the things you are comparing are relevant and thus gives you a focus for gathering information and writing your essay.

Comparison, methods of organizing The *block method* consists of organizing your *middle paragraphs* so that you finish everything you have to say about one of the things you are comparing before taking up another. The *point-by-point method* consists of organizing your middle paragraphs so that in each paragraph or series of paragraphs you discuss only one aspect of each of the things you are comparing.

Conclusion The concluding paragraph in your essay provides the chance for both you and your reader to step back from the essay and survey the development of your *thesis*. The conclusion should restate the thesis, tie together the points developed in the *middle paragraphs*, and mention the wider implications of the discussion, if any. A good conclusion will not have substantial repetition of words or phrases from the *introduction*.

Context The social, historical, and/or cultural situation in which a text is written or produced.

Deductive and inductive structure These terms provide the most common way of making a distinction between essays that begin with the *thesis* (deductive structure) and essays that lead up to a thesis at or toward the end of the essay (inductive structure).

Definition: A definition is a detailed explanation of a term or concept. A *definition essay* provides an extended definition of a concept that goes beyond a mere few sentences and may contest common perceptions or assumptions about that concept.

Development, methods of The uses of *evidence* and detail to give substance to a point.

Diction A writer's level of word usage (formal, informal, colloquial) and particular word choices. An aspect of *style* that also contributes to *tone*.

Discuss An ambiguous term frequently used in essay topics. It does not mean "summarize the relevant information." Check the essay topic carefully to determine whether you are expected to *analyze*, *compare*, or *evaluate* a body of information. "Discuss the significance of X in Y" means to analyze the relationship between X and Y; "discuss X and Y" means to compare X and Y; "discuss the validity of X" means to evaluate X.

Evaluate To determine the strengths or weaknesses of something—a plan, a performance, a work of art, or a theory, for example. Evaluation usually examines an idea, position, argument, or viewpoint and often determines the effectiveness or validity of its presentation.

Evaluation, standard of A set of criteria based on accumulated judgments of things of the same kind that you can use as a standard against which to measure the material you are evaluating. The most common standards of evaluation are aesthetic (how effective is the relationship between form and content in the work?), logical (how convincing is the reasoning?), practical (will it work and is it useful?), and ethical (is it morally right or wrong?).

Evidence The factual information, examples, and references to and quotations from authorities that you use to support your thesis.

Genre and subgenre We use the term *genre* to refer to the broad kinds of text (for example, novel, play, film). We use *subgenre* to refer to more specific types within the form (for example, Gothic novel, Greek tragedy, film noir).

Inductive structure *See* Deductive and inductive structure.

Introduction The introductory paragraph prepares your reader both intellectually and emotionally for the essay to follow. It establishes the context by defining necessary terms, giving historical background, and so forth, and indicates the structure of the essay by mentioning, in order, the main points you plan to cover. The introduction usually ends with your *thesis*.

Literary analysis The analysis of a literary text or performance that focuses not only on the *theme* or *thesis* of the work but also on the presentation and *style*. For example, a film may be about dogs, but the film may present the theme of dogs as a comedy, a tragedy, or a documentary. Therefore, literary analysis will consider the *genre and subgenre* of the work through *subject*, *structure*, *development*, *tone*, and *theme* or *thesis*.

Middle paragraphs Paragraphs between the *introduction* and *conclusion* that explain and illustrate subpoints of the *thesis*. The purpose of each paragraph is defined by a *topic sentence* that links the paragraph to the thesis. Middle paragraphs usually contain both explanations of the point made in the topic sentence and specific details illustrating that point. Transitional words and phrases show how points, explanations, and details are related.

Middle paragraphs, order of There are four common ways of organizing a sequence of middle paragraphs.

1. *Chronological order:* The arrangement of material according to units of time. The simplest chronological order starts with events furthest away in time and ends with events closest in time.

2. *Spatial order:* The arrangement of material according to locations in space. Spatial order may move from near to far, top to bottom, right to left, and so forth.

3. *Logical order:* The arrangement of material according to a chain of reasoning. The order in which material is presented is determined by the need to establish one point so that it will serve as the basis for the next.

4. *Order of ascending interest:* The arrangement of material to lead up to the most important or most interesting point. An order of ascending interest may also accommodate a chronological, spatial, or logical order. *See also* Comparison, methods of organizing.

Peer-reviewed Often called "refereed," peer-reviewed materials are publications that have been examined and approved by experts in a particular field of study. The information and analysis in these publications are usually considered reliable, current, and consistent with the scholarship in the field. Such publications are used as *secondary sources* in a *research paper*.

Persona The mask or second self created by the author, especially in poetry and in ironic essays where the stated thesis and the implied thesis are completely different. In "A Modest Proposal" (Readings), for example, Swift creates a persona who argues that eating the poor is the best way to solve the problems created by them. Swift's real thesis is that his readers need to see the Irish poor as human beings and find a humane solution to their problems.

Primary source Any first-hand source of information, such as the literary work you are analyzing, a performance you have seen, your own observations and experience, the raw data from a scientific experiment, or the historical documents on which historians base their interpretations of events.

Process analysis *See* Analyze.

Research paper An extended analysis, comparison, or evaluation essay that includes information from *secondary sources* as well as from *primary sources*. A research paper is not merely a summary of other writers' ideas; it is an essay in which you develop your own opinion on your subject and use your research material as part of your evidence to support that opinion.

Secondary source Material that provides information about, or criticism and analysis of, a *primary source*. A historian, for example, may write a book (secondary source) interpreting the meaning of historical documents (primary sources). An anthropologist may collect data (primary sources) about various cultures and write an article comparing those cultures (secondary source). A literary critic may write a review (secondary source) of a new novel (primary source). In secondary sources, material is selected and presented to support a particular point of view.

Structure   The selection and ordering of parts in a written work or performance. *See also* Middle paragraphs, order of.

Style   The distinctive way of writing that belongs to a particular writer. For analytic purposes, it is helpful to see style as consisting of a writer's use of *diction*, image and symbol, figurative language and allusions, and sentence structure.

Subgenre   *See* Genre and subgenre.

Subject   The text, issue, theory, or proposal that a writer writes about. If your essay topic is "Assess the role of the peasants in the French Revolution," the subject of your essay is the role of the peasants in the French Revolution.

Systems analysis   *See* Analyze.

Theme   The main statement made about a subject in fiction, drama, poetry, film, and imaginative literature generally.

A theme is usually implied, whereas a *thesis* is usually stated directly.

Thesis   The main statement made about a subject in nonfiction. The purpose of the essay is to develop and confirm the thesis. In your essay, the thesis statement will consist of an opinion with one or more reasons to support it. Like the hypothesis in a scientific experiment, the thesis is the statement or assertion you are proving.

Tone   The attitude a writer takes to a subject and to a reader, the equivalent of "tone of voice" in conversation. The tone of a work can be described as serious or light, witty or ponderous, condescending or apologetic, and in many other similar ways. In your own essays, think of tone as a product of *diction* and pronouns of address.

Topic sentence   The sentence in a *middle paragraph*, usually at the beginning, that states the main idea of the paragraph and shows how the material in the paragraph supports the *thesis* of the whole essay. Topic sentences are thus the bridge between the generalization you make in your thesis statement and the specific details you give in your middle paragraphs. An "umbrella" topic sentence covers points made in more than one paragraph.

Index